NO CUNNING PLAN

Sir Tony Robinson is most famous for playing the role of Baldrick in *Blackadder*, but he made his first professional appearance at the age of thirteen in the original stage version of *Oliver!* and went on to appear with the Chichester Festival Theatre, the RSC and the National Theatre. He wrote and starred in *Maid Marian and Her Merry Men*, and presented *Time Team* for twenty years. He has made numerous factual series, including *The Worst Jobs in History* and *Tony Robinson's Time Walks*. He is a multi-award-winning children's television writer and has authored many children's books, including the history series *Tony Robinson's Weird World of Wonders*. He has also written several books for adults.

TONY ROBINSON

NO CUNNING PLAN

My Story

PAN BOOKS

First published 2016 by Sidgwick & Jackson

This paperback edition published 2017 by Pan Books
an imprint of Pan Macmillan
20 New Wharf Road, London N1 9RR
Associated companies throughout the world
www.panmacmillan.com

ISBN 978-1-5098-1549-4

A Different Kind of Weather: A Memoir by William Waldegrave
© 2015, published by Constable.
Extract from *Who Is Sylvia?* © Terence Rattigan, 1950. Reprinted with
permission from Nick Hern Books Ltd.
The picture acknowledgements on page 422 constitute an extension of
this copyright page.

1 3 5 7 9 8 6 4 2

A CIP catalogue record for this book is available from the British Library.

Typeset by Ellipsis, Glasgow
Printed and bound by CPI Group (UK) Ltd, Croydon, CR0 4YY

Visit **www.panmacmillan.com** to read more about all our books
and to buy them. You will also find features, author interviews and
news of any author events, and you can sign up for e-newsletters
so that you're always first to hear about our new releases.

For Louise

And in memory of
Leslie and Phyllis Robinson

As I get older, it seems that peace of mind may be most often found among contemporaries who have mastered a craft, and left examples of their craftsmanship. If there are rules and disciplines, and one has fulfilled them, perhaps one has achieved all that can be achieved. Happiness may not be something to pursue directly, perhaps it is a side-effect of working hard at something to the best of one's ability.

William Waldegrave, *A Different Kind of Weather*

CONTENTS

PROLOGUE

I learnt I was about to become a knight when I was lying on my hotel bed with a belly full of pork and pastry. I'd been shooting a story in Parramatta, New South Wales, about an eccentric nineteenth-century showman and pastry cook called the Flying Pieman, and the director had wanted endless retakes of the part where I had to eat one of the Pieman's signature dishes, so I was feeling a bit queasy.

My iPad pinged. My PA, Heli, had Skyped me, and was waving an official-looking letter.

I'd heard a rumour that secret conversations had taken place, my name had been looked on favourably, and in the near future there might well be some official recognition of my contribution to politics, entertainment, charity, education and whatever else might justify a gong, so I'd consulted my daughter, who has a much keener understanding of this kind of thing than I do.

'Strewth! What do you reckon it'll be, Laura?'

'An "O", I should think, or maybe an "M".'

'Excuse me?'

'Order of the British Empire, Member of the British Empire . . .'

'There's hardly any British Empire left. The Isle of Man, I suppose, Gibraltar, Tristan da Cunha maybe . . .'

'Oh, come on, Dad. It's a massive honour. Being picked out for service to your country, how cool is that?'

So when my wife Louise and I had left for Australia, I'd

asked Heli not to open any letter that looked like it might have come from Buckingham Palace, 10 Downing Street or some other fancy address, but to call us immediately.

And now there she was twelve thousand miles away with a sealed envelope in her hand that clearly said 'On Her Majesty's Service, Return Address: 1 Horse Guards Parade'.

It should have been a dramatic moment. I'd been expecting something embossed, with lots of sealing wax and a big coat of arms, not a piece of paper that looked like the reminder you get from the dental hygienist about your six-monthly check-up. But it definitely said 'The Prime Minister has asked me to inform you, in strict confidence, that he is recommending that Her Majesty may be graciously pleased to approve the honour of . . .' Although what honour it was she might be graciously pleased to approve was a mystery. The trouble with trying to read something that's being Skyped from the other side of the world is that the image tends to pixelate.

'What's it say, Lou?' My eyesight isn't the greatest.

'I haven't got my lenses in.'

'Shall I read it?' asked Heli helpfully.

'No! No! Tony's got to hear first.'

'What's the first letter?' I said. 'Is it an "O"?'

Lou put her glasses on.

'Nope!'

'An "M"?'

'Nope!'

'Flippin' 'eck! It's not a "C", is it?'

'What's that?'

'Commander of the Empire. That really would be a big deal.'

'Nope!' There was a long pause followed by a squeak. 'It's a "K",' Lou yelled. 'It's a fucking "K"!' and she started bouncing round the room.

How do you keep a knighthood quiet? We weren't supposed to tell anyone until the formal announcement a month later. OK, in the great scheme of things it didn't matter a jot. It wasn't like I'd been kidnapped by Islamic State or contracted Ebola. I wasn't going to be given a castle, or dressed in armour and made to fight at the Battle of Agincourt. Nevertheless it was an extraordinary thing, like Bristol City winning League Division One and the Johnstone's Paint Trophy in the same season, and I couldn't stop thinking about it.

Lou and I developed our own secret signal. Wherever we were, whoever else was around, we'd catch each other's eye and draw a discreet circle with our forefingers, followed by a tiny stabbing motion. It was supposed to represent a very small knight wielding his sword. It worked. Nobody ever guessed what it signified. If they noticed anything at all, they probably thought we were trying to get something nasty off our fingers.

The only people we told were Laura, and my son Luke. We knew they wouldn't blab. But before the story broke we wanted to share the news with Lou's mum. So as soon as we got back to the UK, we phoned her and told her we were coming straight up to the Wirral.

'Why?'

'Why what, Pam?'

'Why are you coming up?'

'To see you.'

'You can't come up just like that. I need to clean the house, sort out the dogs . . .'

'Don't worry. It's no big deal.'

When we arrived, the whole family was there. Lou's mum looked tense.

'Lovely to see you, Pam.'

There was a pause then 'Get on with it,' she said.

'Get on with what?'

'The news.'

'What news?'

'The news you've come all this way to tell me.'

'It's nothing,' I said. 'Except . . .'

Pam reached for her ciggies.

'I'm going to be knighted . . . which means your daughter will be a lady.'

Pam put her fags down again.

'Thank Christ for that,' she said, and breathed a sigh of relief. 'I thought you were going to tell me you'd been exposed for having sex with underage girls in the seventies!'

On the night of the big announcement we had a dozen friends round to dinner. We'd told them it was to celebrate our return from Australia – we'd been away the best part of four months. At a quarter to ten Lou sneaked out of the room and came back with a big cake, blazing candles and lots of plastic knights stuck in the icing. That's when we made the announcement, and everyone got a slice with a knight on it.

On the stroke of ten we turned on the telly, and I was the lead story. More important events had occurred that day, but the earthquakes, race riots, ministerial resignations, and train crashes hadn't offered the news editor an excuse to play the clip from *Blackadder* where Baldrick is made a lord and enters wearing an ermine cloak. OK, maybe it didn't deserve quite such extensive coverage, but being the first item on the BBC news still felt a pretty big deal to me.

Tuesday, 12 November 2013, 6.30 a.m. The night before I'd been reading my latest book to a bunch of kids at a literary festival in Kilmarnock, and I'd just got off the sleeper at Euston. I walked across the station to the cab rank, frowzled, tousled and a bit flustered.

It wouldn't be my first time at Buckingham Palace. In 2006 Channel 4 had asked *Time Team* to create a week-long live TV extravaganza. As we were in the middle of the Queen's eightieth birthday year, we'd suggested an excavation at Buckingham Palace.

The palace authorities were initially sceptical, and we didn't blame them. I was a republican, so was Mick Aston, our lead archaeologist. The Windsor press office wouldn't want us recording any royal high jinks and selling the story to the *Socialist Worker*. But they relaxed a little when we appointed Laurence Vulliamy as series producer. He'd orchestrated a number of televised royal events, was thought to be a safe pair of hands, and eventually, though nervously, it was agreed we should be given royal access, although not before I'd been taken to one side by their press office and asked for reassurance that I wouldn't cause any offence.

Of course I wouldn't! We were old hands at this on *Time Team*. You had to keep on the right side of the punters, that was part of the job. We'd wrecked every garden we'd ever filmed in. Mechanical diggers had ground their way across the lawns of England, flowers beds had been destroyed, enormous trenches dug across paths and through vegetable plots. It was extraordinarily generous (not to mention a bit daft) of anyone to be prepared to make such a sacrifice, and the least we could do in return was be polite and respectful to the occupants. We'd treat the royal family in exactly the same way. Furthermore, I said, I didn't feel any animosity towards the Queen, who I thought had done a remarkably good job in extremely trying circumstances. How many other rulers would have dealt with losing the largest empire the world had ever known with such good grace? It wasn't HRH I was opposed to, it was the principle of monarchy – the fact that the Queen could veto proposed new laws, could nominate bishops to the House of Lords, was the head of just one sect among Britain's many religions, that she sat on the throne only because her father . . . but by then the press attaché's eyes had glazed over. We'd both made our points. Any further conversation was redundant.

The first part of *Time Team*'s 'Big Royal Dig' was shot at a royal garden party. Laurence's idea was that in our first sequence we'd ask the Queen if we could dig up her garden, and she would regally say yes. But, on principle, Mick refused to attend, and our chief digger, Phil Harding, said he'd only turn up if he could wear what he wanted and didn't have to comb his hair.

There was much agitated discussion, at the end of which this was agreed, and we finally arrived at the garden party and stood in line, with Phil sporting a beige safari jacket and cowboy hat that made him look like one of the Village People. After an excruciatingly long wait, the royal family finally processed out of a tiny insignificant-looking door at one side of the palace, the men mostly tall, thin and stooping, the women short and dumpy with round faces. There were royal handshakes and brief bursts of conversation. I don't think the Queen had any idea who I was or what I was doing there, but following a whispered briefing from an aide, she asked me a carefully constructed question about my interest in archaeology to which I gave a nondescript reply. Then I asked her if we could dig her garden, and she said yes. Job done!

Prince Philip was a different kettle of fish. 'Archaeology?' he harrumphed. 'There's bugger all archaeology here. Won't be much of a programme. The whole bloody place has been dug up twenty times already!'

It was reassuring to find that he was exactly like I'd always imagined him to be. Thirty years previously I'd read reports of his rudeness and had been appalled, but now I found him amusingly straightforward, like someone pretending to be Mr Magoo. He was very bright. He argued with me for far longer than he was supposed to given the length of the queue, and when I tried to explain why we were optimistic about what we might find, he cited a long list of reasons why the area was likely to be barren.

He eventually moved on, I had an animated discussion with the Duchess of Cornwall about traffic problems on the M4, then we all went off for a sandwich and a slice of lemon drizzle cake.

The show had been billed as a live dig, but it was actually 'as live'. In other words, to avoid the necessity of excavating in the dark, we taped it an hour earlier than it was transmitted.

This led to a lot of confusion, not least when, during rehearsals, I told the floor manager I was going to slope off for a pee, thinking there was an age before our cameras rolled, and he replied that recording was starting in seven minutes – and no, it couldn't be delayed.

I was in a quandary. The portaloos were round the other side of the palace, much too far away for me to reach in time, but I was a middle-aged man, and there was no way I could survive a whole hour with a bladder about to split asunder.

I proceeded with some urgency down the little slope that led to the main body of the garden, and after a brief reconnoitre of the ornamental trees, found a hornbeam which obscured the palace windows sufficiently to allow me to have a slash without causing offence.

I was halfway through when I heard a whirring sound. Looking up, I saw a security camera which was fixed to the top of the trunk and was currently pointing straight down at me. I tried to finish as quickly as I could, but it's difficult when you're being observed. I struggled on for a while but was interrupted again, this time by a figure bursting through the shrubbery. It was a copper, complete with a stab jacket and a very large Alsatian. He looked me up and down, the dog sniffed my legs, and they moved off again.

'I bet everyone wishes they could do that,' he murmured before disappearing back into the undergrowth.

The programme was a great success. While I'd been excavating at Buckingham Palace, Alice Roberts and our archaeologists were digging at Windsor Castle, and they'd discovered the Round Table!

Sadly it wasn't King Arthur's original Round Table; it was the rubble-filled foundations of a massive circular building Edward III had built in the fourteenth century to house the Knights of the Garter. They used it to dress up and indulge in acts of old-fashioned chivalry, and in honour of their ancient forebears they named it after the most famous piece of furniture in early British history. It may have been nothing more than a piece of medieval show business, but this building was one of the most significant excavations ever conducted on *Time Team*, rather eclipsing the tiny hundred-year-old lead horse which was my best find. On the day Prince Philip hadn't been mistaken. There was bugger all archaeology at Buckingham Palace. Still, my chipped little toy gave me something to be enthusiastic about.

So now I was back at the palace again, this time with my thirty-four-year-old son Luke, tall and handsome, with designer stubble and a sharp grey suit, Laura, wearing a permanent look of pride and affectionate amusement, and my beautiful wife Louise, dressed in Alexander McQueen, with a foxy heart-shaped hat tilted over one eye.

A hundred and seventy-six UK and Commonwealth citizens were to receive their awards that day. They were milling around in the long gallery, framed by the palace's lush red, white and gold decor, honoured guests at a swanky party where no one knew each other and there was no alcohol. But ten of us were singled out and directed up a small flight of stairs into an ante-room where we were offered white wine. Obviously the 'C's and 'K's were regarded as special people who could hold their liquor, unlike the 'O's and 'M's who'd have made idiots of themselves if they'd even sniffed a spritzer.

I got chummy with a chap called Sir Peter Caruana who'd served as Governor of Gibraltar and was now being given the obscure, although apparently great, honour of the 'Knight Commander of the Most Distinguished Order of Saint Michael and Saint George'. He was an unaffected and very funny man who kept me giggling inanely throughout the whole event with his subversive, whispered commentary. We were like two naughty boys at the back of the class.

There were a few people I vaguely recognised – a po-faced Liberal who was being made a Companion of Honour, a director from one of the great theatrical families, and a retired general who used to get wheeled onto the telly whenever we invaded a

Middle Eastern country. I could only see one woman, and she had her back to me, talking to two servicemen in dress uniform. When she turned round, my head spun a little. It was the Queen. Well, not the real Queen, but as good as. She'd certainly always been a queen to me.

When I was seventeen I hadn't had much time for Hollywood actresses. They'd seemed so silly: either vulgar and over the top, or bland, vacuous and as authentic as Minnie Mouse.

There was Marilyn Monroe, of course, but she was from another planet. Claire Bloom was English. She was troubled, and it showed in her eyes; attractive, but like a real person, not cartoon attractive; vulnerable but smart, and you wouldn't mess with her. No wonder she was cast as women who answered back. Other actresses seemed diminished by the smouldering presence of Marlon Brando, Rod Steiger and the new breed of male actors, but Claire Bloom always shone.

She must have been in her eighties by now, but she was still stylish, vital, and looked amazing. 'Hullo, I'm Claire,' she said. If I'd had a penknife, I'd have slashed open my chest and offered her my aorta. Instead I mumbled something inane, then something else twice as inane. She returned my wild-eyed stare with a look of mildly charmed curiosity.

'Excuse me, Mr Robinson.'

There was a discreet tap on my shoulder. A very well-spoken palace official was suggesting I might like to be briefed before proceedings began. I raised my eyes, and smiled at her by way of apology. 'I've got to go and be given my notes,' I said, then realised this was the most dicky, actory thing I could possibly have said, and confirmed my dickiness by exchanging slightly fumbled cheek-kisses with her.

The instructions were straightforward. Prince William was going to be doing the knighting. I had to bow, kneel on a stool, call him 'Your Highness' when he talked to me, then when I'd been knighted, step back, turn right, and move off. It was child's play. Frankly I was more worried about him. He was new to this investiture business; I just hoped he wasn't going to mess up.

A few minutes later we were made to stand in line, and led crocodile-style through another side door into the ballroom. Five hundred people were looking at us. My name was called, I stepped forward, and amnesia set in. What was I supposed to do? I looked at the Duke of Cambridge; he looked at me. I smiled at the Duke of Cambridge; he smiled back. It was like the duel scene from *High Noon* – one of us would surely die. Then his eyes flicked downwards, I gratefully took my cue and knelt. Whoops! I'd forgotten to bow. His sword bore down towards my shoulder in slo-mo.

This was extraordinary. What was I doing here? Why was I being singled out? How come I'd been allowed to snog Claire Bloom? Why had I been the number one story on the news? There'd certainly been no cunning plan.

'Arise, Sir Anthony Robinson.'

I stood up. I forgot to call him 'Your Highness', but he didn't seem to mind. We talked about *Blackadder* – he was a big fan. He asked me if there were going to be any more episodes. I suggested that if there were he should have a small part, and he agreed. We could have nattered on all morning; he seemed a good bloke. But there were another 175 people behind me, so it would have been a bit selfish.

The conversation ended. I stepped back, turned left, and bumped into the rest of the queue.

1

THE ROCK STAR

For the best part of three hundred years my family lived in the East End of London. All the smelly jobs – tanning, brewing, boiling bones and the like – were done there; anyone with a few bob in their pocket eventually left because it stank so much. But my family couldn't afford to move more than a few streets. They were what the Victorians called 'the deserving poor'. They had jobs like matchmaker, seamstress and shoebox maker. We did boast one entrepreneur: Thomas William Parrott, my great-grandfather on my mum's side, set up a business called Parrott's Popular Pickles. He had a handcart, two small barrels and two ladles. A big ladle of pickles cost you a penny, a small one a halfpenny, but it didn't catch on. His son, my Grandpa Horace, was a steward for the Union Castle Line and worked the South Africa run for half a century.

My Great Granddad Francis on my father's side was a box cutter and died in the workhouse. His wife and their five children, including my Grandma Ellen, struggled on for another fourteen years until in 1915 Julia caught diphtheria and died in St George's Workhouse Infirmary. Ellen was terrified of ending up in the workhouse too, and worked obsessively all her life to fend off poverty.

My dad and his brother Cyril grew up in a different world. They were the early-twentieth-century products of universal education, better healthcare and tap water that didn't make you vomit. Dad won a place at London University, but didn't go because Grandma Ellen said they couldn't afford it. Instead he worked for the London County Council. Ironically, his first job was as a clerk helping to wind down East End workhouses like the ones in which his grandparents had died.

In those days the LCC was structured a bit like the army. There were officers and other ranks, and my dad was at the bottom. He met my mum at a badminton club near Clapton Pond, but they didn't go out much. Most evenings she went round to his parents' house and knitted, while he read textbooks and wrote essays.

He had a good mind and, like his mum, was a hard worker. In 1937 he passed the LCC administration exams with distinction and became a junior administrator. In those days if you were an East Ender with aspirations, you moved to Essex. It was leafy, respectable and only a few miles away from the rest of your family. He put down a deposit on a semi-detached house in South Woodford which cost £998. His friends said they were mad to spend that kind of money on a house. Nobody should be saddled with a debt that big, it would weigh you down for the rest of your life. But they were in their mid-twenties and wanted to get away from the East End and raise a family. It's how the whole *TOWIE* thing started. Today's Essex boys and girls are the great-grandchildren of ambitious white working-class East Enders like Leslie and Phyllis Robinson. That's why they've got those cockney accents and chipper wit.

Mum and Dad got married in June 1939, but their new life lasted less than three months. Hitler invaded Poland, Dad joined the Royal Air Force and was stationed at Peterhead, hundreds of miles away on the Scottish coast. He hardly ever saw Essex or my mum anymore. He didn't have what people describe as 'a good war'; he didn't battle his way through the deserts of North Africa, or parachute into Nazi-occupied Crete. He was a corporal fitter, patching up Hurricanes and Spitfires so posher young men could fly into the clouds and shoot down Jerry.

Not that he had much time for those heroes. Early in 1940

he'd been huddled over a Spitfire fixing its engine when, out of the corner of his eye, he saw Squadron Leader Archie Hamilton striding towards him. He was wearing a brown leather flying jacket with a high wool collar, and his white silk scarf was flapping jauntily in the breeze. He was a legend. He had twenty kills to his name, and was an inspiration to the other pilots.

Dad jumped down from the fuselage, and saluted. 'It's an honour to be making your little beauty fighting fit, sir. Good luck to you, and all who sail in her.'

'Farrk Awff!' replied the squadron leader. From then on Dad waited to see if he returned from each sortie, and was disappointed when he did.

Dad did have one moment of glory. It was dusk, and he was standing solitary guard at the perimeter of his airfield, when he saw a plane coming in low from out at sea. Something about its shape seemed odd, so he picked up a pair of binoculars. There were black crosses on its wings.

He raced towards the nearest machine gun post and yelled for help, but the post wasn't manned. It seemed the defence of north-east Scotland was entirely in Dad's hands. He'd only had half a day's gunnery training, but he knew what he had to do – line the plane up in its sights and fire in short bursts so the gun didn't overheat. It was less than half a mile away now. He pressed the button and a hail of bullets erupted from its twin barrels. The plane seemed blithely unaffected, but Dad kept firing. On and on he blasted. The whole sky was alight. The sound of the weapon was a deafening roar, echoing and re-echoing round the surrounding hills. Eventually it stuttered to a halt, and however hard he pressed the button, it refused to restart. But a little white plume was rising from the plane's cockpit like a tiny smoke signal, then it flipped over onto its back, pirouetted and dropped silently into the sea.

Dad stood there panting, his mouth wide open. His mates raced over to find out what the bloody hell was going on. Only one of the plane's wings was visible now above the waves, then that too disappeared. The men lifted Dad onto their shoulders, and carried him to the NAAFI canteen. He was the man of the moment. There were strains of 'For He's a Jolly Good Fellow!' and a sergeant bought him a drink, which was unheard of.

Next morning Dad was summoned to the station commander's office. Was a medal on the way? Was he to be mentioned in despatches? Apparently not.

The station commander was in a foul mood. 'I claimed that Heinkel last night on this aerodrome's behalf!' he snapped. 'But it appears that every other machine gun post in the vicinity did the same thing. So unless thirty-nine Jerry planes were shot down yesterday within a twenty-mile radius of here, you've made a complete tit out of me. I'm charging you with the wanton destruction of a machine gun.'

Dad had hoped to be promoted. He'd wanted to see action, and become a rear-end gunner on a Lancaster bomber, a job brimful of excitement, but with a very short life expectancy. This episode put him off the business of war completely. From now on he sought other, more entertaining ways of occupying himself.

There were hundreds of Canadian airmen in that part of Scotland, and some of them had formed a dance band which was the toast of Aberdeenshire. British musicians could play a serviceable foxtrot, but the Canadians swung. The band was short of a pianist, and Dad could just about find his way round a keyboard, so he volunteered. This heralded a massive change in his wartime career. His playing became better and better and, as he was a cheeky chappy with the gift of the gab, he became the star of the show, belting out Fats Waller's 'Your Feet's Too Big' and Hoagy Carmichael's 'Up a Lazy River'.

He was five foot three inches in his socks, with a little moustache and glasses, and people called him Wiggy, a nickname he'd acquired because of an accident he'd had as a little boy. He'd contracted ringworm and had been taken to Hackney Hospital to have radiation treatment, along with six other boys.

The machine was switched on, the boys were left unsupervised, and something went wrong. Exactly what, no one seemed to know.

The children were only supposed to be in treatment for a couple of minutes, but half an hour later when a nurse popped in to check on them, the machine was still switched on, pumping out X-rays. Two boys died, and a couple more suffered severe burns. Dad was lucky. He'd been fighting with another boy, and they'd rolled away from the machine into a corner. He was taken home, given his supper and sent to bed. In the middle of the night my grandmother woke to the sound of screaming. When she went into Dad's room, all his hair was on the pillow and it never grew back. He was given free wigs for the rest of his life. As a child it didn't bother me – I thought all dads wore wigs. And it didn't seem to bother him either.

While Dad was having the time of his life boogieing his way round the church halls of north-east Scotland, Mum was left at home audio-typing. Her bosses would dictate their letters on a reel-to-reel tape recorder, and she'd type them out wearing earphones the size of soup plates. She grew bored and lonely, so she joined the Women's Royal Air Force, became a clerk, and was stationed at an aerodrome near Slough. Like Dad, she blossomed. The highlight of her social life was amateur dramatics. I've got ancient photos of her standing on rickety stages wearing heavily applied greasepaint, and pulling a variety of dramatic faces. My favourite is of her dressed in a bloodsplattered nightie looking down at a dead man in pyjamas with a knife by his side. Nothing's written on the back of the photo, so I'll never know whether she was the murderer, or the innocent dupe who found the body.

In later years Dad implied that he'd had a string of wartime girlfriends, and I assumed Mum was the innocent victim of these shenanigans. But a few years before she died we visited her in her nursing home and I got a rude shock. Her dementia had recently become more acute, and she'd often spend visiting time staring at the wall. On this particular day we tried to engage her attention by showing her wartime photos of her friends. There was virtually no reaction till we came to a snap of a suave-looking officer.

'That's Stuart,' she said.

'Who was Stuart?' I asked.

'My boyfriend,' she replied with a hint of irritation, as though it was a stupid question.

What did she mean? Did they make passionate love under khaki blankets, surreptitiously hold hands under the tables of country pubs, or were they simply mates? It remains an unexplained but tantalising secret.

When the war ended, Dad got a great job offer. The guys from the dance band were going pro; would Wiggy like to join them in Canada? The answer was no. Mum and Dad were home birds at heart, and having bought their semi only a few years previously, they weren't thrilled with the prospect of exile. So they returned to 14 Raymond Avenue, South Woodford, Dad went back to the LCC, and within a few months Mum was pregnant. The labour wasn't easy; I was premature, weighed around four and a half pounds, and was covered from head to toe in black hair. Apart from that I was apparently unscathed, but Mum wasn't. The birth damaged her insides, and she was afflicted with stabbing pains for many years.

Dad bought a shiny black baby grand piano which, with great difficulty, he managed to squeeze into our little front room. So from the start, music was at the centre of my life. The house rang to the sound of Gilbert and Sullivan, Glenn Miller, Schubert and Ted Heath.

Mum kept up her acting; there were lots of amateur groups around – it was that kind of neighbourhood. People prided themselves on being respectable but fun. There were social gatherings at neighbours' houses with cheese balls and Sun-

Pat peanuts on the tables, the men drinking Truman's Ale in half-pint tumblers, while the women sipped Babycham or Snowballs.

The Wanstead Players were the most envied of the local am-drams. The company was run by John Gibson, a sophisticated and languid young bachelor and the son of a department store owner in nearby Ilford. Harrison Gibson provided the actors with elaborate props, made the scenery, supplied the lights and donated swathes of material for the costumes. The shows were put on in the elegant surroundings of the Royal Wanstead School, whose chairman, Sir Winston Churchill, was the local MP and which overlooked the swans on The Eagle Pond.

Most of the Wanstead Players were posher than Mum, so she became a bit of a dogsbody. She'd be given the task of assistant stage managing on one show, selling programmes on the next, and occasionally she got the small parts which no one else wanted. But she was happy, loyal and tenacious, and the Wanstead Players was the centre of her social world.

Dad volunteered to run the box office. For six weeks prior to each new show, we were exiled to the kitchen to eat our Sunday roast, because the dining table was covered in a green baize cloth, piled on top of which were seating plans, tickets, letters and piles of money. Each seat in the theatre was represented by a box on the plan, and an X was drawn through it when the seat had been sold. I loved the excitement of watching the Xs accumulate as we edged towards another full house, which happened phenomenally quickly when the show was a George Bernard Shaw or a Noël Coward, but was painstakingly slow if it was an unknown play, particularly one of those modern European ones about guilt, anxiety and the trauma of loss.

I was sent to Woodford Green Preparatory School, an establishment far less impressive than it sounds. It was a small private school, buried away down the end of an alleyway behind a row of terraced houses. Its teachers were poorly paid and looked perpetually depressed and irritated. Our uniform was a bright red blazer and cap, with grey flannel trousers and a striped tie, and for five shillings a term our parents could buy extra tuition, including elocution from Miss Myfanwy Phillips who visited us twice a week to polish up our East End vowels. Her passion was poetry: Shakespeare, Wordsworth, Walter de la Mare and John Masefield. Her dream was that her little charges would learn to love their poems as much as she did, and from my very first lesson I did. I was hypnotised by the rhythm and the swing of the writing, the way the words rolled round my mouth, and the pictures they created in my mind. Soon I was catching the 179 bus to visit her crumbling mansion in Chingford every Thursday after school, and then on Saturday mornings too.

She entered me for a poetry competition. It was called the Wanstead and Woodford Eisteddfod, which made my dad laugh. I won lots of prizes. She put me in for competitions in other counties, and for speech exams at the Trinity College of Music.

I became known as the boy who was 'good at elocution' and was given a part in a show for the Wanstead Players. I played a cheeky cockney kid in a Terence Rattigan play called *Who Is Sylvia?*. My first words ever on stage were, 'I've been knocking on this door for half a bleedin' hour.' The shock of such a profane word springing from the lips of a young child (I was eleven but looked about eight) brought the house down. I had no idea why the audience was laughing, but I liked the sound of it a lot. Next night I hit the word 'bleedin'' twice as hard, but there was a deathly silence. The leading man told me, 'Less is more . . . unless it's in your pay packet.'

A few months later my Mum showed me an article in her *Daily Express*. It said they wanted a London boy to star in a film called *The Boy and the Bridge*. She asked me if I'd like to go for an audition, and I said yes, why not, it would be a laugh. We had to travel all the way across London, which took about two hours. Twickenham Studios were vast, with long corridors covered in pictures of film stars wearing cravats, smoking cigarettes and staring moodily into the distance. The studios themselves were the size of aircraft hangers, with chunky ropes dangling from the ceiling, and banks of lights clicking and ticking even when they weren't switched on. There must have been a thousand twelve-year-old boys and their mums there.

The casting directors asked us questions, gave us lines to read and took our photos. It was boring, but exciting too. By lunchtime there were only a hundred of us left, by teatime fifty, and at 9 p.m. just two.

We sat in the green room for ages, with earnest half-heard discussions taking place next door. Then the director came in and took me and my mum to one side, put his arm round me and said the other boy had got the part. Before I had a chance to take this in, he carried on: 'What we want to do is this. We're going to write you a special little part – the boy's best friend. Is that all right? You're not going to cry, are you?'

Cry? Of course I wasn't. I'd never dreamt I'd get the main part in the first place. That was the sort of thing that happened to Mickey Rooney or Judy Garland, not an ordinary kid like me. But the best friend? Yeah, sure. I could do that. It'd be brilliant.

A few weeks later we were on our summer holiday staying at a farmhouse in Pembrokeshire. There were only the three of us. Mum's 'women's disease' had got worse and she'd had an operation which meant I couldn't have any brothers or sisters. That was fine by me!

I was sitting on a stone wall playing with bits of sheep's wool when Dad came over looking sad. 'I've had a call from the film people,' he said. 'They tried writing you that part, but it apparently didn't work for some reason. They say you're not going to be in the film after all.'

That's when I cried.

But it didn't put me off acting, and it didn't put Mum and Dad off either. They were as excited as I was by this alien new world the three of us had blundered into. We never knew what would happen next, and if I'd got close to success already, maybe something even more exciting would be waiting just round the corner.

There was another reason why I wanted to be a child actor. I'd passed my Eleven-Plus, I was at my new grammar school, Wanstead County High, and I hated it. The other kids said I was cocky, a show-off, too big for my boots, and my teachers were always getting at me. This became the bane of my life. As a child actor I was encouraged to be funny and to draw attention to myself, but when I did it at school I was hammered by everyone.

The killer blow had been delivered by Mr Trencher, my English teacher. For our homework he'd told us to write an essay about the sea. I knew everyone else would scribble out a 'what-I-did-on-my-holidays' piece, or a lame story about a storm at night, but I decided to write something that was the complete opposite: no action, just dazzling description like the first few minutes of a moody play. It would be called 'The Wreck of the *Tiger Lil'*, and the only bit of plot would be a shark approaching, its eye glittering as it caught sight of a shoal of herring. It might not have much of a story, but it would bask in a host of luxuriant adjectives.

The following Tuesday Mr Trencher brought in our marked exercise books. He called Davida Woodall to the front and asked her to read her essay out loud. It was called 'The Night of the Great Storm' and, as usual, it was pretty good. When she'd finished, everyone applauded, and Mr Trencher gave her nine out of ten.

Then he called me up. I read out 'The Wreck of the *Tiger Lil'* as dramatically as I could, and waited for my pat on the back. Instead Mr Trencher took my exercise book from me, and held the essay up to the class.

'He always has to be the clever little performer,' he said. 'But look at that margin!'

I'm left-handed like my dad, and still struggle to draw a straight line, even when I use a ruler.

'Now look at the handwriting.'

Again, probably because of my left-handedness, I write like a five-year-old with a paralysed thumb.

'And these spellings! Is this really how you spell "effervescent"? And how about this – does "maritime" have a "y" in it? I think you should learn how to spell "dyslexia", Robinson, that's a word you'll need quite a lot!'

The class turned on me; they rocked with hilarity and jeered with derision. Once again I'd got my comeuppance. But if Mr Trencher thought I was going to try to write a good essay ever again, he couldn't have been more wrong.

Mum had started buying *The Stage*, and found an advert in it that said someone was looking for children to be in a show – 'no previous professional experience necessary'. Dad got me an appointment and took me to a huge house in Chiswick with a board outside that said 'Phildene Academy'. He immediately smelt a rat. It was a scam. There was no job – the advert had been placed by the Wisbys who owned a small stage school and were looking for potential students. But Dad didn't walk away; he said I should audition for them to get a bit of experience. I recited John Masefield's 'Quinquireme of Nineveh from Distant Ophir', and an extract from *Wind in the Willows*, and the Wisbys got very excited, or pretended to be. So I did the mechanicals scene from *A Midsummer Night's Dream* with all the different voices, and they laughed in the right places and said they wanted to take me on.

Serious negotiations then opened. There were two Wisbys: Miss Wisby was short and intense, with bright red lipstick and a lisp; her mother, Mrs Wisby, was birdlike and theatrical, with tough eyes. They said that although their stage school was expensive, I was so talented that I was bound to earn lots of money, so Mum and Dad wouldn't have to worry about finding enough for the fees. I was desperate for them to take me on, and kept slipping Dad pleading looks. Oh, to be freed from another five years' incarceration at school! But Dad wasn't keen. Education was a big thing to him; he was proud that I'd passed my Eleven-Plus, and was adamant that I should stay at Wanstead. I could be a child actor, but not at the expense of my schooling.

Finally a deal was struck. I'd remain at grammar school, but the Wendy Wisby Theatrical Agency could put me forward for professional acting work, and would receive 10 per cent of any money I earned. Dad seemed to think he'd got what he wanted.

Oliver! became the most successful British musical ever to be mounted on a West End stage, but it didn't have an auspicious start. No producer would touch it because it was about poor Victorian cockneys, which wasn't the sort of subject likely to appeal to West End audiences. The selling point was its talented young collaborators: writer Lionel Bart, director Peter Coe and designer Sean Kenny, all in their twenties. They'd recently had a minor hit with a musical adaption of an eighteenth-century comedy which they'd retitled *Lock Up Your Daughters*, on the strength of which they finally managed to persuade Donald Albery, who owned a few theatres around St Martins Lane, to mount their new show, although he insisted on a shoestring budget. The cast were all to be unknowns, and the show's gimmick would be a gang of London boys who'd play the inmates of a workhouse and the members of Fagin the miser's gang.

The Wisbys sent me to audition at the Wimbledon Theatre with Mum in tow, and once again I found myself among a crowd of hopeful boys and their even more hopeful parents. I joined the other children swarming all over the stage and the stalls, but by now this kind of hurly-burly was familiar to me and I enjoyed the excitement and the larking about. Again the number of kids rapidly diminished, until after six auditions spread over two weeks there were just fourteen of us left. An Ilford boy, Keith Hamshere, was offered the role of Oliver Twist, Martin Horsey, from south of the river, was to be the Artful Dodger, and the rest of us were the cheeky cockney chorus. The job, we were told, would mean taking two months off school. I'd only been on the Wisbys' books for three weeks, and already my plan for avoiding Wanstead High had come to fruition!

First Mum, Dad and I had to go and see Mr Ingham, the headmaster, to get his permission. I'd only been in his office once before, when I'd been caught leaving school without wearing my cap. He'd given me four of the best with the cane he kept wrapped up in a Union Jack, then shook my hand and said, 'What do you think would happen if all the boys unilaterally decided they didn't want to wear their caps, Robinson?'

I'd replied, 'I suppose we'd be living in a capless society, sir,' which he seemed to find very amusing.

He must have kept an eye on me following that beating, because he knew all about me and my 'speechifying', and said he thought I might one day make something of myself, so yes, he'd allow me time off to attend rehearsals.

They lasted six weeks, and mostly we came and went as we pleased. We were supposed to be overseen by a chaperone called 'Chappie', who was fierce, with yellowy bleached hair, red lipstick, and an exotic sweaty smell. But there were fourteen of us and only one of her, and she was always either nattering on the phone, or gossiping with the wardrobe department, so we usually managed to avoid her. A tutor was drafted in too, a kindly, vague lady, who had no idea what she was supposed to be teaching us. I told her I was happy to do my own studying, and brought in a pile of books. I had a series of hardbacks called the Heirloom Library with full-page illustrations: *Heidi*, *Tom Sawyer*, *The Children of the New Forest*, *Pinocchio*, and the like. I must have read the entire cannon of classic children's literature while I was rehearsing for *Oliver!*

We got paid more money than we'd ever had in our lives: five pounds a week for rehearsals, ten once the show started, plus Tube fares and lunch money. Our parents banked most of it for us, but our pockets bulged with cash. We bought vast quantities of cigarettes and sweets, and splashed out on grey Robin Hood hats, black and white herringbone overcoats, and black sunglasses from Woolworths so we'd look like Frank Sinatra's rat pack. The effect must have been a bit muted though, given that we were thirteen years old and had been chosen for our lack of height.

The writer and composer Lionel Bart was the first man I ever knew who wore scent. Apparently it was Guerlain and very expensive, but it seemed weird to me. No men in South Woodford dabbed themselves with scent. They smelt of armpits or booze and fags. One of the girls in the chorus told me Lionel had written 'Living Doll' for Cliff Richard and was a millionaire. He certainly dressed smartly, like a small Italian gangster with shiny cufflinks and Cuban heels. He was kind, soft-spoken and seemed genuinely interested in us boys. Later he bought a mansion in Kensington with twenty-seven rooms, remote-controlled curtains and suits of armour on the staircase. He threw showbiz parties for hundreds of guests, where they passed round a silver tray covered in drugs, and another covered in money. Eventually he went bankrupt.

In the show, the character of Mr Sowerberry the undertaker was supposed to be scary, and the actor who played him was perfectly cast. He was in his mid-twenties but looked like an old tramp. He wore a shabby overcoat, had dirty nails, long, ragged hair and smoked roll-ups incessantly. He was fresh off the boat from Australia and his voice was a like a croaking bird. His name was Barry Humphries.

After five weeks of rehearsals we were introduced to Sean Kenny's set. It was weird, wonderful and very dangerous. There were two huge scaffolding towers on metal rails criss-crossed with rough wooden slats, and in the centre of the stage a revolving turntable. The whole assembly swung and careened around creating constantly changing Victorian slums and crowded streets. It was so complicated, and its movements needed to be organised so exactly, that it was first erected on the stage of the Princes Theatre (now the Shaftesbury), which didn't have a show on at the time, so we could rehearse on it for a week while the carpenters did running repairs. It wasn't a child-friendly environment. All of us kids had narrow escapes, particularly when we weren't concentrating or were mucking about. Eventually my friend Brian Lewis slipped and trapped his ankle during one of the dances when two trucks were passing close to each other. We heard a crack, and stood round watching his face turn white. It took an age to get him free, but we found it very interesting, and talked about it for days. Eventually the set was taken down and re-erected at the New Theatre, (now the Noël Coward) in St Martins Lane. And it was there on 30 June 1960 that *Oliver!* finally opened.

On the first night there were twenty-three curtain calls. Even the stage carpenters took a bow. I was excited – who wouldn't be with such a lot of bravo-ing going on? – but I didn't realise how significant it was. How was I to know that not all first nights ended like this? That when the final bow came, the actors were often greeted by thirty seconds of polite applause, and were back home drunk and depressed by midnight?

But *Oliver!* was special. It wasn't American like *Oklahoma!* or *Seven Brides for Seven Brothers*. Even the apparently British *My Fair Lady* had been written by Yanks. Now at last the UK had a full-scale musical of its own, and it was about London and the drama and fun of being a cockney. The reviews were raves, and it became the number one theatre ticket for foreign tourists.

Being in it was tiring, though. Now we were no longer rehearsing in the daytime, I had to go back to school. I never got to bed before 11.30 p.m., and had to be up again at seven thirty. I'd yawn all day, catch the Central Line Tube late afternoon, change to the Piccadilly Line, get off at Leicester Square, sing and dance all evening, and get collected and taken home by Dad at 10.30. This cycle was repeated every day except Sunday, plus matinees on Tuesdays and Saturdays. We were permanently irritable, never stopped squabbling, and had dark circles under our eyes. I didn't enjoy the constant repetition either. Some actors adore performing the same part night after night. They see it as a mark of true professionalism, but I found it dead boring.

I loved the show, though, and was very proud of it. I knew every word and note from beginning to end. The music was catchy and bitter-sweet, the characters were larger than life, and the cast were brilliant. As for the lyrics, what poetry!

> *In this life*
> *One thing counts,*
> *In the bank*
> *Large amounts.*
> *I'm afraid these*
> *Don't grow on trees,*
> *You've got to pick a pocket or two.*

That was Fagin's instruction to his gang, and every night Ron Moody would sing it to us boys with a thick Jewish accent and a twinkle in his eye.

'Nobody tries to be lah-di-dah and uppity, there a cup-o'-tea for all!' sings the Artful Dodger to Oliver Twist. What a clever rhyme! I wished more than anything else in the world that I could play the Artful Dodger.

On the Tuesday after the first night, Martin Horsey, who was playing the Dodger, bunked off afternoon school and went to the park, forgetting it was a matinee day. A search was conducted, but the whole point of bunking off is that you don't want to get caught, and no one could find him.

The producers had been so immersed in getting the show

mounted that they'd overlooked long-term considerations like recruiting understudies. With fifteen minutes to go before curtain up, the company manager called me into his office.

'Tony,' he asked, 'do you know the part of the Artful Dodger?'

Of course I did.

My dad was working at County Hall, Westminster. I phoned him and told him I was about to go on as the Dodger, and he dropped his biro, sprinted out the building, raced across Westminster Bridge, up Whitehall, across Trafalgar Square, up St Martins Lane, into the theatre and up into the gallery, arriving just in time to see my first entrance.

Even today most people can remember the lyrics of 'Consider Yourself'. I didn't. I went, 'Consider yourself la-la, consider yourself la-la-la-la! La! La! La!' but the audience didn't seem to mind. They apparently warmed to my interpretation of the Artful Dodger as a cheeky, young cockney in the grip of early onset dementia. At the end of the show I got a big round of applause, and all the other actors clapped me too.

Martin Horsey turned up for the evening show looking slightly defiant. I'd hoped they'd let me play the part again that night to punish him for his absence, but of course they didn't. I found it hard going back to being a member of Fagin's gang, but at least I was given the job of Martin's official understudy which meant an extra two pounds a week. And as all the boys had to take a three-week rest every three months, I got to play the Dodger lots more times. It was that experience more than any other that spawned the monster of ambition in me. Being in the chorus was all right, but being at the front of the stage was twenty times better.

Now the show was successful, Decca Records asked us to make an LP. Maida Vale Studios was unique. It was housed in a converted roller-skating rink, a beautiful rococo, white stucco building, over fifty years old, set incongruously among the gloomily uniform red-brick mansion blocks of W9. It's where the

Beatles and the Stones recorded some of their legendary radio sessions a few years later. I live round the corner from it now, and every time my dog Winnie and I walk past, I have vivid memories of the two days I spent there over fifty years ago, being a recording star.

Maybe 'star' is a bit of an exaggeration. I had one solo line in the song 'Food Glorious Food' . . . No, I exaggerate. It was half a line, the words 'What's next? is the question'.

But I was able to make my mark on the record in a far more dramatic way. Keith Hamshere was supposed to recreate Oliver's famous long walk from the wooden workhouse table to where the obnoxious, fat beadle was supervising the doling out of the boys' food. Then he had to say the legendary words 'Please, sir, I want some more,' a request so outrageous that mayhem ensued, and the story began in earnest. But Keith had come to the recording in plimsolls, and when he attempted the walk, the mic couldn't pick up the sound of his feet. I was wearing Chelsea boots, a fashionable innovation that co-ordinated superbly with my herringbone coat and Robin Hood hat, and as they were hard-soled, I volunteered to make that fateful walk instead of Keith. Thus my footsteps were immortalised. I still get a royalty cheque each year for sales of that LP. Usually the sum involved is around £4.85, but it's always gratefully received. Even half a century later I know that somewhere in the world my childish feet are giving joy to an unknown listener.

The other indicator of the show's success was that a whole new gang of boys was employed at the reduced rate of eight pounds per week, to be our understudies and to take over our parts once we'd left. My understudy was a boy called Stephen Marriott. He was six months younger than me, but was beefy and lived in Manor Park, which was considerably rougher than South Woodford. We were supposed to be friends, and in a way we were, but I felt terrorised by him. One minute he'd be my best buddy ever, the next he'd heap scorn and derision on me.

At that time I thought I was the only person he treated like this, but it was just the way he was. He played the guitar, which I thought was very impressive, and I told him I wanted to learn too. He agreed to teach me, and said he could get me one cheap. I gave him five pounds, and a week later he presented me with a small red plywood ukulele. It hadn't been fitted together properly, and when you put pressure on the neck, the strings went 'wow! wow!' Stephen said it was a special effect which was why it was so expensive, and no, I couldn't have my money back. He'd also decided not to give me lessons after all as I was such a moaner.

By now I was in the remorseless grip of early adolescence. Yellow-headed pimples and blackheads mysteriously erupted on my forehead and round my nose, and dark hair was growing on my top lip. Dad refused to let me shave, so in a desperate last-ditch stand to keep my face youthful by warding off juvenile stubble, each night he bleached my putative moustache with hydrogen peroxide instead. It stung, and it didn't work. My moustache didn't disappear, it merely went white, and I looked like a hairy albino. 'Moustachio, Moustachio!' Stephen would chant, and I'd amble off with a look of blithe unconcern on my face, until I'd locked the toilet door and could have a little grizzle.

Every Sunday I went to Manor Park to visit Stephen in his terraced house in Strone Road, but he and his mum were always rowing. They'd say terrible things to each other, and I'd pretend I hadn't heard. So we'd go out, even if it was raining, and we usually ended up at Valentines Park in Ilford. Valentines was a Georgian mansion that had been built by a young captain who'd made his fortune working for the East India Company. But by the early 1960s its grandeur had long faded. It was now owned by Ilford Council, who hadn't a clue what to do with it. It was run-down, had been closed and boarded up, and the park was unkempt and overgrown.

Stephen said we should try some super-strength untipped

cigarettes, which were apparently very manly, a far cry from the menthol Consulates which were the cigarette of choice among us *Oliver!* boys. We bought five Player's Weights, a book of matches and a packet of Extra Strong Mints so our breath wouldn't smell, then hid in the bushes and lit a couple. It was as though I'd inhaled a bonfire. My head span, I was completely discombobulated, and my throat felt like I'd swallowed a Brillo pad. I wanted to stop, but didn't dare show how profoundly I'd been affected. It was bad enough being jeered at for having a white moustache. If I couldn't hold down a Player's Weight, my life would be a torment.

I eventually finished it, nodded appreciatively like a proper cigarette connoisseur, ground the butt manfully under the sole of my shoe, and headed back to South Woodford.

A few years later Stephen became Steve Marriott the rock star, and he wrote a song about Valentines Park called 'Itchycoo Park'. 'What did you do there? I got high!' went the lyrics. I was the first person to get high in Itchycoo Park with the lead singer of the Small Faces, and I was sick three times before I got home.

After nine months, my time in *Oliver!* came to an end. I missed the excitement, but I was totally exhausted, and wasn't too upset about leaving. Except that now I'd have to get my head out of the theatrical clouds, and unless I could find another escape route, the next five years of my life would be nothing but more unremitting misery at Wanstead County High.

2

THE DIVA

Every day I hated school more. It was like the Berlin Wall, cutting me off from everything I wanted to do and be. I was depressed, struggled to get to sleep, and had a recurring nightmare. When I woke up I couldn't remember what it was about, but I'd be terrified and feeling sick.

Then, when I was in my late-thirties, my partner Mary and I went on holiday to the Gambia with the kids. Our hotel was solid concrete but luxurious, like a five-star block of council flats, with barbed wire round it to protect us from the poor people. We were advised not to go out without a security guard because the local population could get a bit aggressive, but on our first morning I checked out the beach and, though it smelt of rotting fish, it was sandy and virtually empty, so I decided to ignore the advice and take a stroll. I watched the terns doing kamikaze dives into the ocean, and crabs rummaging around on the foreshore then scuttling into their holes when they detected my shadow, but my mooch round was interrupted by an eager young man who introduced himself as Eric, and announced that he wanted to be my friend. He offered to take me on a variety of trips, asked me to get involved in his business plans, and invited me to his compound to visit his family and in particular his sister. I turned down these proposals, but then he suggested I might go out with him that evening to the nearby capital city Banjul for a cup of 'special' tea.

I was no stranger to the hallucinogenic experience. I'd read *On The Road* and Carlos Castaneda, I'd wandered the slopes of

the Mendips collecting tiny mushrooms shaped like fairies'
breasts, and I'd built countless three-skinners on the covers of
Dylan LPs. The promise of a trippy encounter with no deadlines
to meet the following day was enticing.

There was hardly any electricity outside the tourist areas.
At night Banjul was lit only by oil lamps and the stark white
light of the moon. The whole place flickered with shadows. It
was the evening of a big wrestling match, so the streets were
packed. Noisy crowds were milling around the rudimentary
shops selling cooking oil, spare parts for transistor radios and
Halls Mentholyptus, and pungent smoke from the fish on
countless barbeques stung my eyes and got up my nostrils.

On the far side of town, across a wonky footbridge over a
muddy trickle of water, was a shack made out of a patchwork
of customised metal advertising hoardings. 'Oxo' said one;
'Made to Make Your Mouth Water' proclaimed the next; 'The
Mint With The Ho—' announced another.

Inside was a wooden bar, four plastic tables and assorted
chairs. 'Pass the Dutchie on the Left-Hand Side' was playing on
the radio. A man with white hair and a pretty teenage girl in a
faded Rolling Stones T-shirt were nodding in time to the music.
They were drinking Pepsi from the bottle, and on the table in
front of them was a chicken in a small wooden cage.

A smiling fat man with gold front teeth brought me a teapot
with Chinese writing on it, and two cups made out of tuna cans.
Eric declined his, but I poured a cup of bright yellow tea, and
he talked to me about how keen he was to come to England so
he could stay with me and further his education. After half an
hour the tea had had no effect so I asked for another. I knocked
it back, but was again disappointed.

I didn't feel particularly cheated. The whole evening had
cost me less than a fiver, including the tip which Eric had
finally accepted after demonstrating acute reluctance to do so.
I'd only been in the country twenty-four hours, but had already

glimpsed authentic Gambian life. How many English tourists locked away in their posh bunkers could say the same? Eric guided me back across town and, as he was worried that if he got any closer the security guards might beat him up, left me 100 yards short of the hotel. I got back to my room, kissed Mary goodnight, and went to bed.

Sometime later I woke up. My head had split open like an overripe watermelon, and bands of bright colour were pouring out of it. I felt intensely emotional. Tears came to my eyes as I remembered the pets of my childhood: Goldie my goldfish, Monty my furry brown and white rabbit, and Ricky my blue budgerigar who'd flown out of the open window when I'd let him out of his cage.

I was blissfully happy. I could hear Laura and Luke fast asleep on the other side of the room, their breath like waves crashing on the shore. 'They're the greatest blessing . . .' I said, and the words echoed round the room like a *Doctor Who* sound effect, '. . . that life has bestowed.' BESTOWED!! What a beautiful word. It glowed and glittered in front of me, then disintegrated into diamonds of light. Slowly I floated off the bed and rose towards the ceiling. When I looked below me, I saw myself on the bed looking up, calm and smiling.

Then the noise began. It was a loud, rhythmic grinding like the engine of an old Victorian milling machine, and it was chillingly familiar. It was the sound of my childhood nightmare.

Out of the darkness a large metal grid was being lowered onto me, jerking like a marionette in time to the noise. It got closer and closer. It was going to choke me, squash the life out of me. When it was almost touching my nose, I looked my metal nemesis full in the grid, and I knew. I was absolutely certain. The grid was the school timetable! My terror was the inescapable certainty that every day, every week, every term of my school life I'd be in thrall to double French, followed by maths, history, R.E. and the rest. There was no pleasure to be had from school; learning was a life sentence. That's why I hated Wanstead High, and why I was so desperate to escape from it.

Relief came when I was given a TV role on BBC Children's Hour in a play called *The Man from the Moors* about a brutal Victorian school. My character was a weaselly tell-tale who finally gets exposed and bursts into tears at the foot of the school stairs. It was a dramatic part, and I thought I was rather good in it, but when I saw it on telly, I was horrified by how unreal my crying was. But at least it had kept me out of my own brutal school for a week.

Then I got a couple of days off to do a drama-documentary film about oral hygiene, in which I had to say the following words: 'What it means, I think, is that scattered all over the body there are various centres of infection where diseases get hold of you: the throat's one, here's another – the kidneys – and the teeth a third, and I don't know how this lark's going to turn out, but I think I'm going to have to start cleaning my teeth soon!' This was a very difficult sentence for a fourteen-year-old to learn.

My next lengthy escape came when the boy who played Anthony Newley's son in the West End musical *Stop the World – I Want to Get Off* had his appendix out, and I played his part for six whole weeks. I was awestruck by Tony Newley; he was intense, anguished, and seemed completely detached from the rest of the world. He never spoke to me – that was part of his mystery – but I watched him obsessively from the wings every night. He'd been a child actor and had played the Artful Dodger in a famous film version in the old days. Now he was grown-up, but still had a cheeky Artful Dodger voice, and sang pop songs with a cockney accent and a wobble in his throat which sent him to the top of the hit parade. He seemed like a grown-up version of me. Every night I mimicked his words, and gazed agonisingly into the spotlight pulling a heartbroken face, just like he did.

And then there were the girls. *Stop the World* was the story of a young man who rises to the top, comes crashing down to earth again, and finally realises that true love is his only salvation. But in order to learn this, he has to go to bed with a lot of beautiful girls, and be very mean to them. This was a path I was eager to tread, if possible with the same girls, although my knowledge of sexual activity was fairly rudimentary. Everything I knew about the adult naked body I'd learnt from the magazine *Health and Efficiency*. Once you'd leafed through its articles on vegetarianism and advertisements for haemorrhoid creams, you came to the real thing – photos of naked men and women playing table tennis in German forests. I didn't realise their pubic hair had been airbrushed. When I had my first below-the-belt experience with a girl of my own age a couple of years later, I was a little put out by the fact that the area round her vagina wasn't silky smooth, but was rough and tufty as though she had an old dormouse snuggling in her lap.

As for the mechanics of sex, I learnt about that from the jokes older boys told me. A fourth-former gave me a long poem he'd laboriously typed out. It began:

> *Good morning, Mrs Henderson, God bless your heart*
>   *and soul,*
> *I tried to shag your daughter, but I couldn't find*
>   *the hole . . .*

There then followed a series of couplets in which the poet described his attempts to enter the correct resting place. It ended:

> *And then I gave her more, more than she could stand,*
> *Now she's selling babies up and down the Strand.*

It was the best poem I'd ever read, witty, highly informative and with a strong narrative thrust, a much finer piece than the work of John Masefield or Walter de la Mare, although I doubted whether Miss Phillips would have appreciated its spirited cadences. My best friend Roger Burbery and I read it out loud over and over again, each time practically wetting ourselves with hysteria.

My first close-up encounter with sex was in Wanstead Park. Our PE teacher was a large, charismatic man called Ron Pickering, who later became the BBC's top sports commentator and a senior athletics administrator. He gave me the nickname 'Mighty Mouse', which stuck with me for the rest of my school life, but he was also a bit contemptuous of me – he was well aware that I'd do everything possible to avoid strenuous physical activity.

My *bête noire* was the cross-country run. The only boys I ever beat were the chronically fat, and asthmatics who'd forgotten their inhalers. But Ron forced me to take part, and there was no escape other than to follow the runners into Wanstead Park, veer off into the forest and hide in the trees. After twenty minutes or so, when they'd slogged round the vast ornamental lake, I could sneak out, rejoin them, and trot back to school.

One morning I ducked into the trees as usual, and wandered about for a while waiting until I could safely reappear. I came to a clearing, and there stood half a dozen of my fellow athletes, their white shorts and pants round their knees, each one holding the penis of the runner to his left, jerking it up and down with a look of rapt concentration on his face.

'Hi,' I said.

'Hi, Mighty,' they chorused, and I jogged off again.

Now every night at the theatre I was in the presence of nine young women who'd been specifically chosen because they'd be plausible fantasies for Tony Newley's character (who went by the faintly ironic name of Littlechap). The only males backstage were the ancient stage door keeper and me, and as far as the girls were concerned, we were invisible. They'd run from one dressing room to the next in their brassieres and petticoats laughing and shrieking, and would make quick changes in the wings, undressing right down to their knickers, oblivious of the fact that I was sitting in the corner studiously reading Graham Green's *Brighton Rock*. What a privilege! I was a Christian at the time – at least I sang alto in the St Philip and St James's church choir – and I thanked God mightily every night that he had given me this blessing. The memory of Jenny Wren, Vivian St George, Janet Allman, her twin sister Jennifer, and all the other young women in the show is etched on my heart to this day.

But above all there was Marti Webb. She was only three or four years older than me, with the face of an innocent child, and the sleekness and elegance of a gazelle. She was also hugely talented, and the only performer on stage who wasn't eclipsed by Newley's charisma. I watched her avidly, giving her smouldering looks whenever she glanced casually in my direction. I knew that one day she'd realise I was just like Tony Newley, only much younger, smarter and more interesting, and that the most sensible thing she could do would be to fall wildly in love with me. But for some reason this never happened. On the night I left the show, I went to her dressing room for her autograph, and before she signed it, she looked at me thoughtfully and said, 'What's your name again?'

At the end of the year, my school report was desultory, and I'd come rock-bottom of the class. I was sent to Mr Ingham the headmaster for a serious talk, but he was surprisingly sympathetic. He said it was mainly his fault I'd done so badly; he'd given permission for me to have a lot of time off school, and this was the inevitable consequence. He'd keep me in the 'A' stream, not because I'd had any success with my school work, but because I'd come top of the entire year in my I.Q. tests (which were long lists of triangles and squares you had to put in the right order, and which frankly were a piece of piss). I'd avoid the ignominy of being sent down to the 'B' stream, and the following year I could continue performing because I was obviously rather good at it, but at the same time I had to get stuck into my school work with a vengeance.

'Do you understand?'

Yes, I did.

'Will we see a marked improvement in your school work?'

Yes, we would .

But no, we didn't.

My third year passed even more miserably than my second. The lessons were harder, and I got further behind. The only way I got even faintly respectable marks was by borrowing my friends' homework and looking over their shoulders during tests.

There were two high points that year, though: the Aldermaston march and meeting Judy Garland. Neddy Knight, a sixth-former in charge of my lunch table, took a shine to me. He had a tiny black and white badge on the lapel of his blazer, which he told me signified he was a member of the Campaign for Nuclear Disarmament. He explained about nuclear weapons, the effects of radioactive fallout, and about Nagasaki and Hiroshima. He said that both America and Russia had arsenals of H-bombs, and threatened each other with them, despite being aware that if even one went off thousands of people would be burnt to charcoal, and others would suffer horrific burns or would give birth to mutant babies.

I was outraged. How could civilised people be prepared to use such disgusting weapons when they knew the consequences? They should be banned. We had to persuade our government to give them up unilaterally, and shame Russia and America into doing the same.

I read everything I could get my hands on about unilateral nuclear disarmament. I debated long and hard with my dad about whether or not it would leave us vulnerable to invasion by a crazed dictator, and went to my first Ban the Bomb meeting. Two weeks later I and a few friends started the Wanstead and Woodford branch of Youth CND.

I wasn't a good organiser. I forgot where the meetings were going to take place, and what time they were due to start. I didn't pass messages on, and got into terrible trouble with the finances. Two years later I discovered a tin box in the back of the bottom drawer of my wardrobe underneath my stamp albums. It contained the money from the sale of Ban the Bomb badges which I'd lost and never told anyone about. I'd like to think that I sent the cash straight back to the CND, but I'm not sure I did.

I was good at persuading other teenagers to join the movement, though, and was even better at chanting. Every Saturday six of us would meet outside Bearmans department store in Leytonstone, and walk round in a circle waving our placards, handing out our leaflets, and chanting, '1-2-3-4, we don't want a nuclear war! 5-6-7-8, we say negotiate!'

It didn't scan properly, but the message was clear.

Then I went on my first Aldermaston march. Dad hadn't wanted me to go as he was worried people would think I was a communist and I wouldn't be able to get into America if I was ever offered a part in a Broadway show. But he believed in the right to free speech, even for teenagers, so he reluctantly acquiesced, and even drove me to the place where the coach was going to pick us up. He tried to put his arm round me to say goodbye, but I shrugged it off like I always did; fourteen-year-old boys can be little bastards.

I loved every minute of the next three days. A hundred thousand people, that's what the organisers said, walking the fifty-two miles from the Berkshire nuclear base at Aldermaston to Trafalgar Square over the Easter weekend. So many people in one long line expressing their opposition to something I thought was supremely important! I kept looking back at them stretching out behind me. It felt as though we were the moral force of the entire universe. How could we possibly fail?

After a couple of hours my feet ached, by midday I had blisters, and by lunchtime I'd had enough of marching. A lorry was driving slowly down the line of marchers carrying kitbags,

suitcases and young people with armbands. I limped up to them
and asked what they were doing.

'We're the baggage marshals,' a girl said. 'We collect everyone's stuff, and leave it at the various places where they're
going to sleep.'

'Can I help?'

'Are you sure you want to – you'd have to miss out on the
marching?'

'If it's important, I'll do it,' I replied nobly, and scrambled up
onto the lorry.

Each bag was numbered and had a brightly coloured ticket
with the owner's name on it and its intended location. All day
we sorted through the bags, drove to the various designated
church halls, and laid them out in long lines according to their
numbers. The other marshals were sixth-formers who belonged
to the Labour Party Young Socialists, politics students from
the London School of Economics, and members of the Young
Communist League. We chatted about films I'd never seen,
books I'd never heard of, and politics I only vaguely understood.
I had a great time.

Two and a half days later in the centre of London I left my
fellow baggage marshals and the lorry, and walked the last
half-mile to Trafalgar Square. Crowds lined the pavements
applauding us for our commitment. Looking faint and exhausted
like John Mills struggling through the North African desert in
Ice Cold in Alex, I wearily nodded my thanks.

As the year went by I got more little parts from the Wisbys
which meant more time off school, although sometimes only a
few hours. Steve Marriott and I spent an afternoon modelling
jumpers for the front covers of Fair Isle knitting patterns in the
basement of Raymond's Revue Bar in Soho. Steve was a snappy
dresser, and the cardigans and scarves looked great on him.
But I looked like a refugee. He'd just sung the part of the Artful

Dodger on a new budget LP of *Oliver!* 'Nice one!' I said, but through gritted teeth.

None of us minded too much if we got small parts rather than big ones. Doing anything in a show or on TV got us off school and earned us good money.

Word went round that the famous Hollywood star Judy Garland was in London to make a film called *The Lonely Stage*, and two hundred fourteen-year-olds were needed as extras. Mum and Dad drove me to central London in the middle of the night, we met up with a crowd of yawning teenagers on Northumberland Avenue, ten coaches arrived, and we clambered in. I was the smallest and most nimble, and managed to get the best seat in the back row by the window. I was looking out for Gregory Phillips who I'd worked with a couple of times before, and who'd been cast as Miss Garland's son. I was told he wouldn't be coming with us as he was being driven down to location in a chauffeur-driven car. If it had been anyone else, I'd have hated them, but Greg was always smiling and shared his cigarettes, so I couldn't resent his new status.

We drove for an hour and a half, entertaining ourselves by reading *The Beano*, passing wind, playing with our yo-yos and telling dirty jokes. I was good at all those things except the yo-yo, so time passed quickly enough.

We eventually arrived in Canterbury. The King's School was in the shadow of the cathedral, and looked very old, like a castle or a stately home. It was still early, and if it hadn't been for the dawn chorus, it would have been absolutely silent. We poured out of the buses, were herded into the school hall and given our public school uniforms. They were ridiculous clothes, like the sort a butler might wear in an old-fashioned comedy – black suits, white shirts with black ties and wing collars. Did kids really wear this kind of thing? The trousers they'd given me were far too long, and the bottoms trailed along behind me, so a wardrobe lady with half-glasses on a ribbon round her neck and a fag in her mouth sewed them up for me. She told me what the plot was about. Miss Garland was playing a Hollywood star who'd fallen in love with a young English doctor in New York, and she'd become pregnant and had a baby boy. But she'd grown needy and neurotic, and was taking lots of drugs and drink.

'So it isn't going to be much of an acting challenge for her,' the wardrobe lady added, and raised an eyebrow.

Miss Garland's character was so ruthlessly ambitious that she didn't want to look after her little boy, and the doctor had taken him back to England, after making her promise she'd never try to see him again. Now it was thirteen years later, her career was on the rocks, and she'd been invited to give a concert at the London Palladium. She'd met up with the doctor again, and after she'd made a big fuss, he'd agreed to take her to their son's public school so she could see him for one final time, and in the scene we were about to shoot, she was going to watch him playing rugby.

Thus briefed, I was sent off for breakfast. It was the first time I'd ever worked on a feature film, so it was also my introduction to location catering. Imagine everything that might be put on your plate if you ordered a full English breakfast. Now imagine a few more things that you'd like to get, but probably wouldn't. All of them were served up that morning, and when you'd finished you could go and get more without being glared at.

At nine o'clock we were led to the rugby pitch and placed round various parts of it. There was a hiatus while we waited for Miss Garland to appear but she didn't, so the director orchestrated a few shots of rugby players running around and throwing the ball to each other while the rest of us cheered. At eleven o'clock there was a short break while we were served ham and cheese sandwiches on large trays and plastic cups of orange squash. After that there was more waiting around. Some of the King's School boys had come out to watch us, dressed in their stupid butlers' uniforms. We told them to bugger off and fetch us some gin and tonics, and when one of them made a sarcastic comment implying that we were all queers, we chased him back into the school. A short time later he appeared at a window with his mates and they pulled their earlobes and stuck their tongues out, so we booed them and gave them 'V' signs.

Next to the pitch were two large Winnebago camper vans with gold stars and numbers on the doors. Number one belonged to Miss Garland, and number two was for Dirk Bogarde who was playing the doctor. At about midday a catering man took a plate of food into Winnebago one, there was a crash, and he came out again minus the food. Then one of the producers knocked on the door, went inside and he came out again. Another producer did the same, except that when he came out, he knocked on the door of Winnebago two and went in. Then Dirk Bogarde came out of Winnebago two looking very cross, went into Winnebago one and came out again. There was no sign of Miss Garland.

For lunch we had chicken, great piles of it on huge tin trays – chicken wings, chicken legs, chicken thighs and chicken breasts. Chicken was so expensive back then that at home you only got it on special occasions, so we scoffed it with gusto, along with shovelfuls of chips and mounds of tinned peas. For pudding there was black forest gateau or strawberry instant whip, or both.

After lunch we were told that Miss Garland had been indisposed, but would be joining us on set soon. At three thirty there were fairy cakes and Penguin biscuits, and at four o'clock we were told we could go home, but were asked to be ready to finish the scene the following day. This was the best news possible. Not only would we get more chicken, but we'd only been expecting to get paid for one day, so now we'd double our money.

Day two followed a similar pattern to day one – a long, dark journey, breakfast, waiting, elevenses, more waiting, chicken, etc., etc., and being sent home at four o'clock. It was a bit more boring than day one though, because some of the time we had to sit in our coaches as the school had made complaints about our behaviour. Day three was the same, although by this time I was getting a bit sick of the chicken.

Mid-morning on day four I wandered into Greg's dressing room, because if I was talking to him, I wouldn't get sent back to the coach. It wasn't really a dressing room, just a large classroom with lemonade and comics on the teacher's desk, but it had his name on the door, so it was still pretty impressive.

He was sitting on a desk, and a little girl with a big pink band in her blonde hair was cross-legged on the floor looking up at him, holding a large stuffed bulldog with a Union Jack round its stomach.

'Lorna,' he said in the voice people use when they're talking to little children, 'this is Tony.' She waved shyly.

There was another girl in the room, looking out of a large window. She was about our age, and was wearing lots of make-up. I strolled over to her.

'Hi!' I said, and held out my hand. 'Tony Robinson.'

She didn't reply. The other boys were still on the coaches clowning around. Beyond them on the games field, half a dozen crew members were playing a mock game of rugby.

'A rugby girl, or a football girl?' I asked.

Again she didn't reply. One of the camera assistants was running towards the touchline in slow motion clutching an imaginary ball.

'Three points for a try,' I said, 'another two for a conversion,' which was practically all I knew about rugby. 'See the lads down there? They're supporting artists.' I waved at them, and they pulled moronic faces. 'Idiots, aren't they?'

She turned to me.

'Why are you doing this?' she said fiercely.

'Doing what?'

'Talking to me.'

She was American, and sounded like an actress in *Perry Mason*.

'I don't know,' I said, nonplussed. 'Because . . . the night is young?'

The look she gave me would have turned a lesser man to stone.

'Come on, Lorna,' she said, grabbed the little girl by the hand and left the room.

'What a bitch!' I said. 'Who was she?'

'Miss Garland's daughter.'

'Christ, why didn't you tell me?'

'I thought you knew. She's all right actually.'

'No, she isn't.'

'Well, she's fine with me,' said Greg. 'I think she fancies me,' and he rolled his eyes.

In the lunch queue I was besieged by the other lads.

'Was that the daughter?' someone asked.

'Yes,' I replied. 'Liza.'

'What were you doing?'

'Just chatting,' I said, 'about this and that. She's all right actually. I think she fancies me.'

Her presence certainly seemed to work wonders on her mother. Half an hour later the entire unit was summoned onto the pitch, and Miss Garland came out of her trailer and thanked us all for being so patient. She had been brought low by a nasty virus, she said, but had now recovered. She looked forward to working with us tomorrow.

On the next and final day we got to do the big scene at last. Greg was supposed to be playing scrum-half for the under-fourteens, and when he was tackled and disappeared under the ensuing scrum, Miss Garland would appear, and the ref would blow for half-time. A boy was then needed to carry a plate of quartered oranges onto the pitch to give to the rugby players. This might only be classed as glorified extra work, but it was an important role, which required an interesting-looking boy, who was professional and had good movement skills.

Following some prompting, Greg volunteered me for the

part, the director agreed, and after four days of anonymity I was suddenly, for a few minutes, the centre of attention. Even Miss Garland talked to me, although I didn't take in what she said, because I was worried the oranges might fall off their plate.

The scene couldn't have gone better. Miss Garland, swathed in fur, was struggling through the pitch-side mud. She lost a shoe, leant on the manly Dirk Bogarde for support, then laughing like a slightly mad young girl, continued round the pitch barefoot. At that moment a young man, sensitive but intellectual, dressed smartly in his traditional school uniform, walked past them expertly bearing fruit for the rugby players. They followed him with their eyes, their son was revealed, and they looked proudly on.

I shot the long walk in one take, and was congratulated for my professionalism – at least I think I was. Shortly afterwards the first assistant called a wrap, and I went home for the final time.

By the time it was released, the film had been retitled *I Could Go On Singing*, which was the name of Judy Garland's big song. I told everyone about my role as the boy with the oranges. Five of us went to watch it at the Plaza in George Lane, South Woodford, but to my horror, my part had been butchered. I was on screen for three and a half seconds. (That's not an exaggeration, I've timed it.) My friends thought this was hysterically funny, and told the whole school. I was mortified.

At Wanstead life went from bad to worse. There was only one silver lining. The dad of one of the boys in my class died, and the bereaved lad had to take so much time off school that he got even further behind than me, so at the end of the year I came second to bottom rather than bottom.

By the fifth year I'd given up on school work, and my teachers had given up on me. I was now a master at bunking off, because I had one major advantage over other truants – the teachers never knew whether I was supposed to be at school or performing somewhere. I'd leave home after breakfast, go down to South Woodford library for a few hours, pop into school for a spot of lunch and a game of football, leave again, hang round the bus stop for a bit, then meet up with my mates on their way back home.

Even when I was at school I had an uncanny knack of getting away with my crimes. I smoked like a chimney but was never caught, won a wanking competition during physics without the teacher noticing, and regularly stole the key to the stock cupboard and took armfuls of exercise books.

My luckiest escape was in the Cottage. Wanstead High was built at the turn of the century, but at the bottom of the games field there was an early nineteenth-century workers' house which was occasionally used as an overflow classroom. It was strictly out of bounds because it was so far away from the rest of the school. Once inside you were completely unobserved, which was of course what made it so attractive.

The card game of choice was three-card brag. It's a brutal game requiring a combination of luck, ability and sufficient money to hammer your opponents into submission. On this particular morning there were half a dozen of us in the small upstairs room, and I was having a rotten run of luck. Roger Burbery dealt and I picked up my hand – the two of diamonds, the three of spades and the six of clubs. Absolute rubbish. In disgust I threw my cards down, dogged out my cigarette, picked up my money, and walked over to the window to watch the sixth-form girls playing rounders in their white aertex blouses. At that moment the door burst open, and our maths teacher pounced. He whisked the other boys off to the headmaster and I was left on my own. Later, when I sneaked back into school, the rest of the card players had gone home. They'd been suspended for a week for smoking and gambling. On their return

I told them how guilty I felt, but they said, 'Shut up, you jammy sod,' which I thought was uncalled for.

Soon O-levels were looming. This was a big problem. On one hand I'd done no school work for years and the thought of revision made me feel physically sick. On the other hand if I did badly, Mum and Dad wouldn't let me go out into the big wide world and become an actor; they'd force me to sign up at some dreadful private college in Ilford and swot for a couple of years. At least if I could get into the sixth form I'd be OK. Everyone knew it was a doddle; for a start you only had to do three subjects. But you needed five O-level passes. How on earth was that going to happen? One solution presented itself – cheat!

We had to sit eight O-levels. Spanish was incomprehensible, I was good at music but couldn't be bothered to learn the theory, and I'd definitely fail maths. (In retrospect my loathing for the subject was absurd. I was the school bookie from the age of fifteen. I had exercise books full of bets. If anyone put two bob each way on a horse at 7 to 2 and it won, I could do the sum in my head. 7 to 2 is 3½ to one, so that's seven bob, plus a quarter for the place is one and nine pence, plus the original stake of four bob is twelve shillings and nine pence in total. But I didn't think that was maths, it was just me being a bit dodgy.)

So that left five subjects, all of which I needed to pass. I ought to be able to bluff my way through English language, English literature, history and geography. So I'd have to cheat in French.

The night before the exam I made a list of the most impressive-sounding words in the French dictionary, and wrote them down on the inside of my right arm. Then, during the examination, I took off my blazer and hung it on the back of my seat. Now I was able to slide my shirt up and down, and access the words through the little vent between the button and the top of my wrist. Thus I could pepper my French essay with sophisticated vocabulary. The only problem was I'd forgotten to write down next to the French words what they meant in

English. So I put them in at random. If my essay had been translated back into English, it would have sounded like a James Joyce novel.

Title – 'What I Did On My Holiday'. 'The sun was shining, the birds were singing and the flowers were INCONTROVERT-IBLE. I bought my bucket and VACCINATION, and built a castle in the EPIGLOTIS . . .'

When the exam results finally came out I found that my dazzling use of language hadn't impressed the French examiner. He'd failed me! I had only four O-levels – I was doomed to incarceration in Clarke's College where all the other half-wits who failed their exams went if they had pushy parents.

But once again Mr Ingham came to my rescue. He said my long absences from school had inevitably meant I'd missed a lot of the curriculum, and consequently I'd failed exams I would otherwise have passed. He was quite confident I'd do well at my A-levels, so he was prepared to give me special dispensation and let me into the sixth form. I was off the hook again.

If my first five years at Wanstead had been hell, my final year was a scholastic paradise. Everyone understood I was dead set on an acting career, so my grades didn't matter anymore. If I kept my head down, no one would bother me.

Ironically, once the pressure was off, I immersed myself in school life like never before. I studied Aristotle and Plato on Friday lunchtimes with an earnest German master, started a project on early Christian heresy with my R.E. teacher Mr Turner, learnt how to roll a cigarette one-handed, and played bridge and Texas hold'em in the school library.

I also listened to a lot of music. I'd always been a music fanatic. The first record I'd ever owned was Elvis Presley's 'Teddy Bear', which was free when you sent in the tops of four bottles of Corona fizzy drink. Mum and Dad didn't have a radiogram so I took my new record down to Susan Pears, the girl next door but one, who had an old gramophone with sharp needles that you screwed into the stylus. It was made of floppy plastic and when we put it on the turntable, the needle cut into it. We watched in horror as the record went round and round with no sound coming out, until after two minutes it had cut a spiral all the way to the middle. 'Teddy Bear' had become a slinky.

Mum and Dad gave me a blue and cream Dansette record player for passing the Eleven-Plus, and I bought records by Buddy Holly, J.S. Bach, Frankie Lane and Ludwig Van Beethoven. It didn't occur to me that some of them might be classified as 'pop' and others as 'classical'.

Later my obsession became modern jazz. I spent hours sitting in the school library fantasising that I was a beatnik in a duffel coat and blue corduroy trousers, staring moodily out of a Manhattan club window, wearing my CND badge and clicking my fingers along to the John Coltrane Quartet.

I had to write a few essays, but I enjoyed English. I found Jane Austen's clever, sexy, teenage girls very funny, I liked Robert Browning's ironic stories, but my absolute favourite was Gerard Manley Hopkins. I thought I knew a bit about poetry, but when he described his feelings being like a kingfisher catching fire, that was just like Coltrane's music.

Dad and I were summoned to school.

'We want you to try for Oxford,' said Mr Ingham.

Aaaaarrghh!

Were they mad? A place at Oxford would mean getting an O-level in Latin, another in maths, four A-levels at grade 'A', not to mention the Oxford entrance exam. What had I managed so far? Even when I'd written the answers on my arm I could only get four measly O-levels. What was I going to do? How could I tell my dad I didn't want to go to the greatest university in the entire world?

There was one alternative. I didn't want to do it, I didn't need to do it, but going anywhere would be better than the nightmare of studying for Oxford.

'No thanks,' I said. 'I'd like to go to drama school.'

3

THE BEARDED ELF

It was my first day at the Central School of Speech and Drama. I sprang jauntily up the stairs at Swiss Cottage Tube station in my donkey jacket, black and white dogtooth knitted jumper, blue jeans, and pinned to my lapel my ever-present Ban the Bomb badge. I was a promising young performer about to wow my fellow students. I was talented and experienced; a few tips and tweaks and I'd be a first-class actor.

I was confident my new teachers would be able to show me how. At my audition the head of drama, John Blatchley, had dazzled me with his authority, his theatrical flair and his left-wing passion, and he'd clearly warmed to me and found me interesting. He'd talked to me at length about Brecht and Stanislavsky, both of whom I'd heard of, although I wasn't sure exactly what they did.

Swiss Cottage was surrounded by interesting neighbourhoods. Camden Town was sleazy and hip, Hampstead arty and sophisticated, and Kilburn full of dangerous Irish people and prostitutes with small dogs. But Swiss Cottage didn't seem to have a clue what it was. The cottage itself was a pub and looked like the kind of place Heidi's dad would have sloped off to when he got irritated by his tediously twee daughter. As a watering hole it had a massive drawback. It was on an island in the middle of a one-way system on the main road heading north out of London. If you fancied a beer, you had to risk your life crossing five lanes of traffic.

Close by, though, peacefully hidden away among tree-lined

streets, was the Embassy Theatre, which for the best part of seventy-five years had been a prestigious outer-London theatrical venue, until Central – which up until then had been squeezed into the top floor of the Albert Hall – had moved in.

The Embassy wasn't a glamorous-looking theatre. A casual passer-by might have mistaken it for a synagogue or a church of the Seventh-day Adventists.

But I bounded enthusiastically up its wide stone steps through some big glass-panelled doors, into what had once been the theatre foyer. Sandwiches were being scoffed, hair was being combed, solitary students were huddled in corners gesturing with their hands as they silently mouthed their lines, and there was a lot of cuddling going on.

There were thirty-five of us in the new acting intake. We were shown into a large room with a battered sign on the door announcing 'Rehearsal Room A'. It was bright and empty and had long ago been painted light blue. It had a high ceiling, full-length mirrors, a practice barre for dancers, and a big bare wooden floor on which we sat in a sophisticated we-don't-need-chairs kind of way.

A door opened and the staff walked in. We instantly sat up straight while trying to look relaxed at the same time. Hang on! Where was John Blatchley? Where were all the teachers who'd interviewed me and been so excited about the possibility of working with me? Not a single one of them was there. Had I come to the wrong place?

A tall hawk-like woman with a lazy eye announced herself as Gwynneth Thurburn, the school principal. She said some of us might be puzzled by the change of personnel, but that there had recently been a difference of opinion about training methods. She'd become perturbed that several students were damaging their voices because of changes in their posture brought on by their exercises. She had asked for the exercise regime to be altered, but the head of drama had declined to do this. Consequently, after much discussion, he and several members of the team had resigned. So now Central was about to set off in an exciting new direction, and our new head of drama was to be . . . George Hall.

Who? I'd been expecting John Blatchley, a giant of the theatre, with flowing locks and the voice of Zeus. The man who now joined Miss Thurburn was small, with a silly little black beard, beady eyes, a black roll-necked jumper, and black tights which drew far too much attention to his spindly legs. Who was he? I didn't want him! John Blatchley had worked with the finest actors in the world. This man looked like a naughty elf in a seaside pantomime!

He was certainly confident, though. He squatted in front of us like a wolf-cub Akela and, in a soft but firm voice, told us emphatically that good actors had to understand their bodies. They must control their breathing, make sure they keep their throats open and relaxed, and have long, flexible spines and good balance. They must be able to fence and dance. They must be supple and strong.

I didn't care about any of that. I didn't need to run a mile in four minutes or dance the fandango. I just wanted to be able to stand up on stage and convince people I was a real person.

When the elf had had his say, our first class began. It was called 'movement'. We squeezed into ridiculous black tights like the ones the elf was wearing, with ballet jockstraps over them which pushed my balls up in the direction of my naval.

The movement teacher was another weirdo. Had they got her cheap? She looked about ninety years old, and was swathed in black rehearsal clothes like the walking dead. She had a German accent, was hunchbacked and wrinkled with hooded eyes, and her grey hair was tucked up in a rudimentary bee-hive. Every time she spun round, hairpins flew out of her head.

Her name was Litz Pisk, and eventually I grew to have a deep love and respect for her. She'd worked with the great inter-war German theatre practitioners, and represented all that was fine in the European dramatic tradition. I didn't know that at first, of course. As far as I was concerned, she was a peculiar old midget. But I did discover one remarkable thing about her very quickly: she could mimic the way we walked with unerring accuracy to demonstrate what was wrong with our posture. Her impression of me made me feel sick. This strange, bent old lady suddenly became a teenage boy with tense shoulders almost up to his ears, a tight fore-shortened neck, a chin pointing to the stars, a body slightly twisted with the weight thrown over to the left, bowed legs and flat feet. I'd thought I looked like a prowling cat, mysterious, predatory and alert, but she portrayed me as a teenage neurotic riddled with physical tension. I didn't like her classes, and lurked at the back of them. They were exhausting, and my lack of mobility and balance humiliated me. But gradually I realised how much she could teach me. The problem was I didn't want to learn it.

That first afternoon we sat in a circle and talked about ourselves and why we wanted to act. When it came to my turn I ran through my CV, which was far more impressive than anyone else's, and modestly explained that I knew I could do better, and was here because I wanted to improve.

When we'd finished our life stories, George told each of us what we needed to work on during our first term. Eventually he came to me.

'Tony!' he said, and cocked his head to one side.

'George!' I replied, smiling.

'Oh dear, sir,' he said.

'Oh dear,' I replied, still smiling.

'You know that of everyone here, you'll have the toughest job.'

Whaaaaaaaaaaat? I thought.

'As a child actor you've picked up some dreadful habits. It's not your fault, it's just what happens. You, sir, are going to have to unlearn everything, I mean *everything* you think is good about your acting. Then you're going to have to build yourself back up from scratch. We'll help you, but we can only do it if you take on board how important it is to do so. It'll be tough.'

I nodded thoughtfully and with a committed look on my face, but inside I was thinking, *You bastard! You bastard, with your bastard little legs and your bastard little beard! What do you know?*

I was still living at home, and as Swiss Cottage is about ten miles from South Woodford, getting there and back was a slog. But it was much easier once I had a car.

On my seventeenth birthday I'd applied for my driving licence, a few weeks later Dad decided to get rid of his old car, and as I'd got some money saved up from my earnings as a child actor, I bought it from him for £300.

It was a Triumph Herald – 948cc of Italian panache. It was jet black, with little fins on the back to give it extra style. It was light and bright with big windows, and a turning circle as tight as a London taxi (which impressed other drivers but made my tyres bald). It had twin carburettors whose precise function was a mystery to me, but which meant it could accelerate from nought to sixty in an eye-watering twenty-three seconds. And most important of all, it had a wireless, so I could tune into the new pirate radio stations whenever I wanted, which was all the time.

My driving test was booked in for just before Christmas, and I was determined to pass. I'd get up early, drive my dad to work at County Hall, Westminster, take the Tube to Central, get another one back to Westminster in the evening, pick up my dad and drive home. At the weekend we'd tootle round Epping Forest or drive down to Southend. When the day of my test came I was quietly confident. By now I considered myself a pretty experienced driver.

The examiner was a middle-aged, grey-faced man with a nondescript brown sports jacket and brown leatherette gloves. He burped quietly but regularly, and then said, 'Excuse me.' I was scrupulously courteous to him, and tried to give him the impression that I deeply respected his age, wisdom and knowledge of the road. I drove through the streets of Ilford checking my mirror every few seconds. I slowed down to a snail's pace whenever a pedestrian came remotely close or when a cyclist needed to be overtaken, and if no perceived danger lurked, I gently accelerated to twenty miles per hour but no more. I was the epitome of the careful, mature driver who understands his responsibilities to other road users.

The examiner began sighing and tapping the glove box with one leatherette finger. Finally he snapped. 'Stop bluffing!' he said, in a tone I found unnecessarily hostile. I felt as though I'd been told off for overacting. I sped up to 30mph. 'That's better,' he said tersely. No further incidents occurred.

At the end of the test he told me I'd passed. 'But only just!' he added.

From then on I drove like Stirling Moss. I was hooted at, shouted at, fingers were raised at me, but I didn't care. I was free! I borrowed a shiny black-peaked sailor's cap from Central's wardrobe. It was my special driving hat. It seemed ironic and devil-may-care, and maybe people thought I'd picked it up in Carnaby Street, although it's more likely they mistook me for a trainee bus conductor.

Now I was mobile I could travel further afield. Coffee bars were springing up all over my part of London. There was La Fiesta in Wanstead, The Calypso in Woodford Bridge, and in George Lane, South Woodford, The Bamboo (or 'The Boo' as we regulars called it). They had complex decors – an eclectic mix of Cuban, Hawaiian and Benidorm beachfront – and my mates and I sat in them for hours stirring a solitary cappuccino and talking about girls and their irritating ways. The music on the jukebox was divine: 'Tell Him' by the Exciters, 'Our Day Will Come' by Ruby and the Romantics, 'Baby, I Love You' by the Ronettes – exquisite three-minute musical jewels about regret, loss and how to get a nice boyfriend. I even started to quite like coffee, although it was rather bitter so I stirred in a lot of sugar.

It was in 'The Boo' that we heard trouble was brewing. Some lads from Harlow or possibly Loughton had gone down to a dance hall somewhere near Tottenham and had behaved violently in an unspecified way.

My mates were outraged, and so was I. These intruders were out of order. Such a territorial slight couldn't go unpunished.

Two evenings later The Boo was much fuller than usual. There were lots of young men I'd never seen before in motorbike jackets. There were mods in parkas, and scary-looking boys in lace-up boots and shirts with rolled-up sleeves.

I wore my collarless Beatles jacket and a tight blue and white checked button-down shirt. I felt I gave off an aura of smartly dressed violence, although this was slightly undercut by the Ban the Bomb badge which I obviously wasn't prepared to forego.

When we went outside I was taken aback by the number of vehicles. There must have been at least thirty Vespas and Lambrettas parked up, with racoon tails dangling from the aerials fixed to the backs of their saddles. There were a dozen or so motorbikes – Triumph Bonnevilles, Vincents and Nortons – and an old greengrocer's van which a Leytonstone boy I vaguely knew had borrowed from his dad.

Whether it was because I was appalled by the potential level of violence, or possibly because I wanted to be helpful, I volunteered to drive round to the other two coffee bars, to tell our allies that the main force had already left for Harlow, and to pick up any stragglers.

Everyone set off, but by the time I'd fulfilled my co-ordinating role I was about half an hour behind everyone else, and given my hazy knowledge of the Essex road system, was even further behind by the time we got to the outskirts of Harlow. In my excitement I'd forgotten to ask for clear instructions about the location of the dance hall which was to be the scene of our punitive action, so I pulled into a layby to have a look at my map. Suddenly I heard a cacophony of jangling bells, and shortly afterwards about seventy scooters, motorbikes and other assorted modes of transport came hurtling back out of Harlow pursued by police cars.

There were three boys in the back of the Herald, and another in the passenger seat. They flung themselves into their respective footwells, and when the headlamps of the police cars illuminated my car, all that could be seen was a solitary young driver perusing an AA Road Atlas, shaking his head in confusion at having mistaken the A1169 for the A1025.

We waited for some time until the ringing sound had faded away, then began to drive cautiously back towards London. Epping Forest was dark and threatening, and I feared a roadblock round every bend. Instead we were confronted by the greengrocer's van which had come off the road on a curve. A posse of passengers was scrambling around in the forest loam trying to get it back on the tarmac. This seemed a pointless exercise as the front axle was so bent that one of the front wheels was now at right angles to the rest of the vehicle.

'My dad'll kill me,' the driver moaned.

A ginger lad who I'd met previously at the church youth club pleaded for a lift home, and I took pity on him, although a little reluctantly as the car was already full. But as he opened the door, three other boys pushed their way in. There were now nine of us in one Triumph Herald, practically a physical impossibility, all of us wishing the night was over.

'What happened?' I asked.

A muffled voice from among the tangle of bodies replied, 'It really kicked off. Some daft wanker brought a shotgun and fired it in the air. The ceiling came down and everything.'

I didn't dare drive straight back to South Woodford for fear of the old bill, so I weaved my way round a jumble of country lanes until we eventually arrived at Chingford station, where most of my passengers clambered out. I lay awake all night fearful that there would be a knock on the door, and a police sergeant would drag me out of bed and charge me with assisting in the perpetration of a violent crime, but no such knock came.

The next day the papers said that sporadic violence had occurred all over East London and West Essex. I'd almost completely lost touch with Steve Marriott by now. He'd been getting a lot of good acting jobs, he'd even been in an episode of *Dixon of Dock Green*, but he'd lost interest and wanted to become a musician. I heard that he and his guitar-playing mate Ronnie had been caught up in the same trouble a few miles away in Loughton. Some blokes had mugged them with a broken bottle and a piece of wood with a nail in it, and they'd ended up in casualty. I never found out which side they were on or whether they were innocent bystanders, but given Steve's previous record, the latter seemed unlikely.

I was finding Central hard going now, mainly because I was so young. I'd been seventeen years and two weeks old when I went there, and everyone else was considerably older, some in their mid to late twenties. They seemed like my parents' friends rather than mine. And it wasn't as though I was a mature seventeen-year-old. I had a veneer of sophistication and a superficial ease in most situations, but I'd had no experience of life other than in the theatre, and absolutely no self-awareness. And whereas all my contemporaries were living in shared flats and bedsits, I was still at home with Mum and Dad.

I would have quit if I hadn't occasionally got so excited by some of the lessons.

'How do you look like a king?' George had asked us.

'By acting regal?' we suggested. 'Keeping your spine straight? Flashing your eyes?'

We waited for the answer.

Mainly, he said, it was about how you were treated by those around you, their body language, and their deference. Don't play being a king, play his character. The kingliness will come from the other actors. That's what ensemble acting is all about.

Another question: how do we avoid being self-conscious about the language we're using, particularly when it's old-fashioned like Shakespeare or George Bernard Shaw?

We learnt a scene from *Richard II* and acted it out. We were terrible. Then George told us to do it again, only this time while carrying the rehearsal room piano from one side of the room to the other. The moment we had to cope with the sheer weight of the damned piano, we forgot our hang-ups about language, and the words came out naturally. The scene was ten times better.

Not all my classes went well. One project was to study an animal, then recreate it physically and emotionally. We got free passes to London Zoo and stared at the caged creatures for hours on end. Most students chose to watch big cats and antelopes, and Caroline Maudling, the daughter of the Tory Chancellor of the Exchequer, was a panda. But I was a timid rabbit, which spoke volumes about my state of mind at the time. In fact, my rabbit was so timid that on the day we were supposed to perform our animals to the rest of the school, I didn't turn up.

If my confidence was low at Central, it was sky-high elsewhere. St Philip and St James's church youth club, or 'Pip and Jim's' as we called it, was only a few streets away from my house. For some years I'd sung in the church choir and could read music quite well, but my interest in the *St Matthew Passion* and Stainer's *Crucifixion* had waned when I started listening to Buddy Holly and began noticing girls in their flared skirts and pedal pushers. Apart from table tennis and snogging in alleyways, Pip and Jim's also put on occasional shows, which at first I acted in but was now directing. I loved doing this, partly because it was fun, but also because it gave me a taste of power, something I wielded far too frequently when my reluctant performers weren't fast or funny enough. The shows were getting slicker and more imaginative, and I began to realise that what I was learning at Central was having a big influence on me.

But the high point of my life at this time had nothing to do with acting. My mum's best friend in the Wanstead Players was Iris Brown, a glamorous middle-aged woman who wore bright lipstick and lots of gold jewellery. It felt really weird lusting after someone my dad fancied.

Iris's husband Ken had a business in Stepney called Sharpe's Ships Victuallers. It was a big yard, surrounded by high red-brick walls and heavy wooden doors, in which there were warehouses where ships' provisions were stored. It was here that I worked in the holidays. Ken gave me a brown storeman's coat, a little Austin van, and a job as a driver. I'd drive down to Canary Wharf, the King George V Dock, or all the way through the Kent and Essex countryside to Tilbury and the Isle of Grain. Then I'd cross the wobbly gangplank onto one of the boats, find the galley and the cook, make a list of the things he wanted, and drive back to London. Next day I'd make up the order, load my van with huge cans of beans, massive bags of flour, hundredweight sacks of spuds, and sides of beef and lamb, and drive back to the ship.

On my first day at Sharpe's I got through my deliveries as quickly as possible, and was back at the yard by lunchtime. But Big Michael, the senior driver, took me to one side.

'Slow down, son!' he said. 'You're making us look like a bunch of lazy twats.'

That was the last thing I wanted to do. I was besotted by the drivers. When I was with them the rounded vowels I'd learnt at Central melted away, and I became the Artful Dodger again. Except that the drivers were the real deal, proper, chipper cockneys. Compared with them Steve Marriott, Tony Newley and all the rest of us showbiz Dodgers seemed painfully phoney.

They were great days! Massive fried breakfasts, the *Daily*

Mirror racing section, grown-up dirty jokes, bacon sandwiches for elevenses, pulling into a layby for a couple of hours and reading Robert Graves and Albert Camus. But above all there was the card playing.

The drivers played 'hearts', a game I'd never come across before, and because they were all on good wages, they played for what I considered to be high stakes.

The card school took place in a prefabricated tea hut dominated by a long trestle table surrounded by an assortment of chairs, with threadbare armchairs in the corners for those who weren't in the game. I'd watch the cards and the betting intently, learning the game, and sipping burning hot tea from a chipped enamel mug. One lunchtime I plucked up the courage to ask if I could play too. They were initially reluctant – maybe they thought they'd get into trouble if they took money off a callow teenager – but eventually they agreed, and given that virtually the only skill apart from acting I'd acquired in life was card playing, I did pretty well, and was soon up £23, which was about two and a half week's wages.

But then out of nowhere, a bit of needle started to creep into the game. 'Oi,' said Big Michael. He was bald and stocky, and always did the talking if there was trouble with the management. 'I saw that!'

His words were directed at Terry, who was sitting at the far end of the table, and who'd recently come back to Sharpe's after having been away for some time. Dennis, the trainee butcher, told me he'd been inside, but I suspected this was a wind-up.

'Saw what?' said Terry.

'That. What you did.'

'Did? I did fuck all!'

'You fuckin' didn't do fuck all. You fuckin' looked at that card, and then bet blind.'

'Didn't.'

'You did, didn't he, Tone?'

'I don . . . I don . . .' I said helpfully. I was pretty sure he hadn't, but I wasn't going to argue with Big Michael.

Terry's face was mean now. 'You calling me a fuckin' cheat?' he said.

'I am, son. I fuckin' am.'

Terry grabbed the big trestle table with both hands and threw it to one side. Cards, tea, money and old newspapers flew everywhere. He barrelled his way across the room and hurtled into Michael. The two men hit the door with a crash and tumbled outside.

Dennis kicked the door shut. 'Leave them to it, silly gits,' he said.

Outside there was yelling, yelps of pain, and the sound of fists on flesh. Fat Lewis picked up a copy of *The Sport*, and sat down to read it.

'Tone,' he said, 'clear this shit up, will you son.'

I crawled round the floor in a daze picking up mugs, righting the table and collecting the coins.

There was silence outside now, then slowly Big Michael came back in.

'I think I've fuckin' killed him,' he said softly, dropped into an armchair and put his head in his hands.

More silence. Then he murmured through his fingers, 'Sorry about the game, lads. You all know what you started with, don't you?'

'Don't worry about it, Michael,' said Dennis gently. 'We'll just divvy it up. Forget it ever happened, eh?'

One after another we went to the table and took our original stakes from the pile of money.

'Sorry about that, Tone,' said Big Michael. 'You were doing really well.'

'It's not an issue,' I said. 'What are you going to do about Terry?'

Bang! The door burst open and there he was. 'Wind up! Wind up!' he shouted, and the others joined in.

All that palaver so I wouldn't win £23.

'You bunch of fuckers,' I said, and we all roared with laughter. For the first time I truly felt I was one of them.

4

THE LIBERTINE

I'd been reading an Agatha Christie novel in which a dozen people are stranded in an island hotel, they're bumped off one after another, and none of them has a clue who'll be the next to go. That's what it felt like sitting on a bench outside George Hall's office.

He came across to most people as a kindly man with his cute little beard and his impish smile, but those of us who were close to him knew he had a ruthless streak. Once he'd decided a student wasn't up to it, he'd send them packing, and no amount of pleading, however dramatically executed, would change his mind. He wasn't going to encourage someone to persist in a profession in which, as far as he was concerned, they were bound to fail. Thirty-five of us had started the first year, and we were now down to the mid-twenties. The final year was when we'd be seen by agents and casting directors. We'd also be the first fruits of George's teaching. No one wanted us to look sub-standard. It was the last day of my second year, the final cull was about to take place, and I was pretty sure I was one of the lambs about to be sent to the abattoir.

It wasn't that my work was awful; the problem was I was virtually invisible. I had enormous difficulty getting out of bed before lunch so my attendance record was dreadful. I didn't excel at anything, I found a lot of classes boring, I even yawned through the ones I liked. George had said I'd find the three years tough, but I was finding them soporific. As a child actor

I'd thought I was special; here I felt miserable, isolated and permanently exhausted.

Word had got round the London media that George was doing interesting work at Central, and our class was given the honour of a half-hour programme on the new TV channel BBC 2. The show was conceived by Litz and was called *Explorations*. It was about the Black Death, was intensely physical and dramatic, and I hated it. When I see photos of it now I'm struck by the fact that my fellow classmates are flinging themselves round the TV studio being demented medieval peasants, while I'm hovering on the sidelines looking like I'm waiting for a bus.

'Tony,' George's voice rang out. 'Can you come in, please?'

I stood up like Sydney Carton on the steps of the guillotine, and walked heroically towards my fate.

'A turbulent year, I think.'

'Yes, George.'

'Could we have worked a little harder?'

'Yes, George.'

'And graced us a little more often with your presence?'

'Yes, George.'

'Good.'

He paused and made a little steeple with his fingers.

'Well, sir . . .'

Oh, for Christ's sake, George, I thought.

'I'd be misleading you if I said there wasn't a place for you in the professional theatre . . . and we would of course like to see you here again in the autumn, but . . .'

There were no buts. I was coming back. I was going to make it through the three years! Nothing else mattered.

George lectured me for another five minutes or so with an intensely serious look on his face, but I wasn't listening. All I can remember is his little black tuft bobbing up and down on his chin, and a feeling of complete happiness.

As I walked back towards the rehearsal rooms, something

he'd said came back to me. He wanted me to leave home and live in London. Well, that was fine by me.

I got a bedsit off the Finchley Road with a fellow student called Will Knightley. I was short with glasses; he was tall and gangly, with high cheekbones. Our room on the ground floor of a huge terraced house in Frognal had vast dirty front windows and even dirtier net curtains, two single beds at right angles in one corner, and a screen covered in coloured pictures cut out from the *Sunday Times* magazine which blotted out the view of the Belling stove and the pots and pans. The communal toilet and bathroom were down a long, draughty, lino-covered corridor.

Will and I were East London boys who didn't know much about anything, and we bunked off to watch exotic new Hollywood movies starring actors from Lee Strasberg's actors' workshop. These were a new breed, unlike any performers we'd seen before. Marlon Brando blew us away. He was so real you couldn't understand a word he was saying, so true to his part that he was prepared to sacrifice not just coherence, but narrative, storyline and wit. He was sexy, laid-back, troubled, and as cool as a menthol cigarette. He epitomised the way Will and I wanted to live our lives. Previous generations of actors may have had panache, but Brando had authenticity; he became for us what Mick Jagger was to die-hard pop fans.

We went back home most weekends, and as the Knightley family lived a stone's throw from mine in Belle Vue Road, Walthamstow, I'd give him a lift, and got to know his mum Vi and his dad Bill quite well. Will took his craft as an actor extremely seriously, but in a long career he never got the accolades he deserved. Thirty-five years later I was driving past the end of Belle Vue Road and saw a huge poster on the bus stop at the junction. It was an advertisement for *Pirates of the Caribbean* and Will's daughter was slap bang in the middle of the picture looking feisty and glamorous. It was a pity Vi and Bill weren't still alive to see it.

*

I don't think I'd ever been truly happy until my final year at Central. I'd once told Litz that I always had a headache, and when she asked me what kind I said, 'Just the kind everyone has.'

'Most people don't have a permanent headache, darlink,' she said. 'You put all your emotions in your shoulders. You hold your neck like a tortoise in order to vard off all those imaginary blows. Tuck your chin down a little, loosen your neck, and stop vorrying. You'll be fine!'

Other drama schools worshipped at the shrine of Ibsen and Chekhov, but George was a song and dance man.

'Ya-ta-ta-ta! Ya-ta-ta-ta!' he'd chant as he beat his little drum, dancing from one side of the stage to the other in his black tights while we tentatively tried to emulate him.

For our opening production that year he chose a late nineteenth-century piece of froth by the French farceur Labiche, called *The Italian Straw Hat*. It was the story of a young woman whose hat is eaten by a horse while she's meeting her lover, and can't go home to her husband till it's been replaced. Will played Fadinard, the leading man, and I had the relatively minor role of Tardiveau, an aging soldier who is permanently in a sweat. I enjoyed the rehearsals. George had a remorselessly accurate theatrical eye, and persistently tweaked the moves and our performances to make the production slicker and wittier. But the story was so trivial that I doubted whether his nit-picking was worth the bother.

Our dress rehearsal was performed to the rest of the school – a couple of hundred trainee drama teachers, speech therapists, stage managers and actors, the bitchiest, most critical audience you could possibly imagine.

I listened from the wings. It didn't seem to be going too badly; a few titters, and a smattering of applause at the end of some of the less turgid scenes. Then it was my turn. I crept onto the darkened stage and into my sentry box. The lights came up. I waited for a few beats, stepped out of the box, stopped, looked balefully at the audience, produced a large red and white handkerchief from my pocket, mopped my brow, looked baleful again for three more beats, and finally said, 'I'm so hot!'

There was a moment's silence, then an explosion of laughter. It was exactly like the moment eight years previously when I'd made my debut with the Wanstead Players and said, 'I've been knocking on this door for half a bleedin' hour.' The reaction was heart-warming, exhilarating and completely unexpected.

As the scene ran its course my laughs got bigger. For my second scene they were bigger still. At the beginning of my third scene, I stepped out of the sentry box and the audience was laughing even before I started speaking.

At the interval I sat in front of my dressing room mirror and stared at my reflection. I'd never been good at make-up, and my attempts at aging myself had been ruinous. Black and white greasepaint was splattered across my face like a badger in a road accident, and my beard was daubed with what appeared to be icing sugar. I looked bizarre. A nineteen-year-old attempting to fool people he was an old man – and failing. But the audience had liked me. They'd believed in my character.

When I came into school the next day, everyone was talking about Tardiveau, even my classmates, who I'd thought regarded me as a complete waste of space. Litz said, 'Of course you were capable of ziss. The only person who didn't know vas you. Vy do you zink we haff been taking so much time and trouble viz you, my darlink?'

And George said, 'Losing a little bit of the child actor at last, are we, sir?'

'Yes, George, I think we are.'

For the next three evenings I experimented with my performance, playing with the pauses, teasing them out to see how long I could leave the audience hanging before delivering the laugh line, but underplaying too so they'd be drawn in, rather than being beaten over the head by my gags. And I got a glimmer of the notion that acting could be a craft, that a good performer doesn't drop into the world fully formed. Each new show, every new experience, could be a chance to build your skills. I'd never be perfect, but in a way that was fine. It meant I'd always have a purpose: constantly trying to get better.

By day I strode the corridors of Central like a small colossus. Everyone wanted to talk to me, students I didn't recognise smiled at me, younger actors asked my advice.

The Embassy's original box office next to the foyer had been converted into a student tea bar. It was small, always full and was run by a charming wheeler-dealer called Gerry and his wife Marianne. He had thick-lensed glasses that made his eyes seem tiny; she was hard-working, and passionate, with hairy armpits and an Austrian accent. She ruled the tea bar like it was the Sudetenland.

I was queuing for a Coke when three pretty first-year girls from the teachers' course beckoned me over – one blonde, one red-haired and one brunette, like the trio of girls who might befriend the G.I. hero in a fifties musical. This was the kind of person I was going to be from now on, someone like Gene Kelly, constantly dancing over to a table lured there by beautiful women. We talked about the show, the school, and how much they were enjoying the course, until out of the corner of my eye I saw Marianne glowering at us because we were taking up a table while other students were queuing, so I went off to my voice class.

When I came back a couple of hours later, the brunette was there again, this time on her own. Although I was enjoying my newfound status, I certainly wasn't confident enough to approach her so soon after our first meeting, so I hovered nearby, lifting up the top slice of my bread to check that Gerry had given me enough cucumber in my cheese and cucumber sandwich. When I glanced at her again, she patted the chair next to hers, and I went over and sat down. She was even more stunning than I'd remembered: smart, funny, ironic and with big quizzical eyes.

I don't know how I got round to asking her out – I suspect she did most of the heavy lifting – but we agreed to go to the Swiss Cottage Odeon to see *Cat Ballou*, and afterwards, as a sophisticated touch, I suggested a Berni Inn.

That evening I was as nervous as I'd been on the first night of *The Italian Straw Hat*. She'd told me her name was Bardy, short for Barbara, which was a weird name and I knew I wouldn't remember it if I got nervous, so I'd written it on my hand in case I was struck by temporary amnesia.

The date went well apart from the fact that my hands got sweaty, the ink ran, and her name became virtually unintelligible. We agreed to meet again the next night. By the third evening we were boyfriend and girlfriend.

I couldn't have been happier, except that a burden weighed heavy on my shoulders. Unlike every other student at Central, I was a virgin. I didn't want to be; I always carried a johnny. In fact, my johnny was such a permanent part of my wardrobe that if I ever took it out to replace it for a less frayed one, its imprint would stay embossed on the leather of my wallet. But it had never been called into action. I didn't find it too difficult to get a snog, and sometimes quite a lot more, but no girl had ever offered me entry into her secret garden of delights, which really pissed me off.

Bardy, though, not only appeared to like me, but had agreed to visit my bedsit the following evening for a meal, so who knew what might happen?

'Tonight! Tonight!' as Richard Beymer sang on my *West Side Story* LP.

'Tony! Tony!' as Natalie Wood replied. (Although actually, as I told Bardy later, it was Marni Nixon. Natalie's voice was dubbed because her voice wasn't strong enough.)

I managed to banish Will for the evening and cooked my first ever meal. I'd decided on pork chops in Heinz tomato soup with grated cheese on top, which I thought would be tasty and easy to prepare. I made the bed, emptied the ashtrays, and put an attractive tea towel over the side lamp. The doorbell rang, Bardy came in, we kissed, and the whole night went to plan – swimmingly!

Later I walked triumphantly down the hall to the bathroom in my Marks and Spencer's dressing gown and slippers. I looked at my refection above the washbasin, and nodded at it in a masculine, conspiratorial way. My reflection nodded back. Finally I'd done it! Four minutes of unalloyed pleasure. I was now a man!

Shortly afterwards Bardy and I decided to move in together. There were two people I needed to tell: Will and my mum. Will was magnanimous; Mum didn't speak to me for three weeks.

My new home was an airy, spacious top-floor flat in Mowbray Road off the Kilburn High Road. We shared it with the two other girls I'd met in the tea bar. Debbie Galloway was the redhead. She was bouncy, bubbly and never stopped talking, and Christine Bosher, the blonde, was pretty, posh and fancied by every bloke at Central. The flat was some distance from the school, but I was quite happy ferrying my girls to and fro in the Triumph Herald. I was like Noddy with three Big Ears.

I enjoyed chatting with the people who came to visit us at Mowbray Road. They were different from everyone else I knew. Debbie came from Chorley Wood, and Christine was from Gerrards Cross, so most of their friends were Tories. I'd thought all Conservatives looked like Sir Alec Douglas-Home, with a skull for a head, half-moon glasses and plus-fours. But these were young businessmen and trainee lawyers with fashionably long hair down to their collars, and debutantes who were training to be models and had haircuts like Mary Quant. I couldn't believe they had such dreadful politics. I did my best to make them see the error of their ways, but I don't think I convinced anyone, even though I often argued brilliantly.

My favourite visitor was an acting student from the year below me called Vivian MacKerrell. My class were a slightly fuddy-duddy lot. Brown herringbone jackets were sometimes worn, the occasional tie, even cavalry twills and brogues had been spotted. But in the year since we came to Central, a profound change had occurred in teenage Britain. The new girls looked like Jean Shrimpton and were charmingly neurotic. They fell in love, then out of love, got dreadfully upset and had to visit discreet private clinics. The boys wore clothes like the Rolling Stones, had chiselled faces and the confidence of film stars. The most enigmatic of them by far was Vivian. He was tall, elegant and wore an immaculate 1950s tailored suit, with a long purple scarf which he tied like a cravat, and genuine rose-tinted spectacles. If Evelyn Waugh had dropped acid and written a film script of *Brideshead Revisited* set in the 1960s, Vivian would have been cast as Sebastian Flyte.

He came round to our flat one evening with Debbie. I'd hardly ever spoken to him previously, and thought that after a few minutes in his company, my essential squareness would be ruthlessly revealed. But instead of immediately disappearing into the bedroom as was the fashion, he began nattering to me, until we'd worked our way through a couple of bottles of cheap red wine. He was gentle, honest and perceptive, and a puzzling contradiction: a boozer, a drug-taker and a libertine, but with elitist political opinions somewhere to the right of Debbie's Tory friends. I didn't understand him, but I was riveted by him.

The following morning after he'd gone, Debbie giggled her way into the kitchen, a little outraged by the challenging bedroom requests he'd made the previous night, which I admit impressed me even more.

Another actor in his year, Bruce Robinson, left Central early to play Benvolio in Zeffirelli's film of *Romeo and Juliet*, then embarked on a dazzling Hollywood career. He wrote a screenplay about his Central friends called *Withnail and I*, and although some of it was clearly based on other students from his year, Withnail himself was undoubtedly inspired by Vivian. Vivian never had great success as an actor, and died of cancer aged only fifty-one, but I like the fact that his life has been immortalised in Richard E. Grant's bravura performance. We remained friends for the rest of my time at Central, although I suspect that, like me, a lot of people believed they knew him far better than they actually did.

After six weeks Bardy still hadn't told her parents about us, so she invited me to her house in Alsager, near Stoke-on-Trent, to test the waters. I was happy to go, but the night before we were due to head up there, she asked me an odd question.

'You do like football, don't you?'

'Whaaat?'

'I mean, really like it?'

How could she not know? OK, I might have let *Match of the Day* slip a bit in the first flush of love, but *like football*? I was a Spurs supporter. Of course I liked football.

I'd first been taken to White Hart Lane in 1958, and had been an avid fan ever since. Jimmy Greaves was the great goal-poacher of his age, but he caused me to have a major ocular disaster. I'd recently started wearing contact lenses, the old-fashioned hard ones, and I was jammed in the terraces close to the away goal when my right eye began to water.

Under normal circumstances I'd have washed my hands, removed the offending lens, cleaned it with the appropriate soothing fluid, and popped it back in. But White Hart Lane wasn't the appropriate circumstances. I took it out, and slipped it in my mouth to wash it. But at that moment Terry Venables sent a looping pass over the opposition's defence to Jimmy's feet, he dummied the opposing full back, sashayed into the area, and shot.

'Oooh!' The crowd drew their breath as one. Greavsie had sent the ball a few inches the wrong side of the goalpost.

Unfortunately my intake of breath had sent my contact lens down my throat and into my stomach. I stuck my fingers into my mouth and began to gag, hoping to bring it straight back up again, and even though the terrace was full to bursting, a six-foot ring of emptiness immediately appeared all round me. But sadly I failed in my quest, and had to watch the rest of the match with one eye closed. For three days I humiliated myself with a sieve and a fork, but I never found it.

So yes, I did like football, I was passionate about football, and yes, I had paid my dues.

'. . . only my dad's chairman of a football club back home.'

This sounded like it might be interesting.

'Non-league?'

'No.'

This was definitely interesting.

'Port Vale?'

'No.'

Had I broken out in a cold sweat?

'Is it Stoke City?'

Stoke City were in the First Division. This was the First Division before football was turned upside-down by the money men. There was no Premiership, no Championship. The First Division really was the First Division. Stoke were up there with Liverpool, Man U and, of course, Tottenham Hotspur. Apparently the next weekend I was going to watch Stoke at home to Fulham, I'd be sitting in the directors' box, and I'd have to wear a suit. A suit at a football match? How weird was that?

That Friday afternoon we drove up to Alsager, a well-heeled Cheshire suburb a stone's throw from Stoke. The Firs, Sandbach Road, was a big detached house in its own grounds. It reminded me of the posh people's homes in the *Just William* books. Bardy's mum, Kathleen, was a burlier, slightly more pugnacious version of her daughter. She and her frenzied boxer puppy came bustling out of her side door to greet us. She was courteous, if a little terse, and helped me take the bags in.

Bardy had asked her if we could share a room, but had been told firmly that we couldn't, and if she heard even the faintest creak in the upstairs hallway overnight, we'd both be sent straight back to London. Given that we were still in the early days of our relationship, this diktat seemed almost unbearable, like something a fascist regime might impose, but we stoically agreed to suffer without complaint.

Albert Henshall was a tall, gangly man with a grey moustache, who dressed in a slightly rumpled pin-striped suit. He wore the vague look of someone whose mind was elsewhere, then something would amuse him, his eyes would twinkle, and he'd nod in appreciation before retreating into his own thoughts again.

His son Richard was even taller and ganglier. He was a few years older than his sister, and was by all accounts a bit of a rogue.

The plan was that the five of us would nip out to the local for a Friday night drink, then head back to The Firs for a meal. But various friends and acolytes kept popping into the pub, the conversation flowed and so did the alcohol. I've never been much of a drinker. I'd like to be, but I don't seem to have enough room in my body to process the alcohol. While others are quaffing their fifth pint and knocking back shots, I'm trying desperately hard to stay awake.

I managed to sip my way through a few halves without nodding off, but this must have weakened my resolve, because when Richard suggested whisky chasers, I happily acquiesced. Soon I was having trouble communicating. I knew what I wanted to say, but my jaw wouldn't allow me to form the words properly. I sat down heavily at a quiet corner table and propped my head on my chin, but my elbow kept slipping and I'd lurch forward. Bardy was on the other side of the room laughing with some mates of her former boyfriend. I had a sneaking feeling her family were deliberately trying to set me up.

After an interminable amount of time we left the boozer and went back to The Firs. There must have been a meal, and it must have involved carrots and sweetcorn. I sat on their vast sofa, my head spinning like a carousel with a broken brake, and Richard switched on the radiogram. The record was Beethoven's Ninth played at full volume. When 'Ode to Joy' kicked in, he dropped his trousers, and began conducting with great vigour. Kathleen wiggled out of her dress and danced round the room in her bra and slip. Bardy was sitting next to me squeezing my hand; Albert was in his armchair nodding and smiling. Was this really happening? Yes, it was.

I don't remember being put to bed, but I do remember spending most of the night in the bathroom. At one moment I vomited so hard I thought I'd ripped my uvula out of its normal position, and that it was now dangling from my mouth.

Next morning death would have been a blessed relief. Bardy came breezily into my room and, although she demonstrated kindness and concern, insisted that I get up because her mum had made me a special fried breakfast. But however much I would have liked to please her, I was physically unable to move. Sometime later she came in again, slightly less solicitous than previously, and said I absolutely had to get up because it had been arranged that we would visit her grandmother mid-morning. Apparently without her stamp of approval, any relationship with the family would be in tatters.

I crawled into my clothes, but couldn't bear to wash or shave. Every stair was a station on the road to Calvary. I walked straight past the breakfast room and its smell of fried kidneys and into the car. Bardy drove.

We met her grandmother, an austere old woman who kept giving me sidelong glances. Bardy chattered away about our exciting life in London, and I sipped a cup of tea and ate the corner of a piece of cake. I found it hard to keep my eyes open.

When we got home again Richard suggested 'the hair of the dog', which seemed slightly foolhardy, but it worked. I was able to speak a little now, and my headache gradually downgraded from stroke-inducing to severe.

At half past one Kathleen decided it was time to send us off to the football, although I didn't have to go, she said a little edgily, if I was feeling too poorly. I bravely pulled myself together, climbed into the back of Albert's Ford Scimitar, and we hurtled along at the speed of light towards the Victoria Ground.

Twenty-two thousand fans rose to acclaim their team as they trotted out. Only Albert and his fellow directors remained seated, although Albert applauded and nodded. He was a modest man; no one in the away end would have known that all this, the size of the crowd, their First Division opponents, the quality of the team, were down to him and his ability to negotiate the return to the Potteries of England's greatest ever footballer.

Stanley Matthews had been a Stoke-on-Trent boy, but had risen to the pinnacle of his success at Blackpool FC. He was an attacking forward who was legendary not just for scoring goals, but for making them for other players.

After fourteen years at Blackpool, he had become increasingly disenchanted with the board of directors because he didn't think they recognised his true worth, and after one particular row, Albert 'just happened' to turn up in Blackpool, Stan 'just happened' to put him up, and within a week, to the footballing world's complete surprise, Stan 'just happened' to become a Stoke player again.

Mind you, he was nearly forty-seven years old, and most footballers retired in their early thirties. But his age didn't matter, the crowds flocked in. Stoke had been watched by an average of 8,000 supporters that season; but on Stan's return 36,000 spectators turned up.

The money rolled in, and the following year Stoke were promoted back to the First Division, with a policy of revitalising the careers of talented older players who other teams thought were fit only for retirement. And all of this was down to canny, unassuming Albert, and his manager Tony Waddington. I sat behind Albert in the directors' box. A story had gone round that he'd paid Blackpool the £3,500 transfer fee out of his own pocket. When Stoke scored I patted him on the shoulder. He'd have had no idea why, but it was a mark of respect.

The following day we drove back to London. 'I think that went quite well,' Bardy said.

I didn't reply.

'I mean it. Flash southern boy who's screwing their daughter. He goes up there, can't hold his liquor, pukes all over the bathroom floor, doesn't say a word the whole day, but perks up when he's allowed to go to the football. Very funny! They'll dine out on that for months.'

Still no reply.

'But you weren't flash really, were you? And you were nice to my mum, and said please and thank you. And you obviously like Dad, and you know your football. Even if you are a Spurs supporter, I think they liked you.'

'Good . . . great!'

'Mind you, Gran thinks you're a bit of a wanker!'

I never got another part at Central as good as Tardiveau. George said he wanted to stretch me; he didn't want me to get stuck in a comedy rut. So I played a lot of roles I was barely suited for, and was by no means a star of my year. But I can't blame George for that. I was still lazy. I was often the last one to learn their lines, I forgot my moves, I missed rehearsals; sometimes I just wasn't very good.

But I had one other important triumph that year. Shortly before I left, I got a note through the post. 'I've been watching your performances,' it said, 'and I'm quite a fan. Can we meet to talk about representation?' It was signed Penny Wesson, and the note was headed 'The William Morris Agency'.

William Morris was the biggest, most powerful theatrical agency in the world. Two thirds of the stars of Hollywood and Broadway were on their books. And they wanted to represent me?

Yes, I thought. *I might consider that.*

5

THE NAUGHTY ACTRESS

Cis Berry was in her late thirties with smudged lipstick and a fag constantly hanging from her mouth. She looked as though she'd crawled out of bed five minutes ago in the clothes she'd partied in the previous night. She used the word 'fuck' more than anyone I'd ever met, and was by far the sexiest teacher at Central.

She had a passion for words, and tried to drum into us the fact that language was essentially a physical activity. We'd perform a sonnet for her while throwing ourselves round the rehearsal room like trainee banshees. Our diaphragms would ache, our lips would twitch, but the poetry we spoke while we panted and puffed was authentic and muscular.

To me she was a kindred spirit. My fellow students were primarily interested in character, motivation and the other tools in the actors' toolkit, but I was especially passionate about the sound of the words, and the way intense feelings could be encapsulated in one well-crafted line. She gave me a lot of encouragement at a time when I felt permanently bottom of the class.

Shortly before we left Central she invited a few of her favourite students to perform some poetry at the College of Education in Welwyn Garden City. It may not have been the London Palladium, but George didn't like his students acting outside the college before they'd completed the course, so this felt like a first tentative step into the outside world.

The show was called *Impression of a Life*, which we all

thought sounded a bit la-di-da, so to lighten it up, three of us put together a musical comedy act and sang 1940s songs between the poems, like Fats Waller's 'Your Feet's Too Big' which Dad had taught me as a little boy.

Maurice Colbourne, who twenty years later would star as the heartthrob Tom Howard in *Howards' Way*, was six foot five inches tall with a chocolatey baritone voice, Steve Bradley was a tenor of middling height who strummed the guitar, and I was five foot four and a half and sang falsetto like Frankie Valli of the Four Seasons. We sounded ridiculous, but looked even more daft because when we sang, we danced stupid little steps with deadpan faces like Cliff Richard's backing group, The Shadows. Central could be so over-serious that it was a relief to be able to break out and be zany for a while, particularly with Cis's stamp of approval.

Rumours about our ridiculous trio must have travelled up the M1, because we were phoned by the casting director at the Phoenix Theatre, Leicester, and she told us they were about to premiere a new play called *Dante Kaputt* by Rex Harrison's son Carey, and needed some comedy actors who could play instruments and impersonate ex-public schoolboys.

'Are you genuine musicians?' she asked.

'Yes.'

'Can you play rock and roll?'

'Eddie Cochran is one of our greatest influences.'

'Can you speak like young Etonians?'

'Yah, absolutely.'

'OK. Money? I don't suppose any of you have got an agent?'

'Yeah, William Morris,' I said in the most matter-of-fact voice I could muster.

'Get you!' she replied.

The William Morris office was in Brook Street, opposite the bijoux high-end shops of South Molton Street. It was where

Hollywood film stars were cosseted when they came to London, and was decorated with scarlet flock wallpaper, crisp white eggshell paint, and thick mid-blue wall-to-wall carpet. While I waited for Penny, a young secretary in a shiny black miniskirt gave me two chocolate fingers, a cappuccino, a glass of water and the smallest croissant I'd ever seen. I was very impressed. Penny was only a few years older than me; she was tall, friendly and well-spoken, with front teeth like a little rabbit, and I liked her very much. She phoned Leicester and got me £2 more per week than they'd originally offered. In a couple of weeks my three years at Central would come to an end, and I'd already got a job on good money. As I walked back up Brook Street there was a strut in my step.

The first two weeks of rehearsal took place in a Hampstead church hall. On day one Carey Harrison, a charming, soft-spoken man, made a little speech about what a privilege it was to have his play performed by such a talented ensemble of actors, and showed us a model of the set. Then we read the play, and broke for lunch.

When we got back an hour later, Miriam Margolyes, a busty, bubbly young woman fresh out of Cambridge University, was nowhere to be seen. We waited a while, then started without her. Half an hour later she burst in and said, 'Sorry I'm late. I've been on the Heath wanking off a park-keeper.'

There was a gasp, a roar of laughter, then the moment passed, and we moved on. Well, everyone moved on except me. Miriam's phrase echoed round my head all afternoon. Had she really said that? Was this what life in rep was going to be like, people wanking each other off all the time? Would I be involved? The possibility took my breath away. Or maybe it wasn't true; perhaps it was just a brilliant excuse for being late? Either way it was the filthiest, most outrageous thing ever. How brave! How absolutely obscene! How unlike anything I'd ever heard a woman say before! I was profoundly impressed.

Since that day Miriam has said countless things to me that

have been far more disgusting. She's got the unique talent of being able to puncture any awkward moment with a well-honed strategy of smutty subversion. But nothing since has captured my imagination like her entrance into St John's church hall on my first day in rep.

A fortnight later Maurice, Steve and I piled into the Triumph Herald and drove up to Leicester where we met Julian Wright, the assistant stage manager who was going to double up as the fourth member of our quartet. He was enthusiastic and generous, and so was his mum; she let us sleep on her floor for the next month, surrounded by open suitcases, dirty ashtrays, half-full cups of cold tea and ketchup-stained plates.

The songs we wrote, and the way we sang and played them, was excruciating. Fortunately, because the show was a comedy, most people assumed our ineptitude was deliberate. We seemed to fool Carey too, who thought we were very funny; indeed he seemed happy with everyone. He was the most laid-back director I've ever come across.

Leicester town centre was covered in posters advertising the fact that Steve Marriott's band the Small Faces were going to perform a gig at the Granby Halls. I hadn't seen Steve for a couple of years. When 'Whatcha Gonna Do About It' had been released and got to number 14 in the charts, I'd felt very proud, with hardly a twinge of jealousy. But apart from 'Sha La La La Lee', his following singles hadn't done particularly well, and I assumed it wouldn't be long before he picked up his acting career again.

On the day he was due to arrive in Leicester, I dropped a note at the stage door of the Granby Halls saying I'd pop in after the show, and when our curtain came down, I headed off to see him.

I couldn't get near the place. The roads round it were packed; I'd never seen so many people except on Ban the Bomb marches or at football matches. This was the kind of reception

the Beatles and the Stones got, not my mate Steve and his little
bunch of cockney mods! I wormed my way through the crowd
until I was a few yards from the stage door. Suddenly it burst
open, and there was a loud collective scream that reverberated
off the walls.

Four small figures surrounded by police and security guards
shuffled and pushed their way through the throng towards a
parked coach with black drapes across its windows.

'Steve!' I called. 'Steve!' But everyone was surging forward
now. I was lifted off my feet and propelled along until my head
smacked into the stomach of a security guard. The bridge of my
glasses snapped in two; one half of my spectacles was now dangling from my ear, the other half had dropped on the pavement.
I dived after it, curling into a ball to prevent myself from being
trampled. I grabbed the broken bit, and struggled back to my
feet again, by which time the scrum had reached the coach, and
the engine was revving. The door began to close, and I could see
my friend sitting alone at a table.

I gave one final despairing shout: 'Steve!'

He looked up. I think he recognised me, but I'm not sure. He
looked tired, his eyes were red, and his face was puffy. Then the
coach drove off.

I never saw him again except on telly. I followed his career,
of course, everyone did. The following year 'Itchycoo Park'
became a national anthem, with Steve's voice sounding like a
cross between Little Richard and the Artful Dodger. He and his
band went from triumph to triumph, then he turned his back
on his mates, went to America, achieved superstar status with
his new band Humble Pie, and did virtually the same thing
again, rejecting America and returning to England, skint and
feisty as ever. He spent his last few years touring English pubs
and clubs supported by a handful of friends and admirers. I
didn't go and see him. We lived in different worlds; I doubted
we'd have anything to say to each other.

He died in 1991 at his home in Essex. People say he fell

asleep with a fag in his hand, and it set fire to his bedclothes and then to his house. When I heard the news, I felt I'd lost part of my childhood. He'd been difficult to like, and he'd made me cry more than once, but he was magnetic, talented, and there was always a seductive air of danger around him. I suppose for thirty years I'd had a bit of a crush on him.

When *Dante Kaputt* came to an end, I went back to our flat in Kilburn, and in the evenings drove over to Woodford and directed my final youth club show, *One Over the Other*, which I'd written in Leicester. We hired the biggest hall in Woodford for three nights, a massively expensive gamble for a youth club, but it paid off. Bardy and I thought the show was patchy, but it was a colossal hit and sold out. I felt flat and depressed when the final curtain fell. I'd got new friends and new interests now. I doubted I'd see much of South Woodford any more.

Meanwhile a bunch of students who'd left RADA at the same time as I'd gone up to Leicester had formed their own theatre company called The Vanbrugh Theatre Group and were about to set off on a tour of *Tartuffe*, an eighteenth-century play by Molière, in a translation written by a celebrated old actor called Miles Malleson. It was seriously heavyweight fare in rhyming couplets and, as all the actors in the group were in their early to mid-twenties, they needed someone with a bit more gravitas in the cast. The oldest actor from our year at Central, Jim Walker, was now thirty-one, and they asked him to play the lead role. Then when someone dropped out at short notice, Jim suggested I should join them.

I'd imagined I'd get a minor role but, for reasons unknown, I was cast opposite Jim as Orgon, the foolish, rich idiot who is systematically ripped off by the fake religious guru, Tartuffe.

I was nineteen, but looked four years younger. It was difficult to imagine how any audience would be persuaded that I was a middle-aged businessman with a sixteen-year-old daughter.

But I adopted the traditional actor's standby of a limp and a stick, swathed myself in padding, plastered my hair with white liquid make-up, and made the best of it.

The play creaked like a pair of old French windows. It opened at the Corn Exchange, Falmouth, and zigzagged its way north, terminating at the Pier Pavilion, Southport. We had an elaborate set, lots of bulky costumes on two long rails, and a cast and crew of ten. Our producer Bill Horne came up with an inexpensive way of solving our transport problem. During rehearsals he bought a very old forty-seater Bedford coach, which we gutted to make room for the sets and costumes, leaving only the first few rows intact for the company. But who'd drive it? Hardly any of the actors had passed their driving test, and of those who had, none of them fancied handling this juggernaut. And what about the insurance? Shouldn't the driver have an HGV licence? Bill swore blind that all the paperwork was in order so, after behind-the-scenes negotiations which involved me receiving an extra £1 a week in my back pocket, I volunteered.

I loved driving my coach; she was a two-tone mauve and cream goddess. She had no acceleration, and was as noisy as a tractor, with virtually no clutch. Every time I changed gear I had to perform an operation known as double de-clutching, which involved lots of revving and yanking the gearstick up and down, and as I've got short legs, I had to bounce backwards and forwards in my seat while I was doing it.

Occasionally when my leg muscles started twitching, I'd try a normal gear change, but that would produce a hideous grinding sound, the whole vehicle would judder, and it would seem as if the engine was about to drop through the floor. So I didn't do that very often.

I drove long distances – I think Swansea to Bury St Edmunds was the furthest – and my biggest problem was that the fuel gauge was broken, so every fifty miles or so we'd stop, I'd unscrew the petrol cap, push a long stick into the tank and

Mum and Dad in the Royal Air Force during World War II.

Dad's wartime band. He's on the far right playing an invisible piano!

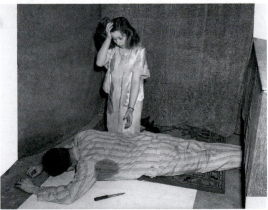

Mum in a wartime am-dram. Was she the killer or an innocent bystander?

First day at Woodford Green Preparatory School, 1951. Taken in our back garden at 14 Raymond Avenue.

Mum and me posing in the garden.

The moment I said, 'I've been knocking on this door for half a bleedin' hour' for the Wanstead Players in *Who Is Sylvia?*

As the Artful
Dodger in *Oliver!*

The *Oliver!* boys with
retired US General
Battley, who was
apparently a big fan.
Bottom row: second-
left Keith Hamshere
(Oliver Twist),
fourth-left Martin
Horsey (The Dodger),
and me far right.

My first year at Wanstead High. I'm bottom left talking to Roy Truscott. Roger Burbery, who shared my taste in music and dirty poetry, is sitting behind him.

At Wanstead High hanging out with the older boys.

Dancing self-consciously with my mum at a hotel in Chichester where we spent Christmas 1961. Note the ubiquitous Ban the Bomb badge.

The Black Death from *Explorations*, performed by my year at the Central School of Speech and Drama. I'm choking to death somewhere in the middle of this heap.

George Hall, head of drama at Central. A huge influence on me.

My comic breakthrough in *The Italian Straw Hat* at Central.

Dante Kaputt, Phoenix
Theatre, Leicester.
First job out of drama school.

*The Victoria Palace
of Varieties*, Victoria
Theatre, Stoke-on-Trent.

My long-time friend and
partner in crime Sylvie,
with her son Jason.

'Bennie' in
Big Soft Nellie,
Victoria Theatre.

With Bardy in
Cannon Hill Park,
Birmingham.

Directing the cast of *Little
Malcolm and His Struggle
Against the Eunuchs*, Midlands
Arts Centre, Birmingham.

Our wedding at Alsager, Cheshire.
L–R: Debbie Galloway (bridesmaid), Bardy's
dad and mum Albert and Kathleen, me,
Bardy, Mum, and Guy Pierce (best man).

Bardy and me in Brighton.

Sue Macready and
me in *Simon Says*,
Leeds Playhouse.

test how much fuel we had left. But sometimes I forgot, or my calculations went awry, and we'd come to a halt and have to wait for the RAC man. When we finally got back on the road again, I'd feel a wave of seething resentment from behind me which I thought was extremely unfair. I did all the driving, surely someone else could be in charge of the bloody stick!

But I exacted my revenge. The Bedford's finest asset was her ability to stop. I only had to touch the footbrake and she'd immediately come slap bang to a halt as though she'd driven into a concrete wall. So if any of the cast expressed criticism of my driving or fuel management skills, I'd pretend there was a hazard in the road and slam the anchors on, causing my passengers to lurch forward, then spin backwards in their seats at speed to halt the advance of the costume rails which by now would be hurtling towards them.

The brakes, though, were my downfall. The day after the show ended and I'd said a heartbroken farewell to my Bedford, I picked up the Herald from Mum and Dad's house, and drove back towards Mowbray Road. It was an autumn day and the road was wet and leafy. On Forest Road, outside Walthamstow town hall, a bus came to a halt in front of me. For a moment I thought I was still in the driver's seat of my coach with its hyper-efficient brakes. And when I finally attempted to stop far too late, I drifted slowly and ineluctably into the bus. My beloved Herald was a write-off.

This tragedy meant I couldn't drive to Stoke's away matches anymore, so I'd hitch a lift with Albert in his Ford Scimitar, a beast of a car which he drove with intense, silent abandon at a hundred miles an hour. He was often stopped by the police, but his celebrity and his handshake were enough to ensure he wasn't hindered even if his speech was a little blurry. Eventually, though, when he was negotiating his way out of the carport, he reversed over one of Kathleen's new dachshunds, after which she insisted on a degree of sobriety when he was driving.

We now travelled in the team coach. This was the high point of my week because sometimes I sat next to Gordon Banks or George Eastham, who were among British football's all-time greats, although I always tried to look casual, as if their celebrity was a matter of complete indifference to me. Sadly our trips to Alsager came to an abrupt halt when Bardy got an irate phone call from her mum after we'd been staying with her for the weekend. She'd found evidence of the hanky-panky she'd always feared on the Axminster carpet in Bardy's bedroom. I was barred from the house till further notice. We didn't protest; it was a fair cop!

On the strength of *Dante Kaputt* and *Tartuffe*, I got several more jobs, but after nine months I'd still only performed in single shows before moving on somewhere else. My first chance to work over an extended period with an ensemble came when I was offered a season in Stoke-on-Trent, a few miles from Bardy's home.

The configuration of the Victoria Theatre was 'in the round', with the stage in the middle of the auditorium and the seats surrounding it. It was one of the most innovative theatres in the country, and had been founded by a brilliant young theatre practitioner called Stephen Joseph, who also created the theatre at Scarborough where Alan Ayckbourn's original productions were, and still are, produced.

The boss at the Vic was a hyper-energetic director called Peter Cheeseman who had a national reputation. His production of *Zigger Zagger*, a play about Stoke City fans, had transferred to the West End, where I'd seen it a few months previously with the Stoke team the night before they played Spurs at White Hart Lane. I don't think they found it particularly interesting, but the rest of the audience were enthralled.

Peter and Stephen Joseph fell out, there was a power struggle which Peter lost spectacularly, and Stephen, who was in

Scarborough, dying of cancer, appointed a replacement director to run Stoke, with the task of building a fresh company of actors. The man given this impossible job was Terry Lane, who had a solid reputation as a director of shows 'in the round' having founded the Traverse, a similar type of theatre in Edinburgh. But Terry wasn't suited to the emotional maelstrom in which he found himself. He was gentle and shy, but with an irrational streak of stubbornness. Gwynneth Thurburn, the head of Central, was an old friend and fan of Stephen's, and she suggested to him that I might be a suitable new recruit. I was blissfully unaware of what had been going on at Stoke, and wasn't sure I wanted to be away from London and my life with Bardy for five months. But my agent Penny was all for it. She thought it would be good for me to be at a theatre of the Vic's status, and I'd get a chance to play plenty of big parts. So up to Stoke I went.

I was still banned from The Firs, so for the first few weeks I shared a house with a fellow actor, but it wasn't a happy experience. It was February, and the only heating came from a tiny coal fire which it was virtually impossible to keep alight, so some nights we slept not only in our pullovers and trousers, but in our coats and gloves too.

But the temperature in our little house was balmy compared to the atmosphere at work. The first play in Terry's season was Shakespeare's *Julius Caesar*, and several of Peter Cheeseman's actors were still in the company working out their contracts. They were furious that their boss and mentor had been sacked. So there was a split of Grand Canyon proportions between Peter's supporters and the newcomers. We had no interest in taking sides in this power struggle, but the old guard viewed us as scabs.

Our presence was undoubtedly provocative, and I was particularly gutted about this because, in the two years I'd been coming up to Stoke to visit Bardy's parents, I'd watched Peter's company on many occasions and respected them hugely. There was the outrageous comic Ken Campbell, and the young leading man Robert Powell; they were first-class actors, and I wanted them to be my friends. But whenever I approached them, I seemed to get it wrong. Either I was too friendly and looked a creep, or I left them to their own devices and came across as stand-offish.

Eventually I sneaked into the theatre office, got hold of Peter Cheeseman's phone number, called him and asked if I could go and see him to explain how uncomfortable I was feeling. In retrospect this was an insensitive and dumb thing to do. He got very angry, and told me there were only two sides: his side and the sell-out side. I'd clearly shown which one I'd chosen, so I should get out of his house right now.

News of our row got back to the other actors, and their attitude towards me grew even more hostile. I tried to ignore the sarcastic face-pulling and barbed comments, and did my best to get on with the day-to-day business of putting on a play. Eventually, after what seemed an age, *Julius Caesar* opened. It was remarkably good given the sour environment in which it had been created, but I'd been given a ridiculous leather miniskirt to wear which showed my little hairy legs, so I don't think I was particularly convincing as Octavius Caesar, the ruthless emperor of the entire world.

It ran for three long weeks, then Peter's actors left, the rest of Terry's company arrived, and the sun shone. The first show under the new regime was Henry Livings' comedy *Big Soft Nellie*. It was a smash hit, got lots of good news coverage, and gave Terry and the rest of us a blast of confidence, which was particularly welcome as so many people had told us we were doomed to fail.

The next few shows were received equally enthusiastically, and I started having the time of my life. People came up to me in the street and wanted to talk to me about the plays, I was interviewed by local newspaper reporters, and blushing sixth-form girls waited outside the theatre to ask for my autograph.

I was the size of a jockey, with glasses and a beaky nose, but suddenly I was being treated like George Best or Billy J. Kramer, albeit only in the few square miles of the Potteries. Sadly this tiny bit of adulation went to my head. I enjoyed the attention I was getting from female fans, and even though I missed Bardy, I didn't behave at all well, although I enjoyed myself enormously.

I became friendly with a girl called Rita who worked in the Co-op on Hartshill Road. She had a beehive hairdo, which, unlike Litz Pisk's, was immaculately coiffured and smelt of Sunsilk hairspray, which I found particularly exotic. But our friendship came to a swift end when she told me her boyfriend was about to be let out of prison, and was going to come and get me.

The actors at the Vic had been given free passes to a night-club called La Boom Boom, an exotic, if seedy, Potteries hideaway that became my passport into a world I hadn't previously known existed. It was home to half a dozen drag acts who wanted careers in showbiz. Every Tuesday night, they'd totter onto the tiny wooden stage in their high heels, and mime to tracks by Dusty Springfield and Sandy Shaw. I was fascinated by their wit, and touched by their fragility and courage. One in particular, a boy called Bobby, whose wig made him look a bit like Natalie Wood, took a shine to me. He'd bat his eyes and give me suggestive looks. It was very confusing, and I had no idea how to process his come-ons, particularly as I fancied Natalie Wood so much.

One evening an agitated Rita ran into the club and told me her boyfriend was in the car park and was planning to sort me out. Geoffrey Todd, who played Big Soft Nellie and was both big and soft in real life, told me not to worry. 'I'll look after you,' he said.

A few minutes later a young man stormed into the club, sat down opposite me and started waving his hands and shouting at me. It was obvious that whatever I said would only make matters worse, so I kept quiet and let him rant. He wasn't much taller than me, but had the physique of a boxer, spiky hair like a mongrel and psycho eyes. Geoffrey wandered over with a couple of beers, pulled up a chair, and pushed a beer over to Psycho with a friendly smile. He was joined by Alan, a bulky Australian who was our deputy stage manager. But their mere presence seemed to incite my nutty new friend even more. He raved incoherently about knives and bricks, and how he was going to summon up a whole army of friends who would stamp on me, blind me and, only much later, kill me.

Then the drag queens arrived. They were wielding gin and tonics and flashing their razor-sharp eyes. They squeezed round our little table, and my agitated companion ground to a halt. Bobby patted my arm and suggested that I and my friends go home now, because the girls wanted to have a word with 'Psycho'. I started to protest that I didn't want them risking— 'Now!' said Bobby firmly. We did as she requested. As we left, I could see the terror in Psycho's eyes.

I never went back to La Boom Boom, which was a pity, and I never saw Psycho again, which was something of a relief. I moved into a cosy flat with Guy, our young assistant stage manager, his wife Sylvie, and their baby, Jason. The three of them swiftly became my best friends. Guy had the kindest of faces, and blond curly hair down to his shoulders. Jason's hair was similar. Together they looked like the Laughing Cavalier and the baby Laughing Cavalier.

Sylvie had been a wild child. She had full lips, a home counties accent, wore big red beads and diaphanous hippy dresses, and had eyes that flashed with curiosity and emotion. She'd been educated at a school for the children of army personnel in Devon, but she'd found it oppressive, more like a holding area than an educational establishment. When she was fifteen she ran away with an older man who sold purple hearts in the West End and said he'd deserted from the French Foreign Legion. She was nineteen now, and like me she'd had virtually no education and was hungry to know more about the world. We became fascinated by the New Left, a coterie of young intellectuals who despised Westminster politicians, were opposed to the Vietnam War, and wrote about the possibility of revolution breaking out all over Europe. But the streets of Stoke-on-Trent were seldom filled with flag-burning insurrectionists, so our interest remained purely theoretical.

The biggest hit of our season was a documentary about the Edwardian music hall called *The Victoria Palace of Varieties*. It was the perfect vehicle for me. I recited cheeky cockney poems, told naughty jokes, and sang risqué songs in drag.

> *I feel just as happy as a girl can be,*
> *Upon my word it's true.*
> *I'm so very happy that I don't know which*
> *Or what I'm going to do.*
> *For I'm in love and just engaged*
> *To a man who ploughs the sea.*
> *He fishes for a living, and he fished last night*
> *On land, and he caught me.*
>
> Chorus:
> *And he calls me his own Grace Darling,*
> *He says that I'm his pet.*
> *I fill each plaice with his sole,*
> *That ain't no cod you bet . . . etc.*

I pouted at the audience, flirted with them, and tossed my long, flowing hair. As for my dress, I loved it! Not only did I look good in it, I also found it liberating. It didn't squash my bits and pieces like trousers did. The thought slowly dawned on me: *Oh my God, I like wearing dresses! I'm gay! I fancy Bobby! I'm totally well and truly bloody gay!!*

But if that was the case, what was I going to do about it?

There was an actor in the show called Roger who'd been making playful passes at me for some time. Previously I'd pretended not to notice, but now I made my move.

'Oh, Tony!' he said for the hundredth time. 'What am I going to do with you?'

'I don't know,' I replied, fixing him with a smouldering stare. 'What are you going to do with me?'

He didn't say anything, but his look told me he'd got a good idea.

A few nights later he turned up at our flat, and asked Sylv if we could put him up for the night.

'I've locked my keys in my flat,' he said, and gave me a sly smile, and a tiny wink.

Half an hour after we'd all gone to bed, I was still wide awake staring at the ceiling, when I heard the hall floorboards creak, my bedroom door slowly opened, and a voice whispered, 'Are you asleep?'

'No,' I whispered back. There was a rustle which I assumed was his dressing gown dropping to the floor, and he slipped in beside me.

'What would you like me to do?' he said softly. I didn't reply, partly because I was terrified, but also because I had no idea what choices were available at a moment like this.

He pulled me to him, and kissed me. He smelt like a male changing room. I tried to join in. I wiggled around and even played with his willy for a while, but it felt slippy so I let go. Then realisation dawned. I was straight. I'd lured poor Roger into my room, but now I wanted him out again as quickly as possible.

I apologised, stuttered, started to make detailed excuses, but they petered out. He was very decent about it. He kissed my cheek, ruffled my hair and left the room. We never referred to the matter again. Thanks to Roger, I had trodden the winding path beloved by Oscar Wilde and Kenneth Williams, but now it was time to return to Straight City. I could go back to London pretty sure I knew where my sexual preferences lay.

Shortly after the season ended, the board of directors at the Vic met again, and a counter-coup was engineered. Peter Cheeseman was reinstated and Terry Lane's contract was terminated. I was never asked back. Stephen Joseph died the following year.

Twenty-five years later when I was vice-president of the actors' union Equity, I met Peter again. He was now a fiery champion of Britain's drama schools and was still brimful of energy and passion. We worked together to try to ensure that drama schools got better funding and a higher status. He seemed to have either forgotten our original rancour, or had decided to put it behind him, and we became close colleagues.

6

THE MAN WITH THE CLICKING TEETH

I was feeling pleased with myself. I'd been working non-stop since I left drama school, and had returned to London with a sheathful of newspaper clippings from the Stoke-on-Trent *Sentinel* testifying what a big hit I'd been. I was on an unstoppable trajectory. Soon there'd be a TV series on offer, a call from the National Theatre, perhaps even a small part in an American film. All I needed to do was be patient, and wait for the phone to ring.

But it didn't. A week went by, the week became a month, and it still didn't ring. After six weeks I asked the GPO to check the line, but there was nothing wrong with it. After two months I was running out of money. Penny tried her hardest. She was determined to get my face on television, but every time I read for a part, I was turned down flat. I was either too short, too fat, too thin or just too rubbish.

Eventually I got my old ships' victualling job back, but was fired a couple of weeks later, which was horrible. It was the summer holidays and Ken Brown had temporarily employed a student, the son of a neighbour. Ian was innocent and well-spoken, the exact opposite of the drivers, who prided themselves on being wheeler-dealers. At the end of each shift we'd walk out of the yard with big brown paper bags under our coats bulging with fruit, vegetables and joints of meat. We also claimed far more overtime than we were due, particularly on the long runs to the Isle of Grain and Tilbury. But Ian would drive there and back like Donald Campbell, just as I'd done when I first started at Sharpe's. He didn't seem to understand that by doing this he was showing up the other drivers. Eventually Big Michael took me to one side and asked me to hammer into the young lad that he had to massage his hours. Ian agreed, but was useless at covering his tracks. He lived round the corner from Ken, brought his van home from work, and Ken soon realised he was claiming overtime for hours when he was at home. He was summoned to the office, said I'd pressurised him into claiming the extra money, and I got the push.

I was pissed off that he'd grassed me up, and felt guilty that I'd been caught cheating by a man who'd been so kind to me, but mainly I was gutted that my days with Big Michael, Dennis and the rest were now well and truly over.

After three jobless months, I was spending virtually all my time staring out of the window feeling sorry for myself. I got in touch with Tony Cliff, a radio producer friend in Manchester, told him I was skint and miserable, and he contracted me to read the *Woman's Hour* serial. It was the story of a northern working-class lad's attempts to cope with poverty and disability, but it was so bleak and painful that the audience switched off in droves. The BBC put the episodes out in the wrong order, and there wasn't a single complaint! I was grateful for the work, but it hardly felt like the next step on my road to stardom!

Just when I thought I'd never get a decent job again, Penny phoned me in a state of high excitement to tell me I'd been offered the guest lead in an episode of the BBC cop series *Softly, Softly*. I read the script, and my heart flipped; my part was an absolute belter, a young loser who fancies a fourteen-year-old girl, stalks her, and when she finally succumbs, is put in prison for having sex with her.

I couldn't wait for rehearsals to begin. I was practically splitting in two with anticipation. Finally the day came, I went to the designated church hall in Notting Hill, and we read through the script, after which the producers went into an animated huddle. They told us to take a break, and we wandered into the next room where there was coffee, biscuits and a table tennis table. I'd played a lot during my youth club days, and after half an hour I hadn't lost a single set.

The assistant floor manager interrupted us; the producers wanted to have a word with me. They were kind and apologetic, but said they were going to have to let me go because there'd been a casting mix-up. The whole point of the episode was that my character was supposed to be in his sixties, which made his relationship with the girl dark and paedophiliac. Unfortunately I looked practically the same age as her, so with me in the role, the story was more like a cockney *Romeo and Juliet*. The director Paul Ciappessoni told me it was his fault, he was sorry for any embarrassment he'd caused me, and of course he'd give me another part as soon as a suitable one became available, but he never did.

Then at last, out of the blue, I got a call from my old boss at Stoke, Terry Lane. He was now director of productions at the Midlands Arts Theatre in Birmingham, and wanted to know if I'd like to join him there. The Midlands Arts was a children's theatre company, and Penny made it abundantly clear that this wasn't the sort of work she wanted me to be doing, but I was practically going out of my mind with boredom, so off I went.

When I got to Edgbaston, I turned right at the county cricket ground and was immediately engulfed in an explosion of mauves, yellows, pinks and a dozen different varieties of red. It was as though I'd been dropped in a jar of boiled sweets. This was Cannon Hill Park in the middle of its yearly tulip festival.

I crossed an ornamental wrought-iron bridge, and ahead of me was a neat turning circle surrounded by yet more tulips, in front of which was a cluster of low buildings clad in light wood, a hexagonal tower, and to one side a small stone amphitheatre.

I parked up and was confronted by a pair of giant glass doors, above which was a large wood carving announcing

'The Midlands Arts Centre for Young People'. Inside was an exquisitely crafted light-wood reception desk and an equally exquisitely crafted young receptionist. Terry skipped down a flight of terracotta-tile stairs, gave me a typically shy and diffident welcome, and showed me round.

The Arts Centre was an artist's paradise. There was a painting studio, a photographic studio, a pottery workshop, a carpentry workshop, a print room and an enormous space for making sculpture. There were meeting rooms, rehearsal rooms, exhibition rooms, puppet-making workshops and a puppet theatre, and at the centre of this swirl of creativity a two hundred-seater studio theatre, home of the Midlands Arts Theatre Company.

We went upstairs and I was introduced to the big boss, John English, in the huge office he shared with his tiny, loyal wife, Mollie, who chattered non-stop in a broad Birmingham accent which she attempted to make sound posh. Terry and John couldn't have been less alike, and it was obvious they didn't get on. Terry looked as though he was a 1950s Parisian philosopher, tall, thin and languid, with long artistic hands and a wispy beard. John was built like a bullock, wore an ill-fitting grey suit and constantly tugged at his waistband which was forever slipping off his little potbelly. He strutted about like a self-made millionaire in the middle of a takeover bid, his neat-trimmed beard jutting aggressively from his chin, his ill-fitted false teeth clicking like flamenco dancers.

He told me about his passion for the arts, how they could be a life-transforming experience for young people, and why a professional company of actors was at the heart of his strategy. But I soon learnt that this vision was fraught with problems, particularly as far as personnel were concerned. Terry's predecessor, a talented young director called Mike Leigh, had left the company after a big bust-up and was now working in TV. Then when Terry took over, tension immediately developed between him and the older members of the theatre company, many of whom had worked with John for years and hated change. A cloud of gloom hung over the rehearsal room.

This magically disappeared, at least temporarily, when we opened our first show, *Hansel* (played by me) *and Gretel*. Our young audiences adored it. John Blundell, Britain's foremost puppet maker, designed the show. He and his black-clad puppeteers created a constantly moving forest populated by a host of birds and animals, and a cottage made of intensely appetising-looking sweets which the witch used as bait to lure little children into her clutches. The children were invited up on stage to break bits off at the end of the show and there was always a stampede, followed by disappointment and tears when they realised they were being offered polystyrene, not sugar. The witch was played by a camp old actor in drag, and was terrifying. The theatre rang with screams every time he made an entrance. Whatever differences John English may have had with Terry, he begrudgingly admitted it was one of the best shows the Arts Centre had ever put on.

On the Sunday before the season ended, I devised and co-directed a farewell revue for friends and supporters. I had the luxury of a fully equipped theatre, professional technicians, and a team of young writers, musicians and performers at my disposal. We satirised the Tories, the Labour government, John and Mollie, the Arts Centre, the prohibition of soft drugs, old-fashioned attitudes towards sex . . . virtually everyone and everything except ourselves. The other shows put on in that theatre felt cosy and safe, but this one didn't, particularly as John and Mollie were sitting in the fourth row, and were the butt of most of our jokes.

Next day I was summoned to John's office. I felt pretty combative. He could say what he liked – my contract came to an end in six days' time.

'Excellent!' he said. 'Very funny.'

That floored me.

'How would you fancy directing here?'

'How? When?'

'The Arts Council gives bursaries to theatre companies to train young directors. If I nominated you, we'd be in with a fair chance for next season.'

I grunted some sort of noncommittal reply, the kind you give when you're gobsmacked but don't want to show it.

'By the way,' John added, 'I might have something for Bardy too. Ask her to give me a ring.'

It didn't need much thought. All I'd done since the age of thirteen was act; it was all I'd ever wanted to do. But I was frustrated, and felt trapped by the shortage of meaningful opportunities. As a director I'd be able to play around with my own ideas, and I could count on Terry's support. The interview with the Arts Council was a formality, and I was offered a scholarship to be a trainee director at £20 per week.

Bardy was given a job too. She'd been up to the Midlands Arts a number of times, and her energy, commitment and vision had made a big impression on John. As soon as she left Central she was going to become the co-ordinator of the Arts Centre's Junior Arts Club, a new initiative for younger teenagers which she would set up from scratch.

Penny wasn't happy about my proposed career move. She'd invested a lot of time trying to get me TV work and high-status theatre jobs. She thought training to be a theatre director was at best a sidetrack, at worst a major setback. But she was patient and generous-hearted, and set to work trying to find me a job that would fill the five-month gap before I went back to Birmingham.

Prospect Productions was the most prestigious theatrical touring company in the British Isles. A job with Prospect was an opportunity to work with some of the country's best actors, and to play to audiences ten times bigger than those I'd been performing to since I'd left Central. The downside was that the part I was offered was tiny. The show was John Gay's *The Beggar's Opera*, and I'd been asked to be Nimming Ned, one of the anti-hero Macheath's gang of highwaymen. I'd virtually be a member of the chorus, a bitter pill given that only a few years previously I'd been playing major roles on West End stages. I told myself that size wasn't important, I was building an adult career from scratch, and our director, Prospect's co-founder Toby Robertson, wasn't the kind of man who would treat me disrespectfully because I was playing a small part. Unfortunately this assumption was undermined by two incidents that occurred on the opening night.

Every cast member was given a show programme, and when I looked through mine I discovered that my photo, my biography, and even my name were totally absent from the cast list. I stormed into the company manager's office, but got no satisfaction apart from an embarrassed apology. He certainly wasn't going to pulp the offending programmes and, given that a thousand copies had already been printed and distributed, I'd have to wait several weeks before he could amend the mistake. I breathed deep, told myself that this humiliation was good for my ego, and went back to my dressing room.

An hour later I realised that, while the other actors' make-up mirrors were festooned with cards, letters and good luck telegrams, I had nothing to look at apart from my own reflection. I went to see the stage door keeper.

'I'm Tony Robinson, where are my cards, please?'

'Toby Robertson?'

'No, Tony Robinson. Toby Robertson's the director.'

'Sorry, mate, I didn't know. I probably gave them all to him.'

I stuck my head round the door of Toby's office. All my cards were stuck round his mirror. I suppose it was an easy mistake to make, but I felt unrecognised and totally humiliated.

I could have had a dreadful ten weeks on tour, but I didn't, and that was entirely due to our deputy stage manager. Tash was only four years older than me, but she was graceful and mature, and I was besotted by her. She was fascinated by Eastern religion and philosophy, had an ethereal quality about her, and spoke in a measured and thoughtful way. She had high cheekbones, a full, sensual mouth like a Mayan carving, and I was deeply flattered by her attention. She taught me about fine art, fine wine and, most importantly, fine food. She had a private income, something I'd only heard about before in nineteenth-century novels, and when we went to restaurants she'd found in *The Good Food Guide*, she always picked up the bill.

She asked me to stay for the weekend in a cottage she owned outside High Wycombe, an invitation I conveniently forgot to mention to Bardy. At dinner on our first evening together she presented me with half a weird green fruit which had a knobbly skin and a hole in the middle with a brownish salad dressing in it. On one of my Grandpa Horace's trips as a steward on the Union Castle Line, he'd brought a box of avocado pears back from Durban. They'd been rock-hard, 'Solid, Jackson!' as my mum used to say. She'd put them in the airing cupboard to ripen, but they'd shrivelled and she'd thrown them away, so I never got to taste one, and had no idea how they were supposed to be eaten.

I didn't want to show Tash how naive I was, so I pretended they were as familiar to me as Heinz spaghetti. She went to the kitchen to sort out the next course, and I was left alone to confront the alien starter. I poked it, stabbed it, chased it round the plate with my fork, and eventually drank the dressing, had a couple of nibbles at the unappetising-looking green flesh, and left the rest in its bowl half hidden under its little fork and spoon. When Tash returned I said it had been lovely but I was full now, thank you. That was the low point of the weekend – it got better after that.

The show transferred to the Apollo Theatre, Shaftesbury Avenue, which meant I was now playing a bit part in a theatre only a few doors down from where I'd appeared with Anthony Newley in *Stop the World*. I probably should have lightened up and enjoyed myself, but I was in a dilemma. Bardy and I had seen so little of each other over the past year that we'd drifted apart; she'd already moved up to Birmingham to start her new job, and I was due to join her. What was I to do?

There was a lot of heart-searching, late-night phone calls and tears, but eventually we decided to try and make a go of it. I made my painful goodbyes to Tash, left the West End cast and the little cottage in High Wycombe, and headed back to the Midlands. What would have happened if I'd stayed? Certainly my subsequent life would have been entirely different. But I suspect I was too young and unsophisticated for Tash, and we'd have broken up pretty soon. I'd tried desperately hard to emulate her maturity without much success, but she'd shown me the direction in which maturity lay, and for that I was inordinately grateful.

When I got back to Birmingham Terry had vanished. Maybe he'd had one too many shouting matches with John English, maybe he'd resigned or been given the push. No one seemed to know. I was now the only theatre director at the Midlands Arts, the new season was about to start, there were casting sessions to be held, sets to be designed and built, programmes to be compiled, and a hundred other jobs which need to be attended to right away. I was a twenty-two-year-old trainee and before I'd even put on a single play, I was virtually running the place. This was difficult enough, but was made doubly so by the fact that John and Mollie had jetted off to Egypt for a series of arts seminars, and it was impossible to get in touch with them.

Fortunately I had the support of our company manager, David Gordon, a waspish but shrewd old trooper who knew the business inside out, and while I ricocheted from one crisis to the next, David smiled seraphically, made sensible suggestions, and fuelled himself with gin and optimism.

The season opened with *Little Malcolm and His Struggle Against the Eunuchs*. It was the perfect play for a callow, young director. Set in contemporary Huddersfield, it was the story of a group of arts students who form a new political party, the 'Party of Dynamic Erection'. All the characters were the same age as me, their preoccupations, their fantasies and their failures were similar to mine, the jokes were funny, the story was well told, and the cast was sufficiently enthusiastic to cope with a novice director who was a paranoid perfectionist. On the opening night there were cheers and a nearly-but-not-quite standing ovation. A few days later John and Mollie flew back home, saw the show and loved it, and John instantly promoted me to associate director.

But then the shit hit the fan. John had mentioned that he was surprised by the number of four-letter words in the play, and I'd explained that rather than using the bowdlerised version which had been performed at other theatres, I'd gone back to the original uncensored text which I thought reflected the play's characters better. John had simply shrugged and moved on to the next subject.

But a few days later a party of sixth-formers from a Catholic girls' school came to see the show along with a couple of nuns. Halfway through the first act there was the sound of seats slamming as they walked out. Somehow the press got hold of the story and we were hit by a storm of outrage. The theatre company's judgement was called into question, there were demands that the play be pulled from the repertoire, and questions were asked about whether we should continue to receive Arts Council funding. The story even reached the national newspapers after the play's writer David Halliwell went public and criticised us for using the uncensored text in front of impressionable young people. John asked me whether every 'fuck' in the show was actually in the script, and I had to admit we'd added a few. He ordered me to remove the additional profanities forthwith, and I huffily agreed. He told me firmly that I wasn't to talk to the press, which I thought was an outrageous curtailment of my right to free speech, and while I

sulked, he dealt calmly and reasonably with each new reporter
and defended me to the hilt.

As he predicted, the fuss soon died down, but I was pretty
shaken by the episode. I didn't admit it to anyone except Bardy,
but I felt overwhelmingly guilty. It had been my judgement that
had been faulty, I'd brought the organisation into disrepute,
and the fact that John had been so decent about it only made
me feel worse.

I'd started smoking copious amounts of weed. I'd roll a joint
when I got back from work, puff away till the early hours, then
crawl out of bed the following morning feeling dozy and with a
thumping headache. It was a seven-day-a-week pursuit, which
allowed me to forget how unhappy I was at work.

This had nothing to do with the problems of putting on a
play. I enjoyed engaging with actors, teasing out the meaning
of the text, challenging them to produce interesting performances. Of course there were parts of the job at which I was useless – I didn't know how to light a stage, and I once OK'd a set
that didn't have a door in it – but these were skills I could learn.
The big issue was my relationship with the rest of the company.
I was now twenty-three years old, and although I had a veneer
of sophistication, I was insecure, felt inept, and covered this up
with bluster and pomposity. I started to believe that everyone
in the theatre company hated me, and this may not have been
far from the truth. I was certainly a rotten boss.

Five spliffs a night may not be the best antidote for dealing
with rampant paranoia, but it anaesthetised the hurt, and it
had another attraction too. Our old friend and flatmate Debbie
Galloway often came to stay, and we turned her on for the very
first time. She'd never even smoked a cigarette previously, and
puffed nervously to no effect whatsoever. But by the third joint
she was confident nothing bad was going to happen to her, and

began sucking away as though she'd received instructions on drug use from The Grateful Dead.

Suddenly she was well and truly stoned, and shook her head in disbelief at the curious state she found herself in. For a long time she didn't speak, then she smiled beatifically and said, 'I don't have to try anymore, do I?' I knew exactly what she meant. All my life I'd been driven by ambition and nervous energy. But when I was stoned, the pressure melted away.

I don't think our drug-taking affected our working lives much. Bardy's Junior Arts Club was a runaway success, and its members adored her. She was a superb teacher and director, and gave her students enormous confidence in their own abilities, a talent that was fully recognised thirty years later when she became dean of RADA. Fuelled by coffee and chocolate, I was working hard too and shouldering a lot of responsibility. I still felt waves of hostility from the company, but I was a non-stop theatre-making machine. I directed a couple of Chekhov plays, wrote a full-length children's entertainment, directed a celebration of Britain's most influential contemporary playwright Edward Bond, created a puppet show about Dick Whittington, and mounted various theatrical events around the building, in the amphitheatre and in Cannon Hill Park. John didn't see the need to employ another director, and neither did I.

Bardy and I decided to get married. Although I undoubtedly loved her, it was probably foolhardy, and I suspect had more to do with our mutual craving for security rather than a desire to spend the rest of our lives together. But we were young and our parents disapproved, so tying the knot seemed rather romantic, like a song by Del Shannon or Ricky Nelson. The wedding was at the parish church in Alsager, with Guy as my best man. I didn't invite anyone from the theatre company. Kathleen had forgiven me by now, so all Bardy's family were there, including her gran. My parents came too, with Mum looking like Queen Elizabeth's stunt double. Bardy wore a white minidress, and

I was in a purple velvet suit. Time might not have been kind to my fashion sense, but it was 1969, and I thought I looked amazing.

What a successful couple we must have appeared! We were both well paid, had fulfilling, creative jobs, a smart flat in Moseley, and I'd even bought a brand-new Mini Cooper with the last of my earnings as a child actor. But dope has its downside, and it was about to bring me low.

7

THE SECURITY GUARD

I didn't see mankind's first steps on the moon because I'd fallen asleep in front of the telly. In fact, most issues of high drama and political importance passed me by in a haze of marijuana smoke. Our social life was suffering too. Early one evening Bardy and I smoked a couple of joints, and were overcome by an attack of the munchies. We tucked into some cold chicken, a can of beans, a slab of Cadbury's Fruit and Nut and an Arctic Roll, which we topped off with a bottle of cider, and settled down to an evening in front of the TV. *Monty Python* would be on in a couple of hours and we didn't want to miss that.

Shortly before eight thirty the telephone rang.

'Are you still coming?'

'Who is this?'

'Tony Cornish. Are you still coming round to dinner?'

Tony was the senior radio drama producer at Pebble Mill. A few weeks previously he'd asked us over, a fact that had been totally obliterated from my mind. He wasn't just a friend, he also occasionally employed me. This was a man I didn't want to piss off on either score. I drew a deep breath.

'Yes, of course, Tony. Sorry if I sounded a little vague. We've sprung a leak.'

'Is it serious? You sure you still want to come?'

'Absolutely! We're looking forward to it, aren't we, Bardy?'

I shouldn't have looked at her. Her glassy stare was terrifying.

We blundered into the night. I drove at the pace of a hearse

while Bardy attempted to read the tiny writing in the Birmingham *A to Z*. It was an age before we arrived at Tony's house.

We stood on their step with no wine, flowers or chocolates,
and with virtually no brain cells. Tony's actress wife Linda
came to the door and introduced herself. She was all smiles and
friendly concern.

'What an evening!' I said. 'What a nightmare bloody evening!'

'You didn't have to come,' she said sympathetically. 'Is everything all right now?'

'It'll dry out,' said Bardy, 'eventually.'

They served us prawn and celery cocktail, a Robert Carrier
roast beef dish with garlic and red wine sauce, and crêpe
Suzette. Bardy was brilliant. She talked non-stop. Sometimes
she lost her thread and had to think for a while before continu-
ing her story, but our hosts were enthralled.

I on the other hand was having problems eating and sitting
up straight. My teeth refused to chew, my throat refused to
swallow, and my stomach wanted to eject everything that was
being crammed into it. The evening wore on, and I could hardly
keep my eyes open. Eventually I told them I'd got a migraine
brought on by our flooding crisis, and we left. I was riddled
with the intense self-loathing you feel when you've lied to a
friend, but when we got home I rolled a joint and we forgot all
about it.

In fact, I blotted it out of my mind completely until the read-
through of an episode of *Blackadder II*, twenty years later.
The plot involved Ploppy the jailer and Mistress Ploppy (no
relation) the last-meal cook, who only ever had sausages on the
menu. The actress playing Mistress Poppy said I probably
wouldn't remember her but this wasn't the first time she'd prepared food for me. Her name was Linda Polan and we'd had
dinner together many years previously with her former husband in Birmingham. I made sincere apologies for my behaviour
that night, but she didn't know what I was talking about – all

she could remember about it was that the crêpe Suzette had been a bit floppy.

I don't know how long I could have kept up this double life of intense hard work and narcotic stupor, but it swiftly came to an end. The Christmas holidays are a tough time for those who want to take drugs. Dealers, like most young people, tend to go home during the festive season, stay with their parents, eat turkey, borrow money and get their washing done. The amount of cannabis on the street diminishes, it becomes more expensive, and ultimately unobtainable. We faced a bleak New Year.

But there was a rumour that some opiated hash was out there somewhere, and I eventually managed to purchase a small brick of this alien substance in Balsall Heath. The hash we normally smoked was either a dark brown pliable resin, or green and hard, and crumbled into dust when you scratched it. This substance was light grey with white streaks running through it like a piece of unpolished marble, and it was so solid it was impossible to break it into pieces small enough to put into a cigarette.

After hacking at it fruitlessly for quarter of an hour, our friend Ted Barker, an elegant young hippy who was a talented artist and cartoonist, had an idea. We loped across the park to the Arts Centre, which was locked for the night. After a great deal of hammering, the Arts Centre's security man came to the door. His name was Bob Johnson, and he was a cheery soul with a droopy jet-black moustache and a way with the girls. He was currently going out with our gorgeous receptionist, which made us all intensely envious.

Ted explained that we needed access to the art department as he'd been asked to draw some sketches over the holiday and didn't have the materials he needed. We trudged home with a box of charcoal and some art paper, the paper being a red herring to obscure our need for the charcoal. We heated it on a tin plate, and once it was glowing placed a large chip of the hash on top of it. When it was alight we sucked the fumes into our lungs via the cardboard tube from a roll of toilet paper. This improvised shisha pipe proved very efficient – in fact, far too efficient. Within half an hour we were slumped silently in our seats, looking like the kind of addicts Victorian heroes blunder across in East End opium dens when they're searching for their best friend's fallen lover.

I was basking in an aura of bliss when the heebie-jeebies kicked in. Every doper has the occasional attack. Usually a short walk and a few breathing exercises will ward them off, but not this time.

Panic came in waves. I went to the kitchen for a glass of water and began automatically wiping up the dishes. But my mind veered off elsewhere, and eventually I realised I'd screwed our tea towel into a tight, crumpled, neurotic ball. I staggered into the bedroom and lay down. Nothing seemed real. It was as though I was hurtling up and down in a fast lift and wanted to get off at a floor called 'Normal', but the lift wouldn't stop however many times I pressed the button. How terrifying was that? Everything was a figment of my imagination, which meant I could change what I wanted just by thinking about it. I tried moving the bedroom door from one wall to another, and it worked. A second previously it had been in its normal place opposite the end of my bed; now it was on the side wall. Why had it done that? If I could move the door at will, how would I ever know where the real doorway was? Was there a real doorway? Would I ever be able to get out of my bedroom? I was trapped.

Another terror engulfed me. If I was imagining everything, who was Tony Robinson? Tony the actor wasn't real, he was only a machine spouting someone else's words; his ideas weren't real, they were second-hand opinions he'd read in books. Tony the director was a grouchy control freak wearing the mask of a grown-up. Tony the husband, Tony the hippy, Tony the socialist, all fakes, two-dimensional characters from a badly written play. Tony Robinson! Tony Robinson! Even his name sounded phoney. I could see an image of him looming out of the darkness dressed in rags. He had the face of a teenager, but it was covered in age lines crudely drawn on in stage make-up, and tears were dribbling from his eyes. Bagpipes were playing a terrifying dirge, and he was jigging and capering in time to the music.

Eventually I must have fallen asleep. The next thing I remember was the dawn light. My heart was still racing, but the hallucinations had stopped, and the bedroom door was in its usual place. I pulled on my slippers and shuffled into the sitting room. Bardy was snuggled up on the sofa clutching a cushion and Ted was asleep on the floor. The TV was still on even though it was early morning. Someone was talking about what the new year might have in store for Great Britain. It was New Year's Day 1970. The bagpipes had been real. They'd been played by the Royal Highland Fusiliers on Andy Stewart's Hogmanay show. I shuffled into the kitchen and slowly spread blackberry jam on a piece of bread.

It took me a long time to get over the events of that night. For the first few days I stayed in the flat and pretended I'd got the flu. This was quite plausible, I certainly looked rough. Then I made my first tentative steps out, which was fine as long as our front door was in sight, but as soon as I turned the corner, the terror came back. After a week I returned to work and, as I wasn't directing a show at that time, was able to sit on my own in my office, reading the *Guardian* and drinking peppermint tea. I'd go to the shops, become overwhelmed by panic, and have to find a phone box and call someone to come and rescue me.

Bardy took me to Kings Heath to learn the basics of transcendental meditation from a man in a brown corduroy suit who gave me my secret mantra. That helped. Gradually my strength came back, the worst of my panic disappeared, and I began to realise that what I'd experienced had been more than a nightmare – it was a series of unpleasant and very important insights. 'Tony Robinson' was indeed a ragbag of delusions, prejudices and redundant childhood habits. My notion of reality was nothing more than shadows on a wall. My non-stop ambition, my constant searching for the next big break, were empty and meaningless. I needed to become more aware of the constant chatter in my head, quieten it down, and learn to live a life that was less about me! me! me!

Change came, although not necessarily in ways I expected. I hadn't played cards since I'd begun smoking weed; high-stakes gambling and the temporary inability to count to ten don't make for happy bedfellows. But I'd sworn off drugs now, and wanted to do something enjoyable that would take my mind off my fit of craziness, so why shouldn't I go back to the card table? I was a good gambler – probably very good – so I might make some serious money. One of the drama teachers at the Arts Centre ran a poker school in Moseley, and I usually found myself up a few pounds by the end of the evening.

After one game I got into conversation with a man I hadn't met before; we analysed a few hands, discussed various betting tactics, and he mentioned that there was a professional school in Birmingham city centre most nights. If I fancied trying my luck, he could probably get me in.

I was flattered that he thought I could hold my own in professional circles, and the following week I turned up at the front door of Tiffany's in the Bullring. It was the most unprepossessing club I'd ever seen. No flashing lights, no illuminated sign over the entrance, just a solid metal door tagged with graffiti. I pressed the buzzer, announced who I was, and went in.

The club was the size of a large cupboard, with a round green baize table in the middle of it. There must have been other rooms, but apart from a dark and rudimentary toilet, I never saw any. Not that I was there for long. I sat down at 10.15 p.m. and by midnight I'd been cleaned out. I was offered credit, but declined. Losing money is always unpleasant, but I wasn't too distressed. These things happen. You get a bad run of cards and, no matter how skilful you are, you're going to lose. The knack is to minimise your losses, and though I'd had a bad night, I hadn't racked up any debts, so I'd done the right thing.

The next week I went back and again lost everything. I'd brought an extra twenty quid as back-up this time, and even that had gone. But two losses give you an advantage. The other players begin to think you're no good, and when the high cards start coming, you can take advantage of their mistaken belief, and fleece them for all they've got.

No, that was bollocks! After being cleaned out for a third consecutive week I had to face up to a stark reality. I wasn't the gambler I thought I was. I'd got enough know-how to take money off friends and acquaintances, but nothing more. I'd believed I was Marlon Brando in *One-Eyed Jacks*, but I was simply a young man who thought too much of himself. Oddly this realisation, though painful, was almost pleasurable. I never gambled again.

My final play at the Midlands Arts Centre was Bertolt Brecht's *The Caucasian Chalk Circle*. Brecht was the playwright most admired by the seventies left, but although I paid lip service to his work, I'd never really understood him. So rather than adopting my usual default position of pretending to know more than I did, I gave myself a couple of weeks' thinking time before I began work on the play in earnest.

This coincided with the International Student Drama Festival, which was held each year in a different European city. Passionate young people from all over the western world would act out pieces of Shakespeare, Arthur Miller and the fashionable German romantics like Georg Büchner. They'd fall in love, laugh, cry, then go back home to their private schools and well-endowed universities nursing their broken hearts.

1970 was different, though. The Midlands Arts Centre was hosting the event, and virtually all its five hundred young guests had been infected with the anger of the New Left. For them the Arts Centre wasn't what it seemed; it was a symptom of bourgeois democracy's desire to control the masses. It was an agent of capitalism, no different from Rio Tinto Zinc or the United States war machine. In fact, it was worse. Capitalism was only interested in profiteering and made no bones about it, but the Midlands Arts Centre practised cultural imperialism, using the language of art to get inside the heads of the young and infect them with the ideology of consumerism.

To show their contempt for us, these young revolutionaries stole Twix bars from the canteen, smoked in the non-smoking areas, and walked across the flower beds. Their plays were mostly performed naked, and they poured red paint over the stage which was very hard to get off.

The local hippies and sixth-formers who usually inhabited the centre fled in the face of this righteous wrath, but I was intoxicated by it. Of course I disapproved when they drew hammers and sickles on our reception desk with their felt-tip pens, and declined to flush the bowl when they'd been to the lavatory, but I'd never seen such fearless devilry.

I was still too shaky to talk to any of these fearsome terrorists, but I invented excuses to hover in their vicinity, particularly the Austrians, Germans and Swiss who appeared to be the ringleaders. They looked back at me with stony eyes as though I was an arch-quisling, an oppressor disguised in a kaftan and beads, and I couldn't avoid their accusing stares. They were right. I was a creature of the state in thrall to the pernicious fantasy of show business.

After they'd gone, the Arts Centre reverted to normal. The shiny wood was re-sanded, waxed and polished, the toilets flushed and the flower beds replanted. But the young anarchists left a big hole in my life. Ever afterwards the MAC seemed tame. I missed their righteous anger, the smell of their Gauloises and their acres of pubic hair.

I began thinking afresh about *The Caucasian Chalk Circle*, and decided to blow the play wide open, just as the European anarchists had blown open the culture of the Arts Centre. I used pop music, masks and a host of theatrical devices. I rewrote the first act so it was about contemporary issues rather than the preoccupations of Brecht's time. I employed a large cast and used their combined presence as an additional character, a powerful force that could transform the stage into a mountain range or a snowy waste.

I adopted a similar physical approach to the one Litz Pisk had used in our BBC television show *Explorations*. At the time I'd thought it was arty nonsense, but now I had an inkling of what she'd been trying to do, and was inspired by it.

'Darlink Tony,' Litz used to say, 'you alvays say no to me. No! No! No! All zer time. Then eventually you say yes, and everything's fine. Vy don't you say yes sooner? You vaste so much time and energy with your no's.'

I said yes now. The heroine, Grusha, had to flee across a bridge with her baby. The entire company used their bodies, their flexibility and their strength to create this bridge. It was a huge, rickety monster that stretched from one side of the stage to the other, and I was very proud of it and my company's imagination.

Towards the end of the season Bardy was headhunted; Central wanted her to come back and teach voice technique to the student actors. She felt she'd achieved her goal at the Midlands Arts. She'd created a thriving arts club, and with fresh leadership, it could go from strength to strength. Reluctantly John let her go. She suggested Debbie Galloway should apply for the post; she did, and she got it.

We invited John and Mollie to dinner to thank them for

everything they'd done for us. While we were having coffee, John asked me to come back the following autumn as director of productions.

'You've virtually been doing that job for the last few months,' he said. 'We should recognise that.'

How ironic! Ever since I'd been offered the trainee director-ship, my ambition had been to run the company. I'd only recently convinced myself that this was a narcissistic delusion, yet now it could become a reality. Except that I no longer wanted it. I didn't have the emotional wherewithal to run a theatre company, just as I wasn't cut out to be a professional gambler. When I told John I wasn't going to stay, he was typic-ally generous, told me he'd thought 'no' would be my answer, and wished me well.

The MAC was the starting point for a lot of glittering careers; even our security man Bob Johnson changed his sur-name to Carolgees, and became an international superstar along with his dog, Spit. As for me, what did I want to do now? I had no idea.

8

TINKER BELL

It was a rat, definitely. At first I'd thought it was the tail end of a nightmare. But no, I was awake, and it was the tail end of a large rodent, which had padded across my prone body and was now burrowing its way into a pile of discarded T-shirts and tracksuit tops in the corner of the bedroom.

The early morning light was flickering through the tatty net curtains, and Caroline lay beside me, snuggled under the fur coat that had once belonged to my mum. Dad had bought it for her before the war, and she'd asked me to give it to the Oxford Committee for Famine Relief along with some old tops and handbags, but I'd filched it from the carrier bag because it looked like something you'd wear if you were on the sleeve of *Sergeant Pepper*.

It had certainly come in useful the previous night. Portable Theatre were interested in art, not administration. As usual there'd been a cock-up with the accommodation, and we'd sat around in our dressing rooms for an hour or so after the show till our digs were sorted out. Eventually the secretary of the Lancaster students' union had arrived looking harassed, he'd brought us to this dingy flat, and handed us over to some engineering students, who'd been totally disinterested in our plight. They'd nodded towards this freezing room and gone back to their game of Cluedo. There was only one bed, which wasn't very appropriate given that Caroline and I were work col-leagues, and she'd made it quite clear that she didn't want any hanky-panky, which I thought was a bit rich given that I hadn't

offered her any. But the earnest lad from the students' union
had now fled, and we obviously weren't going to be given anywhere else to stay, so we'd kept our clothes on, and gone straight
to bed. The temperature had dropped even lower during the
night, and we'd huddled together for warmth. Had Caroline
meant what she'd said about no hanky-panky? How did I feel
about that? What would happen if . . . ? I thought about Bardy
in a tragic motorway pile-up and that did the trick. I fell asleep
almost immediately.

The job with Portable was tailor-made for me. My drug-
fuelled nerves had calmed down, but my attitude towards life
and work had changed radically. I certainly didn't want to go
back into rep. What was the point? The audiences always
looked the same – middle-class, middle-aged and white – and I
suspected most of them would rather have been anywhere but
at the theatre. Watching a play was a pointless ritual. What did
Molière or George Bernard Shaw have to do with their lives?
The world was at boiling point; workers and students were on
the streets, nuclear weapons threatened to fry our planet, and
a white republic had been declared in Rhodesia. I didn't want
to be an old-fashioned actor with a cravat and a neat haircut,
with elegant spirals of smoke drifting upwards from the cigarette held in my exquisitely manicured hand. I wanted to
engage with the real world, and I wanted to challenge audiences to do the same.

Portable Theatre had been the brainchild of Howard Brenton, a big teddy bear of a man with gappy teeth, David Hare,
who was glamorous, haughty and a rising star of the theatre,
and Andrew 'Snoo' Wilson, who had an untamed writing style,
but was brimful of ideas. These three playwrights shared a
common vision: theatre as an art form was bankrupt, they
should create new plays that exposed the fact that Britain's
imperial might was at an end, and the country was spinning
into a terminal crisis. Some of their plays were brilliant; others
crashed and burned. They were the products of young arrogant

minds, and could often be wilfully obscure. But whatever their shortcomings, most Portable Theatre shows were head and shoulders above those of their young contemporaries.

Snoo offered me a part in his new play, *Portable Pericles*, a reworking of Shakespeare's lumbering masterpiece. I wasn't sure I understood it, but he said he was interested in me not only because of what I might offer the production, but because he relished my contempt for traditional theatre. This was exactly the kind of thing I wanted to hear from a director. The money wasn't good, and we'd be touring to some fairly out-of-the-way places, but I couldn't refuse, even though Penny groaned when I told her.

I soon realised that the rest of the company couldn't make head or tail of Snoo's adaptation either, but we rehearsed with gusto and conviction, jumped in an old red Transit van, and set off for the Midlands. The tour could have been a complete disaster, and I suppose in many ways it was – an obscure Shakespeare tragedy reworked to make it even more obscure – but it was far more exciting than any of us could have expected.

Most of the performances were in student venues, and Britain's students were in a ferment, inspired by continental activists who'd been demonstrating, occupying buildings, barricading streets, burning tyres and generally expressing outrage against international capitalism, the war in Vietnam, and the shortcomings of the university curriculum. A mini version of these events was currently being played out in British universities, with the bumbling authorities making the situation worse by the incompetence of their response, see-sawing between doing nothing, and threatening police raids and mass expulsions. It was in this febrile atmosphere that we performed, and it was intoxicating. However obscure our play might have been, it was clearly on the side of the students, and wherever we went we were given a rapturous reception. We felt like messengers from the gods of socialism, spreading the word from town to town, and from performance space to performance space.

Our greatest triumph was in Liverpool where we'd been booked to play at the university theatre. We arrived to find that Leftist students were occupying the Senate House so we cancelled the advertised show, and asked our audience to follow us to the Senate to perform to the occupiers. It was like a scene from *The Battleship Potemkin*. The doors to the Senate House had been barricaded by burly young men in rugby shirts, but the piles of chairs and inverted ping-pong tables were heaved to one side as we made our way in, followed by the audience still clutching their programmes and boxes of Bassett's Allsorts.

The occupation had already lasted three days. Those inside were red-eyed, unshaven and dishevelled, but bubbling with excitement. It was a venue unlike any we'd played previously. There was no stage, only a tiered horseshoe of seats surrounding a small rostrum. I suggested we play the show in the round like we used to do at Stoke, and given how crowded the Senate was, with people standing five-deep at the back and in the aisles, this meant we had to make our entrances and exits by shoving our way through the audience and clambering over the seats.

When we took our final bow we held our left fists high in a gesture of solidarity, applauded the occupiers and sang 'The Red Flag', although not everyone knew the words.

I don't know for certain how the revolutionary actors of the Paris Commune, those on the steps of the Winter Palace or in the streets of Havana behaved, but I'm pretty sure it would have been much like us, and I bet at least one of them would have been wearing his mum's fur coat.

When the tour ended I slept for the best part of a week. The tide of revolutionary anger ebbed, and apart from a few expulsions, the students were soon back at work feverishly swotting for their exams. I doubted that I'd want to work for Portable Theatre again until the next wave of revolutionary fervour swept Britain. I'd been put off by the rat.

*

Back in London, Bardy and I stayed with Sylv and Guy. They'd moved down once the Stoke season had finished and Sylv had now transformed herself from harassed teenage mum into queen hippy of West Hampstead. The flat she and Guy rented in Cumberland Mansions had become a mecca for the radical young artists of the area. The air was scented with grass, patchouli and home-made chocolate chip cookies, Jefferson Airplane played non-stop, and pop singers and assorted musicians wandered in and out looking for pretty girls, drugs or a natter. Terry 'Copkiller' Ford moved in too. He was an American drama student studying at LAMDA who would soon achieve reflected glory when his elder brother Harrison started doing rather well in Hollywood. Terry's middle name was ironic; he'd fly into rages, but was as gentle as a kitten. He got arrested on an anti-Vietnam War demo, and Sylv and I went round his various friends trying to raise his bail, but no one was prepared to stump up, which I thought was a bit sad.

Then Sylvie and Guy split up, and he set off for India on his motorbike. One night in the south of France he pitched his tent, and woke up to the sound of Sylvie calling his name. He drove straight back to West Hampstead, but when he got there, Sylvie said he must have misheard. So he drove off again, and I lost touch with him for a long time.

Now Bardy was in London full-time we needed a place of our own, and eventually she found us our dream flat. A long-haired entrepreneur called Charlie Ware had converted an Edwardian house in Camden Town into small, modern apartments ideal for young professional couples. But he'd been hit by a potentially disastrous cash-flow crisis, and was prepared to sell us the top-floor flat for £4,500. This still seemed an enormous amount of money to pay for somewhere to live but we loved it at first sight. So we borrowed fifteen hundred pounds from my dad, took out an additional loan, I sold my car, and the deal was done.

I'd often dreamt of owning somewhere like 253 Camden Park Road. It was the complete opposite of the dingy flats and bedsits I'd lived in previously. There was no wallpaper, just freshly plastered walls painted bright white, and no hallways. The front door opened straight into a kitchen/dining room which we decorated with framed posters of modern jazz festivals. To the left were two bedrooms. We lit them with candles and a lava lamp, and bought exotic Middle-Eastern throws for the beds from a sale at John Lewis. In the middle of the right-hand wall were double doors which opened onto a small balcony overlooking Camden Square, an ideal place for our new miniature dachshund, Herman, to poo. But the most unusual feature of the flat was a discreet curve of stairs which led up to a mezzanine where the attic would once have been. It was too low to stand up in, but ideal for sitting cross-legged meditating, or lying on scatter cushions reading Krishnamurti or the latest edition of *Which?*.

We'd spent every penny we'd earned buying our exquisite new unfurnished flat, so had to fill it with heavy dark-brown tables, chairs and cupboards our parents wanted to get rid of. Occasionally, if I got a job or a repeat cheque, we'd buy something in light wood or a fancy uplighter from Habitat, and we laid wall-to-wall carpet throughout, which we bought from Cyril Lord. It had red, green and gold swirls, and some of our friends thought it looked a bit vulgar. But it had a rubberised back so you didn't need to buy underlay, which we thought was very practical.

I could see myself living there for the rest of my life, but my initial stay didn't last long because, despite my newfound reluctance to perform plays in repertory theatre, I was about to become the first actor to tread the boards of a major new playhouse.

In the early 1970s Leeds was a tired old monster of a city with few signs of its former glory. The vast warehouses were boarded up, the once-great Liverpool-to-Leeds Canal was a cesspool, and urban blight abounded. But there was an optimism about the place, a belief that it could re-invent itself. People dreamt it could become a city of culture, with new concert halls, galleries and theatres as good as, if not better than, the ones down south.

Alfred Bradley, the Leeds BBC radio drama producer, had been a strong supporter of mine since my time at Stoke, and for many years had been heavily involved in an ambitious bid to create a repertory theatre in the city's heart. Now Leeds University had constructed a building to house it, the money had been raised for seats, lighting, dressing rooms and a stage, and the Leeds Playhouse was about to become a reality.

Alfred persuaded Bill Hays, the newly appointed director of productions, to employ me as the hero in a brand-new play called *Simon Says* which was going to open the theatre. I thought about saying no, but I had great affection for Alfred and didn't want to let him down. I was also excited by the prospect of working with its author Alan Plater, who had the knack of writing about working-class lives in a way that touched the hearts of popular TV audiences. He'd adapted a play called *Close the Coalhouse Door*, which was about the miners' struggles against the pit owners and politicians, and how by joining together in the face of hardship, they'd gradually won their rights. Bill had directed it, and it had been a big hit on the telly. I felt this was the kind of work I should be doing.

It was only when we started rehearsing that I realised there were two big drawbacks. Firstly *Simon Says* wasn't a 'brand-new' play; it was an old play that had been lying at the back of Alan's cupboard for some time, and was frankly a mess. The second drawback was that Bill wasn't the right person to deal with this *Mary Celeste* of a script. He might have been a capable TV director, but he had no idea how to cut, rewrite and generally knock *Simon Says* into shape.

The upside was that he'd been able to attract a team of very talented young actors to take part in the season, plus some experienced older performers like Alfred Burke, who'd starred as the superbly understated Frank Marker in the long-running

Thames TV series *Public Eye*. It felt like a good team. The question was, though, would they be able to rescue the show from the disaster which seemed to be looming?

On the first night the theatre was full to overflowing. Local people were out in force, the mayor and the Leeds MPs were there, as were senior Arts Council administrators and several national theatre critics who had somehow stirred themselves to review a show outside London.

We stood in the wings in our circus costumes listening to the excited buzz from the auditorium. We were nervous, but pumped full of adrenaline. The play's circus metaphor represented the state of Britain today, and I was the sad-faced clown, an everyman, buffeted by Capitalist lion tamers and various other reactionary forces.

The houselights faded to black, followed by a few seconds of darkness, then a single note sounded, and a spotlight illuminated my white face. I inclined my head courteously.

'Welcome,' I seemed to be saying. 'You and I have arrived. The show can begin.'

Applause broke out, and it went on and on. It wasn't for me, of course, no one had a clue who I was, all I'd done was nod. It was the sound of three hundred people congratulating themselves on their long years of work and commitment which had finally paid off. The clapping showed no sign of coming to an end. I looked round, as though I had no idea where the sound was coming from, and shrugged. There was laughter and even more applause. I let it continue for as long as I could (I was really enjoying myself), then finally held up my hand to indicate that enough was enough. Most of the audience stopped, but a hard core continued. I waved a finger of admonition, and there was another gale of laughter. I'd always been useless at mime, but at that moment I felt like Marcel Marceau. Eventually there was silence, I nodded at the musical director, the band struck up and I began to sing. The audience hung on my every note (boy, oh boy, this was fun!). When I finished there was yet more applause, and a beautiful female clown entered. She was played by Sue Macready who I'd known since our Central days, and although we were only friends, there'd always been a strong stage relationship between us. (Have I mentioned how much I was milking this?) I greeted her shyly but with love in my heart. She looked back in wonder. One after another the actors made their entrances and were greeted by the audience with rapture, at least for the first half hour. But gradually the enchantment seemed to dissipate. Was I imagining it? I glanced at Sue, and she looked back as if to say, 'Christ, we're losing them.' The laughter grew less intense. There was no longer applause at the end of each scene. The audience was finding me a little less charming, and a little more irksome. I suspected they were asking themselves the same question Sue and I had been asking for the last few weeks: 'Why have they chosen this crappy play to open our lovely theatre?'

Halfway through the second half they clearly decided they'd had enough. Programmes were read and rustled, there were whispered conversations, and people left early to catch their buses. When we took our final bow there were no cries of 'More!'

A reception had been organised in the freshly painted restaurant on the first floor, to which all the actors had been invited. We should probably have given it a miss, but we'd seen the trays of canapés being laid out and there was free wine, so we decided to go.

There are stories of leading actors on Broadway who, after their first-night curtain has fallen, have entered Sardi's restaurant, whereupon the other diners have risen from their tables and spontaneously applauded. This was not my experience that night. When I arrived, no one looked up, or if they did, it was a shifty glance and a swift look down again. No one tried to engage me in conversation, or ask for my autograph. It was as though I was at a gospel meeting dressed as a black and white minstrel.

The other actors were clustered round the buffet being

similarly ignored, but were managing to disguise their embarrassment by wolfing down platefuls of cooked meats.

Bill Hays came bouncing up to Sue and me, the crumbs from his quiche Lorraine tumbling down his chin. 'Great show! Great show!' he said. We didn't reply.

A couple of weeks later there was a civic reception for the theatre's supporters at the town hall, and I devised an entertainment for it. It wasn't unlike the one I'd put on at the Midlands Arts, and it got a similar reaction. The outcome was similar too: Bill asked me to direct a series of late-night shows at the theatre. I came up with some ideas but my heart wasn't in it. I didn't want to start directing again, and if I did, it would be to put on shows far more subversive than Bill would allow.

I left Leeds as quickly and discreetly as I could, and went back home. Not that Bardy seemed particularly pleased to see me. Things weren't going well between us in the way they had previously. Her job at Central was a success, and she had a new social life which I wasn't part of. I felt jealous of her circle of friends, but also bored by their company. So our paths hardly crossed anymore, and neither of us made much effort to rectify that. At first people didn't notice, they said we were like brother and sister, and meant it as a compliment. But the trouble was they were right. We were like siblings, not husband and wife.

My gloominess was considerably relieved, though, when Penny got me a 'champagne' job, a part at the Royal Court Theatre. It had been the ambition of every serious young actor to perform at the Court since the mid-fifties when it had first put on John Osborne's *Look Back in Anger*. The play had transformed the English theatre. Its anti-hero Jimmy Porter epitomised the rise of a new, angry, articulate working class. Encouraged by the Court, a host of talented young playwrights appeared as if out of nowhere and because they used the English language in an innovative, authentic and naturalistic way, there was suddenly a proliferation of great parts for actors.

So it should have been good news for me, but unfortunately

the run of bad luck I'd been having hadn't come to an end. The playwright Don Howarth had recently had a big hit with a play called *A Lily in Little India*, and our show, *Ogodiveleftthegason* was the follow-up. Unfortunately, like *Portable Pericles*, it was obscure and impenetrable, and, like *Simon Says*, was written by a playwright who audiences rated highly, but whose expectations weren't met by this play. The first night came and went, the reviews were dreadful, and the ticket sales desultory. The only silver lining was the friendship I struck up with Dudley Sutton. He was of the generation that produced Albert Finney and Tom Courtenay; he'd been expelled from RADA, but after appearing as a gay biker in *The Leather Boys*, he had become highly successful, culminating in playing the lead in the original production of Joe Orton's *Entertaining Mr Sloane*. But his career had been on the wane for the last few years and he'd acquired the same kind of dissolute charm that had made Vivian MacKerrell so attractive. One night after the show I was propping up the bar of the pub next door to the theatre with the rest of the cast, consoling myself with whisky sours. Cocktails were a novelty for me; after a few I felt like Ernest Hemingway. But Dudley was growing restless. He was in recovery and was fed up with orange juice, so he suggested I go back to his place in South Kensington for a smoke.

I'd recently broken my promise about giving up drugs, and we rolled joints till dawn. I woke up mid-morning and staggered into the kitchen. Dudley was already there, rifling through the ashtray. He found the crushed dog-end of a spliff, smoothed it out, we smoked it, then had several more. I don't know which of us first realised it was a Saturday and we had a matinee to perform.

'I don't . . .' I said. 'This is very . . .' I tried to stand up but failed miserably.

'It's not a prob . . .' replied Dudley, 'not . . .'

He crawled to a chest of drawers, heaved himself onto his

feet, opened a drawer, waved a small cardboard box in the air and tipped out a handful of plastic phials and a couple of disposable syringes.

'In . . .' he pointed vaguely in my direction.

'What?'

'. . . your arse.'

'That isn't . . .'

'Smack? No, you lunatic. It's, er, whatcha call . . . vitamins. Like shooting up vegetables.'

We dropped our trousers, both injected a phial full into a buttock and waited. It seemed to work. After a minute I tentatively got to my feet. We headed off towards Sloane Square like a pair of comedy drunks.

It was the afternoon from hell, not just because we arrived at the theatre late and everyone was panicking, or because of the looks of disapproval on the faces of the other cast members, or even because of the struggle I had with my lines. The real problem was trying to remember who I was, where I was, and what I was supposed to be doing. Was I asleep in our Camden flat, running through my words on the Tube or, horror upon horrors, standing on a London stage acting in front of eighty-odd people? My mouth flapped up and down like Peter Brough's dummy in *Educating Archie*, and my head pounded from the effort of trying to concentrate, but the purpose and meaning of it all was lost on me. And when eventually, by sheer force of will, I managed to yank myself back into the play, I caught sight of Dudley, his face grey-white like one of the un-dead, and I knew that the entire audience must realise I was stoned, because if he looked like that, I must be looking ten times worse.

Since that dreadful day I've never taken anything stronger than Pepsi Max before a show, or indeed before any public engagement. But whenever I watch a rerun of *Lovejoy* on TV, and see Dudley's middle-aged face transmogrified into Tinker Bell, Ian McShane's hapless and raddled sidekick, that afternoon comes flooding back to me, and I die a little.

My self-esteem was at an all-time low now, which wasn't helped by the continued collapse of my relationship with Bardy. I doubt whether either of us was more to blame for the mess we were in than the other. We were still in our early twenties and had only been married for a couple of years, but were imbued with the ethos of the late 1960s, and had no idea that relationships needed to be worked on. Friends tried to help us repair the damage. Ted Barker had got work in London on the *International Times* and later had his own cartoon strip in *The Observer* called 'The Largactylites'. He came to stay, we revelled in his newfound celebrity, and for someone as laid-back as Ted, he showed remarkable and tender concern for us. Sue Macready gave us some money to go on a camping holiday in the Lake District, but it never stopped raining, and we came home more depressed than when we'd left. I soldiered on, though. In fact, I don't think I realised the state I was in until the night of David Alistair's party.

July 1970 was the fourth anniversary of my class leaving Central. David had recently had some success as the desk sergeant in a cop series, and offered to host a 'do' in his little flat in Kilburn. About twenty members of my course turned up, plus a few friends like Bardy who'd been closely associated with us.

It was what you might call a 'social gathering' rather than a full-blown party. I don't remember music playing, only the chatter of polite conversation. People were sitting on sofas with their shoes off, others were lounging on the floor. Two ex-students had flown in from the United States, and were regaling us with their adventures off-Broadway. Old photographs were passed around. There were Twiglets and a modest buffet.

I don't know why I got so dreadfully drunk, but I did, and very quickly. And in those days, when I got pissed I tended to develop kleptomania.

I went over to the little dining table where the food was being served, picked up a handful of knives and forks and slipped them inside my new blouson jacket. I crossed to the bookshelf pretending to be browsing, and pocketed a Penguin book about the beat poets and Lawrence Durrell's *Bitter Lemons*. I pulled open one of David's new Laura Ashley curtains and gazed into the night, which gave me the opportunity to raid the fruit bowl.

'You're slurring your words,' said Bardy, 'and staggering. We should go.'

She took my arm and steered me to the front door.

'So soon?' said David solicitously.

'Sorry, he's got an early start tomorrow,' lied Bardy.

I nodded with due seriousness, and turned to leave with my arm clutched round my stomach to support the weight of my newly acquired treasures.

David followed us down the front garden path.

'So lovely to see you,' he said.

It was so lovely to see him too. I was overcome with affection and sadness, and held my arms open wide to embrace him. A shower of knives and forks rained onto the path and oranges bounced into the flower beds. I took the paperbacks out of my jacket and handed them back to him.

'Great books!' I said, and lurched off into the night.

Not that my life was entirely miserable. I'd been worried that Alfred Bradley, whose recommendation had got me the job in Leeds, would be disappointed by the brevity of my stay there, but his reaction was entirely unexpected. He'd become disillusioned by the set-up at the Playhouse too, and felt bad for having persuaded me to take the job. The BBC were about to televise *Big Soft Nellie*, and he suggested to its director Mike Newell that I should reprise the role of Bennie which I'd played with some success at Stoke. Mike agreed and I spent a happy, untroubled fortnight in Manchester working alongside top-rated comedy actors like Brian Pringle, and a chubby apoplectic comedian called Roy Kinnear. The show was well received, which put a bit of a spring back in my step, but although I was grateful for the praise, I secretly thought I could have done ten times better. I'd acted the part as though I was performing to a theatre audience, rather than using the subtlety required for the television camera. It was a lesson it would take me decades to learn.

When I got back to London I found that a few of my friends had been cast in *The Darwin Adventure*, a feature film about the great nineteenth-century evolutionist. There was a tiny part in it that hadn't yet been filled, and someone persuaded the director to give it to me. It would only be two or three days' work, but it would pay more than I'd earned in a whole month slogging away in Leeds.

After my final scene the director asked me if I could do him a favour. The following Saturday he was going to shoot a sequence in which Darwin gives a lecture to the members of the Royal Society, and is jeered and heckled when he unveils his theory of evolution. This would involve employing a couple of hundred extras who'd have to sit for twelve hours on hard, wooden benches dressed in heavy Victorian clothes, wigs and beards, listening to him proclaiming the same bits of his diatribe time after time in a variety of different shots. They'd inevitably get bored and a bit hacked off. Would I come in, stand behind the camera, warm them up, and get them to look interested, thoughtful, amused or scornful as required?

'How do I do that?'

'Oh, I don't know,' said the director. 'Just clown about like you always do.'

I wasn't aware that I did clown around – well, not that much; I only knew a few jokes, and I was certainly no Tommy Cooper. But I was willing to give it a try. In fact, I was rather intrigued by the idea, particularly as it would earn me another day's filming money.

For the next few days I trawled through the sketches and monologues I'd written since my late teens, wrote some new ones, and asked friends for their favourite jokes. I turned up at the Wigmore Hall bright and early the following Saturday ready for the fray.

I performed my jokes when required and got the necessary response from the extras. I outlined a number of interesting facts for them to listen to when they needed to be serious, which they duly were, and mimicked Edward Heath and Willie Whitelaw when they had to boo, which they did with gusto. All in all it was a great success. The problem was that I ran out of material after ninety minutes, and it was a twelve-hour shoot, so I had to do the whole routine all over again. It went down even better the second time, because the audience knew what was coming and reacted in advance of the punchlines. But by the end of my third repetition they were flagging, and so was I.

During the lunch break I popped over the road to the shops, and newly armed with some props, returned to the battle. From then on I improvised. I said anything that came into my head about Charles Darwin, his grandfather Erasmus, the Galapagos Islands, evolution, location catering, my life, apartheid, and the seductive politics of the Parisian Situationists. When I couldn't think of anything else to say, or wasn't getting enough laughs, I took an egg out of a box and cracked it over my head, or tipped a bottle of orange juice into my shoe.

I was riffing like a musician, although I was probably more like Acker Bilk than John Coltrane. But I could learn to do better. Everyone was laughing now, even the crew. Whatever this thing was that I was doing, I could do it quite well. I knew that some of the laughter was at my desperation to glean yet another response from 200 bored extras, but that was fine too, it was part of the joke.

Years previously, during my final year at Wanstead High, I'd been cast in a play called *Semi-Detached* at the Queen's Theatre, Hornchurch. The part of my character's grandfather had been played by Edgar K. Bruce, an old-school theatre actor with a plummy voice and a different bow tie every day. During rehearsals he'd casually mentioned that the opening night would coincide with the fiftieth anniversary of his career on the professional stage, so the theatre arranged a surprise party for him. The night arrived, and after the final bow, the leading actor stepped forward and paid tribute to Edgar. Then the stage manager appeared from the wings with a birthday cake and fifty flickering candles, and we all sang 'Happy Birthday'. The cast remained on stage after the curtain fell, and we toasted him with sparkling wine, and gave him a pair of cufflinks and a Parker pen. Then everyone had their photo taken with him. It was very touching and highly appropriate. The following year a friend of mine was working at the Palace Theatre, Watford, and told me that a heart-warming event had taken place at the theatre the previous Saturday night. Apparently it was the anniversary of the actor Edgar K. Bruce's fifty years in the professional theatre, and they'd thrown a surprise party for him!

John David, one of the actors at Hornchurch, had gone on to become a theatre director at the Bristol Old Vic. He'd seen the TV version of *Big Soft Nellie*, liked my performance, and remembered me from *Semi-Detatched*. He was currently casting the play *Little Murders*, there was a part in it he thought would suit me, and he gave Penny a call.

The timing was perfect. Everything had become so difficult with Bardy that I'd moved out of Camden Park Road, and was temporarily lodging at Sue Macready's flat in Hammersmith trying unsuccessfully to housetrain her cats. I was desperate for an excuse to get out of London. I packed my rucksack, unaware that the dark cloud that had hung over my life for the last few years was about to disappear, and that the following day I'd meet the woman who would eventually become the mother of my children.

9

THE BLUE-EYED BOY

When I was a little boy, my best friend was Susan Pears who lived next door but one. One day we were let off early from school. This had never happened before, and we got a bit over-excited. I pretended to be a chicken, and Sue chased me up Bressey Grove with a stick.

'Stop it!' ordered Sue's sister, Ann. She was three years older than us, and we always did what she said. 'Don't you know what's happened?'

We shook our heads.

'King George has died.'

I pulled a face like a basset hound begging for its dinner, which made Sue laugh.

'Tony, show some respect!'

'Is that why we're going home? Hooray! Thank you, King George!' I shouted, and sang 'God save our gracious King, Long live our noble King!' all the way back.

It was daft to have been so happy about being given the afternoon off, because when we got to the Pears' house we didn't get out the dressing-up box or do fuzzy-felt pictures, we played 'school' like we always did. Everything we'd done in the previous few hours we repeated, with Ann as the headmistress, Sue and me as the teachers, and Sue's dolls and teddies as the students. This constant repetition meant we could read by the time we were three, and write when we were four. In the girls' bedroom was a glass-fronted bookcase with twenty leather-bound volumes in it called *The Children's Encyclopaedia edited by Arthur Mee*. We'd stand on a chair, pull out a book, open it at random, point to an arbitrary line, and start reading to the assembled teddies. We told them about marsupials, volcanoes, X-rays, the life cycle of the dragonfly, and the Chinese. No subject was safe from them. Nobody praised and patted us for our erudition, but we weren't doing it to earn parental approval. It was like my dad's wig, just part of the way things were.

Unsurprisingly both sisters became teachers, and Sue was now deputy head of physics at a comprehensive school in Bristol. A couple of days before I left London, I gave her a call and asked if I could sleep on her floor till I found a place to stay. She said that was fine but she'd be away in Swindon on an A-level marking course for a few days, so Mary Shepherd would let me in. Did I remember Mary Shepherd?

Of course I did. When Sue and I had passed the Eleven-Plus and gone to our respective grammar schools, our relationship had fizzled out. For a while I'd still gone round to her house after school, but her new friends would already be there, smart, supercilious girls in dark blue skirts and blazers and white blouses. I'd try to make them laugh, I'd tell them interesting stories about being a child actor and the stars I'd met, but they'd look at me as though I had three eyes and a pair of tentacles, and wander into the next room giggling and whispering while I was still talking. One of these girls had replaced me as Sue's soulmate. Mary Shepherd was taller than me with an oval face and a little nose that tipped up slightly at the end. I tried hard to make her my ally, but whenever she looked at me, she made me feel a fraud, and eventually I was getting the same reaction from Sue.

Apparently Mary was now working in Bristol too, and was flat-sharing with Sue and another girl. I was intrigued to see what sort of person stuck-up Mary had become, but I was also a bit nervous. I'd taken quite a battering over the last couple of years and was almost back on an even keel; now was not a good time to be undermined by the humiliations of childhood.

I heaved my motorbike out of the guard's carriage at Bristol Temple Meads station, and pushed it along the platform. I'd sold my Mini Cooper, and because I'd read Rousseau and a new American book about pesticides, decided I wanted a more authentic relationship with the world around me, and had bought a bright red second-hand Honda 50 instead. I liked the wind in my face and the chill on my cheeks, but I certainly wasn't going to ride it from London to Bristol. It had the power of an electric lawnmower, and a top speed of forty miles an hour. But its slow and steady pace reflected my new state of mind. I wore a pair of leather bike boots which I'd painted pink, an afghan coat, and a grey crash helmet on which I'd stuck coloured stars like the ones children are given at primary school when they've done a good painting.

I tootled up Jacobs Wells Road admiring Clifton's elegantly understated Georgian architecture, and felt at peace. No one here would judge me, and no one would have any expectations of me – except perhaps Mary Shepherd!

I wheeled the Honda up the garden path of 111 Pembroke Road, Clifton. It was a tall house with a big, overgrown front garden; the kind of place where a respectable young officer of the British merchant fleet might have deposited his wife and children while he sailed off to loot the British Empire.

I knocked on a side door marked 111A and while I waited for someone to come, ran through the procedures I needed to adopt in order to avoid making an idiot of myself. I must talk quietly, and not too much; I must listen rather than harping on about myself; I must be polite and helpful; I mustn't be manipulative; I mustn't tell lies in order to impress; and I mustn't try and cop off with someone who'd previously made it clear she thought I was a complete wanker.

The door opened.

'Hullo, Tony,' Mary said, and smiled. 'I like your helmet.'

She had a tan, was poised and at ease, and wore a floral hippy dress that reminded me of Judy Collins on the sleeve of *Both Sides Now*.

I chained my bike to a tree, then she helped me heave my rucksack up the long, steep stairs to the top of the house, and put the kettle on.

The flat was huge: three big bedrooms and a sit-down kitchen. In the voluminous lounge was a vase of fresh flowers, small pot plants, little tubs of moisturiser, pots of cotton buds and cotton wool, piles of fresh washing, and an ironing board with the iron plugged in. I made a space for my sleeping bag in a corner and put my clothes in tidy piles. Mary came in with some peppermint tea. She sat down in the armchair opposite me. I'd remembered her as taciturn and a bit detached, but she immediately started chatting. She'd recently got back from travelling round Australia. She'd ended up in the Queensland outback cooking for forty cowboys, the only woman in a hundred-mile radius. 'Quite a challenging experience,' she said enigmatically.

We talked for half an hour or so, and all the while I was poised, waiting for the barbed comments. But none came. She asked me about myself, I told her a few bits and pieces, but didn't say too much in case I started bullshitting.

She said she needed to do a few hours' work. She was training to be a French teacher, and had an exam in a few days' time. I read her copy of Ted Hughes' *Crow*, then went for a walk. I bought a newspaper and a few bits of shopping, came back and made cheese on toast with grilled tomatoes. I knocked on her bedroom door. She was sitting at her desk, with one arm propping up her chin, reading. She looked a bit like Natalie Wood. I put the cheese on toast in front of her, then left again.

At about five thirty the light began to go, and she wandered into the sitting room.

'Thanks for the grub,' she said.

'I don't suppose you're a football fan?'

'Two, two, the lily-white boys!' she sang.

'Spurs?'

'Always!'

'I thought I'd go to Ashton Gate tonight. City are playing Blackpool,' I said casually.

'Sounds a feast of fun.'

'Fancy it?'

'It's a long walk.'

'I've got a spare helmet,' I said.

'I hope it hasn't got any of those bloody stars on it.'

City won 3–1.

The Bristol Old Vic was based at the Theatre Royal down by Bristol docks. It was the oldest continually operating theatre in England, a little Georgian masterpiece, but it was undergoing a major refurbishment, so its shows were temporarily being mounted at the Little Theatre, a three-hundred seater, part of the Colston Hall where the big music acts played.

Our first rehearsal for *Little Murders* was on the Little's stage. The big news was that the script demanded we eat a full-scale dinner during act two. We were on paltry rep wages, and free grub every night would be a welcome subsidy. But eating and acting at the same time is remarkably fiddly, so we were to be given exactly the same dish every night in order to ensure we got the timing right. We had three options: lasagne, lamb casserole or chicken tarragon. We voted overwhelmingly for chicken tarragon.

At lunch I got talking to Howard Davies, the assistant director. He was a year older than me with a large head, receding hairline, bright blue eyes and a very serious face which would occasionally be illuminated by an openhearted smile. We discussed the Vietnam War, the failure of the Labour Party to provide a socialist alternative to free-market capitalism, and who fancied Julie Christie most. He asked me if I wanted to go for a drink and a chat that evening, but I said I was meeting up with a childhood friend.

Mary had bought tickets to see Buster Keaton's *The General* at the Bristol Arts Centre. After that I took her for a meal at the Rajdoot in Park Street which I'd checked out earlier. It was impressive, not your run-of-the-mill Indian restaurant – the waiters dressed in aquamarine Indian costumes with elaborate headdresses, and they melted gold strips into your curry.

The following evening she had a meeting with her tutor, so I went round to the flat Howard shared with his wife Sue. It was in Clifton Village, a quaint network of old-fashioned shops and tiny alleyways, a bit like Camberwick Green, but with greasy pubs that sold rough cider.

I got back to Pembroke Road about 11 p.m., unrolled my sleeping bag and clambered in. Half an hour later the key rattled in the door.

'Do you want a nightcap?' Mary called.

'What you got?'

'I picked up half a bottle of Bell's.'

'Very nice.'

'It's in the bedroom if you want some.'

I rolled up my sleeping bag, and didn't unroll it again for a long time.

When Sue came back a few days later she wasn't very enthusiastic about our new sleeping arrangements. She'd met Bardy a few times, and didn't want to collude in a sordid affair. I told her the marriage was over, something I hadn't quite admitted to myself previously, but the admission made it a reality. Sue was, to some extent, mollified by my explanation.

Then the girl who occupied the third bedroom came back from a sporty week in Carmarthenshire. Her name was Barbara Engstrom and, by an eerie coincidence, her mum had been in the Women's Royal Air Force with my mum. She was even more disapproving than Sue, and I had to go through the whole

mollification process all over again, although this time it took
a couple of days for the air to clear.

But the aggravation was worth it. Mary and I were now
inseparable. We were both fans of Adrian Mitchell and Sylvia
Plath, Tony Benn, Che Guevara, Stan Laurel, Stan Freberg,
and molten metal on our masala. There was an intensity about
the way we shared small pleasures, a kind of intimacy I'd forgotten. She admitted that when I was a teenager she'd thought
I was a little git, and that I'd probably always have that character trait, but she'd heard some fairly good things about me
before I'd arrived, and I'd definitely matured. She also said her
previous boyfriend, an Australian called Kenny who'd been a
drummer on the *Queen Mary*, was even smaller than me, so my
size wasn't an issue. All this was music to my ears, apart from
the bit about the dwarf drummer.

Little Murders was a comedy by the American satirist Jules
Feiffer, but its acerbic style didn't go down too well with Bristol
audiences and was a bit of a flop, although the chicken tarragon
was sensational, at least at first. The problems began when
Terry Bird, the assistant stage manager in charge of props,
began rehearsals for his next show, so had less time to prepare
it. He became very slapdash. One night he forgot to buy any
tarragon and sprinkled mint on instead, which was disgusting.

We'd have forgiven and forgotten a single cock-up, but by
now we'd eaten over twenty identical meals, and even a perfectly cooked one would have been received with indifference.
Instead we got unwashed carrots, potato peel in the mash, and
plastic wrapping in the gravy. Our nightly treat became a
nightly trial. The final blow occurred when the actress sitting
next to me spat out a mouthful of chicken because it was slimy,
and realised there was blood running down her fork. When she
gagged, she sounded like a donkey braying.

For the last show, another of the actresses cooked us a surprise spaghetti bolognese. It was difficult to act while winding up long strings of sauce-covered pasta, and most of us got dribbles down the front of our costumes, but it was infinitely preferable to yet another chicken bloody tarragon. From that night on I vowed that neither meat nor fowl would ever pass my lips again.

Howard wanted to attract more young people to the Old Vic. Ticket prices were high, the plays dreary, and the experience of going to the theatre was turgid compared with the excitement of a live music gig. He put together a late-night project, a series of 'alternative' shows which would start at 11 o'clock on Friday nights, and be targeted specifically at the students at the university and the polytechnic.

The first play, *Christie in Love*, had been written by Howard Brenton for Portable Theatre. It was about the serial killer John Christie who'd killed eight women in the late 1940s, and how society had sensationalised him and his tawdry acts of violence. I was to play Christie.

The set was a bleak representation of the murderer's back garden where some of the bodies of his victims had been found. It was strewn with torn, dirty newspaper a metre deep. A few minutes into the play, I was to rise out of this mire wearing a grotesque mask. There were no curtains, so the set would be in full view while the audience took their places. Consequently I'd need to be under the paper for a good half hour before the play started.

I was fairly confident that the meditation techniques I was now familiar with would prevent me from getting restless and claustrophobic, but I wanted to make sure about this, so I decided to bury myself for the half hour prior to the dress rehearsal as a try-out.

I found a discreet area upstage where I wouldn't get trodden on, lay down, covered myself with newspaper, and began to recite my mantra. Soon I was relaxed, calm and only faintly aware of the outside world. I heard feet pacing around the stage, and later more feet, but I didn't pay them any attention. There were voices, puzzled perhaps, a little concerned maybe. I continued chanting. There was the whirr of a motor, a lighting bar descending from the flies perhaps, the clank of metal, a stepladder possibly, and more discussion. I decided it would be prudent to get out of the way of whatever was happening, so I stood up.

There was a howl of terror. Two stagehands jumped off the stage, a third backed into the wings mumbling, 'Jesus! Jesus!', and the stepladder toppled over. I stood there apologetic in my hideous mask. I've never been able to create a moment of terror like that on stage since, and it was all because a bulb needed changing.

But the reaction when I did the same thing that night was almost as good. People had been queuing round the block for nearly an hour. I'd seldom heard so much chatter before a show started and, almost as soon as the house lights dimmed, the audience was hooked by Brenton's bleak and hard-edged writing. It was the perfect play for an intelligent, young audience, and the evening was a big success.

Unbelievably the next week's show went even better. Three young journalists were currently on trial for publishing obscene material in *Oz* magazine, an underground publication which specialised in mild outrage. The offending material was in an edition called *Schoolkids' Oz* and included articles on sex, drugs, corporal punishment, and a picture of the children's cartoon character Rupert Bear having sex. While those who brought the case clearly thought they were protecting the country's morals from the forces of anarchy, its readers and supporters saw it as yet another example of the British state's desire to ban anything it didn't like. The trial was a battle between the libertarian sensibilities of the early 1970s, and the old-fashioned conservatism of those in power.

Celebrity barristers rallied to the cause, writers and academics gave evidence for the defence; there couldn't have been a more appropriate subject for a late-night show.

We had to be careful, though; the issue was *sub judice*, public comment might be deemed to affect the course of the trial, and could get the theatre into very hot water. To stay within the letter of the law we could only read edited extracts from the transcript, and even that was a grey area. Wasn't the act of editing a comment in itself?

The playwright Dave Illingworth did a sterling job. The script was coherent and balanced, yet managed to highlight the essential absurdity of the trial. The atmosphere in the theatre was extraordinary. It was as though the cast and audience were at the Old Bailey watching the day's events unfold as they were happening.

Oz lost its case and the three editors were fined and sent to prison, but the verdict was overturned on appeal. Some people see the trial as an important milestone in the forward march of our country's sexual and cultural liberation. Others say that though *Oz* posed as a champion of the permissive society, it was misogynistic and exploitative of women, and it's certainly the case that a number of leading liberals declined to defend it in the witness box because they had reservations about the magazine's content.

Nevertheless, at the time *Oz* seemed to represent a new order overthrowing the shackles of oppression, and for a few hours on that Friday evening, both actors and audience felt themselves to be in the vanguard of that order.

When my stint at the Bristol Old Vic came to an end, I didn't want to go back to London. I'd grown to love the city and Mary, and had a new circle of friends. There was Ted Braun, the Russian specialist at the university drama department, who knew everything there was to know about Brecht and Chekhov; the charming but scatty young songwriter and storyteller Julia Donaldson; John Grimshaw, a giant of a man, obsessed with the nonsensical idea that he could raise enough money to lay cycle paths across the whole of Britain; there were architects and artists who wanted to transform Bristol's decaying warehouses into art, film and dance venues; Mad John Connor, an anarchist who sold beans and pulses in St Nicholas Market and was convinced that in a hundred years' time the human species would have wiped itself out because it was treating the planet so badly. Every day there was someone new to talk to, some fresh idea to come to terms with.

But eventually Penny inveigled the BBC into shortlisting me for a job back in London to which I couldn't say no. Each year the BBC children's TV department produced twenty episodes of a drama serial to be shown in schools, featuring key words its young audiences could learn to spell, backed up by books and magazines, and support material for the teachers. This year's series was to be called *Sam on Boffs' Island*.

Penny said no one was better qualified than me to front this project. I'd learnt a lot about kids during my stint at the Midlands Arts, and had become passionate about their education; the new series was going to involve puppets, a field in which I'd got a lot of experience, and although I was now nearly twenty-six, I looked young enough to be the new face of BBC youth! After a brief meeting with the series producer, I was handed the part of Sam – six months' work doing something I cared about, getting invaluable experience, and earning enough money to be able to afford to commute to Bristol each weekend.

Sam on Boffs' Island was to be filmed at Elstree Studios, and as there were twenty-seven puppets and only one human on the cast list, I was given the number one dressing room and all the perks associated with being the lead actor on a movie set, including a chauffeur-driven limousine.

The show's writer was a young poet called Mike Rosen who'd recently completed his BBC traineeship. He was like an enormous tousled St Bernard, an uncompromising egalitarian who, like me, cared deeply about children and was overwhelmingly generous. He had a flat in a mansion block in Paddington, and lent me his spare bedroom as I needed somewhere to stay during filming now that Bardy and I were getting divorced. Every morning at 5.30 a.m. a Bentley T-1 would arrive and my chauffeur would spring out wearing a charcoal-grey uniform and a black cap with a shiny peak. He'd hold the back door open and I'd scramble in and sit in solitary splendour cocooned from the outside world by its jet-black windows. Forty minutes later we'd arrive in Elstree. At the weekend I'd shed my showbiz lifestyle and spend two days pottering around Bristol on my Honda 50 in my pink boots and star-encrusted crash helmet, chanting 'Come on, you Reds' on the terraces at Ashton Gate, and drinking rough cider and smoking roll-ups in the Coronation Tap.

Then every Monday morning back in London a sense of unease would descend again as the chauffeur opened the door, and I got in his shiny black car. I was a socialist. I didn't want to be driven around by some bloke dressed like a stormtrooper. On the other hand I loathed getting up early, and would have struggled to get to work on time and in one piece if I'd had to drive there myself. I wrestled with my guilt for a week or so, then came to a big decision. I'd continue to be driven to work, but from now on I'd sit in the front with the chauffeur. The next day when he opened the back door, I explained the new arrangement. He nodded, took his sandwiches, apple and *Daily Mail* off the passenger seat, put them in the boot, and opened the front passenger door.

We drove in silence. He stared straight ahead, focussed on the early morning traffic. What was he thinking? I had no idea. Should I break the silence, ask him what team he supported, or what he thought of the Bentley's fuel consumption? No, I'd sound like a tosser. The journey back was the same. I sat with my arms folded, occasionally glancing at his inscrutable profile, and at the few millimetres of stubble that had grown on his chin in the hours since I'd last seen him.

The following morning, when we'd been driving for about ten minutes, he finally spoke.

'I'll tell you something funny, Mr Robinson,' he said.

'Call me Tony.'

'OK, Tone, I'll tell you something funny. You know Chalfont St Giles?'

'I know where it is.'

'Right. The other week I'm doing this job in Chalfont St Giles.'

'OK.'

'I've got to deliver something, a parcel or something, to this house, lovely house. And this woman opens the door. Lovely woman. Thirty-five maybe, thirty-six. Gorgeous tom tits, you know.'

I nodded thoughtfully, as though I knew exactly the sort of tom tits he was referring to.

'So I passed the parcel over, and she says, "Hang about, come in, have a cup of coffee," and I'm thinking *hello* . . . !'

I laughed in nervous complicity.

'So I go in, and she's making the coffee, and she's bending over the whatsit putting the sugar in and everything, and she says, "Are you hot? I'm hot. Take your jacket off," and she comes over to me, and she only starts unbuttoning my jacket, doesn't she . . .'

I was trapped in a porn movie, a wank-fest honed and polished throughout those solitary months and years behind the wheel. I'd specifically asked to sit in the front, I could hardly ask him to stop so I could get into the back again, but I'd got no idea how to shut him up.

'Anyway, we're going at it like rats in a sack, and the front door opens, and I'm thinking, *Christ! It's her old man*, but it's this other bird, stacked, arse like a peach, and she says, "This is my next-door neighbour, Shirley." And this Shirley says,

"Hello," and she's smiling like, and she's looking really filthy . . .'

I took off my shoes, sat cross-legged and tried to meditate, but it wasn't easy. Next day I sat in the back.

Mike Rosen's script for *Sam on Boffs' Island* was a gem. The 'Boffs' were tiny, child-like creatures under attack from their enemies, the 'Hairy Gurglers'. Each week I'd rescue them from their latest spot of bother with the help of the 'Say-Birds', a flock of long-necked birds who spouted letters and syllables from their beaks. The puppets' voices were provided by my friend Miriam Margolyes, and two actors from *The Archers*, Judy Bennett who played Shula, and Charles Collingwood, the obnoxious Brian Archer. We wiled away the long filming days putting inappropriate words into the mouths of the cute little puppets, which gave the film crew a great deal of amusement, but produced terror in the heart of the sound recordist, who feared that What-Boff's requests for a blow-job might be inadvertently broadcast.

Mike's work was effortless; simple and yet sophisticated. It made me realise that virtually everything I'd written for the Midlands Arts had been facile and derivative. If I was going to create my own shows for children, I'd have to try a whole lot harder.

By the time the final episode had been recorded I'd decided that, though London was the hub of English theatre and TV, I couldn't bear to stay there any longer; I wanted to live in Bristol. It was reckless – there was very little work available in the south-west, and I'd be cut off from my London contacts – but I didn't care. Ted Braun and his wife, Sarah, offered us their spare bedroom in Redland and, as Mary had recently become a fully fledged teacher, we'd have some money to survive on, so we moved in.

The director of productions at the Bristol Old Vic was Val May, a tall, thin, stooping man with a hooked nose. I didn't like him much or his attitude towards the theatre, and my feelings were reciprocated. His play choice was archaic, his attitude towards his actors patrician, and his plans for the refurbishment of the Theatre Royal were dire. His theatre was a jewel, Georgian design at its best, but the foyer he was about to slap onto the front of it was a piece of brutal modernism devoid of function, charm or meaning. It made the building look like the regional headquarters of an insurance company.

The production Val had chosen to celebrate the unveiling of his architectural masterpiece was *Trelawny of the Wells*, a piece of nineteenth-century froth by Arthur Wing Pinero, about an actress, Rose Trelawny, and her sweetheart Arthur who runs away to become an actor at the Bristol Old Vic! Apart from the moderately amusing conceit that the play was being performed in the theatre in which it was set, I could see no reason for putting it on other than that it might make money when it inevitably transferred to the West End. It certainly didn't seem to be a particularly inspiring statement of intent on the reopening of Britain's oldest regional theatre. But I didn't want to appear a Jeremiah, and as a number of my friends were in it, I went along to the first night.

At the interval I bumped into someone I hadn't seen since we'd both left drama school six years previously. During our first couple of years at the school, Central's young actors didn't have much to do with the stage management students. While we were pretending to be animals, they were busy learning about fuses, amplifiers, and how to make props as cheaply as possible. It was different in the third year. Suddenly we were reliant on them to get everything right, and the two courses became much closer. The acting students in my class became particularly fond of one young stage manager because he was so geeky and ham-fisted. He wore glasses and a tatty green home-knitted jumper with the left elbow completely missing. 'Oh, Cameron!' we'd chorus when he made yet another mistake.

But he wasn't wearing an old jumper when I saw him that night at the Theatre Royal. He was dressed in an elegantly tailored dinner jacket and a black bow tie – an amazing transformation!

'Hi, mate,' I said. 'Nice to see you. Involved in the show?'

'I am,' he replied.

'A.S.M?'

'No.'

'D.S.M.?'

'No.'

'Company Manager?'

'I own the show,' he replied, a little steelily.

'Blimey!' If tubby little Cameron Mackintosh was now a theatre producer, I'd completely lost touch with who was who in mainstream theatre.

One night we were round at Howard and Sue's with Dave Illingworth and his girlfriend Kate, with whom we'd remained good friends since I'd left the Old Vic. We were complaining that none of us was happy about where we were living. Ted and Sarah Braun had been very generous, but their spare room was no solution to our long-term housing needs. Howard and Sue were thinking of having a baby and needed an extra bedroom, and Kate had three children from a previous marriage and no place for them to come and stay.

Dave came up with the suggestion that we buy a dilapidated house in Clifton, do it up and divide it into three flats.

'If we had one big kitchen,' I said, 'it would give us lots more room.'

'And a shared sitting room next to it would be sociable,' suggested Kate.

'We could do bulk buys,' said Dave. 'Toilet rolls, washing powder and stuff.'

'And have a shared fridge, washing machine and deep-freezer,' suggested Howard.

There was a thoughtful pause, then Mary said, 'So what you're all suggesting is that we set up a commune?'

Thus the idea was born.

10

LITTLE HOPPING ROBIN

'Lot 27 . . . 9 Frederick Place, Clifton, a fine example of a five-storey early Victorian residence, located between the university students' union and the shops of Park Street. In need of some renovation, but would make a superb family home or an ideal investment opportunity. I'm starting at £4,000. Who'll give me £4,000?'

The auction rooms were an almost infinite number of nooks, cubby holes, corridors and pokey rooms crammed with old furniture, aspidistra pots, chamber pots, cooking pots, umbrella stands, teapot collections, chipped metal shop signs, tubs of cutlery, tubs of old tools, and a stuffed buffalo. There was a small mountain of precariously piled metal fire grates into which someone had stuffed peacock feathers and plastic flowers, and beyond it was a corner which had been cleared of junk, dominated by a rostrum with an old church lectern on top of it. Behind it stood the auctioneer, surrounded by about twenty potential bidders: middle-aged women with hawk eyes and plaid coats, dealers wearing trilbies and holding roll-up cigarettes in their cupped hands, and a couple of estate agents in dark suits and brown shoes. Dave, Howard and I had agreed to take responsibility for the bidding, but we stuck out like bomb-throwing revolutionaries in this sombre crowd, with our long hair, tank tops and bell-bottom jeans. I was pretty sure the other potential bidders would collude to ramp up the price and bring about our financial downfall, but Howard said they couldn't – we'd decided what we could afford, and if the price went beyond it we'd walk away, end of story!

'£5,000! 5,500! Do I hear 6,000?' The auctioneer had a triangle of light blue silk handkerchief peaking from the top of the breast pocket of his dark blue sports jacket. He looked as though he'd dressed for his next appointment in the bar of Clifton Golf Club with his chums from the Rotary.

'6,500, 7,000!'

Bardy and I had managed to sell Camden Park Road without too much shouting and door slamming; its value had rocketed in the previous eighteen months, so we were able to walk away with enough money to start again. Not everything went smoothly, of course. I'd put my heart and soul into that flat, and felt very possessive about it. When I wandered in one day and discovered a young Welshman I vaguely knew wearing my Marks and Spark's dressing gown, making scrambled eggs in my mum's old non-stick saucepan, and stirring it with one of her wooden spatulas, it took some time before I could summon up the grace to apologise for having arrived unannounced.

'8,000, 8,500, 9,000 . . .' The auctioneer was hurtling towards our limit and we hadn't even started bidding yet.

Bardy kept the furniture and Herman, and I took my LPs, some books, and the Casio electronic keyboard she'd bought me for Christmas.

'9,500, 10,000, 10,500 . . .' Jesus Christ, when was he going to slow down!

Dave hadn't wanted to make the bids, and he and Howard had agreed that, given my lack of height, the auctioneer might not see me, which I thought was bloody patronising. But I was happy for Howard to act for us. He had a pugnacious face and a set jaw; he'd be good at the terse nodding required when making a convincing bid.

It was Mary, Sue and Kate who'd found the house. They taught at various Bristol comprehensives, and they'd meet up after work and scour the local estate agents. As soon as they saw 9 Frederick Place, they were convinced it was perfect for us. It was elegant, in the heart of where we wanted to live and, most importantly, would be easy to divide up. Dave and Kate would get the top two floors, including the servants' bedrooms which would be ideal for Kate's kids. Howard and Sue could have the middle of the house which had the least floor area but boasted impressively high ceilings and double doors leading to a balcony at the front. The ground floor would be entirely communal, and Mary and I would live in the cavernous basement, which we had plans to make lush and cosy, 'like a Pasha's seraglio' said Dave.

'11,000. Any advance on £11,000?'

Suddenly Howard interjected. '11,750,' he said, and his jaw tightened a little more, as though daring anyone to outbid him.

'That's 11,750! 11,750! Going once, going twice . . . 12,000 from the man at the back.'

Shit! That was it. Time to walk away.

'12,250!' said Howard.

Dave and I looked at him aghast. That wasn't what we'd agreed.

'12,500!' said the bloke at the back.

'12,800!' roared Howard like a roundhead charging a cavalier castle.

'12,800 once, 12,800 twice . . . Sold to the young man in the stripy tank top for £12,800.'

We'd got it! We'd got it! Our own massive and elegant house, built by profiteers dealing in tobacco, alcohol and slaves, but now about to become a socialist paradise. The only pressing problem was explaining to the girls that we'd gone over our democratically agreed limit.

I'd never been so happy in my life as I was at Frederick Place, or 'Fred Place' as it was affectionately known. I'd found five people I respected and, not to put too fine a point on it, had grown to love. We talked and laughed, and laughed and talked, and I don't remember a single row.

Dave was an old-style socialist from a Labour-supporting family in Leeds. He was soft-spoken and kind, wore John Lennon glasses, and had a droopy moustache like Peter Wyngarde in the Jason King series. He and I spent hours together planning the future of radical British theatre. Kate was ten years older than the rest of us. She was one of the West Country Foot family who'd produced the Labour Party politician Michael, the radical journalist Paul, and her father, the Liberal peer Sir John. She was tiny, deeply sympathetic to other people's needs, and had a shrewd intelligence that put the rest of us in the shade. Sue was blonde, pretty and a Christian of the type who, if she'd been South American, would have lived in the jungle patching up the wounds of guerrilla fighters.

Everyone assumed that as we were a commune we spent our time copulating on the stairs, dealing drugs and drinking raw alcohol. Nothing could have been further from the truth. There was seldom any pot smoking, we drank in moderation, and at night were tucked up in our own beds and fast asleep before the last strains of 'Sailing By' had died away. The coffee pot was always on, the front door open, and friends streamed in and out.

Mary and I took great pride in our basement. We covered our woodchip wallpaper with orange paint, stuck chocolate-brown hessian on one wall and in the alcoves, and bought an orange pull-down light from Habitat which we hung above a coffee table inset with oriental tiles from a discarded fireplace. We had a multi-coloured chesterfield sofa, half a dozen massive patchwork cushions painstakingly made by Mary, and big squares of rush matting on the floor. The room was exotic but modern, stylish, cosy, and very, very orange.

One morning Debbie, now Debbie Gates, phoned me in a panic. She'd finished her stint at the Midlands Arts and was living down the road from us in Bath. She'd got married and had a baby, but a job at Radio Bristol had come up, and childcare was proving to be an issue, particularly if she was asked to work at short notice.

'I can't find anyone to look after Genevieve,' she said, 'and I've got to finish making a radio show by the end of the day. Would you mind having her for a few hours? She won't be any trouble.'

An hour later she burst into Fred Place like a hand grenade, dumped one-and-a-half-year-old Genevieve, her dummy and her spare nappies on the kitchen floor, garbled some unintelligible instructions, and disappeared again.

I loved pottering around the house when there was no one else about. It was usually chaotic, rehearsals in full flow, huge packs of toilet paper and boxes of washing powder being lugged about, teachers giving tutorials to noisy, wayward children, music blaring from various transistor radios, the washing machine constantly churning. Genevieve and I wandered round quietly collecting the dirty coffee cups, sorting the messages on the notice board, and emptying the contents of the wastepaper baskets into a sack. She crawled, walked, slid along on her bum, and sometimes I carried her. We wandered to the corner shop and back, and fed the starlings in the back garden. Time whizzed by.

We were in the kitchen cleaning the forks when there was a rat-tat-tat at the front door. I bounded down the hall and flung it open.

'Sorry I'm late,' Debbie said as usual.

'Look, Genevieve,' I called. 'Who's this?'

The little girl toddled up to us, and plunged her face into her mum's legs.

'How . . . did you do that?' Debbie stuttered.

'What?'

'I . . . she . . . she can't walk.'

'Course she can. She's been walking all morning.'

'Where?'

'I dunno. We went to the shops. Down to the basement.'

'But those stairs are like the Eiger!'

'I waited at the bottom.'

'Tony! Tony! She can't walk!'

'Well, she can now.'

Apparently I'd performed a miracle.

There were lots of actors struggling to make a living in Bristol, and indeed in the whole of south-west England. I went along to a meeting of Equity's South-West Area Committee, and heard about Redcoats from the holiday camp in Minehead who'd been refused a clothing allowance, a pantomime dame from Torquay who'd fallen through a trapdoor and damaged his spine, film extras from the South Hams who hadn't been paid, a magician from Keynsham who was worried about the amount of cigarette smoke in the local nightclubs, actors from the Northcott Theatre who couldn't afford to live in Exeter and needed a raise. There were about a thousand Equity members in that long stretch from Swindon to Land's End. They were isolated, their employers were often rogues, and there were times when every one of them needed help and support. After three meetings I was asked to chair the committee, and to my surprise found I was quite good at it. Chairing is one of those skills like playing the penny whistle or making snug-fitting dovetailed joints: it's not that important in the great scheme of things, but there are times when it comes in handy.

Unfortunately our union, Equity, wasn't fit for purpose. It had been set up in the early 1930s by a handful of London-based leading actors. Now the membership numbered tens of thousands, but it was still run like a gentlemen's club, with a rulebook to match. It was more like a medieval guild than a trade union, intent on protecting jobs for its members by keeping new applicants out, rather than welcoming them in. It needed a thorough overhaul, but there were two factions preventing this from happening. The first was the Equity council, the union's governing body. It was made up of establishment figures, haughty and deeply conservative. Their idea of a proper actor was someone who performed in the West End, and they were contemptuous of small-scale theatre, theatre in education and the fringe. Their left-wing counterparts were a new phenomenon, the Workers' Revolutionary Party, hard-line Trotskyites whose behaviour scared the union membership into opposing any kind of internal change.

The WRP believed a people's uprising was going to break out at any moment. All that was needed was a good, firm push, and principled leadership from themselves. It's not difficult to see why they were so successful in the actors' trade union; they weren't any old revolutionaries, they were showbiz revolutionaries. By far the most influential were film star Vanessa Redgrave, her brother Corin, and the playwright Tom Kempinski. They were highly intelligent, dazzlingly elegant, and dominated any room with their presence. They recruited intense young actors oozing with testosterone, and beautiful wide-eyed actresses who pulled faces like Eve tempting you with a cox's orange pippin. Their numbers were small, but they were scary and made a lot of noise, like a wasp in your bedroom, and their influence on the union was enormous. They were the witches in a Disney cartoon, immaculately dressed, seductive and appealing, but equally repellent. A small network of us decided to try taking on the smug conservatism of the council and the messianic gobbledygook of the Trots, but it was going to be a gargantuan struggle, and it would take years before we were ultimately successful.

I'd initially imagined that once I was down in Bristol, I'd stay there. But I was continually being tempted back to London, where a small underground theatre scene was starting to emerge. I was asked to perform the title role in a play called *Little Hopping Robin* at a tiny theatre in Soho known as the Almost Free, so-called because a ticket cost you as much or as little as you wanted to pay for it. My wages were £20 per week plus a room in a squat in Kentish Town.

Little Hopping Robin wasn't only my character's name, it was also the name of his penis. The play was strange and surreal, but once the audience got used to its style, they realised it was a dream, and they could deduce what Robin's waking life was like from what he was dreaming. This being early seventies underground theatre, there was a lot of nudity, culminating in a scene in which my wife and I were asleep, the alarm went off, I got out of bed naked, moved to the front of the stage and shaved in silence for about a minute in front of an invisible mirror until the lights gradually faded to darkness, thus indicating that the craziness and eroticism of the previous night was over, and Robin now had to face the day again.

Theoretically I didn't have any qualms about taking my clothes off in public, but the proximity of the audience to the stage was a little daunting. The theatre was so small, and the seats so close to the actors, that if someone in the front row had sneezed, my Hopping Robin would have quivered in the breeze.

My wife was played by Maggie Ford, an old friend and campaigning feminist who, after the dress rehearsal, expressed some concern about my exposing myself in this way.

'Suppose you get an erection?'

'What?'

'An erection. When you're doing the shaving scene.'

'I won't. I wouldn't.'

'You can't tell. These things happen.'

'It's not an erotic situation. There's no chance.'

I thought the conversation was over, until as an afterthought she added, 'I bet I could make you.'

'You couldn't.'

'I could.'

'Not without grabbing hold of it and wiggling it about.'

'I could.'

'Maggie, you absolutely couldn't.'

I so wished I hadn't said that.

Every night the stage management carried us onto the stage in our darkened bed, there was a long pause during which ethereal music played, after which the lights went up, and I got up and started my shaving routine.

And every night during the blackout Maggie would do something under the covers to try to get Little Hopping Robin to spring to life. Sometimes she'd gently rest her fingertips on my stomach, run a fingernail up and down my inner leg, or press her thigh against mine and start undulating. Once she cocked her leg and tickled the hairs under my balls with her big toe, which I thought was cheating.

Fortunately a combination of rigorous mental discipline, and the terror of giving the audience the sight of a slightly larger than usual Hopping Robin, kept him flaccid.

But on the last night Mum and Dad came to see the show. Objectively there's no reason why a parent seeing your erection should be more shocking than anyone else having a look, but we are not objective animals.

Maggie and I lay side by side in the darkness, and I waited. *Do your worst!* I thought. *No, don't,* myself replied. Five seconds went by and she didn't do anything. Then five more – still nothing. The seconds ticked slowly on, and the fact that she hadn't, but might, was sheer torture. Oh my God! What was it she was about to do? Oh no. Was something stirring? The music ended, and I reluctantly got out of bed, turning away from the audience and back towards Maggie as I did so. Then I thwacked my penis with the back of my hand in case the dreadful anticipation had brought Hopping Robin to life. 'I won,' Maggie mouthed at me, but I didn't dare look down to see if she had.

In the years since Maggie issued her challenge, I've hacked

my way through dense jungle while attempting to dodge donkey spiders, stood waist-deep in chicken shit and dangled from the tallest spire in Oxfordshire. But nothing I've ever done has been as difficult as trying to keep my errant penis under control at the Almost Free Theatre.

The next day Mary and I took my parents to the Lyons Corner House in Coventry Street for Sunday lunch. I wasn't looking forward to this meeting because I'd had my ear pierced. Not many young Englishmen were doing this in 1973, apart from sailors, homosexuals, and a few of the more outlandish pop stars. But I'd felt it would make a bold statement about my devil-may-care anti-establishment sensibility, and I was confident I could carry it off. I don't remember much about the actual piercing, other than that I needed to sit down quietly for about twenty minutes afterwards. But I was pleased with the result, even though the little sleeper wasn't often visible because it was covered by my long hair.

Mum was a conservative, both with a big and a little 'c'. She liked men who were smart, preferably dressed in a pressed white shirt and jolly tie, and with a short, tidy haircut. My various Seventies fashions were a constant disappointment to her, although she bore them with moderately good grace. I was fairly sure she wouldn't approve of my new adornment, but the sooner I broached the subject the better.

I sat opposite her eating a rum baba with double cream, waiting for her to spot the offending item. An interminable amount of time passed, the conversation batted to and fro, but she still hadn't seen it. I tried tossing my hair boyishly, looking sideways at the next table so she'd catch my profile, leaning on my chin and tilting my head at an angle, but nothing worked. Eventually I said in an affectionate and teasing voice, 'You haven't noticed then?'

'Noticed what?'

I smiled, ran my fingers backwards through my hair, leant forward and presented her with my naked ear.

'Aaaaarrgghhhh!' The cry echoed round the entire restaurant.

'It's OK, Mum. It's only a—'

'Aaaaarrgghhhh!' Everyone was looking at me now, the delinquent who'd forced this blood-curdling death cry from the mouth of his own mother.

'You've mutilated yourself,' she sobbed.

Dad looked non-plussed; Mary was desperately trying not to laugh.

Then Mum delivered her *coup de grâce*.

'You did it to hurt me,' she intoned like Joan Crawford in a sixties horror film.

Oddly Mum was far less upset by my stage nudity than she was by my earring. A few weeks later when she'd forgiven me, I asked her if she'd been disturbed by seeing me flaunt my naked body. 'No, Tony. You looked very nice,' she said and patted my hand as though I'd been modelling a well-tailored suit, which in a way I had.

My forays away from Bristol weren't limited to London. I spent a month in Surrey making a TV film of which I became inordinately proud. Picture the scene:

It's Christmas Day in the imbeciles asylum at Caterham in Surrey sometime in the mid-1930s. A few battered Christmas decorations and half-inflated balloons hang on the walls, a 78 rpm record of Alexander's Ragtime Band is being placed on the turntable of an HMV gramophone by a portly superintendent, and twenty or so patients in dingy clothes are about to dance. Except they don't. Instead they stare at the lighting, the cameraman and at the director who leaps to his feet and paces

round the ward, enthusiastically waving his arms and shouting, 'Animate, loves! Animate!'

This was the BBC drama documentary *Joey*, and director
Brian Gibson's problem was that the location in which we were
filming was the original asylum, St Lawrence's Hospital as it
was now known, and in order to make it as realistic as possible,
he'd asked for volunteers from among the present-day patients
to play their 1930s equivalents. Understandably these extras
didn't have a clue about the niceties of making television, and
had no idea what was required of them. This was going to be
another long day.

It was a continual struggle to recreate this hideous institution with any degree of authenticity. But it was while working
there that I encountered one of the smartest and most courageous people I've ever met. Joey Deacon's mum had fallen
down the stairs when she was pregnant with him, and he was
born in 1920 with severe cerebral palsy. He couldn't walk, his
limbs constantly jerked and twitched, his head waggled like a
flower in the wind, and he could only speak in a series of gruff,
strangled, inaudible grunts. He'd been incarcerated in St Lawrence's since the age of eight, and for years was classified as
educationally subnormal and consequently unable to take
responsibility for himself. But there was nothing wrong with
his mind, he was merely trapped in a body which wouldn't do
what he wanted.

His salvation came when a young man with a similar,
though much less severe condition, arrived in the same ward.
Ernie Roberts understood Joey perfectly. At first the doctors
thought he was putting words into Joey's mouth, but after
rigorously testing them both, they realised he could translate
Joey's apparently meaningless grunts, and that Joey wasn't a
gibbering idiot, but a bright and alert man with a prodigious
memory.

One day in 1969 Joey began collaborating with Ernie on
writing down his story. It was a slow process. Joey would say a

few words, Ernie, who couldn't read or write, would repeat them, a third patient, Michael, would write them down in longhand, and a fourth patient, Tom, painstakingly typed up the words. Fourteen months later they'd produced a slim manuscript which was published by the National Society for Handicapped Children in the series 'Subnormality in the Seventies'. It was called *Tongue Tied*; and became the talk of the medical world. Brian, an ex-medical student and currently a TV director working on the *Horizon* strand, was inspired by it and decided to turn it into a drama-documentary.

He needed actors to play the parts of Joey and Ernie as young men, and approached Britain's leading casting director Miriam Brickman for help. She was too busy to do the job herself but asked her bright new assistant Joyce to take on the task. Joyce Middleton had been an old school friend of Mary's, one of those smart and terrifying teenage girls by whom I'd been plagued over a decade previously at Susan Pears' house. She'd recently married John Nettles, a promising young actor renowned for his mellifluous, baritone voice, and this was her first proper casting job. She thought I looked a lot like the young Ernie, suggested me to Brian, and he agreed.

I researched the part for weeks. A Harley Street dental specialist made a set of teeth for me identical to Ernie's, I listened to tape recordings of his voice repeatedly, and the BBC filmed him getting out of his wheelchair and walking a few paces so I could copy his wild, staggering gait and the way he used his arms to propel and steady himself.

Once I'd gone through the process of learning how to reproduce Ernie's physicality, I had to forget that side of my performance and concentrate on understanding who Ernie was and what he was feeling, so I visited his ward in Caterham to get a sense of what life would have been like for him.

The imbeciles' asylum had been built in 1867 to care for the poor, sick and confused of metropolitan London – the 'idiots' as they were known. It was a colossal and daunting edifice, like an enormous early nineteenth-century mill. When it had been built, it was at the forefront of enlightened medical care, but now it was crumbling, the paint was peeling, and on the morning I arrived it was raining, the roof was leaking, and there were puddles of water on the floors of the endless corridors. I saw patients with twisted limbs and tiny deformed bodies. Some had huge heads, staring eyes, and long attenuated hands. One poor misshapen soul slipped in front of me and crashed down into a puddle, before being whisked away by an apologetic nurse.

I talked to the patients, played and laughed with them, and felt relatively at ease. But at lunchtime I was sitting in the staff canteen eating shepherd's pie and Surprise peas, and listening intently to a specialist in cerebral palsy explaining about the neurological problems that cause this dreadful disease, when I detected a hair in my mouth tangled up in the minced beef. In other circumstances I'd have removed it discreetly from my mouth and put it on the side of my plate. If I'd been feeling particularly squeamish, I might have decided not to finish my grub, but I wouldn't have made a song and dance about it. Now, though, I was overwhelmed by revulsion. The food had obviously been prepared by a crazed lunatic who'd not only failed to wear a hairnet, but had probably coughed over it, dribbled in it, and generally infected it with madness. Outwardly I was listening to the specialist, but inside it was as though I was warding off a chainsaw-wielding maniac. I might have thought I was a sensible, modern kind of guy, but when I was confronted by physical deformity and psychiatric disorder, my reactions were positively medieval. I was exactly the kind of person who should watch the TV programme I was making!

But strangely I didn't feel disturbed by Joey. His limbs were never still, he was constantly dribbling, and communicating with him via Ernie was achingly laborious, but his eyes twinkled, and his responses were playful and laced with little jokes. He also had a steely quality about him. He wanted to know how we were going to tell his story and what we wanted from him, but he had his own priorities too. He was happy to go along with our plans, but not if they conflicted with his. He and his friends weren't victims, they were four thoughtful men who happened to have physical disabilities.

Joey won a BAFTA and the International Golden Rose of Montreux. The real Joey and Ernie played themselves as older men, and for a while became national celebrities. *Blue Peter* championed them and raised enough money for them to live in their own home in the grounds of the hospital, although they later moved out, and lived fiercely independent lives in a house a few miles away. I was proud of the programme, and of my role in it. I wish every piece of work I've done over the years had been as fulfilling.

All the theoretical discussions we'd had about the arts at Fred Place over the previous few years finally came to fruition. Early in 1974 Dave and I received £1,000 from the Arts Council, and another £1,000 from HTV. We could now create our own left-wing theatre company.

The Labour Arts Minister, Jenny Lee, had freed up a significant amount of money for small-scale touring theatres, and all over the country companies similar to ours were emerging. They had imaginative names like Forkbeard Fantasy, Monstrous Regiment and Mrs Worthington's Daughters, but we gave ourselves the prosaic title the Avon Touring Theatre Company, which simply described what we did and where we did it.

There was no shortage of volunteers. One of our first recruits was Old Vic stalwart Tim Fearon. He was six foot two inches tall and when he and I appeared on stage together the audience laughed before we'd even said anything, Chris Harris was a talented clown and the finest pantomime dame I'd ever seen, Chrissie Bradwell had a keen business brain and a brother, Mike, who had founded the well-respected Hull Truck

Theatre, Sue Macready came down from London to help us out, and Tim Munro, an ex-Central friend of mine, was an actor, singer, writer and political firebrand who swiftly became totally devoted to our new company. Our most notable acquisition, though, was Howard Goorney. The actors who made up companies like ours were invariably in their twenties and with limited experience, but Howard was in his mid-fifties and looked twenty years older. He had been one of the original members of Joan Littlewood's celebrated Theatre Workshop in Manchester, but had grown disillusioned when she moved her company down to London and began relying on the income from creating West End hits. He'd recently moved with his family to Bradford on Avon and wanted to relive his past as a young communist actor on the road. His experience, fatalism and mournful, lugubrious face were an enormous asset to us.

The appearance of a radical new theatre company in Bristol attracted a lot of attention in the local press. No one revelled in this more than I did, and I used the publicity not only to promote Avon Touring, but also to criticise the Old Vic for having failed to respond to the needs of the city's diverse communities. Unfortunately Val May took exception to my public tirades and made it clear I was no longer welcome at his theatre. This was annoying because the Vic had been the source of a significant part of my income, but on the other hand to be blacklisted, like a Hollywood actor in the McCarthyist witch hunt of the 1950s, did seem rather romantic, although at the time I had no idea that it would be another ten years before I'd be walking back through the doors of the Theatre Royal with my head held high.

Avon Touring put on plays about prostitution, punks, Queen Boudicca, and the national building workers' strike. Some were good, others were pretty dreadful, but they invariably had bucketsful of energy and commitment. I'd imagined that being on tour with like-minded actors performing socially committed plays would be an uplifting and pleasurable experience, but it seldom was. We never stopped arguing. We rowed about what hours we should work, what gigs we should accept, and how we should divide up the work involved in running a theatre company. We argued about how much we should spend on repairing our van, and when it finally came to a juddering halt we argued about how much we should spend on a new one. We were a co-operative, but a very uncooperative one, a collective, but disunited. The problem was we were socialists and visionaries, but without a shared vision. We were good at debating, but our debates brought us to a standstill.

We were at our least argumentative when rehearsing the plays, and that was due in a large part to the calibre of the outside directors we employed, young tyros like John Caird (whose later work included big West End musicals like *Les Misérables*), Mel Smith (who became a TV comic and film director), and of course Howard Davies. I directed a number of shows too, but the job always made me miserable and my actors even more so, so eventually I stopped.

Avon Touring survived for over a decade, visiting countless schools, church halls and community centres. It never achieved great success or huge audiences, but was part of the spirit of the times. It left me with a belief that theatre as a genuinely popular art form was a thing of the past. It might have been able to galvanise the imagination of the masses in the days of Aeschylus, Shakespeare and Bertolt Brecht, but now it had been superseded by the mass media. Theatre could still be a serious and entertaining middle-class diversion, but if I wanted to touch the hearts of ordinary people, I would have to build a career in television.

11

THE CHAT SHOW HOST

'Can you ride a motorbike?'

'Yes.'

'Course you can! You've got that little scootery thing, haven't you?'

'That is a motorbike, Penny.'

'Is it? Good Lord! Can you ride a proper one?'

'I've just bought a 250.'

'And that's bigger, is it?'

'Considerably.'

'And you've passed your test?'

'Penny, why are you suddenly so interested in my transport arrangements?'

'Do you think you can drive well enough to be a motorcycle messenger?'

'Christ, things aren't that bad, are they?'

'In a film.'

'What kind of film?'

'A feature film. Shot over here. American money.'

Had I misheard?

'Who's in it?'

'John Wayne.'

'*The* John Wayne?'

'*The* John Wayne. It's called *Brannigan*. The producer wants to see you as soon as poss.'

'I'll get my stuff together.'

'Great. Er, Tony?'

'Yeah?'

'You won't wear those pink boots, will you?'

Shepperton is a two-and-a-half-hour bike ride from Bristol. By the time I got there, the afternoon's filming was well underway. Two figures were sitting close to the camera conferring. 'Jules Levy – Producer' was stencilled on the back of one canvas chair; 'Douglas Hickox – Director' proclaimed the other.

The set was a rickety office with a blown-up photo of the London docks behind it. Three large men were rolling their shoulders and stretching their necks in the time-honoured fashion of actors before a take. The studio bell rang, the warning light flashed red, and someone yelled 'Standby!' One of the actors lay on the floor as though he'd been shot dead; the other two went to their positions marked with little bits of white tape. One of them I recognised as Mel Ferrer, the American actor who'd been married to Audrey Hepburn. He was dressed as a corrupt lawyer, with a sharp suit and shiny shoes. The other was greasy and unshaven with a podgy face and a blood-stained bandage round his hand. The camera assistant clapped his board, announced, 'Thirty-seven, take one,' and Doug Hickox shouted 'Action!'

For a few moments nothing happened, then there was a rattling sound, and a muffled voice said, 'I can't open the fucking door.' It sounded suspiciously like John Wayne. No one laughed. 'Cut!' shouted Doug Hickox.

Assistant directors and carpenters raced out of nowhere like Israeli commandos on a deadly mission. In thirty seconds the edges of the big door at the back of the set had been re-planed, re-sanded and re-oiled.

'Thirty-seven, take two,' said the camera assistant.

'Action!' shouted Doug Hickox.

Bang! The door exploded open, sugar-glass shattered, and in burst John Wayne, practically as big as the door.

The two actors cowered, the dust settled, and Wayne said, 'Knock! Knock!'

'Brannigan!' roared the greasy gangster, and lunged for the gun on the table.

'I wouldn't,' drawled Wayne, 'unless you wanna sing soprano.'

'Cut!' shouted Doug Hickox, 'Print it! Moving on, please. Mr Ferrer's close up.' Lights and camera were moved, an extra piece of wall was brought in, and make-up began touching up Mel Ferrer's face. The producer and director were deep in conversation. I hovered for a while, hoping they'd notice me, but they didn't. Eventually I chipped in.

'Mr Levy?'

'Yeah. You got a parcel for me?'

'No.'

'You collecting something?'

'No, I'm Tony Robinson.'

'From . . . ?'

'I'm an actor.'

'What? Christ! I thought you were a motorcycle courier.'

'No, I'm an actor who's come to see you about playing the part of a motorcycle courier.'

'You came dressed for the part?'

'No, I came on my bike.'

'Fuck!' said Jules, 'that's funny.' He was middle-aged, American and a much more convincing gangster than the two on the studio floor. 'You hear that, Doug?'

Doug Hickox, who was spry and very English, said yes, he'd heard it, and it certainly was amusing.

Jules turned to Mel Ferrer.

'You see that?'

'See what, Jules?'

'This guy! He walks in, I think he's a motorcycle courier, but he's a fucking actor who wants to play the part of a motorcycle courier. Isn't that the funniest fucking thing!'

He repeated the story to three or four members of the crew, before turning back to Doug.

'He's gotta be our guy, right?'

'Has he?'

'He's gotta be our guy, right?' he said again a little more emphatically.

'I suppose he has, Jules,' replied Doug Hickox.

'Funniest fucking thing,' repeated Jules, and wandered off towards the catering table.

Doug turned to me. 'Can you act?' he said.

'Yes,' I replied.

'We'll see you in about ten days then. Thanks for coming.'

Brannigan was going to make me serious money. Sixty pounds for each day in front of the camera, plus a retainer of sixty pounds a week until filming was completed. Crazy! But more fool them. I'd be happy to spend it! It was the school holidays, and I had ten days to kill. Mary and I hired an Austin Allegro and drove to Snowdonia.

Who knew there was anywhere so beautiful? We yomped up Mount Snowdon, but got stuck on a knife-edged ridge, and didn't get back to the car till after dark. We climbed Cadair Idris and raced and tumbled down its scree slopes like crazy people. We took up ornithology and saw wheatears, a sedge warbler, an osprey with a fish in its mouth and a peregrine falcon. We paid good money for walking boots which crippled us, but still managed to walk all day with ham and cheese sandwiches, ordnance survey maps, two novels, and a bottle of Tizer in our rucksacks.

At five minutes to six each evening I'd phone Penny to see if I was needed on set the following morning. If she'd said yes, we'd have driven all night to make it, but it seemed worth the risk. Eventually I got a message that I had a fitting the following Monday, so we had a leisurely drive to London over the weekend, then Mary took the car back to Bristol.

The unit base was in the Windmill Street car park round the back of Piccadilly Circus. Twenty or so big white vans and lorries were parked up, half a dozen Winnebagos, a catering van and an old bus to eat in, a cluster of black limousines with their drivers, a few Mercedes, a Sunbeam Talbot and a Triumph Stag. Various young men and women in jeans were wandering round with walkie-talkies. It looked as though a small invading army was hidden away behind the salt beef bars and strip joints of Soho.

A security man at the front gates pointed out the production office, a portacabin set back from the jumble of vehicles. It smelt of coffee and too many fags. A harassed young production assistant in a tie-dye smock was sitting at a desk with two phones ringing. She introduced herself as Mags, and said there'd be a lot of hanging around to do, so I'd been designated a dressing room where I could wait, although unfortunately I'd have to share. She gave me a small key with a little pink plastic fob on it bearing the number 2.

Dressing room two was in a Winnebago. On the door a typed sign said 'Richard Attenborough', and below it a smaller one had been added saying 'Tony Robertson'. I corrected my name with a biro, knocked and entered. Inside were two large rooms, with a shower and toilet between. I pushed open the door to the right. It contained a row of motorcycle jackets on hangers, and a bowl of fruit in front of a large mirror surrounded by illuminated light bulbs. I lay down on the couch and reread the call sheet.

There was a discreet tap on the door.

'Come in!'

I'd seen Richard Attenborough a hundred times in black and white movies on afternoon telly, playing the brave young

British officer, baby-faced, stiff upper lipped, but deep down with a glimmer of sensitivity. The Richard Attenborough I was looking at now was much older, though, with a round head and body, like one of those plastic toys your budgie tries to knock over. He had ridiculously large sideburns, a small moustache, and thinning salt and pepper hair combed back to obscure his bald patches.

'Hello, old love,' he said. 'I'm Dickie. Welcome to the madhouse.'

We chatted for a while. He was friendly and gossipy like British actors invariably are on set. He said the American producers had no manners, they thought English actors were a bit stupid, and were bullying Doug Hickox. I asked him about John Wayne. Was he a nice bloke? Was he approachable? Was he easy to work with? Dickie raised his eyebrows and said nothing.

Eventually he was called away, and I was left to my own devices. I read my *Guardian* and Dickie's *Telegraph*, and failed dismally with both crosswords. An excitable wardrobe man with a florid shirt and red-framed glasses bustled in. He made me try on several sets of motorbike gear, and chose a brown jacket with yellow writing on it which he thought looked cute. When I told him I didn't think that was the effect the producers had in mind, he pretended not to hear me. Then someone from props turned up and tried to measure my head for a crash helmet, but he'd only got a wooden ruler, so he went away again.

Around midday I asked Mags if I could go home, but she said that after lunch the guys from transport would want to talk to me about the kind of motorbike I'd like to ride. I wandered down to Piccadilly Circus to watch the shoot. They were working on a sequence in which Mel Ferrer had to drive his white Rolls Royce up to a postbox which was standing conveniently next to the statue of Eros. He then had to post £250,000 in ransom money into it, apparently unaware that some dodgy English criminals had dug a tunnel below it from the London sewers, and were poised ready to replace the ransom with envelopes full of torn newspaper.

About a hundred extras had been employed as members of the general public, and had been orchestrated to cross camera at specially designated times. Bizarrely they included thirty or so young women dressed as nurses who were marching along holding banners demanding more pay, presumably to reassure American cinema audiences that the NHS was indeed in a state of terminal collapse. It was a complicated scene, involving several cars arriving at particular points at different times, and a member of the crew with a walkie-talkie lying flat in the back seat of each one receiving instructions. It was clearly going to take a long time to complete, and tempers were already flaring. I walked back to the unit base. There was a short queue for lunch which I joined, put a trout with almonds and a crème caramel on my tray and headed back towards the Winnebago.

Dickie came in with a duck *à l'orange* and a raspberry pavlova. While we ate he told me showbiz stories about Noël Coward and working with Steve McQueen in *The Great Escape*.

He'd also played John Christie in the film *10 Rillington Place*, and we were speculating about what drove Christie to perform such horrors, when Jules Levy barged in with the wardrobe man in tow. He ignored me – obviously his amusement at my mistaken identity was long forgotten – and insisted that Dickie immediately try on a variety of suits.

'But Jules, I haven't finished my—' Dickie began.

'So you wanna hold us up?' snapped Jules, and moved the pavlova out of Dickie's way to emphasise how pressing the task was.

When he'd gone we sat in silence for a while, then I burst out, 'Dickie, maybe I shouldn't say this, but you're world famous. You're respected. You've directed your own movies. Why do you put up with this crap?'

He didn't say anything, his mouth was full of pavlova. He merely put his hand in his inside jacket pocket, pulled out his wallet, and waved it at me. Then he put it back, and polished off the rest of his pudding.

Halfway through the afternoon, Mags poked her head round my dressing room door.

'The transport people are tied up with the postbox scene,' she said. 'It's running behind, and it's all getting a bit shouty if you know what I mean. You pop home, I'll get them to call you in the morning, and we'll see you again on Wednesday.'

Two days later I was riding down St Martins Lane past the various theatres where I'd worked over the last twenty years, and finally arrived at the big post office on the junction with William IV Street. Then I did a big loop and repeated the journey again . . . and again . . . and again! Eventually the first assistant flagged me down and told me the shot was in the can. So far so good!

They set up the next shot, which involved me pulling up at the post office, getting off the motorbike and going inside. The bike they'd given me was, not to put too fine a point on it, shit. Transport hadn't called me to sort out a decent vehicle as promised, and I'd ended up with a BSA Bantam, faded green and at least fifteen years old. It was a nightmare to start, the clutch and brakes were virtually non-existent, and from the cobwebs woven among the spokes and on the brake light, it looked like it had been lying unloved at the back of a garage for a very long time until yesterday when someone remembered that they were supposed to supply the unit with a motorbike. The most hazardous operation was putting it on its stand. It hadn't seen a drop of oil in years, and one of the springs had broken. It was just about possible to operate, but it required superhuman strength and good balance, two qualities which I had in short supply.

On the first and second take I couldn't get the stand down, and on take three I got it half down, walked towards the post office, and the bike crashed onto the pavement. On the fourth take I performed the whole operation elegantly and with aplomb, but a member of the public came bustling out of an office next door and asked me what I was doing, thus ruining the shot.

On the eighth take the bike toppled into the road and a car was forced to swerve to avoid crushing it. Doug then decided to axe the shot. At the beginning of the day the American producers had been all smiles, but now they glowered at me. I'd confirmed their prejudice that British actors were numbskulls. I tried to explain that the bike was defective, but my case wasn't helped when someone from props picked it up off the road and put it on its stand in one effortless movement.

The final shot of the morning involved me approaching a post office counter and collecting the big envelopes which the cops thought contained the ransom. I then had to leave again, closely followed by Dickie and John Wayne. It would take some time to set all this up so while I was waiting, I went for a breath of air down William IV Street. I bought a quarter ounce of Golden Virginia and a packet of red Rizlas at a tobacconist opposite Charing Cross station, rolled myself a fag, and leant against a wall watching the hustle and bustle of the Strand.

A man came towards me with the air of a London down-and-out. He was wearing a grubby suit that had once been white, a battered pair of American-style plimsolls, and a purple and green Hawaiian shirt. His gaze was aimed directly at me, and he clearly wanted something. Should I be a good Samaritan? Perhaps I'd rather be a selfish Pharisee knowing that the poor wretch would probably rave incoherently at me for a very long time, and wouldn't go away again till I'd given him enough money for a bottle of meths. Before I had time to come to the honourable decision, he loped up to me, greeted me like an old friend and cadged a roll-up and a light. At first I thought he recognised me from TV, or had worked out that I was with the film unit round the corner. But apparently not. He began talking about the weather, which was remarkably balmy for the time of year, fast cars, which he loved, Harold Wilson, who he hated, and MI5, who had been following him for a number of years and he had the papers to prove it. He had the vocabulary of an educated man and the confident demeanour of an estate agent, but his sentences were halting, he broke off in mid-thought, and every few seconds his passionate enthusiasm became clouded by suspicion. There was also something jocular about him, as though he was aware of the ridiculousness of his situation and was laughing at it. His face was vaguely familiar. Had I met him before but in a different guise, like when you visit your bank manager and discover he was in your class at primary school? Then I remembered. I'd seen him countless times.

Simon Dee was one of the first DJs on Radio Caroline. He left for Radio One, moved to television and had eventually been given his own twice-weekly chat show, *Dee Time*, which regularly topped the ratings. The words 'It's Siiiiiimon Dee', which announced the beginning of each show, became a national catch-phrase, one which was now echoing round my head as he began yet another rambling yarn. I knew something had gone wrong for him a few years previously. He had a reputation for being quarrelsome and getting fired, had made himself unemployable, had been arrested for various silly misdemeanours, and had eventually disappeared from view. But now here he was.

He asked me for another roll-up, I gave him the packet of tobacco and the fag papers, and wandered back to the post office. Later I saw him trying to make conversation with the cameraman and a couple of the crew. Everyone gave him the time of day, but I don't think they knew who he was. I last saw him walking towards Leicester Square, alone and deep in thought, the victim of some terrible crisis I knew nothing about, or perhaps just someone brought low by the weight of their own celebrity.

*

That afternoon I rode the bike from Leicester Square to the London docks, while John Wayne and Dickie shadowed me at a safe distance. I was being filmed by a camera which was mounted on a truck in front of me and kept stopping without warning, and given the quality of my bike's brakes I was lucky not to have been severely injured, particularly as it took us two hours to get to our destination. We drove past Buckingham Palace, then to St Paul's, back to Westminster Bridge and across to the Tower of London. Only a madman or a highly unscrupulous cabbie would have taken that route, but it enabled us to be filmed passing virtually every iconic building in London, so it made the producers happy.

Then I was stood down for yet another week. The motorbike might have been useless and the storyline naff, but making a feature film had its compensations! This time Mary and I went to Cornwall for a few days.

'There's no dialogue!'

'I know, Duke. They didn't write any for this scene. How about we improvise?'

'How about we what?'

John Wayne, the Duke as he was known to intimates, sat staring into his mirror while someone fiddled with his eyebrows.

'Maybe we should ad lib something?' suggested Doug.

'Maybe the scriptwriter should do his fucking job,' replied the Duke.

The day of my scene with the great man had arrived. I had to ride through the gates of the King George V Dock, park my bike (or hopefully lean it against a wall), cross a small metal bridge, and throw a bag containing the ransom envelope into the water. The Duke would then appear behind me and throw me into the dock; I'd retrieve the bag, he'd open it, and discover there were only bundles of newspaper inside. He'd been suckered. I was a red herring, an innocent who'd been paid by a stranger to put him off the scent.

'So when I see him swinging the bag,' suggested Wayne, 'I'll say "Hold it!"'

'Good, Duke! Excellent!'

'And then I'll say, "Can you swim?" and he'll say, "Yes".'

'Are you OK with that, Tony?'

'Fine.'

The Duke clearly wasn't an improviser in the free-flowing Woody Allen vein. He was thinking at the speed of a steam-roller.

'And how about, before I push him in, I say, "Go and get it"? Or is "Go get it" better?'

'Your call,' said Doug. 'They're both great.'

The Duke's trailer was huge but right now it seemed over-crowded. Apart from Doug and me squashed up against his toilet door, there was his personal assistant, his personal make-up artist, his personal wardrobe assistant, another American producer who'd just flown in with his personal assistant, and, most important of all, the wig man.

The wig man was a middle-aged Californian with a sand-coloured teddy boy haircut, freshly pressed Levi jeans with a knife-edge crease, and a Levi jacket with the collar up. He had more power on the set than anyone, including Doug. He was the last person to leave the Duke's side before a shot, and the first back after each take. If a hair was out of place, he'd whisper in Doug's ear, and shooting would be stopped immediately. If the lighting didn't show the wig to its best effect, he'd insist the lights were changed, and if the camera didn't favour the Duke's best angles, he'd escort Wayne from the set until the problem was fixed.

As for the wig itself, it was as perfect as Michelangelo's *David* or the Trevi Fountain. If you'd given it a push, it would have stayed in place; if you'd thrown rocks at it, they'd have bounced right back at you; if the Duke had turned fast, it would have stayed still. Dad still had some of his old NHS wigs in a cardboard box. If I'd borrowed one and he'd worn that, it would have looked far more realistic, even if it did smell of Brylcreem.

'So I open the envelope and its full of torn-up newspaper?'

'Correct, Duke.'

'And I'm pretty pissed, right?'

'You are indeed, Duke.'

'But I get what's happening – instantly!'

'That's the kind of guy Brannigan is, Duke.'

'OK, I'll say, "They pulled a Murphy."'

'What's a Murphy, Duke?'

'A Murphy! A Murphy! Come on!'

'A Murphy?'

'That's what I'll say.'

'Fine, Duke.'

He started to unbutton his shirt. His wardrobe assistant moved silently forward, took over the unbuttoning, and pulled the shirt gently off him. It was hard not to gawp. He had the biggest scar I'd ever seen. I knew he'd had cancer, and all the papers had said he'd beaten it in typical John Wayne fashion, but in order to extract the tumour, the surgeon had made an incision from his throat to his waist, then along his belt line, and had opened him up like a big book. How strange! This giant of a man, the twentieth-century version of the god Hercules, was wearing twenty thousand dollars' worth of hair from the head of a third-world peasant, and had a scar that looked like he'd be savaged by a great white shark.

He looked at me for the first time.

'So you're in the water, and I'm walking away. What do you say?'

'Err . . . I suppose something along the lines of . . . er . . . "I'll sink with these boots on . . ." or, er . . . "What about me?" . . . something like that.'

Wayne looked at me as though he was disappointed by my shoddy homework.

'But you wouldn't say it like that,' he drawled. 'You'd be really scared.'

The King George V Dock wasn't an appealing sight. I'd delivered vast hams and gigantic cans of beans to this very dockside when I was working at Sharpe's, but that was before the bottom had dropped out of the London shipping market. There'd always been at least a dozen massive ships tied up here bearing flags from all over the world, but now it was virtually empty, bleak and dilapidated. The only vessel in sight was a Chinese meat ship having its hold cleaned out by men in windcheaters wielding jet hoses.

I had a horrible realisation. The dock I was about to jump into was full of Chinese meat juice, rat wee, and other foul unpleasantness. I found the first assistant and asked him what precautions had been taken to ensure I wouldn't contract a terrible disease. He said he'd ask.

A little while later he brought Jules Levy over.

'Yeah?' the producer enquired in his usual friendly tone. 'And you are what?'

'I'm the motorbike courier . . .' I said, '. . . in the movie,' and laughed to remind him how funny that was.

'And your problem is?'

I explained to him that I was going to have to say my lines while I was splashing about in the dock. I showed him how choppy the waves were, and how this would inevitably mean that water would get in my mouth. I showed him the filthy red liquid cascading from the hold of the meat ship. I explained I knew this dock quite well and that for hundreds of years ships similar to this one had been dumping their offal and human waste in it. I asked him if there'd been any kind of risk assessment of this site and whether there were injections I could be given to ensure I'd be properly protected.

He put his arm around me in a paternal fashion and pulled me to him.

'Naaah!' he said. 'You'll be fine.'

'Well, possibly, but—'

'You're an actor, so act!'

Then he turned to the first assistant. 'That's why we pay him the big bucks, right?'

I could have said no there and then. I could have told him my life was at risk and they'd behaved irresponsibly, so if I walked away it would be down to them. I could have explained that he had a choice. He could sort it out now and cancel the day's filming, or reshoot all my scenes at another time with a different actor. I could have said that, but I didn't. Maybe he was right – after all he was paying me £60 a day; I'd made more money on this movie than I'd earned in the last six months. And what was it I wanted him to do? Pump chlorine into my bloodstream? Drain the dock and fill it with tap water? I said nothing. Instead I stared into the cold, black, oily dock, and thought about Simon Dee and John Wayne, and their very different lives.

12

THE PROMISING PLAYWRIGHT

In the summer of 1975 I fell in love with archaeology. Chichester town centre was peppered with holes of various sizes, and in them were scruffy young people like the ones with a dog on a string who ask you for your change outside Tesco. But these weren't beggars; they were graduates from the archaeology departments of our finest universities, attempting to locate evidence of Roman Chichester which lay under the present-day shops and pavements.

Mary and I were fascinated by the scale of this project, and by the commitment of the diggers. We'd watch them sweating under the summer sun, until eventually one particularly hirsute young man asked us if we wanted to help.

After that we spent every day up to our elbows in plastic bowls of cold, muddy water scrubbing small shards of pottery. Mary proved particularly adept at fitting the tiny pieces together which impressed the senior archaeologists. She was eventually given a trowel, and the responsibility of scraping away at the multi-coloured earth, trying to work out the comparative dating of the layers. But I couldn't get my head round these subtle alterations in colour, and spent most of my time standing around watching, something at which I became extremely skilled.

I'd first arrived in Chichester the previous Christmas to take part in a new show called *Follow the Star* written by Wally K. Daly, the theatre's electrician-turned-playwright. Wally was a working-class Liverpudlian with a personality that was half straight-talking wisecracks, and half over-the-top sentimental-ity. His play was similar – the nativity story told from the point of view of a small posse of angels who'd been instructed to keep an eye on the baby Jesus. Although they were played by young adults, these cherubs behaved like educationally challenged kids in their last year of primary school, constantly getting into scrapes as they defended the tiny deity from the clutches of baby-killing King Herod. My character was Angel Chicago, a parody of the cigar-chomping gangsters played by Edward G. Robinson in the movies, but of course, this being a children's play, Angel Chicago neither dealt drugs nor pimped prostitutes, but was slightly naughty with a heart of gold.

Follow the Star may have been a little too cute for my liking, but it was funny, the music was catchy, it had a strong storyline, and kids loved it. It was immensely successful, played for many more Christmases at Chichester and in London, and we tele-vised it for the BBC. Angel Chicago was an intensely physical part; at one point I had to bounce up a flight of stairs, jump off a ten-foot-high rostrum, land on my feet, and start singing. I'd always been too puny to get involved in competitive sport, but my old friend Ted Braun, who was now a senior drama lecturer, had managed to get us passes to the Bristol University gym and he, Howard and I had been playing a lot of squash there for the previous few months. I was much fitter than usual, my diet was good too, and I'd stopped drinking, so I enjoyed the challenge of getting stuck into Angel Chicago's dance routines night after night, and Chichester's Artistic Director, the Austra-lian actor Keith Michell, was sufficiently impressed to ask me back to his theatre six months later for the summer season.

The Festival Theatre was one of the finest in the country, a thousand-seater with a thrust stage that was both grand and intimate like a Greek amphitheatre. Chichester is in one of the loveliest parts of southern England, and the Festival was able to attract leading actors and international stars from all over the world who fancied a summer break. I had my differences with Keith – we had such opposing sensibilities that we instantly irritated each other – but I'll always be grateful to him. He gave me the opportunity to play big parts alongside celebrated performers in a theatre that received national attention.

Our first production was Ibsen's *An Enemy of the People*. I played Hovstad, a leftist newspaper editor who ultimately betrays and destroys the man who has befriended him. It was a weighty part to give such an untried actor, but I tended to wear my politics on my sleeve, and I suspect Keith thought I could wander on stage, say the words, and be convincing. But I found it a difficult part, made doubly daunting by the fact that I was playing alongside one of Britain's theatrical giants, Donald Sinden, who'd recently triumphed at the Royal Shakespeare Company as King Lear, and had followed that up with a smash hit comedy series, *Two's Company*. I worked hard in rehearsals, tried every fresh nuance I could think of, and plundered my soul for innovative line readings, but to no avail; my performance wasn't working.

Michael Elphick, a long-time friend who'd been born in Chichester, had gone home to visit his mum and dad. I asked him to watch the dress rehearsal and tell me what I was doing wrong. He'd trained at Central, had been in the legendary *Withnail* year, and understood George and Litz's way of working. I was confident he'd be able to put his finger on the problem.

At the end of the rehearsal I made my way to the back of the stalls.

'Well? What should I do?'

'Talk louder,' he said.

'What?'

'Louder,' he repeated.

I thought about this.

'Is that all?'

'Yup.'

'Nothing more? Am I understating the subtleties of my character?'

'Nope.'

'Am I trying to play the totality of Hovstad's inner life from the beginning of the play, rather than gradually revealing his complexities?'

'Nope.'

'Just talk louder?'

'Yeah. I couldn't hear you.'

So I did. The following night was the first public performance. It went very well. There may even have been the odd 'Bravo!' when I took my bow. Certainly the *Guardian*'s Michael Billington said I was an actor of promise and one to watch, which made me feel pretty good.

Mike Elphick wrestled with alcoholism all his life. He was one of the finest actors of my generation, but he died young, and his stellar career was cut short. To this day, though, if I'm struggling with a part, I take his wise words to heart, and talk louder!

The play wasn't only a great showpiece for me, it was also one for Donald. He'd been a celebrated stage and screen performer for half a century, and I suspect would have ranked alongside Olivier and Ralph Richardson if his voice hadn't been so plummy, like an old-fashioned actor-manager. But he was a powerful force on stage, and my mum had adored him for decades.

He and I had a somewhat edgy relationship. I think we both enjoyed what the other did on stage, but politically and artistically we were at the opposite ends of the spectrum. He was a supporter of the Equity council with which I was constantly doing battle. Like Val May, he thought I was a shit-stirrer, while I saw him as the embodiment of the old ruling class destined for the dustbin of theatre history. But Mum wanted to meet him, so I asked him if I could bring her round to see him after the show, and he concurred.

She was ridiculously excited. I met her at the stage door, but when we got to dressing room number one, it was crammed with well-wishers drinking warm white wine and telling him how super he was. I tried to catch the great man's eye, but it was hopeless. I took Mum back to my cottage in Havant, made her a cup of tea, gave her a slice of specially purchased Victoria sponge cake, and settled down to watch the *Moira Anderson Show* on TV.

Half an hour later there was a thunderous crash at the front door and Donald burst in, his great eyebrows bristling like wicked Uncle Abanazar in *Aladdin*. Mum stood up and curtsied, and Donald regaled her for half an hour with stories about the old days in the theatre, how much better they were than the new days, and how young puppies like me had no idea what they'd missed. Occasionally, to emphasise a point, he'd take her hand and pat it, and when he was describing how stunning Ava Gardner had looked, he lightly stroked her hair and said, 'In some ways she wasn't unlike you, Phyllis.' Then, as swiftly and as noisily as he had entered, he kissed her gently on the cheek and left. It was a magnificent performance.

My other role that summer was in a new play written by Andrew Sachs, better known as Manuel in *Faulty Towers*. It was called *Made in Heaven*. Patricia Routledge played a suburban mum, and I was all seven of her children, who came and went at such speed that sometimes it seemed as though several of them were on stage at the same time. This trick required a team of dressers stationed at various vantage points backstage, and lots of fast and furious costume changes. My favourite of these kids was an eight-year-old girl with a shower of long curly blonde hair, a yellow party dress with short puffed sleeves, short white socks, and red Start-Rite shoes. I looked bloody gorgeous – at least I thought I did until the technical rehearsal, when we had to show ourselves to the director and the costume designer. I skipped confidently on stage, and stood waiting to bask in the coos of appreciation.

'That is foul!' said a voice out of the darkness.

'Excuse me?'

'You look disgusting!'

'Why?' I asked indignantly.

'Your hair, Tony!'

'Is it sticking out under my wig? I can fix that.'

'Your body hair! It's everywhere! It's even poking out the top of your dress. You look like a transvestite!'

I went back to my dressing room dismayed. My dresser, a kindly Chichester matron with strawberry blonde hair, took me in hand like a favourite auntie.

'Don't worry, dear,' she said, 'you can shave it off.'

'But it would prickle, and it grows so quickly I'd end up having to shave my entire body every day.'

'There's cream. But it's a bit messy and it takes forever.'

'So why don't I go to one of those waxing places?'

'It's not much fun.'

'I can handle it.'

'It's not much fun at all.'

Bless her! I was a man. I could deal with a few dollops of warm wax.

The theatre booked an appointment for me at a beauty salon in North Street. I told the young woman in the white coat that, except where modesty dictated, I wanted all my body hair removed.

'Are you sure?'

'Absolutely.'

'There's a lot of it.'

'I'm all yours.'

There followed two and a half hours of unspeakable torture. If she'd been in the Gestapo and I'd possessed secrets on which my comrades' lives depended, I'd have shopped them within five minutes. The pain was bad enough, but the noise was even worse: a dreadful tearing sound as strip after strip was ripped from my body. The worst part was when she attacked the insides of my legs. The skin was loose and floppy, and stretched a good six inches before the foul waxy paper finally came away with my hair stuck to it.

I eventually blundered out of the salon, staggered home in a state of shock, lay prone on the bed, and slept for hours until Mary shook me awake. She said I had to get back to the theatre straight away for the dress rehearsal. But how could I? The surface of my skin had gone into crisis; I looked like a Sainsbury's plucked chicken. If either leg brushed against the other, the pain was unbearable. I couldn't walk unless I bowed my legs like an ancient cowboy.

Mary drove me to work and opened the passenger door solicitously. 'Are you going to be able to make it?' she asked. I nodded bravely. I knew I'd have to soldier on. I'd been brazenly confident of my ability to take my waxing like a man. I couldn't come back like a road-accident victim. That evening I gave the performance of my life as a relaxed and pain-free hero. I'd have got away with it if it hadn't been for the quick changes. When my trousers were wrenched off and my tights yanked on, my suffering was like Christ crucified. I'd made the ultimate sacrifice for my art, now I must endure the agony.

Back in Bristol, Fred Place rang with the chatter of young voices, and the stairs thumped to the sound of their remorseless feet. Children had arrived, and their presence transformed the commune. The first were Kate's three teenagers. The youngest, Mick, was chatty and totally at ease in the company of adults. The oldest was Andy – tall, soft-spoken and constantly pained by the injustices of life. On his sixteenth birthday I'd lent him my Honda 50, even though everyone told me I was mad. Predictably he forgot to lock it, and it was stolen the next day. But the hurt and confused look on his face was so heartrending that I couldn't be angry with him for more than an hour. Joanny was sophisticated, articulate, and academically brilliant. We doted on her, and when she was fifteen and didn't come home one night, we all sat round the table worrying, phoning the police and hospitals, and drinking copious amounts of tea. She came back the next morning. She'd spent the night with her Brazilian boyfriend, and was feeling very irritable.

'Six parents!' she said. 'Can you imagine the pressure that puts me under?'

Then babies started coming. Howard and Sue produced Hannah, Dave and Kate had Huw, and Mary gave birth to our wonderful Laura. In the mid-seventies very few dads witnessed the birth of their children, but, for all its faults, Bristol Children's Hospital was progressive in that respect. The eleventh of April 1976 was one of the most magical nights of my life, although Mary was a little less enthusiastic about the experience. When she and Laura had finally fallen asleep, I tiptoed out of the maternity ward and stepped into a lift. Another dad joined me.

'How much did yours weigh?' he asked.

'5lbs 3,' I replied.

'Mine was 10lbs 2,' he said. 'Twice as big!'

'Twice as big,' he repeated as he got out at the ground floor, bursting with pride.

Laura hardly had any time to get to know her new communards, because six days after she was born, the three of us drove down to Chichester for another few months. The weather on the south coast that summer was extraordinary: week after week of blazing sun and cloudless skies. It was an idyllic time. Once the shows were on I could spend all day with Laura. I carried her round the garden and showed her the flowers and the light dappling through the leaves. When she cried I tied a papoose round my front, and sang her to sleep with Stevie Wonder's 'Isn't She Lovely?'. I'd known that having a baby would involve compromises, but I hadn't appreciated that my love for her would make the very notion of compromises irrelevant. Nor had

I realised the unconditional love I'd get back from her. I adored being a dad, and still do forty years later.

That summer would have been perfect if it hadn't been for Rex Harrison. He was a huge Broadway and Hollywood star who'd played the dapper English gentleman in countless shows and films, and had recently had a big hit as Professor Higgins in *My Fair Lady*. He'd flown to England from Hollywood to play the lead for us in a farce called *Monsieur Perrichon's Travels*, in which he was a well-off French merchant whose pretty young daughter is pursued through the Alps by two suitors. I hadn't had a great deal of experience of movie stars, but the ones I had met had all been a bit odd. Rex, though, was the worst; although he was nearly seventy and should have known better, he was vain, petulant and a classic bully, the exact opposite of his charming son Carey who I'd worked with in Leicester in my late teens. In any room Rex would pick on the weakest person, and during rehearsals for *Monsieur Perrichon* that meant being mean to the assistant stage manager. We were aghast at this, but no one wanted to offend him in case he walked out.

I tried to show my disapproval in ways that wouldn't cause too much offence. 'Can we have that nice Dr Doolittle back, please?' I'd say. But he detected the hostility in my tone however hard I tried to disguise it, and I probably wanted him to anyway.

My outrage was counter-balanced by the enormous respect I had for his talent. His timing was immaculate, his delivery spot on, and there was something classy about his filigree comedy that I'd never have been able to emulate in a million years. His was a tough role – he was on stage for virtually the entire play, whereas I came on at irregular intervals, got a few laughs, then disappeared. Whenever we did a scene together it was a duel, with him subtly expressing his irritation that a young know-it-all was interrupting his flow, while I was signalling 'I can get my laughs too. You can't touch me. I'm as tough as you!'

All this was, of course, kept under wraps in typically British fashion, until a couple of days before his final performance. As was so often the case in those days, I'd been asked to direct the end-of-season revue. It hadn't occurred to me to ask Rex to be in it; why on earth would I want him to be? But Keith, our Artistic Director, suggested it would be a good idea to approach him, and I was happy to let bygones be bygones, so I took him to one side and asked him if he'd sing 'I've Grown Accustomed to Her Face', a song and a performance, I said, that had been iconic for so many of us. He graciously agreed in the way royalty does when bestowing a gift on a commoner, I arranged an accompanist, and thought no more about it.

The next evening, he steamed into my dressing room un-announced, and demanded to know where the sheet music was.

'What sheet music?' I asked bewildered.

'For my song!' he said.

'You don't need sheet music.'

'Don't tell me I don't need sheet music.'

'Haven't you got any?' I retorted. 'What do you want me to do? Drive up to Denmark Street overnight and buy you a copy?'

'I don't care how you do it,' he said, and swept out of the room. 'Get me the sheet music,' he bellowed as he strode down the corridor, 'Or your little party piece will be missing its star turn.'

'You don't need the fucking sheet music,' I yelled back. 'You've been singing the fucking song for twenty fucking years,' and as an elegant *coup de grâce* I added, 'Wanker!'

We played *Monsieur Perrichon* that night with hate in our eyes. I knew I'd blown it. My star had just written himself out of our show.

But I was wrong. He turned up the following night, sang 'I've Grown Accustomed to Her Face' immaculately, and got a standing ovation, even from me. All without sheet music.

That autumn, when we returned to Fred Place, Dave died. He was thirty-four years old. He'd had a medical a couple of years previously because he wanted health insurance, but he'd been turned down. He wasn't sure why, but didn't pursue the matter. Then he got a lump on one ball. From a teenager his testicles had itched. Kate used to tease him about how he always had his hands down his trousers, but he laughed it off. The doctor told him he should have it removed, 'to be on the safe side'. Even after the specialist broke the news that the lump was cancerous, I don't remember any of us being particularly concerned. Lumps got removed, then everything went back to normal; that's why you went to the doctor. But a few months later he got another one. It was on his neck and it was a secondary cancer.

He had chemotherapy and radiotherapy, but it soon became clear that it had spread to his lymph nodes. For the best part of a year he carried on writing plays, he even applied for a teaching job at the university, but then Julia Donaldson and her husband Malcolm came to stay with us, and Malcolm was a doctor. Dave asked him to be candid, and he was. We'd been fooling ourselves with our gung-ho optimism. There was little hope of him surviving long. The cancer carried on spreading, and he got thinner and weaker.

None of us had any experience of being close to a young man who was dying, but it wasn't a maudlin time. Dave was fascinated by what was happening to his body, and although his last few weeks were punctuated by bouts of intense pain, there were always the morphine cocktails to fall back on which he greatly appreciated. We gave him our love, and he gave us his. We were concerned for his wellbeing, and felt protective towards Kate and his parents, but there was a fierceness about our behaviour. It was the most terrible thing that we had ever experienced, but we were going to face it together.

Eventually he couldn't stand up any more, hardly ate, and the cancer entered his lungs. The medical team wanted him to go to the hospital to die, but he adamantly refused to leave Fred Place. In the last few hours the pain became unbearable. It was my turn to be with him along with Tim Munro, our close friend from Avon Touring. Dave was flinging himself round the floor in a vain attempt to ease the agony. We persuaded Kate to let the medics take him to the Bristol Royal Infirmary, although in retrospect I don't know whether we were right to do so. Kate got in the ambulance, Tim and I drove behind. By the time we'd parked up, Kate and Dave had disappeared into its bowels, and when we eventually found where they'd been put, Dave was dead.

Kate and Dave had planned to get married on 30 October 1976. Instead that was the day she signed his death certificate.

It was drizzling on the day of the funeral, the cemetery was muddy underfoot, and a solitary cello was playing. We had multicoloured golf umbrellas to ward off the rain. I read something, Howard spoke and Julia sang. There were cakes and a lot of laughter. Death had always been the big unspoken fear in my life. I'd had no idea how I'd cope with it. But Dave taught me that it was possible to be dignified and concerned for other people even in the grip of terminal pain.

He was a good man, whose socialism was neither angry nor timid. He believed in the dignity of human life, and had a burning conviction that while we can't do much to change the course of the world on our own, together we can move mountains. I wanted to be like him, and missed his friendship and example. I still do.

13

THE TATTOOED LADY

It was easier for me to take on work in London once I'd got a second home there. Mum had hated Hackney, she'd got out of it as soon as she could, and loathed going back there. She tried to make my new flat more genteel by calling it a *pied-à-terre*, but it was actually a bit of a shithole. Dad liked me living there, though, because it had belonged to Grandma Ellen and Grandpa Jack.

At the end of World War One Jack had come home from the trenches. Dad was five, my Uncle Cyril was eight and they hadn't seen him for two years. This strange man walked into their house in his uniform, Grandma Ellen spread some old newspapers on the parlour floor, and he stripped naked. The boys huddled on the settee and watched him as he meticulously wrapped his clothes in the papers, and placed them neatly on the tiny coal fire, where they smouldered and burned until all that was left was a charred black lump. Then he went upstairs to bed, and never mentioned the war again. By the time I knew him he had white hair that smelt of brilliantine. He was charming, funny and wore a slightly vacant smile.

Always the grafter, Grandma Ellen eventually made enough money to buy what became Robinson's Newspapers and Confectionery, and got up at half past four every morning to mark up the papers for the delivery boys. Meanwhile Jack had dabbled in a variety of jobs, but none of them worked out, and eventually Ellen, who usually had a large roll of cash stashed away, bought 138 Amhurst Road, a big run-down house oppos-ite her shop, and set him up in it as a stationery salesman.

When she died, Uncle Cyril took over the shop, and occa-sionally on a Saturday morning Dad would drive me up the Lea Bridge Road to Hackney to see him. Mum never fancied coming with us. Uncle Cyril would give me an enormous brown paper bag and tell me to fill it with all the sweets I wanted. Dad couldn't stand him, but I thought he was great. He and Dad would disappear into another room to talk business, and I'd be left on my own in the little parlour with my bitter lemons, span-gles, blackjacks and flying saucers, surrounded by huge piles of magazines. I read *Reveille*, *Woman's Own*, *Good Housekeeping* and *Amateur Gardening*, but my favourite by far was *Punch*. It was hysterical; a whole magazine devoted to cartoons and funny stories. It was *The Beano* for grown-ups. I didn't under-stand the jokes, but I was fascinated by the way it was written, as though the writers were taking the micky, but so cleverly that no one could possibly tell them off.

Dad and Cyril would eventually finish their business, which I later learnt was Cyril borrowing money off Dad, and Dad making Cyril promise that this time he'd pay it back, then we'd go over the road to see Grandpa Jack.

Amhurst Road had been built in the 1860s when, for a few years, the middle classes had flooded into Hackney with their carriages and parlour maids, and the scruffy old borough had been transformed. This injection of money hadn't lasted long, though, Hackney had reverted to its former shabbiness, and the big houses peeled and crumbled. I'd wander up and down the five draughty storeys of number 138. It was cold and echoey and I thought it was probably haunted. Jack's business never seemed to make any money, but he obviously enjoyed buying stock; every room was piled high with stationery. He'd give us a box of envelopes to take home, but they'd be so old the gum wouldn't stick, and we'd have to fix them down with Sellotape.

Grandpa Jack died in the mid-1950s, and even though I'd

never seen much of him, I missed him. He had a fund of daft stories about his life, and each time he told them they got more exaggerated, a trait he passed down to his grandson. Cyril sold the shop and moved to Essex, and Dad inherited number 138. The stationery business was long gone, and the house was now sub-divided into pokey flats. Dad didn't do much with it. The rent paid for its upkeep and minor renovations, but there was hardly any money left by way of profit. I think he only kept it on for old-times' sake.

But he knew I was growing increasingly unhappy about sleeping on friends' floors every time I came up to London, and when the top flat became vacant he suggested I take it over. He only charged me £6 a week, and when I wasn't there I sub-let it, so even though I was usually pretty broke, I could afford to keep it on. Suddenly a house that had been unloved for the best part of a century became a family project. Mary and I decorated the new flat with blue and white Laura Ashley wallpaper, and spent an entire summer hanging woodchip wallpaper up in the common parts, painting the walls brilliant white, and the bannisters pink, with Fleetwood Mac's *Rumours* playing non-stop as we splashed the Dulux about. The only major problem was the brothel next door. The house constantly reverberated with ska and reggae, and when fights spilled over the wall into our back garden, there were thumps, cries of pain and occasional ominous silences.

Gradually, as the other tenants were driven out by the noise levels and my tasteful colour combinations, my friends moved in: Tim Munro and a few other actors from Avon Touring, left-wing musicians, a gay playwright, a Maoist composer and Gareth, one of the singers from The Flying Pickets. The front doors of the flats were always ajar, and we meandered from one to another drinking vast amounts of tea and complaining about the commercialisation of pop music, the iniquities of Margaret Thatcher, and the pubic hair in the plughole. My heart was still in Bristol, but life in Hackney was buzzy, and even though the public transport wasn't up to much, it didn't matter. I could whizz round London on my Honda 250. I had a metal hoop cemented into the front wall, and chained the bike up at night so it didn't get nicked.

Early one evening after I'd finished rehearsing a radio play at Broadcasting House, I popped back to Amhurst Road to pick up some Equity papers. It didn't seem worth taking off my crash helmet because I was going straight back out again. I bounded up the stairs, my front door ajar as usual, and walked straight through the kitchen into the sitting room and started sorting out the documents laid out on the stripped-pine table. I sensed something, a movement maybe, or perhaps a cough. Christ! Was there someone else in the room? Had I disturbed a burglar? Slowly I took off my helmet and turned round. Standing naked in front of the blazing gas fire, frozen in the act of making love, were Gareth and the girl from the flat below.

'Hullo, Gareth,' I said.

'Hi, Tone,' he replied.

'Hi, Anne.'

'Hullo, Tony,' Anne said.

'I'm just sorting out some papers,' I explained.

'I can see that,' said Gareth.

I put all the documents I needed into little piles, then placed each pile into a separate folder with a rubber band round it, all executed slowly and deliberately in order to demonstrate that I wasn't flustered.

'See you!' I said.

'Bye,' they replied.

'You two look great,' I added, and left the room, discreetly pulling the door shut behind me.

It had been a bit of a shock. I'd never previously seen Gareth and Anne speak to each other, let alone shag each other. But they'd been cool about it, and so had I. You look great! That had been good. They'd been fucking in my front room, for goodness' sake, but I'd shown no resentment about the fact that they were in my place using my gas; I'd merely made a passing appreciative comment about their erotic goings-on. I smiled to myself and continued down the stairs.

Shit! Shit! Shit! I'd left my crash helmet on the table! What was I going to do now, wait for them to finish? Knowing Gareth, I could be twiddling my fingers for another hour and a half. I was supposed to be chairing a meeting in twenty minutes. I made the long ascent back upstairs, and went into my flat, this time knocking on the sitting room door before I entered.

'Hullo!' Gareth called.

'I forgot my er . . .' I called back.

'What?'

'My crash helmet.'

I opened the door. They were in exactly the same position.

'Sorry,' I said. I crossed to the table, picked up my helmet and buckled it up. 'See you.' I turned to go again.

'Perv!' said Gareth.

'What??'

'You wanted to cop another look, didn't you, you little monkey?'

'I didn't, I . . .' but whatever I'd said next, would have appeared to confirm his allegation. I left, and went off to my meeting. From cool to dickhead in thirty seconds – the story of my life.

It was at Amhurst Road that a handful of us did our political planning and plotting. We drafted Equity motions, wrote letters and articles, amended resolutions, and generally made ourselves a pain in the bum of the right-wing council. We were serious and desperately enthusiastic, a bit like the kids in the Enid Blyton stories, except that they weren't socialists in their late twenties. *The Stage* newspaper called us 'The Magnificent Seven', and the name stuck.

But it wasn't just us who were trying to reform the union. A new generation of young actors was emerging who were much more politically engaged than their predecessors. The Equity 'deputies', the nearest thing we had to shop stewards, were particularly militant, so were the chorus at the London Coliseum, the actors in most of the long-running TV series, the performers at the RSC and the National, and virtually everyone who worked in the new small-scale companies, theatre in education and the repertory theatres.

Matters came to a head over the Industrial Relations Act which the Tories had introduced in the wake of the latest outburst of strikes and shutdowns. The act was specifically designed to make effective trade union activity impossible. From now on any union which was prepared to abide by the stipulations of the new law would be given special privileges, while the others would be harried through the courts. Most unions gave two fingers to the government's plans, but Equity's council didn't, and consequently we were thrown out of the Trade Union Congress for failing to hold the line.

This expulsion was the tipping point. We didn't want to be government lackeys; we wanted to fight for better pay and conditions. We started a campaign called CRAPE, possibly the worst acronym ever devised. It stood for the Campaign for Reaffiliation And Progress in Equity – 'Reaffiliation' meant rejoining the TUC, 'Progress' meant kicking out the council and rewriting the union rulebook. I was involved in raising money for the campaign, and soon realised that I'd seriously underestimated the resolve of our nation's senior actors, a lot of whom weren't remotely anti-union. The most talented and innovative actress of her day was Dame Peggy Ashcroft, and she and the comedy actress Miriam Karlin bankrolled us for the first few months, and gave us significant donations for years afterwards. John Alderton and Pauline Collins helped, as did Timothy West, Prunella Scales, and many others. Our campaign was built round the hard work and commitment of unknown jobbing actors, but the fact that some of our major stars put their heads above the parapet gave us status, credibility, and made us newsworthy.

After a two-year battle we won our first victory. A new council was elected, and CRAPE members comprised the majority. They voted to deregister from the government's scheme, our general secretary wrote out a cheque for our TUC subscription, and the Equity office assistant got on his bike, cycled round to Congress House, and delivered it to the TUC general secretary by hand. It had taken a long time, but we'd not only been successful, we'd also eclipsed the Workers' Revolutionary Party as the conscience of the union.

By 1978 I had a new agent. I'd received a tearful telephone call from Penny. New American bosses had taken over at William Morris. Any artist on their books who was no longer seen as potentially profit-making was being released. I'd turned my back on London and a promising career in order to spend my time agitating and working in tiny theatres in the provinces. So Penny was going to have to let me go. It was very painful. She'd been my help-mate and supporter since I'd left drama school. I was bereft without her, and I suspect she felt something similar. It was a sad goodbye on a personal level, but it also meant that the confidence I felt from being part of an international talent agency had been taken away from me.

Kate Feast, my new agent, was the ex-wife of a drama school friend, Mickey Feast. We'd got to know each other when Mickey and I were in a West End Christmas show called *Once Upon a Time*. Mickey had played Tommy Tucker, a young actor called Tim Curry was Jack Frost, and I was 'the Smallest Ogre in the World'. I developed a slow, cockney drawl for the part, which I re-used some years later when I took on the role of a stupid comedy servant on TV. During the run Mickey and I spent long indulgent evenings at Kate's Primrose Hill flat, drinking, smoking, talking bollocks and baby-sitting their daughter Sadie. Then we'd stagger off the following morning to perform the show. It didn't do well, and Tim got a part in a spoof horror show at the Royal Court, so we didn't see much of him after that.

Kate's agency was the polar opposite of William Morris, a single room off Primrose Hill with one assistant. She was scatterbrained and embarrassingly forthright, but was one of the rising stars among theatre agents because of her unerring ability to identify promising young actors. When she recommended you for a part, the casting director listened. At the time I assumed she'd taken me on as a client out of charity rather than because she thought I'd set the British theatre alight. She seemed really surprised whenever I got a good job. After she'd seen me as Feste in *Twelfth Night* at Chichester she said, 'God, Tony, I didn't realise you were that good,' which was flattering, but a typical Kate Feast back-handed compliment.

She became very excited when Brian Gibson, who'd directed *Joey*, asked me if I'd be interested in appearing in his next TV production, a new play by Dennis Potter called *Blue Remembered Hills*. It was a weird piece set in the Forest of Dean in the 1950s, the story of half a dozen seven-year-old children, all of whom were to be played by adults. The script was creepy and I didn't fancy it very much.

'You'd be mad to turn it down whatever you think of it,' Kate said. 'Potter's red-hot, and Helen Mirren's got the lead, so everyone'll watch it.'

Mike Elphick was also in it, as was Robin Ellis, who'd starred in the original version of *Poldark*, and with whom I spent a sublime weekend in Stoke-on-Trent watching The Grateful Dead. Kate was right. A Dennis Potter play performed by this cast was too good an opportunity to miss.

We were based at the BBC's Acton rehearsal rooms, ironically known as 'The Acton Hilton', a small tower block comprising fifteen or so barn-like rooms in which the current run of TV plays and variety shows were being rehearsed. The top floor was a large canteen. Whenever I ate there, I felt as though I was at the very centre of the entertainment world. All the top performers of the moment would be on show. One day I was in the lunch queue waiting for cod and chips, and standing next to me was Victoria Wood. 'Why couldn't you and I play Romeo and Juliet?' she asked rhetorically. 'Only because I'm too fat, and you're too small. It's ridiculous. You don't have to be gorgeous to cop off with someone over a balcony, do you?'

On the third day of rehearsals the *Blue Remembered Hills* company were sitting at a long table covered in scripts drinking tea. Helen Mirren had a tiny tattoo on her hand between her thumb and forefinger.

'What's that?' I asked.

She put her hand on mine so I could see the blue squiggle more clearly, and replied, 'I picked it up in a brothel in Marseilles.'

I'd no idea if she was winding me up, but I didn't care. I nodded wisely and held on to her hand as long as I thought I could without appearing weird.

I was enjoying being surrounded by so many top-class actors, but I was struggling. I was playing the part of Donald, an abused boy who's eventually burnt to death in a barn because the other children don't like him and won't let him out when it catches fire. But I felt I was being encouraged to portray him as an unpleasant person, rather than simply playing the character and letting the audience come to their own conclusions. Brian took me to one side.

'We're going to have to let you go,' he said euphemistically. 'It's entirely my fault. The casting's wrong. You're too sympathetic.'

It was *Softly, Softly* all over again, except this time I'd been fired in front of my friends, actors I desperately admired. As for the accusation that I was sympathetic, it was ridiculous. I knew what I was like in real life – an absolute bastard; selfish, manipulative, controlling; what were they talking about!

In retrospect Brian was right. Colin Jeavons, who took over the part, was far better than I would ever have been, but it took me a quarter of a century to be able to face up to that fact. Even today if someone mentions *Blue Remembered Hills*, I feel a bit sick.

When I'd left Chichester I already knew I'd be back the following year. Keith and I had discussed the fact that there were a lot of talented young actors in the company who had nothing to do once the main-house plays were on, and were ambitious and eager to work. If we put on fringe shows utilising their skills, we could make the Festival Theatre feel much more community-orientated, rather than simply a watering hole for London audiences. I had the experience and the commitment, now he'd found me a budget, and he'd appointed me production associate in charge of 'Chichester New Ventures', twenty or so different events to be put on alongside the company's four main-house productions.

I hired the upstairs room of a pub called the Dolphin and Anchor in the middle of town and we played two shows every night, the second of which started at 10.30 p.m. so the audiences from the Festival Theatre could stop by and see it before they went home. We also put on street theatre, a play in Chichester Cathedral, poetry evenings at the prisons along the south coast, and Saturday morning story times for tiny children in Chichester library.

Anyone in the company who had a project they'd like to try out was welcome to join us. My only stipulation was that if, after a few days, their idea wasn't working, they should move on to something else. In fact, nothing was ever rejected, although there were a few close calls. A junior actress called Roberta Symes had the idea of using live actors to perform the

Happy years at Fred Place, Clifton, Bristol

Below: Dave, Kate and baby Huw.

Christmas 1973. Back row L–R: Sue, Kate; front row L–R: me, Dave, Mary and baby Hannah.

Right: Howard and Hannah.

Above L–R: Hannah, Mary, me and Laura.

Right: Outside the house loading up for a summer holiday in the Dordogne.

First read-through
of the Avon Touring
Theatre Company.
L–R: Tim Munro,
Chris Harris and me.

Avon Touring.
Howard Goorney,
a stalwart of Joan
Littlewood's famous
Theatre Workshop.

Avon Touring.
L–R: Tim Fearon, me,
Tim Munro, John David.

Mary and me.

Brannigan with John Wayne. I'm the one in the water.

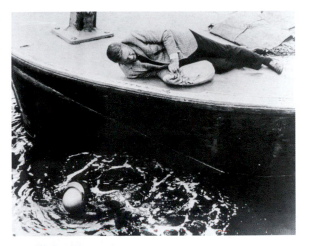

Little Hopping Robin, Almost Free Theatre. Bottom left: me; top left: Bruce Purchase; top right: Malcolm Ingram; bottom right: Margaret Ford.

Showing off my newly waxed body in *Made in Heaven* at the Chichester Festival Theatre, 1975.

With Rex Harrison in *Monsieur Perrichon's Travels* at the Chichester Festival Theatre, 1976.

Highams Park, Chingford. With Laura and Luke in the garden at Mary's mum's house.

With neighbours on the green between Glendale and The Polygon, Clifton. Taken by the celebrated photographer Martin Parr from his front garden.

The cast of the *Oresteia* at the National Theatre.
I'm the short one second from the left.

In the giant amphitheatre at Epidaurus, Greece.

Who Dares Wins – The Pilot, including: far left Denise O'Donoghue (producer), second-left Guy Jenkin (writer) and third-left Andy Hamilton (writer/producer). Bottom right is pilot cast member Brenda Blethyn, who was unavailable for the later series.

Talking about books to a Bristol primary school class, assisted by Luke and Laura.

Odysseus: The Greatest Hero of Them All, shot on the Cornish coast.

The *Who Dares Wins* team. Front row L–R: Jimmy Mulville, Rory McGrath; back row L-R: Julia Hills, Phil Pope and me.

The Black Adder 1983 – Tim, me and Rowan. Presumably this is a rehearsal as I'm still wearing my glasses!

Maid Marian and Her Merry Men. Messing around on set with my mates David Lloyd (to the right), and Mark Billingham (hidden behind me).

Kate Lonergan as Maid Marian, me as the Sheriff of Nottingham and Wayne Morris as Robin Hood.

Mr Robinson,

There is enough muck on TV,-violence, sex and bad language. We understood you wish to have decent entertainments for children, but "Robin Hood" is absolutely disgusting and you are rotten in it! An extremely bad example, especially for children.

Also, the English Programme was smutty, stupid, miserable and boring.

It's a great pity and terrifying that beauty and decency in life is fading away.

                    Five mothers
                    for many others.

A *Maid Marian* fan letter!

text of a *Punch and Judy* show. After a few days of rehearsals it looked like it would be a complete disaster. But we kept working on it, and it became one of the highlights of the season. The evening would begin with a traditional puppet show, then the doors of the puppet booth would creak open, and out would shuffle our actors dressed as Punch, Judy, the policeman, the baby and the rest. It had become a play about brutality, infanticide and arbitrary violence. It was chilling, and great theatre.

To make my employment cost effective, I still had to be part of the main-house company. Unfortunately that meant being in a play by George Bernard Shaw. A lot of people love Shaw – in the first half of the twentieth century he was the most popular playwright in Britain – but I found his work unspeakably dull, his characters two-dimensional, and his dialogue and politics shallow and pretentious. *Pygmalion* has its moments, as does *Arms and the Man*, but *The Apple Cart*, which we put on that summer, is unremitting twaddle. It seemed to me the only reason it was still performed was that its central character, a king who talked non-stop throughout the entire play, was the perfect part for a leading man who wanted to strut his stuff. And as this was Keith's final year as artistic director, he duly strutted.

He obviously found playing King Magnus enormous fun, although I suspect it was slightly less enjoyable for the audience, and for me it was sheer torture. My role was as Britain's foreign secretary. This involved me sitting at the Number 10 cabinet table contributing one line every two or three pages, while looking enraptured by the stream of Shavian wit which poured forth from our leading man. To while away the time I tried playing chess in my head, doing crossword puzzles, and attempting to remember the previous Saturday's football scores. At the end of each evening my brain would be throbbing from the effort of trying to look interested for so long, but it didn't work. Nicholas de Jongh's review in the *Guardian* was excoriating: 'Tony Robinson looked as bored as I felt,' he wrote. I seldom thought much of de Jongh's theatre criticism, but he got that one right.

A couple of days before the season ended, Keith stopped me in a corridor, put his arm round me, steered me into my dressing room, and discreetly pulled the door shut.

'How would you feel,' he said softly, 'about a trip to Australia?'

'What? When?' I replied. 'For how long?'

'I'm going back home, I'd like to take some of the company out there on tour, and it would be good if you came.'

'Fine,' I said. 'Thanks. I'm touched. Count me in.'

'I'm going to be playing Othello, and I'd like you to be—'

'Roderigo?' It was the only funny part in an otherwise bleak play.

'Exactly. And given how well it's been received' – there was a look on his face that unnerved me a little – 'I thought I'd do *The Apple Cart* too.'

Well received? Didn't he read the papers? And as for *Othello*, was that really a play in which Keith would shine?

'The icing on the cake is that before we go, the Saville Theatre would like us to take *The Apple Cart* into the West End for ten whole weeks! That'll be exciting, won't it?'

Fuuuuuuuuuuck! I thought. 'Great!' I said.

Two weeks in Brisbane, Melbourne, Perth and Adelaide, and a month in Sydney; the Australian tour was the stuff of my dreams, but it also confirmed my worst fears. The press hated us. *The Adelaide Advertiser* called the shows 'an uphill struggle', *The Australian* said ours was 'a standard of achievement that theatre companies in Australia would find easy to equal; indeed several would find the much-vaunted Chichester easy to surpass'. And the *Weekend Mail* said of Keith's Othello, 'Michell plays the dull Moor so literally it is difficult to feel any sympathy for the blacked-up goon.' Ouch!

But the weather was balmy, the beaches were appropriately sun-kissed, the locals overwhelmingly hospitable, and we had plenty of time off for exploring. Mary and Laura had come along too so, apart from the evenings spent pretending to be spellbound by Shaw's self-regarding nonsense, it was a family holiday.

Michael Edgley, the producer who'd brought us to Australia, lived in Perth. He'd made a fortune touring the Moscow State Circus south of the equator and his profits had bought him a luxurious mansion on a vantage point overlooking the Swan River. After our first night, the entire Chichester cast was invited there for a barbeque.

We piled out of the stage door, clambered into his air-conditioned coach, and when we approached the grand house the gates opened automatically. None of us had ever seen technology like that before. Every room had sliding doors leading out to the garden, and full-length cotton curtains that billowed in the antipodean breeze. There were massive televisions with swivelling brackets fixed to the walls, and Miles Davis's *Bitches Brew* whined and groaned from a phalanx of gigantic black speakers. Round the pool, tall, tanned Australian women in bikinis were shrieking with laughter as they played with a large inflatable ball.

Laura had been deposited in a magnificently appointed children's playroom. I wandered into the garden, which was tiered in terraces down to the river. Hidden behind a stand of gum trees I found the Australian stage management team, long-haired and wall-eyed.

'Do you want a toke?' asked the sound guy, who was skinny and wore the same pink and orange T-shirt every day.

'No thanks, I—'

'Come on, man,' he said. 'It's Western Australian, the best in the world.'

'I . . .'

'You've never experienced anything like it . . . ever!'

He was right . . . I never had.

On another terrace I was offered a glass of Australian wine. I hadn't ever heard the words 'wine' and 'Australian' in the same sentence before. It went down ridiculously well, as did the next few glasses.

I was hungry, and could smell something delicious. I followed its scent like a wobbly legged bloodhound, and eventually came to a terrace on which a barbeque was glowing. Only two of us were there, me and a flunky in a white shirt, black bow tie, and neatly pressed shorts with a knife-edged crease. He beckoned me over with his large two-pronged fork, presented me with a plate, and put a bun and a burger on it, followed by chicken, pork, two sausages, a couple of slices of bacon and a pair of lamb kidneys. He offered me some salad too, but I declined.

Sometime later Mary found me sitting cross-legged under a bush. The plate had been licked clean. A few gnawed bones were scattered on the ground. The lower half of my face was smeared with grease and tomato sauce.

'Tony,' she said, 'you're a vegetarian!'

It seemed I wasn't any longer.

I became fascinated by Australia, a place that in less than two hundred years had transformed itself from half a dozen godforsaken convict colonies separated by huge burning deserts into one of the most successful and prosperous countries in the world. It began an intense relationship between me and the continent which continues to this day.

When the tour ended, Mary and I flew to New Zealand to stay with her brother Mike, a geographer, or more correctly a geomorphologist, at Massey University on North Island. He taught me about continental drift, and the twenty-seven fractured tectonic plates that comprise the earth's surface. He showed me the massive mountains and fiery volcanoes that were a direct result of the constant bumping and grinding created by these plates when they collide or pull away from each other. I'd had no idea about any of this, and didn't know anyone else who did, but it was extraordinary information, which I felt everyone should be able to share. The Australian economy, volcanoes and earthquakes, Ancient Greek theatre, archaeology; they were all so exciting, and yet were only talked about by tiny academic coteries in a language designed to exclude anyone else from understanding them. When the BBC had been set up in the 1920s, its boss John Reith had said its duty was to educate and entertain, but somehow most people in TV seemed to have forgotten the first of those aspirations. But this combination of education and entertainment was very important to me; indeed it was becoming a moral and political imperative. Although as a Bristol-based actor with four O-levels heading for another bout of unemployment, there wasn't much I could do about it!

In 1979, after several failed attempts, I was finally elected onto the Equity council. My election statement had been uncompromising. I'd demanded root and branch reform of the union, more support for black, gay and women workers, and a big pay rise for performers and stage management. But it wasn't the force of my rhetoric or the quality of my radicalism that had attracted thousands of voters to my politics. No one else had wanted to represent the south-west, so I was elected unopposed.

There were only eight CRAPE members on the new sixty-strong council; all the rest belonged to 'Act for Equity', a faction recently created by the Conservatives, ostensibly to drive the Workers' Revolutionary Party out of Equity, but in practice to clamp down hard on anyone who wanted it to become a proper

union. Looking round the big Harley Street council room where
we had our monthly meeting was a surreal experience. The
familiar, haughty faces opposite me belonged to medical con-
sultants, senior judges, successful businessmen, and senior
army officers – but not real ones. These were the actors who
depicted the upper echelons of society on stage and screen.
Most of them weren't really posh, they were from lower-middle-
class families, and had spent years in damp south London
bedsits scraping a living before their stern demeanour had
made their fortunes. But they'd grown to believe that they were
the characters they played, had joined the Garrick Club, and
had established the right contacts. They weren't very bright;
when they made speeches it was with a dull, plodding formality
or a whine laced with sarcasm. But they had a blinkered single-
mindedness which made them politically effective. We few
oppositionists huddled together on the receiving end of their
dreary invective, but we gave as good as we got, even though
we never won a vote. My greatest ally was Sue Johnston, the
councillor for northern England. Either she or I would propose
an amendment to the latest Act for Equity motion, and the
other would second it. Our speeches would be punctuated by
tuts of disapproval, and the occasional braying laugh from
Kenneth Williams, the right-wing's pet clown. We'd sit down to
stony silence.

Leonard Rossiter was often seated to my right. 'God, you're
fucking boring,' he'd hiss. At first I thought he was probably
right, and castigated myself for not being a more effective
speaker, but Sue and the others bolstered my confidence, and I
developed a resilience which I've never completely lost.

Even though I was part of a tiny minority, the staff encouraged me to get involved in the union's work. I sat on tribunals,
helped redraft contracts, and learnt how to be a negotiator,
attempting to prise better deals from the various theatrical
managements. I enjoyed this; it was deadly serious, but we
played it like a game.

Dancers in the provinces had complained to us that when they were on tour the work was so tough that if they got injured they didn't have time to recover. They wanted each dance troupe to include a 'swing', an understudy who knew everyone's steps, and could take over at a moment's notice.

Predictably the employers had resisted, but we were determined to get a result. We'd already spent three days negotiating the new contract but, even though it had been on the original list of demands, swings hadn't been mentioned. The final day had been a long one, and when we eventually reached agreement on the very last sentence of the very last paragraph everyone was exhausted. The managers put their jackets back on, and started cramming their papers in their briefcases. A few goodbyes were said, and hands shaken. This was my pre-arranged moment to strike.

'Sorry! Sorry!' I said. 'Before we go, there's just one point we haven't sorted out. Sub-section 7C, swings.'

The theatre managers groaned. 'For Christ's sake,' one of them said. 'Why didn't you raise that this morning?'

I ignored him. 'I know you've got issues with 7C,' I said, 'and I think this might take a bit of time. So I suggest we recess for a five-minute toilet break and maybe phone home. I'm happy to go and order pizzas.' The other Equity negotiators agreed and we started compiling a list of Napoletanas, Capreses and the like. The employers looked as though a flock of albatrosses had shat on them.

The recess didn't last five minutes. Two minutes in our general secretary whispered to me, 'We've won. They've given in on 7C.' I screwed up the uncompleted pizza order.

The meeting ended, our side went down the Two Brewers in Monmouth Street, and we all got triumphantly pissed.

14

THE SHORT-SIGHTED SOUTH AFRICAN

In a few hours I'd find out if my life had been transformed forever. ITV had said they'd decide in a couple of months, and that was exactly eight weeks previously. The augurs were good: *Good Morning, Campus* was funny, the premise, about a university lecturer, played by me, who discovers his ex-wife is his new boss, was strong, and it had been produced by Humphrey Barclay who had a reputation for developing successful half-hour comedies like *Doctor in the House* and *Two's Company*.

It hadn't been a smooth ride. There'd been a strike at London Weekend Television, so we hadn't been able to shoot the film inserts, the set was half finished, and we'd only been allowed a small studio audience because so many of the security staff had refused to cross the picket line. But none of that mattered. If the decision-makers knew anything at all about comedy, they'd be able to see our pilot deserved to become a series.

Mary and I had taken the kids to the Kent coast for a week's holiday. It was sunny but cold, and the bungalow didn't have a phone, so I'd have to walk into Deal to make the call. I wasn't sure what time to ring, but I felt cautiously optimistic. The fact that LWT hadn't been in touch during the previous few weeks was a good sign – we were obviously still under consideration. My bet was that there were two shows in the frame for one slot, and they were taking the decision down to the wire. Even now Humphrey was probably running the best bits past the programme controller, and explaining how it would have been even

funnier if there'd been more people available to do the laughing.
I'd leave that call for a while.

At half past four I cracked, phoned LWT, and asked for
Humphrey. 'He's on holiday in New York,' said his PA. That was
a bit of a shock.

'I don't suppose you know anything about *Good Morning,
Campus*?' I asked.

'What's *Good Morning, Campus*?'

'The comedy pilot with Tony Robinson.'

'Who?'

'Do we know if it's got the green light?'

'Hang on, I'll find out.'

I waited an age, every couple of minutes feeding more coins
into the slot. Shortly before I ran out of change she came back.

'Sorry. It was knocked on the head weeks ago. Who are you
again?'

'Tony Robinson.'

'Oh, sorry! Didn't anyone tell you? Ever so sorry.'

The wind had picked up, the sun had disappeared behind a
bank of clouds, and I hadn't brought a coat. Half an hour before,
the Kent landscape had looked like a painting by Constable.
Now it reminded me of that scene in *Great Expectations* where
the scary convict looms out of the gloom and scares the shit out
of little Pip.

Not again! I thought, as I trudged back towards the bungalow. *Not a-bloody-gain!* How many comedy pilots had I made
now? A remake of *The Rag Trade*, one where Thora Hird was in
charge of a bunch of lovable young tearaways and I was the
little nerd; another about a vets' practice; a territorial army one
. . . And there were all the other potential breaks that had come
to nothing. I'd done two episodes of *Doctor at Large* and everyone had said I was bound to become a regular character, but
I hadn't. I'd got down to the final two for the lead in a series
about a cocktail bar, but at the last moment, they'd gone for the
more commercial talents of Richard Beckinsale. It wasn't that

I wanted fame and fortune; well, maybe I did a bit, but it wasn't my prime motivation. The fact was that if people knew who I was, I'd be more likely to get my own projects away, just like writing to prison governors on Chichester Festival Theatre notepaper had got me and my fellow performers into their nicks to perform poetry to the lifers. Or maybe I was kidding myself. Perhaps deep down I'd never lost the ambition I'd had as a child actor. Perhaps I really was driven by a desire to be famous, in which case it served me right if my career had turned to shit.

But I had to snap out of this stew of self-pity. I had a lot to be thankful for. For a start there was Luke. When Mary had got pregnant again, I'd panicked. I'd thought I wouldn't be able to love the new baby enough. I was so besotted by Laura, there couldn't possibly be room for double that amount of love. But on 30 June 1979 he came into the world, I looked into his eyes, and immediately everything was all right. We'd be best friends, I'd take him to watch City play on Saturdays, he'd get a bit weird when he was about fourteen but it wouldn't last long, he'd go to uni and spend three years lying on a sofa watching *Neighbours*, drinking lager and sleeping with dodgy girls, he'd go to prison for a couple of years, he'd get a good job, meet a stormingly beautiful woman, and give me grandchildren who I'd love as much as I'd loved him. And, apart from the prison bit, that's pretty much what happened.

I'd also become a kingpin, or at least a princepin, of small-scale theatrical life in the south-west. Every year or so I directed a show for one of the local professional theatre groups. I was vice-chair of the South-West Arts Drama Panel which handed out Arts Council grants, so I travelled all over Devon, Somerset, Gloucestershire, Wiltshire and Cornwall making financial recommendations about the various companies touring there, I was serving a second term as the south-west Equity councillor, and I'd got involved with the Labour Party, first in my branch, and later at constituency and city level.

At the time a group of Trots was trying to take over the

Labour Party. They were called Militant, and were similar to the Workers' Revolutionary Party, but without the fashion sense.

Their politics were even weirder than their clothes. Their strategy went something like this:

1. The Labour party is rubbish.
2. We'll pretend it isn't rubbish, and we'll join it. (This policy was known as entryism and the various Trotskyist groupings argued long and fiercely about whether or not it was a good idea.)
3. We'll meet in secret to ensure Labour promises to do lots of impossible things like nationalising the top hundred companies without compensation and under workers' control. (Trots called these promises 'transitional demands'. They liked the word 'demands'. It conjures up a picture of an angry customer banging his fist on a shop counter because he isn't being served quickly enough.)
4. The voters will love these demands and will vote Labour into power.
5. Labour won't be able to deliver on its promises.
6. The voters will kick Labour out in disgust and start a revolution.
7. We'll rip off our Labour Party disguises and say to the voters, 'Ha ha! We're the revolutionary leadership, so now we will lead you.'
8. The voters will say, 'That's great!' Britain will become a socialist state, all the countries of the world will do the same thing, there'll be world peace and everyone will get a free puppy.

Militant supporters would probably say I'm being simplistic (actually they'd say I'm being 'reductive', which is pretty much the same thing), But I don't think I am. I'd got no beef with Leon Trotsky. He was one of the great political thinkers of the early twentieth century, and not all Trots were bonkers. I'd worked in Equity with members of the International Marxist

Group for years, and always found them friendly and honourable. The problem with most of the Militants I met was that they were dishonest bullies, and put their faction's interests ahead of the party they pretended to support. They had to be stopped.

Neal Lawson was a young researcher for the Transport and General Workers' Union who lived in Bristol West, the same constituency as me. Whenever Militant members reared their shaggy heads, we'd be on to them straight away. If they attempted to pack a meeting with their supporters, we'd phone round and bring enough of our own people to vote them down. If they tried to get into positions of influence, we'd argue against them and put up our own candidates. Some people might say we were as bad as they were, a charge which can't be completely refuted. That's the trouble with dirty politics: it taints everybody, even those who are trying to clean it up.

The Labour members who took on Militant in Liverpool had to combat political heavyweights. All we had to deal with were a few nut jobs, and maybe we had no effect on them at all. But after a year or so they disappeared from Bristol.

Neal became an adviser to Gordon Brown and is now one of the most interesting and controversial commentators on Labour Party politics. Whenever we meet, we catch each other's eye, and there's a slight swagger in our step as though we're Wyatt Earp and Doc Holliday remembering the moment when we shot the Clancy Brothers in the O.K. Corral. 'Back in the day, we took on Militant, and won!' the look seems to say, even if our opponents were only a few weirdos with beards, beige short-sleeved shirts, and corduroy jackets.

Peter Hall was a round, balding man in his early fifties, with a little beard, and eyes that were both friendly and ruthless. He encouraged banter in his rehearsals, but you never had a moment's doubt who was boss.

He ran the National Theatre, and for a long time had nurtured the ambition to direct the *Oresteia*, a Greek tragedy by the fifth-century BCE playwright Aeschylus. It was a massive piece, three plays in one, with a running time of just under five hours. To put it on in the main house of the National would be horribly expensive, so he wanted to be absolutely confident that the ingredients were right before rehearsals began. The poet Tony Harrison had written a draft script for him, an impressive piece of writing in thundering, rolling, Yorkshire-accented English. But it would need to be properly tested before it hit the stage in order to establish which parts worked and which would need to be rewritten. A dozen actors were asked to take part in these workshops, and I was one of them. Previously I might have declined as there was no guarantee of a proper job at the end of it, but it meant working for one of the greatest theatre companies in the world, and the experimentation might be fun so, now I had my lovely London flat, I was happy to sign up.

One difference between us and Ancient Greek actors was that they wore masks. Should we? What exactly were masks for? We weren't entirely sure. One afternoon I put on a grey, ragged dress from the rack of rehearsal clothes, pulled a mask on, and covered my head with more rags so its outside edges wouldn't be visible. I was Cassandra, the Trojan princess and prophetess who'd been enslaved by the Greek king, Agamemnon. I sat hunched, a young woman with a white staring face, and told my story. I hadn't planned the words I'd use, I'd wanted them to tumble out of my mouth like someone looking through a window and describing a car crash. I was like Claire Bloom in *Look Back in Anger*; fiery, tragic, independent, and very sexy, even in the depths of despair.

When I took my mask off again, I burst into tears. I wasn't feeling particularly sad. It was as though the energy pent up behind it had broken like a dam overwhelmed by a flood.

*

I had another significant storytelling experience during those few months. I was asked to perform my one-man show *The Third Nam* as one of the National's 'Platform' performances. I'd already played it at the Edinburgh Festival in 1980 and had won the Festival Times Solo Award, but was pleased it was going to be on at the National, even though Platform shows were performed in the early evenings before the main productions began, usually in front of less than a hundred people.

The Third Nam was a confidence trick. I'd devised it in Bristol with a friend called Bill Stair who as a young man had worked as a scriptwriter in Hollywood. But he'd hated the brittle vulgarity of Los Angeles life, had fled back to the West Country, and was now buried away lecturing in film at Newport College. He was a brilliant but fragile man, obsessed by the work of Orson Welles.

Seven minutes after the curtain was due to rise, with the audience growing a little restless, I would appear in a suit and tie, introduce myself as the company manager and explain that *The Third Nam* was an elaborate production, a version of *The Third Man* set in present-day Vietnam, but unfortunately the actors, costumes and set had failed to arrive, so would everyone mind being patient for a few moments longer while I tried to establish their whereabouts. I'd return a couple of minutes later to say I'd been unable to contact them, but would be happy to give the audience a rundown of what they would have seen had the performers been there. I'd then proceed to do just that, describing the scenery, the characters' costumes and their dialogue, complete with impersonations of their voices and accents.

But gradually the play would suck my character into it, so that by the end I was no longer the company manager, I was someone trapped inside a play. It was an ideal piece for the Cottesloe, an intimate venue with a theatrically sophisticated audience. What made it particularly bizarre was that behind me was the set for that night's play, a Dublin pub at the turn of the twentieth century, a ridiculously inappropriate backdrop.

The first night went well, but halfway through the second night there was a series of irritating little sounds behind me. Someone was pottering around at the back of the stage. It was Yvonne Bryceland, a celebrated South African actress who was taking part in the *Oresteia* workshops, but was also in the current Cottesloe show.

'Hi, Tony,' she said. 'Warming up?'

'No,' I replied. 'Not really.'

'Rehearsing something?'

'No, no,' I said.

She was as blind as a bat. She had no idea she was facing an audience of nearly a hundred people.

'How about you?' I asked.

'Just setting up.'

'Setting up . . . ?'

'My props. For tonight. I'm in the Synge play.'

The audience didn't seem perturbed. *The Third Nam* was a play about surprises. Why shouldn't the appearance of a celebrated actress be another one.

'You enjoying the workshops?' she asked, as she busied herself with her props.

'Yeah. They're fascinating,' I said. 'Listen, I can't stay gossiping. I'm having a chat with the audience.'

'Wha . . . ?' she began. 'You're . . .'

She fumbled in her bag and pulled out her glasses. The lenses were as thick as submarine portholes.

'Yes, I'm doing a play right now. The rest of the cast haven't turned up and I'm just explaining . . .'

She peered at me myopically, then slowly turned and saw the audience.

'Oh my God! I'm so sorry. I didn't . . . Tony, I'm so sorry.'

The audience fell about. She'd just given the most convincing comic performance ever of an innocent actress who's walked into someone else's play.

'It's not a problem,' I said. 'Do you want to stay and help me?'

'What? No. Oh my God, no. I'm so sorry,' and she began to flee. 'I'm so sorry,' she hissed again as she disappeared into the wings.

'Ladies and gentlemen,' I announced, 'Yvonne Bryceland.'

The audience clapped long and hard.

Yvonne was, like most actors, a bit of a tart, and when she heard the applause, she came back on stage again and took an exaggerated bow. I hugged her, and we gave each other a pair of actory air kisses. She whispered, 'I'm so—'

'Yes, I know,' I whispered back, 'now fuck off!' and I carried on with the play.

Working on the *Oresteia* was fascinating. Every day we were asking ourselves what a play is, how plays began and why, and what their original audience expected from them, questions I'd never asked myself in my quarter of a century as an actor. But it soon became apparent that Peter Hall was dangling a carrot: if we could discover a viable way of making the play work, Tony Harrison would rewrite it, and we'd be invited to be involved in putting on the actual *Oresteia* in a few months' time.

At the end of the workshops we felt positive. We'd gelled as a group, composer Harrison Birtwistle had created some weirdly wonderful plinky-plonky music for us, Tony Harrison was confident about the direction in which his translation was heading, and Peter was smiling like the Buddha on LSD. The *Oresteia* workshops seemed to have been that rare thing: a pilot that had paid off.

No it hadn't. A month later I got a letter from Peter saying,

> *Dear Tony,*
>   *A letter I had written to you, long overdue, was*
> *returned to my office last week. It had sat at the stage*

door for a while and had already missed you. The text of the letter expressed my gratitude for the work you did on the Oresteia *and my sorrow that finally it came to naught because of having to replan this year after our heavy losses . . .*

  Yours ever,
      Peter

It had happened again! I was like some tortured character in a Greek myth, cursed to push my career uphill time after time, only for it to slip out of my hands at the last minute, and go crashing back down to the bloody bottom again.

Although maybe not. I was pottering around the Fred Place basement one morning when I heard a thunk upstairs. On the doormat was a big brown envelope with a blue and white coat of arms on the address label. I knew immediately what it was by its shape and weight. I opened it. Yes, it was a BBC script, and paperclipped to it was a brief letter. Apparently a pilot episode of a new comedy series was about to be mounted – oh blimey, not this again! – it was to star Rowan Atkinson, and would I like to play the part of the comedy servant? Rehearsals were to begin the following Monday, so a swift response would be appreciated. How had this happened? Nobody ever offered me a job on TV without interviewing me at least twice and then making me read the part in front of a phalanx of producers.

I flicked through the pages. It took some time before I found the role they'd mentioned. Baldrick only had about eight lines, and none of them was funny. As for the script itself, it wasn't much better. There were lots of nearly-jokes in it, but nothing that made me jackknife with hysteria. And as for the fact that rehearsals were due to start in five days' time, I knew what that meant: a dozen Equity members had turned the part down already, and the producer was getting desperate.

Should I take the job? I'd got no other work coming up, and it would get me out of the house for a bit. But it wasn't a rib-tickler, and knowing my luck it wouldn't lead anywhere. I picked up the phone, and put in a call to Kate Feast.

On the train to London early the following Monday morning I was feeling a bit more positive. I'd always wanted to be in one of these so-called 'Oxbridge' TV comedies ever since I'd first seen *That Was the Week That Was* as a teenager in the 1960s. It had been brilliant – as funny as *The Goon Show* but as satirical as George Orwell or Jonathan Swift. I couldn't believe anything so dazzlingly modern could be on my television set week after week. It had been produced by Ned Sherrin and starred among others David Frost, Millicent Martin, Willie Rushton and Roy Kinnear. The establishment hated it and wanted it banned, but we loved it. At teenage parties when the shout went out that *TW3* was on, couples would hot-foot it out of the bedroom to make sure they hadn't missed anything. It was unlike anything else on TV, and all my early sketch writing had been a pale tribute to it.

In the years that followed there were a host of other TV shows starring the bright young turks from the Cambridge Footlights and the Oxford University Dramatic Society. Peter Cook and Dudley Moore became world-famous, John Bird and John Fortune wrote countless series starring yet more talented Oxbridge graduates, and eventually John Cleese, Michael Palin and the rest created the sublime *Monty Python's Flying Circus*. I'd have cut off any nominated limb to be given the chance to work with them. I had a fantasy that if I ever did, they'd recognise me as a fellow spirit who had something to contribute. They'd become my friends, and we'd write sketches together, go to the pub together, crack jokes and talk in funny voices about sex and people with amusing names. But I hadn't been to a posh public school like them, let alone Oxford or Cambridge. I didn't even have any A-levels, so although I'd written countless letters offering my services, no response had ever been forth-coming.

The latest Oxbridge incarnation had been *Not the Nine O'Clock News*, directed by John Lloyd, who'd worked on some of the most sophisticated radio comedy shows around, like *The Hitchhiker's Guide to the Galaxy*, and its big star had been Rowan Atkinson. I was in my mid-thirties now, I'd long given up hope of working with bright young Oxbridge things – the new wave were all at least ten years younger than me. But now extraordinarily late in the day, the opportunity seemed to have presented itself. I should seize it with both hands, even if it was only eight lines' worth of opportunity.

The rehearsals were as stimulating as I'd always fantasised such rehearsals would be. The jokes weren't any funnier, and the plot, about a stupid prince who gets into complex vaguely humorous scrapes, was deeply obscure, particularly as it was set in some vague moment of history that nobody knew any-thing about because it had never actually existed! But there was boundless creative energy flying about, and any sugges-tions I made were treated seriously even though I'd never met any of the other participants before, while they all seemed to be best mates. I fell under the spell of Rowan Atkinson's rapier-like wit and enjoyed setting up gags for him because his timing was so good. I hadn't worked with such a fine comedian since my time with Rex Harrison, but whereas Rex had been a crea-ture from a different theatrical universe, Rowan and I were kindred spirits. Richard Curtis, his co-writer, was warm and friendly, as were producer John Lloyd and Tim McInnerny who played Rowan's other sidekick, Percy, the idiotic Duke of Northumberland. I felt I was part of a comedy team, and that even though this unpromising show was unlikely to take off, I might get to work with these people again.

The mystery of why I'd been chosen for the part was resolved at the Thursday technical rehearsal. The BBC's head of comedy, John Howard Davies, who decades previously had played Oliver alongside Tony Newley's Artful Dodger in the film *Oliver Twist*, came to talk to John Lloyd about some internal problem. At the coffee break he came over to me. He was middle-aged, but still looked a bit like Oliver Twist, pale and thin and far too sincere to be a senior TV executive.

'How are you getting on?' he asked me.

'Fine, I think,' I said.

'I thought you would be. I spotted you in that comedy we made in Bristol last year. You played a jockey, right?'

'Yes,' I replied.

'I wrote you down in my little notebook,' he said. 'Small and funny – and you certainly are.'

I was flattered that he'd thought my performance in *Big Jim and the Figaro Club* had been worthy of note, particularly as I'd only been in one episode, but I was a little sad too. I'd hoped that Rowan and his mates had somehow become aware of my work, and had decided they'd like me to be in their gang. Never mind, perhaps they'd warm to me over the next few days.

But the following morning, as it had so relentlessly over the previous few years, disaster struck, and I understood why we'd been visited by the head of comedy. An apologetic John Lloyd announced that due to industrial action at the BBC, we wouldn't be able to record the show, and it would be shelved until further notice. We said our goodbyes in a daze, and I was back in Bristol by lunchtime. I don't remember being upset – I was used to this kind of disappointment by now; in fact, I'd half expected it. But I'd miss my fellow actors. I'd felt special being part of their confident, inventive world. Now I was just another unknown actor again, fast approaching middle age.

There was a silver lining, though. Peter Hall had found the money to put on a full-scale production of the *Oresteia* after all. There was to be another long rehearsal process, followed by nine months of performances in the Olivier Theatre. I signed what amounted to a whole year's contract – the longest piece of acting work I'd ever been offered.

A few weeks later Kate was asked if I was available to record the remounted pilot of *The Black Adder*, and she had to say no. John Lloyd told her he was sorry, but they'd have to go ahead without me, so that was that. My chance of working with that remarkable bunch of comedians had apparently gone forever.

15

SEEING STARS

Sir Ralph Richardson was in his late seventies, but dressed in his black leathers and retro crash helmet and astride his Norton 500, he looked magnificent. Nicky Henson pulled in on the other side of me. He'd been the omnipresent National Theatre leading man for the last decade, and the thunk! thunk! thunk! of his BMW would have warmed the heart of any red-blooded theatre-going biker. I pulled my little Superdream up on its stand, Nicky said something about the mild weather, and we walked away from the bike racks, through the stage door, and off to our respective rehearsal rooms, three theatrical Hell's Angels swallowed up by the uniformly brown-grey edifice that dominated the South Bank.

The National Theatre had been built at a time when concrete was king. I'd often tried to convince myself that it had architectural merit, that it was modern and . . . well basically, it was modern and shit. It looked like the communist party headquarters of an East German town.

Inside, though, was a different matter. In the foyer the various nooks and crannies were alive with coffee bars, chatter and young people reading plays, or at least pretending to. Backstage was equally busy. Floor after floor, and corridor after corridor of purposeful activity; actors, administrators, stage management and technicians all going about the business of trying to get the next play on without having a nervous breakdown.

The *Oresteia* cast had undergone a shocking transformation. Yvonne Bryceland had disappeared, and so had all the other actresses. In their place were fifteen aggressive, northern male actors in rugby shirts and tracksuit tops, plus me. Tony Harrison and Peter Hall had decided that, on the strength of our previous experiments, the play would work better if it had an all-male cast, as would have been the case when it was first performed two and a half thousand years ago. But our original male cast members weren't with us any longer either; they were either working on other shows, or were fed up with being trapped behind a mask eight hours a day. I was the only survivor, and the only southerner.

This was going to be an ensemble production. Initially we'd all play a variety of parts, until after another three months we'd be allotted a role, and for the rest of the five-hour spectacular would retreat back into the chorus. We agreed that in the spirit of ensemble we'd be billed in the programme simply by our names, not by the parts we played. We'd be working as a team, and given that our faces were to be hidden behind brown masks, this anonymity seemed appropriate.

The masks themselves, though, were still proving a problem because they muffled our voices. It took weeks for our designer Jocelyn Herbert to come up with a design that kept our mouths free to speak without the bottom half getting in the way. We also decided to put dark make-up round our eyes so our skin didn't show, otherwise we looked like a bunch of pink-eyed Al Jolsons. But even once they were working properly, their function was a conundrum.

Peter conducted an experiment. He asked our stage management team to pull thirty or so members of the public off the street, and entice them into the rehearsal studio. When they were seated, sixteen figures entered the room, swathed in flowing grey rehearsal robes and mud-coloured masks. We could see the audience clearly, a few programme sellers I vaguely recognised, some potential audience members plucked at random from the ticket queue, and a couple of lads from the skateboard park under Waterloo Bridge. But they couldn't see us, our faces were completely hidden behind our masks. We performed a ten-minute extract from the play, the pulsing metre of the words orchestrated by a pair of drummers, and when we'd finished, there was a smattering of applause. Then we took our masks off, and there was a gasp from the audience. It was as though they'd forgotten we were human beings; we'd been giant, mythic figures striding the ancient world, but suddenly we were ordinary twentieth-century people again, albeit ordinary people with eyes like pandas.

Peter asked a few warm-up questions. He was the consummate chairman, interested in what the audience were saying yet brilliantly manipulative. You could imagine him running rings round the National Theatre board. Gradually our audience members warmed up. They'd liked the acting, though they thought the language was a bit affected, and couldn't always fathom the complexities of the plot. Then Peter came to the nitty-gritty.

'Tell me about the masks,' he said.

Everyone started talking at once.

'They were extraordinary.'

'I'd never have believed it. They changed.'

'What do you mean, changed?'

'Their faces. I knew we were only looking at bits of fibreglass, but it was like a scary sci-fi movie about robots or something. It was as though they came to life.'

'And when did they do that?'

The moments they identified weren't a surprise – they were when characters showed their emotions, when they lied, when they felt lustful or angry. But then disagreements began to emerge.

'Take the moment,' said Peter, 'when Queen Clytemnestra welcomes the captured Trojan princess Cassandra into her house and says to her servants, "This stranger needs looking after. The gods like some kindness from those who have triumphed." What was her face like?'

'Clytemnestra had won,' said someone. 'It was an "I'm-going-to-slaughter-the-bitch" face.'

'Yes, but she looked a bit jealous too. Like she'd no idea what Cassandra and Agamemnon had been up to on the way home.'

'I thought she looked pretty sexy. She was really getting off on the moment.'

'I couldn't see that, but there was definitely a bit of guilt going on.'

'She was nervous. She knew she might blow it.'

The discussion went on and on, but as Peter pointed out, there was no right or wrong answer. What each audience member had seen was what they'd projected onto the masks. The bland little faces may have looked like something on a shop dummy, but they acted as mirrors that reflected each person's imagination.

It occurred to me that my silent comedy heroes Buster Keaton and Stan Laurel did exactly the same thing. Their deadpan looks allowed us to invest emotionally in their comic humiliations. This was a trick that might be worth exploiting at some time in the future.

The mask work was knackering. Each time we made a gesture, we had to stretch and lengthen our arms and necks like ballet dancers, our diaphragms ached from the amount of breathing required to project our voices through the masks, and we were constantly accelerating across the stage in choreographed bursts of energy. In order to keep this up we needed to be fit and flexible. We got very serious about this and a bit po-faced. We did yoga every day, and each lunchtime changed into our running gear, jogged left into Upper Ground, across Blackfriars Bridge, along the Embankment, left again across Waterloo Bridge, and sprinted back to the theatre for a quick lunch.

The petrol fumes almost certainly outweighed the health benefits, but we felt satisfied with ourselves, or at least I did. My only previous experience of intense running had been at school, where the highlight of the event had been hiding in the woods and watching the other unfit boys wanking each other off, but now I was gripped by exercise mania. Sean Baker had run for his county when he was a schoolboy and always came first on our jogs, but I was often third or fourth, which was a triumph that kept me buzzing for the rest of the day. There was definition in my arms and legs now, I'd lost the little barrel of flesh that had lodged behind my belly button for the last few years, and as for my core . . . previously a core had been something other people had; I'd just had a sway back and the inability to stand on one leg. But now I'd got a two-pack which might soon become a four- or even a six-pack, my balance had improved beyond recognition, and I was light on my feet. I skipped and leapt like an antelope on steroids. And that was my undoing.

One morning I was jogging along the National's corridors to rehearsals when I came to a run of seven or eight steps. I was feeling so springy that I jumped down the whole flight in one bound, or at least attempted to. I hadn't noticed that halfway down, suspended from the ceiling, was a large, rectangular metal duct for the heating system. My head hit it in mid-flight, sending me hurtling backwards. My neck smacked into the top step, the base of my spine hit another leading edge, my whole body went into spasm, and I ended up spread-eagled at the bottom of the stairs. I must have passed out, although I don't remember for how long.

As I came round I heard a twittering like a mouse arguing with itself in the mirror. Slowly I opened my eyes. Felicity Kendal was peering down at me. She looked confused and a little aghast, and was trying to engage me in conversation.

I'd never met her before, and had no idea why she was in the building. Perhaps she was rehearsing a new play, maybe she was visiting a friend, or perhaps she was a hallucination brought on by my blow to the head. Everyone fantasised about Felicity Kendal, so that was entirely possible. Or could I be dreaming, and in my dream I'd become Richard Briers in *The Good Life*, and had just had an amusing accident tripping over a garden fork?

I watched her with detached interest for some time. I couldn't understand what she was saying, but I didn't dare lean towards her to catch her drift because I might have broken my neck or my spine, and if I attempted to move, I could spew blood and die. The best strategy seemed to be to lie still, and wait to see what was going to happen next.

I drifted out of consciousness again, and the next thing I heard was Jim Carter, a tall, trustworthy member of the *Oresteia* cast, talking to me in a soft voice and with a concerned look on his face.

'Am I bleeding?' I asked him. I wasn't in pain, but my head was probably wreathed in a pool of bloody brain matter.

'Only a little,' he said. 'You seem to have had a bash on your forehead. Don't worry, a doctor's coming.'

Then I was lying on a bed in A & E at St George's hospital. Someone said no bones were broken but I'd received a heavy blow to the head, and needed stitches and to be kept under observation. This came as such a relief that I immediately went back to sleep again.

After that I remember nothing until I was hobbling up the front path to the door of Fred Place. How I got there I've no idea, but the look and smell of my home were balm to my battered body and brain.

Peter Hall had phoned Mary and suggested I take a fortnight off. The week after that had already been scheduled as a break to allow him time to decide the final casting and to firm up other production details, so I'd get three weeks' rest in total. Hopefully I'd be ready for work again after that.

I'd never felt old before, but I did now. I hobbled everywhere, groaned when I sat down, and groaned even more when I tried to stand up. When I was in bed I'd get stuck, and have to shunt backwards and forwards like a large car in a small parking space before I could get enough purchase to heave myself up and trudge to the toilet. I had mild fits of depression, couldn't remember certain words, and stuttered a little.

Friends came to see me, and brought magazines and boxes of Newberry Fruits. Sylvie popped in. She'd undergone another miraculous change since the days when she'd been the queen hippy of West Hampstead. After she and her husband Guy split up she went to live near Lowestoft, with virtually no money. Her next-door neighbour was an elderly communist with a passion for education. He persuaded her that the only way she could break out of her cycle of poverty and dependency was by getting an education.

She went on holiday to America with Bardy to visit Terry Copkiller Ford, but when she came back, Guy and Jason weren't at the location where they were supposed to meet her. She spent a few panicked days trying to locate her son; eventually they were reunited and ended up buried away in a commune in Malvern.

While she was there she took O-level English, and passed with such ease that she went on to do three A-levels. Her tutor suggested she try for university, the other commune members supported her with childcare, and four years later while she was studying for a Masters at Warwick, she was headhunted to teach law and trade union studies at a tech up the road from me in Gloucester. My former wild-child chum was now a lecturer, writer and well-respected specialist on women and the workplace. She brought me John Berger's *Ways of Seeing* and *The Tin Drum* by Günter Grass. I spent long days in bed reading them, watching *Pebble Mill at One* and chewing jelly sweets.

In the late 1990s Sylv was appointed the chief executive of Reading, and subsequently chief executive of Tower Hamlets, one of the poorest and most problematic councils in the country. We remain friends to this day, and I'm inordinately proud of her.

After a couple of weeks the aches and pains began to disappear, but my brain was still like porridge, and I thought I'd probably sustained permanent mental damage. It would be about a year before I felt like someone in their mid-thirties again, rather than an old duffer in his late eighties.

The depression hung over me for a while too, but there was a good reason for that. Howard and Sue had announced that they were leaving the commune. Howard's career had taken off beyond our wildest imaginings. He'd directed shows for the National, and had now been appointed associate director of the Royal Shakespeare Company. It simply wasn't practical for them to remain in Bristol, and though we were happy for them, Mary and I felt an enormous loss. Only three of the original six commune members were left now, and Kate would need to start afresh soon, rather than live out her days in the place she'd shared with Dave. We knew there'd be no problem keeping Fred Place going; our close friends loved it, and several would be only too willing to buy into it. But our commune had been built round the personalities of six specific people; its ethos, its politics, our attitude towards parenthood had all developed from our shared experiences. Of course all things must pass, but I was sad that in this case they'd pass so soon.

On my first day back at the National we sat in a circle while Peter told us what conclusions he'd come to, what the show's lighting and sound would be like, the look of our costumes, how the music would sound, and how many musicians there'd be. Then it was time to announce the casting.

Greg Hicks was to be Orestes, the princely hero of the

plays. None of us were surprised by this. Greg was the most spectacular stage actor among us, with a soaring but contemporary-sounding voice, and an astonishingly flexible body honed by years of yoga. Jim Carter, young, strong and commanding, was to play Agamemnon; he'd look magnificent in his armour and huge Greek helmet (a mighty general who would one day be transformed into Mr Carson, the curmudgeonly old butler in *Downton Abbey*).

And what about me? The height and bulk of the other actors meant it was certain I'd be cast as a woman – but which one? I hoped I'd get the part of the lonely prophetess Cassandra, but no, Cassandra went to John Normington. Athena was Michael Thomas, Electra was Roger Gartland. So who the hell was I?

Peter came to the end of the cast list. Two of us, David Bamber and myself, hadn't been mentioned. We weren't going to be given parts. We were to be chorus members throughout the whole play. I was so stunned I couldn't speak. I'd been working on this show for longer than any other performer. I empathised with the characters, sang the music well, and could handle the complex rhythms of the dialogue, so why had I been singled out for this ignominy? At lunchtime I wandered across Waterloo Bridge. It was raining, and the Thames was choppy and black.

I went back to the theatre and found David Bamber. He was feeling as numb as I was. Peter Hall was in the canteen surrounded by his acolytes. We asked to speak to him, and he took us up to his office. We told him he'd broken his promise, but he didn't believe he'd made one. He said there weren't enough parts to go round, but we argued that there was no reason why some roles shouldn't be shared, and that we could take it in turns to play whichever roles he was prepared to cast us in. He asked for time to think.

Clytemnestra dies in the first of the three plays, and her ghost appears in the third. The following morning Peter suggested that David and I should alternate as the ghost. It was the best deal we were going to get.

After two more weeks of rehearsals we were back in his office again. The experiment hadn't worked. Our voices were so different from that of the actor playing Clytemnestra that no one realised we were her ghost; they thought we were some new, unexplained character who'd just happened to turn up in a ghostly fashion. Peter offered us each a few lines as messengers instead. If we didn't want to continue, he'd understand and we could leave, but there was nothing else he could do.

We both stayed on. I'm not sure why I came to that decision. Partly I think because David did, and partly because I'd worked so long on the show, and was so interested in the process underlying it, that I couldn't bear to let go of it. But we both felt bitter, and throughout the rest of our time at the National neither of us ever successfully shook off this feeling.

Nevertheless the *Oresteia* was a remarkably fine piece of work, and I wasn't surprised when it received almost universal acclaim. It was tough work keeping the performances up to the required standard, though. The amount of emotion we had to pump into those masks each night was colossal, and when we took them off, intense feelings would spill out. Sometimes we'd accidentally barge into each other on stage or talk over each other's lines, and when we got back into the wings and were once again maskless, would momentarily square up to each other like footballers who'd been kicked in the shin.

But one night after the show Greg Hicks took off his mask and revealed a face beaming with happiness.

'Won the pools?'

'You know I was supposed to give evidence in the trial? I've been worrying about it for days.'

The *Romans in Britain* case was the talk of the National. Howard Brenton had written the play. It was about imperialism, epitomised by the invasion of ancient Britain by the Romans. The metaphor which expressed the Britons' complete subjugation was a Roman soldier, played by National Theatre stalwart Peter Sproule, anally raping a Briton played by Greg.

Mary Whitehouse had been outraged by this scene, and had brought a private prosecution against the play's director, Michael Bogdanov, for gross indecency, even though she'd never seen the play.

'Anyway the case has been dropped,' continued Greg. 'The prosecution withdrew its evidence.'

'You didn't have a problem, though, did you?' I said. 'The defence's whole point was that you only simulated the bottom business. So it couldn't possibly be defined as indecency.'

'Well, that's what I was worried about,' he said. 'It was supposed to be pretend, but just occasionally Peter would push his willy in a little way to make me go "oooh!"'

On the back of the *Oresteia*'s success we were invited to Greece so we could perform the play in its original homeland. Prior to that we were given a week's holiday, and I decided to go to Greece early with fellow company member Sean Baker, so we could see some of the play's original locations.

We took a small tent with us, and I hired a Lambretta so we could ride south through the Peloponnese in a leisurely fashion and join the rest of the company at Epidaurus where the performances were to take place.

It seemed a little peculiar to be exclusively in one man's company for so long, particularly as we didn't know each other very well. But Sean, who at first glance appeared brusque and taciturn, was deeply sensitive, and had fallen in love a week before we left. We spent our days discussing the various land and seascapes, and the agony of his see-sawing emotions. We were the present-day equivalents of the romantic poets, revolutionary artists finding inspiration in the stark scenery of the land where democracy had been born, although Byron and Shelley probably didn't spend as much time as we did trying to find out the English football results. We rode to Athens and saw the Acropolis, to Mycenae where Paris had first seduced Helen, and to Ancient Tiryns, the birthplace of Hercules.

We eventually met up with the rest of our team and had our first sight of the fourteen-thousand-seater amphitheatre at Epidaurus. It was built in the fourth century BC and had astounding acoustics; even the most softly spoken word could be heard in every part of the theatre. Greece had been run by a murderous junta of army colonels, but their rule had recently collapsed, Greece had returned to democracy, and our show was part of a festival where the Greek people were celebrating their newfound freedom. Lots of artists had taken part in the resistance to the colonels, and for them this was a particularly moving occasion. A large and passionate woman enveloped me in her arms and buried me in her breasts. With tears in her eyes she told me she was the new MP for Piraeus, but before the junta seized power she had been an actress, and thirty years previously had played Clytemnestra in this very theatre.

The show itself was an eye-opening experience. The *Oresteia* is peppered with incantations to the sun and moon; it evokes the elements and the seasons, and conjures up images of various birds and animals. At the Olivier Theatre the only sound in the auditorium apart from the audience was the click of the Honeywell thermostat regulating the temperature, but here in Epidaurus dogs barked, frogs croaked, the light and temperature changed dramatically, and once darkness had fallen, the stage lights were bombarded by moths, bats and other scary creatures. Nature itself had become a character in our play, and it wasn't going to be ignored or upstaged.

To see the landscapes where so many ancient heroes and heroines had done great deeds was truly inspiring. It made them more human too. Previously I could only ever have imagined the gods being played by actors like Charlton Heston and Elizabeth Taylor; now I knew their tales could be told by anyone. The *Oresteia* was hard work physically and mentally and was ultimately a personal disappointment. But it transformed my attitude towards performance, and every part I've played since has been influenced by it.

Howard wanted me to be in his production of *Piaf*, a show about the sparrow-like 1950s French singer Edith Piaf which the Royal Shakespeare Company was transferring to the Piccadilly Theatre. It was to be run in tandem with an American play called *Once in a Lifetime*, which had a stellar cast including Zoë Wanamaker, Richard Griffiths and David Suchet, and in which I'd play a hotel bellboy. Unfortunately it turned out to be yet another miserable experience. My dressing room was six flights above stage level, so I spent each evening running up and down the stone stairs like a deranged athlete on amphetamines, and as both shows had been in the RSC's repertoire for some time, there were no exciting moments of discovery in the rehearsals. I was simply a replacement being asked to do exactly what the previous actor who'd played my part had done, repeating the same insignificant performance night after night. It made me feel trapped.

I was far more excited by current Equity politics than by the RSC. The union had always been a strong opponent of apartheid, and had attempted to limit performances and sales of our shows to South Africa as our contribution to the anti-apartheid movement. But some members were opposed to this stand, and were trying to undermine it, both within the union and in the High Court. I became part of the movement to maintain this trade boycott and strengthen it. Every evening I'd cocoon myself in my dressing room organising and writing speeches. I became so enmeshed in this activity that I sometimes forgot to listen closely to what was going on in the theatre.

One night over the tannoy I heard my cue being spoken on stage. I hurtled down the six flights of stairs, bouncing off the stone walls, and yelling to everyone to get out of my way. When

I finally burst on stage, I was met by half a dozen pissed-off faces. The other actors had been wandering around for forty-five seconds, desperately trying to improvise, but not being able to think of anything interesting to say.

After the show I went round to them all and grovelled, and my apology was received with generosity and good grace. But I didn't get the same reaction when I did exactly the same thing, at exactly the same point in the show, a week later. More hurtling, more bouncing, and many more pissed-off faces. David Suchet ordered me sternly to his dressing room and read me the riot act. He was eighteen months younger than me, but I felt as though he was my headmaster suspending me for smoking in the toilets. There was nothing I could say in my defence, I just had to stand there and weather his ire.

By the time my stint at the Royal Shakespeare Company had finished, I was feeling very gloomy. So many opportunities I'd been given had been snatched away from me, and now I'd started letting everyone down because I was so bored and frustrated. I was an also-ran, and unless things started to pick up soon, probably always would be.

Then John Lloyd contacted me. I hadn't heard from him since the day the first *Black Adder* pilot had been cancelled.

'We've got it,' he crowed. 'It's going to happen.'

'What's going to happen, John?'

'The show. The Beeb want six episodes.'

'What, *The Adder*?'

'Yeah.'

'Congratulations, mate. I'm very pleased for you.'

'Pleased for me? You ought to be pleased for yourself.'

'Because . . . ?'

'Are you available next February?'

'Well, yes, but . . .'

'But what?'

'You've already got a Baldrick. The other bloke did the job OK, didn't he?'

'Tony!' said John. 'What did I tell you when our pilot went tits up?'

'I don't know, what did you tell me?'

'That if we got the series, you'd be Baldrick.'

'Did you? I don't remember.'

'You knob! So are you up for it?'

When we'd finished talking I got on the phone to Kate.

'Do you remember John Lloyd saying that, whatever happened, he'd want me to play Baldrick?'

'Err . . . well, yes, I suppose so.'

'You suppose so?'

'Well, it was just the bollocks producers always say, wasn't it? Being nice to avoid being nasty. It didn't mean anything.'

'This time, Kate, it did. It really did.'

16

THE CAGED DWARF

I couldn't believe it! A week before rehearsals were due to begin there was more aggravation at the BBC, another strike broke out, and the plug was pulled on *The Black Adder* yet again.

In other circumstances I'd have chewed the carpet, torn out clumps of my hair and moaned 'Why me? Why me?' But this time my disappointment was cushioned by a very large cheque. I'd signed a contract to make the entire series, so the BBC had to pay me for six episodes at £150 each. Who'd have thought it! The most money I'd ever had in my entire life! Nine hundred quid for doing nothing! And the great thing was, if the BBC ever did get round to making it, they'd have to pay me another nine hundred!

Meanwhile Howard had a play opening on Broadway, and the words 'Howard had a play opening on Broadway' were almost as exciting as 'nine hundred quid'. Mary and I decided to blow the lot, leave the kids with her mum, and fly to New York for his first night. Our hotel was pokey, smelt of cats and was infested with cockroaches, and it didn't stop raining the entire time we were there, but we didn't care. We splashed through puddles like dancing movie stars, wrecked three umbrellas, got soaked at the Statue of Liberty, and doubly soaked on the boardwalk at Coney Island. When we spoke to strangers we exaggerated our English accents because it made them shriek with laughter; we were archetypal, slightly loopy Brits abroad.

The play Howard was directing was called *Good*. It was by

C. P. Taylor, and was a thoughtful piece about a good man, a liberal Jewish professor devoted to his family and aging mother, who becomes vain, selfish and detached from the real world, joins the Nazis, and ends up involved in book burnings, euthanasia and genocide. Alan Howard played the lead, and watching his performance was a revelation. Since my early teens part of me had fantasised about one day becoming a stage actor of international repute. I'd probably live in Hampstead close to the Heath, I'd play leads with the Royal Shakespeare Company, make a couple of arthouse films with screenplays by Harold Pinter and Tom Stoppard, appear on telly in the occasional Shakespeare play or an adaptation of a great Russian novel, and be best buddies with Judi, Juliet and darling Simon. But witnessing the strength, subtlety and profound emotion that Alan conjured up, I knew I could never be as good as him. I'd worked for the National and the RSC, not to mention small innovative companies like the Royal Court and Portable Theatre, but I'd never been singled out for special attention, and though I'd felt resentful at the time, the truth was I didn't deserve to be.

At the after-show party in a candlelit restaurant in Central Park I sat at Howard's table surrounded by some of the finest performers in the world. Actors are often epitomised as noisy extroverts. These weren't; they were softly spoken, unassuming and with a pliant, almost transparent quality about them, as though their hearts and minds were constantly being remoulded by the characters they played. They were angels from the gods, sitting patiently with their wings furled, waiting for their next flight. I could never be one of them. I had the squeaky voice of a London grammar school boy, and the body of an ant. I had wings, but they were comedy wings, short, stubby and brightly coloured. I was convinced there was a place for me in our industry, but I'd never be a Michael Gambon or an Anthony Hopkins, and if I didn't face up to that fact, I'd spend the rest of my life feeling miserable and frustrated.

*

But *The Black Adder* had got the green light again, and everyone at the BBC seemed confident that this time it would really happen. I was still sceptical about whether it would be any good, but somewhere along the line I'd developed an intense loyalty towards the project. Certainly the BBC had high hopes for it. The budget was big, because the show needed to look more like a TV epic than a run-of-the-mill sitcom, and our first three weeks were to be spent filming in the wilds of Northumberland around Alnwick Castle. Ironically this was the seat of the real-life Percy family, who were charming, sophisticated, and heartily amused by our unwarranted attack on their name and intellectual capabilities. The entire area was to be transformed into a movie set, with scores of extras dressed in elaborate period costumes, elegant horses in fine liveries, blazing witches, a dwarf in a cage, and all the other accoutrements of medieval life.

On the train I sat with the other cast members watching the landscape grow ever bleaker the further north we went. John Lloyd was a Cambridge contemporary of Rowan and Richard, but taller, blonder, and much better-looking. His father had been a captain in the Royal Navy, and though he was thought of as quite radical in television circles, he had the demeanour of the officer class. Like most of the younger BBC producers he wore jeans and checked shirts, but would have looked equally at home in a Crombie and cravat. He spoke with a slight drawl and a home counties accent, and put imaginary inverted commas round words he thought were particularly droll. His reputation was sky-high, and everything he put his hand to – *The News Huddlines* and *The Hitchhiker's Guide* on the radio, and *Not the Nine O'Clock News* on TV – had turned to comedy gold. He was liked and respected by his colleagues; men wanted to go to the pub with him, and women wanted to go to bed with him, but he was a deeply troubled man. Superficially he was playful, charming and good fun, but when the mask dropped, there was a deep sadness, sometimes a black despair beneath it. Tim McInnerny said he was a whinger who should realise what a lucky sod he was and lighten up, and the rest of us, ever supportive, thought Tim was probably right.

Just north of Newark, John said something which shook me to the core.

'So how are you going to handle being famous?'

'Ah, the old "famous",' murmured Rowan, who, like John, had a habit of putting words in quote marks.

'There's not much chance of that,' I said.

'Don't be daft,' retorted John. 'Everyone loves Row. They'll all watch the series. And who will they be rooting for? The comedy servant, everybody does.'

'The comedy servant,' repeated Rowan. 'How we all laughed!'

'Mark my words,' said John. 'A year's time and you won't know what's hit you.'

'How about you, Tim?' said Richard. 'Ready for fame, fortune, and more pretty girls than you can shake a stick at?'

Tim didn't answer. He wanted to be a classical actor even more than I did. I'd seen him as Hamlet, although it was on a schools' tour at a comprehensive in Bristol. He was very impressive, but struggled a bit with 'to be or not to be', because the school bell rang throughout the entire soliloquy, followed by hordes of nattering children with large bags crossing the school hall, totally oblivious to the fact that Tim was acting his tights off a dozen feet away from them.

'Tim's problem is his neck,' mused Richard. 'It's like a giraffe's. He'll never look serious enough for tragedy. You're going to have to accept your fate and be funny, Tim. You're terribly good at it.'

But Tim didn't reply.

We'd probably have been warmer filming in Reykjavik. The make-up people had to keep dabbing our faces with concealer so we didn't look like red-nosed reindeer; we had hand-warmers and foot-warmers, menthol-impregnated tissues in every pocket, and needed a break every couple of hours to thaw out in the slightly less icy environment of the castle loo. In one shot, Tim and I counted eight different types of snow landing on us in two minutes and got the giggles.

Rowan still had no idea what he wanted his character to sound like, and spent most of the time cantering around the bleak castle grounds putting on different voices. The rest of us ate pies by day, and drank whisky by night.

I asked the dwarf if he minded being in a cage.

'Nah,' he said. 'Third cage I've been in this year.'

'You don't find it a bit humiliating?'

'This is good work, mate. Better than all that porn I have to do.'

By the time we got back to London and began recording the rest of the show in studio, we knew *The Black Adder* was only going to be half as good as we'd hoped. It was a relief that at last we were in proper historical period rather than the vaguely medieval fantasy time in which the pilot had been set. The show took place in the 1480s, during the Wars of the Roses. But this was problematic. It wasn't like the Tudor or Victorian periods which everyone knew at least something about. The Wars of the Roses were very confusing, a confusion redoubled by the fact that two of our main characters were called King Richard, and trebly confusing because two-thirds of the way through the first episode we veered away from the real world as we had done in the pilot. In our story Richard III, played by Peter Cook, didn't kill the two princes in the Tower as history tells us he did; instead one of the little princes grew up, became Richard IV, and the Tudor succession was delayed by half a century. I apologise if that summary makes the whole shebang quadruply confusing, but that's the way it felt when we were rehearsing it.

In addition, the gags weren't much funnier than previously, and though the personality Rowan had created for himself as Richard IV's scheming son, Prince Edmund, would have been hysterical if he'd been a character actor making the occasional entrance, he was in virtually every scene, and his pliable face and high-pitched squeaking were remorseless. Rowan knew that what he was doing wasn't working and was very distressed by it, but we were powerless to help. If we could have had another couple of months to work on rewrites and rethink our characters, we'd have been fine, but television comedy is a production line; the inserts had been filmed, the actors cast, the sets and costumes made, and the cameramen booked. There was no way we could go back to the drawing board.

The series did have one saving grace: Brian Blessed's performance as Richard IV. Brian was a giant of a man with a red beard reminiscent of a pair of mating squirrels. He had a roaring voice, and a sense of humour like a centurion tank.

One day I bumped into him when I was in the shopping centre on Shepherd's Bush Green. He grabbed me and bellowed, 'I know this man. He fucks old ladies!'

Another time in a crowded Tube he put me in a headlock and yelled, 'I'm sorry, this lad's just done a terrible fart, and he's pretending he hasn't. Can you call the Transport Police please?'

Social niceties aside, he was very entertaining, if a little tiring, to be around. He dominated the screen, gave every scene enormous energy, and his character posed a believable threat to Prince Edmund without undermining Rowan's flashes of subtle comedy.

The series had its moments. Two episodes in particular seemed to show a possible way forward. In 'The Spanish Infanta' my old friend Miriam Margolyes gave a virtuoso performance as a royal nymphomaniac who ravishes Baldrick to within an inch of his life. Jim Broadbent appeared as her translator, and there was something about the nature of their comedy and the quality of their performances which made the episode very classy – certainly classier than Miriam's contributions during rehearsals.

'I was voicing an animated documentary about birth control yesterday evening,' she announced one day. 'I played a cute little piece of spunk who talked like this,' and proceeded to give us a lecture on the comparative merits of the Durex and the diaphragm in the voice of a cartoon duckling.

The other episode of note was about Prince Edmund being ordained Archbishop of Canterbury. Rowan, Tim and I played an extended scene in which we discussed the sale of pardons and indulgences. It showed off our individual strengths, and also the fact that together we made an awesome comedy trio. It was particularly significant for me because, on the strength of it, the scriptwriters went on to write me much funnier and more complex lines.

Edmund: Right, now let's get down to business, shall we? . . . Baldrick has been looking at some of the ways we could actually make a bit of money on this job.

Baldrick: Well, basically, there appear to be four major profit areas: curses, pardons, relics and selling the sexual favours of nuns.

Edmund: You mean some people will actually pay for them?

Baldrick: Well, foreign businessmen, other nuns, you know . . . Moving on to relics, we've got shrouds from Turin, wine from the wedding at Cana, splinters from the cross, and, of course, there's stuff made by Jesus in his days in the carpentry shop: pipe racks, coffee tables, coat stands, bookends, crucifixes, a nice cheeseboard, fruit bowls, waterproof sandals . . . (*picks up a piece of wood that's partly carved*).
Oh, I haven't finished that one yet.

We certainly thought the series had enough promise to justify the BBC commissioning another, but Richard and Rowan had left themselves a major scripting problem. In the final episode the entire royal family, including the Black Adder, drank poisoned wine and died. Only his two servants remained unscathed. If there was another series maybe it would have to be called *Baldrick and Percy*? But that was for another day. For now all we could do was go home, wait for the transmission dates to be announced, then hope we got a favourable reaction from the viewers.

When I closed the front door of our house for the last time, I wasn't as heartbroken as I thought I'd be; I'd been mourning the commune's inevitable end since the day Dave died, and we'd sold it to Robert Spicer, a radical lawyer, whose work on behalf of the poor and disenfranchised keeps the spirit of Fred Place alive to this day.

But now Mary, Laura, Luke and I had a new home. Glendale was a short run of three Victorian workers' cottages built on a terrace at the end of a cul-de-sac on the far side of Clifton, close to its famous gorge. The only access to the front of number 6 was along a small concrete path. Below the terrace was a sloping green dotted with mature trees and primroses, bluebells and daffodils in the appropriate seasons. Beyond it was a curve of about twenty large Georgian houses called The Polygon, accessed by another path. Even though it was only half a mile from the centre of Bristol, this idyllic spot was completely cut off from the rest of the city. There was no traffic, no parked cars, no one but the occasional dog-walker. Children could wander about outside unattended, and given that most of the houses were family homes, there were lots of other kids for Laura and Luke to play with. Our neighbours were middle class, arty and aspirational, and as that's what we seemed to have become, we fitted right in.

I became absorbed by my new life there: the minutiae of the school run, the activities at the community centre round the corner, barbeques on the terrace, sledges and snowmen on the green. When *The Black Adder* was finally transmitted in 1983, a handful of viewers thought it was terrific, but for most people it was just another comedy series, a bit daft, some funny bits maybe, but nothing to get excited about. A few months previously I'd have been gutted by this reaction. But not now; I loved my new house, was enjoying family life, and the phone was ringing non-stop.

Something weird had happened after the first showing of *The Black Adder*. I'd played a supporting role in a series which was at best a niche hit, but it seemed to have projected me headlong into the centre of the world of TV comedy. Writers and directors had apparently been more impressed by *The Black Adder* than the viewers were. I was asked to be a supporting regular in *Alas Smith and Jones*, a sketch series starring Griff Rhys Jones and ex-Avon Touring director Mel Smith. I also performed a sketch on *The Lenny Henry Show* in which he was a fox and I was a badger. (It wasn't great; I had lines like 'I feel dreadful. I was out with the deer last night. It was a stag do,' but no one seemed to think I'd mucked it up, certainly not Lenny.) Most significantly I got a part in an episode of *The Young Ones*, the anarchic new series set in a student flat, written by Rik Mayall, Lise Mayer and the iconoclastic new stand-up artist Ben Elton.

It's impossible to overstate how influential that series was on the minds of the impressionable young. Mary was teaching at Hartcliffe comprehensive school at the time, and one morning she casually mentioned to her fourth years that she was a fan. The looks of non-comprehension were palpable. Why would she watch *The Young Ones*? She was an old teacher, what would she find funny about it? It was their programme, not hers.

My episode was called 'Bambi', and was jam-packed with comedy heavyweights like Mel and Griff, Ben Elton, Stephen Fry, Hugh Laurie and Emma Thompson. It was a pleasure to be confronted by the grown-up Emma. Her dad Eric had been one of my teachers at Central, and when she was a little girl used to sit on my lap some evenings while I played poker with him at their home in West Hampstead.

The scene I was in was very weird. It was set in a Victorian consulting room where Dr Carlisle, played by Robbie Coltrane, was looking through a microscope. My character, Dr Not the Nine O'Clock News, burst in and said:

> Prepare yourself, sir, I have a patient outside whose deformities are so grotesque that you will question how the almighty could suffer such a blasphemy upon His earth.
>
> *Dr Carlisle:* Calm yourself, Dr Not the Nine O'Clock News. We are men of science. We fear no worldly terrors.
>
> *Dr Not the Nine O'Clock News:* Pray remember, sir, he is human. He is a man.
>
> *(Dr Not the Nine O'Clock News exits and re-enters leading an elephant.)*
>
> *Dr Carlisle:* It's an elephant, sir.
>
> *Dr Not the Nine O'Clock News:* You unfeeling bastard, sir!

The stage instruction 'leading an elephant' doesn't accurately reflect what happened during the recording. The animal was little more than a baby, but it weighed as much as a twelve-seater coach. At the afternoon rehearsal it had been coaxed into position by its handler with numerous lettuces and biscuits. So when I took hold of its lead during the show and began to pull it gently onto the set, it knew it was heading towards food, and wasn't going to stop till it found some. My attempts to bring it to a halt were futile. It lumbered across the set, demolished the far wall and the furniture stacked neatly behind it, and only came to a halt when the handler leapt into its path with an entire crate of vegetables. The scene was neatly edited so that the viewers were completely unaware of this act of animal mayhem, which is a pity, because it was bloody funny!

'A seven-day exploration into the geomorphology of the Great Caldera at Santorini, and the archaeology of the proto-minoan civilisation located beneath its tephra.' Mary was flicking through a brochure about the various adult-education courses offered by Bristol University.

'Why do academics write like that?' I said. 'It's gibberish.'

We'd become ever more interested in archaeology since our digging days in Chichester; we even attended lectures on arcane aspects of the subject like the man-made mounds of ancient Jericho and the great prehistoric Turkish site at Çatalhöyük.

'It's partly showing off, partly insecurity, I think,' said Mary, 'and a lot of them don't really know what they're talking about. I thought actors were wankers, but archaeologists . . .'

'These courses are supposed to be about public access. Why don't they bill them with headlines like, "Ancient City Obliterated by Super-Volcano"?'

'Tart!' she said.

'They'd get ten times as many applications.'

'I suppose they would.'

'Do you fancy it then?'

'What?'

'Checking out the geomorphology of the whatsit.'

'Is it actually in Santorini?' asked Mary.

'Yes.'

'Then I certainly do.'

'Do you reckon your mum'll look after the kids? There could be quite a lot of ouzo flowing.'

When we got there our hearts sank. It certainly wasn't going to be the alcohol-fuelled rave-up we'd hoped for. We were the youngest on the course by at least a quarter of a century; indeed some of the others appeared to be even older than the archaeology. Only the tutor Mick Aston was our age, although he seemed pretty ancient too. I had a nasty feeling I'd made a big mistake, but I couldn't have been more wrong. The story of ancient Santorini and its port Akrotiri is like a disaster movie.

It was one of the great cities of the Bronze Age world, but it was destroyed by a volcanic eruption in a few moments. Although the archaeology is as perfectly preserved as Roman Pompeii a thousand years later, there are no skeletons or any other evidence of death. Where the inhabitants of the city went, and whether any survived, no one knows.

Mick Aston vividly brought the story of this awesome moment in pre-history to life. He was staggeringly erudite but wore his knowledge lightly. He was down-to-earth, with the innocence of Winnie the Pooh, and the grouchiness of Eeyore. He wore rainbow-striped jumpers given to him by various besotted ex-students, faded bell-bottomed jeans, little round wire glasses, and had a tumble of curly salt and pepper hair. He looked like a Janis Joplin fan who'd gone to the Woodstock Festival fifteen years previously, and had never returned to civilisation.

Initially there'd been a buzz of interest surrounding the fact that a minor celebrity was on the course, but Mick made no secret of his show business ignorance. He didn't have a telly, he said, and had no idea who I was.

'I've no idea who I am either,' I told him. 'It's not an issue.'

I liked his cranky Black Country integrity. He was a walking contradiction – a hippy who didn't smoke weed, a vegetarian who drove a succession of environmentally toxic campervans, an atheist whose specialism was medieval monasteries.

We wound each other up non-stop.

'Don't pretend you're left-wing,' he'd say. 'You Labourites are all closet Tories.'

'Dressing like Paddington Bear doesn't make you a revolutionary,' I'd retort.

One morning our little group was clustered round a gravesite hanging on Mick's every word. He told us that Akrotiri was some kind of outpost of the all-powerful Minoan society that had prospered in Crete's capital Knossos. This was the civilisation that had brought us the great hero Theseus who rescued Princess Ariadne from the clutches of the Minotaur. 'But Knossos collapsed,' Mick went on. 'The most powerful civilisation in the Mediterranean and whoomp! In a single century it had disappeared. The question is, though, was this because of the Santorini eruption ninety miles away? A tsunami maybe, or volcanic ash wiping out the Cretan crops? The dating evidence seems to suggest . . .'

I never found out what the dating evidence suggested. I'd completely lost my concentration. A little Greek boy had crept up to me and slipped a human skull into my hands. I'd no idea what to do with it, but I didn't want to interrupt Mick's flow, so I nudged Mary, wiggled it up and down a few times, and raised my eyebrows in an exaggerated fashion. She mimed back that I should probably give the little boy a few drachmas as he was now pulling a cross face and trying to snatch it back. I attempted to tuck it under one armpit so I could reach into my pockets for some money, but it kept slipping, and Mary was resolutely refusing to come anywhere near it. I finally managed to offload it into the hands of an elderly student, who swiftly gave it to the woman next to him, and soon the entire group were thrusting it from one to another as though they were playing pass the parcel and the music was about to stop.

Eventually a primary-school teacher from Dursley, who had a crush on Mick and always stood closest to him, seized the skull triumphantly, held it out as an offering and proudly demanded, 'Dr Aston, what do you think of this?'

'Oh, bloody hell!' he replied. He snatched it from her hands, gave it a cursory glance, then hefted it deep into the bushes. The group looked at each other aghast. We were on a site of global importance examining possibly unique archaeological evidence, and in a fit of pique brought on by having his story interrupted, our leader had cast it aside like a rotten cauliflower.

There were glares, sighs, even the occasional tut-tut. But Mick was unabashed.

'What's up?' he demanded. 'Do you think Charlie here is Minoan?'

'Could be,' someone mumbled.

'Didn't any of you notice the edges? Were they worn by age? No, they were practically fresh. And what about the teeth? And did the scuff marks tell you anything? It's some poor old bugger out of the village cemetery who ought to be left alone. He's probably the same age as your gran. The kids dig 'em up like spuds and flog them to the tourists.'

We all looked sheepish.

'But shouldn't we give it to the police?' suggested the woman from Dursley.

'You can if you like,' replied Mick testily. 'But what do you reckon they'll do? They'll stick red tape all around the site, and we might as well go home. No one's seen anything, right?' He fished his leather purse out of his shorts, produced a small coin, gave it to the little Greek thief, said, 'Now piss off!', and carried on with his lecture.

That was my introduction to the interface between archaeology and real life; territory in which I was to spend a lot of my time over the next two decades.

In the evenings we watched the sunset, drank retsina, and I told Mick's kids stories about Theseus the bull-monster and the mystery of the magic skull, peppered with various bits of current political satire involving the evil general Heseltine and the mad witch Margaret.

Making up stories was fun. On summer holidays to the Dordogne I'd told long tales to Ted and Sarah Braun's children about the Michelin Men and their never-ending battles with the evil Osmond Brothers, and I'd devised the Sally stories for Laura and Howard's daughter Hannah about a Greek princess whose job it was to look after the refugee children when the Trojan War had ended. These were long, rambling tales that lasted all summer long. One story for Laura went on for years. It was about a post-apocalyptic yuppy called Programnin whose charred Filofax had been discovered in the bombed-out ruins of twenty-second-century London.

But I never thought of these stories as work. I was enthusiastically useless at playing football with the kids, and my washing and ironing skills left a lot to be desired, but at least I could keep them amused for an hour or two with a string of creative lies. They were part of my contribution to childcare!

Debbie Gates knew I'd become an obsessive storyteller, so when she got an appointment with Lewis Rudd, the head of children's programmes at Central Television, to pitch some stories to him, she asked me not only to help her develop them, but also to be at the meeting.

Her narratives were about a little boy called Henry and the adventures he had in his garden, including meeting a large yellow flower called Fat Tulip. A lot of the plots were strong, but I didn't think they were quirky enough for TV. So I did away with Henry, turned Fat Tulip into a human, and introduced lots of new characters including two heroic young frogs, one called Sylv in honour of my old friend Sylvie, and the other named Ernie, who was a cross between me and Eric Morecombe's partner, Ernie Wise. I knew Lewis would be getting at least ten storytelling pitches a week, so we had to find a way to make him sit up and take notice of ours. We agreed that I wouldn't read the stories to him, instead I'd discard the written words completely and tell them to him as though I was a genial but slightly nutty bloke he'd just met in the pub.

Lewis arrived at Debbie's new house in the smart London suburb of East Sheen, and as soon as she opened the door I began chatting like a banshee, pretending to be all the creatures in Fat Tulip's garden, bouncing on Deb's sofa, hiding behind her curtains, and climbing onto her dining room table. Halfway through she surreptitiously eased open the doors and windows because I was sweating so much she thought it might be a bit off-putting, but it didn't seem too much of a problem for Lewis. He was taken by the zaniness of the stories and the way I told them, and said he'd try to find a slot for us. If he was successful, I feared it would be five minutes on some dreary Saturday morning kids' series, and I'd want to turn it down, consequently upsetting Debbie; on the other hand he would most likely forget us before he'd even got to Richmond station, which would probably be for the best.

When you're an active member of your branch Labour Party, you tend to end up doing all the jobs no other mug's prepared to do. I'd been chair, secretary, political education officer, treasurer, and now two close friends of mine, Helen Taylor and Derrick Price, had persuaded me that it was my turn to stand as Clifton's Labour Party candidate in the Bristol City Council elections.

I didn't want to be a councillor; the thought of sitting through three-hour meetings of the Parks and Highways Committee filled me with dread. Even if I'd wanted to seize the levers of political power, now was not the moment. I had a colossal amount of writing and acting to do, and a host of obligations to Equity and various other charities and political organisations. If I won, I wouldn't have time to turn up to council meetings, and would be exposed as a lazy fly-by-night by the *Bristol Evening Post*.

'It would be irresponsible,' I said.

'You won't get in!' Helen had replied, waving an application form in front of my nose.

'You haven't got a chance in hell,' Derrick had insisted. 'Look at the money round here. It's rock-solid Tory.'

'I suppose you're right,' I said, and filled it in.

But standing for election is an intoxicating process. Leaflets need to be delivered non-stop, money has to be found right now, and party members have to be chased up every day to make sure they're doing what they promised they'd do. For a few short weeks, as far as the public and the local press is concerned, you are the party you represent. Everything they feel about the party is invested in you.

Not everyone felt quite like that, though. One evening I was canvassing students at the Goldney Hall of residence. A young long-haired man opened his front door, and the sweet odour of cannabis wafted out of the room.

'Good evening,' I said. 'I'm your—'

'Wow!' he said. 'How did you climb out of my telly?'

Another equally raddled student joined him. 'Look, Greg! He's at the front door and he's on the telly. How did that happen?'

'Amazing,' agreed Greg.

Behind them a repeat of *The Black Adder* was playing on their TV, and Baldrick was staring right back at us.

A small band of doughty volunteers and I worked our butts off during that campaign, and with only a few days to go it was clear our efforts were making an impact. We were confident we could mobilise the traditional Labour vote, and were making inroads into parts of the ward where Labour hadn't previously had any success. On the eve of poll I sat in the Lion in Clifton Wood totting up our potential votes, and a hideous realisation dawned on me. I ordered another pint, and went through the figures again. At eleven p.m., very much the worse for wear, I knocked on Helen and Derrick's door.

'I'm going to get in,' I said.

'Bollocks,' replied Derrick.

I burst into tears.

'I only did it because you said I couldn't win, and now I am going to win, and . . .'

'Have my hanky,' said Helen. 'If you win—'

'If I win, I'll let everybody down.'

'If you win, the whole country will be on course for a people's uprising,' said Derrick. 'This is Clifton, not St Pauls.'

Next day we chased up all the people we'd identified as Labour supporters, and I drove lots of old ladies to the various polling stations, although I had a suspicion most of them were Tory voters who were simply taking advantage of me. At 5 p.m. we did the final knock-up, then the very final one after that, had a quick Peking duck and pancakes at the Chinese on the Hotwells Road, went to the Council House and waited for the result.

My assessment couldn't have been more wrong. The Tories were triumphant yet again, and we came third. But there was a swing to Labour of 4.75 per cent and I was more than happy with that.

'Rolf the Stonemason' was a drama produced in Birmingham by the *Jackanory* unit. My character was a gargoyle called Prod who was carved in such a well-executed and lifelike way that he came to life, jumped down from his place on the castle roof and rescued his creator Rolf from execution. When the recording was over I went to the BBC bar with the producers, and they asked me what I thought of *Jackanory*. No one had ever asked me that question before, and years of agitated frustration erupted like the Santorini volcano. I said that real storytelling was about the spoken word, but that *Jackanory* relied on actors reading books. Furthermore, I said, these actors read their lines off autocue, which destroyed the possibility of genuine immediacy, and they were stuck in the stultifying atmosphere of a TV studio, so there was no link between what they were saying and the real world. I raved on for about ten minutes non-stop, then petered to a halt when I realised how aggressive, even offensive, I'd been about one of the BBC's best-loved children's programmes.

But Angela Beeching, the head of *Jackanory*, didn't seem fazed by being on the receiving end of a tirade from a man dressed as a stone ornament. Instead she said, 'OK, Tony, so what would you do?'

There and then she took up my suggestion that I create a four-part improvised story about Theseus and film it on location around south-west England. To cap this, a few days later Lewis Rudd came good and gave Debbie and me thirteen episodes of our storytelling series *Tales from Fat Tulip's Garden*. Thirteen? This was a ridiculously large number to be awarded on the back of a sweaty half hour in Debbie's dining room. Coming up with the goods was going to take a great deal of graft and inspiration.

When John Lloyd finally told us the BBC weren't going to recommission *The Black Adder* I was a little disappointed, but my overwhelming emotion was relief – I'd got enough on my plate as it was.

But John was determined to make the BBC change its mind. 'We know how to make *The Adder* work now,' he said. 'It could be brilliant, and they've already spent so much on it that they'd be mad not to capitalise on their investment. It'll happen. I'm sure it'll happen.'

'Sure, John,' I said, 'but with due respect, you're barely thirty years old. You're a kid compared with the grizzled, cynical execs who make the big decisions. Who's going to listen to you?'

17

THE VIRGIN QUEEN

Who Dares Wins a Week in Benidorm was a disaster; not one of those mini-disasters where your friends avoid looking you in the eye for a few days because the show was dreary and you were a bit crap. This was the kind where the producers are summoned to see the head of channel the following morning and he's icy with anger; they're ordered to appear on *Right to Reply* where they're ripped to pieces like trainee gladiators confronted by a pack of lions, anything they say in their defence is twisted by the press and makes things twenty times worse, and board members threaten to resign if any similar programmes ever appear on their channel again. And yet it had all started out so well.

One Saturday night a few months earlier, I had been telling our small invited audience a joke during a *Black Adder* warm-up, when I'd been distracted by a young woman who'd arrived late and was struggling to get to her seat in the middle of a row. She was petite, attractive, and well-dressed in a media-chic way. When she finally got to her place she turned to me and smiled. It was a smile that lit up the whole studio, a frank smile that said she'd made a faux pas, but I wouldn't mind because I was such a charming man. I smiled back in similar fashion, which was pretty big of me given she'd just messed up my punchline.

A few weeks later when I was in studio for *Alas Smith and Jones*, I met her again. Jimmy Mulville, our script editor, strolled into my dressing room with the mystery girl on his arm. I liked

Jimmy. He'd been president of the Cambridge Footlights a few years previously, but he wasn't in the usual run of urbane, ex-Oxbridge types. He was a working-class Liverpudlian with a lethal wit, he was utterly fearless, and ridiculously combative, with a hatred of pretention, authority, and politicians of all shades. His girlfriend's name was Denise O'Donoghue, and I knew her by reputation. She ran the Independent Producers' Association, a job which involved trying to squeeze fair deals out of hard-nosed, tight-fisted television accountants. Rumour had it that in the negotiating room she was lethal.

We went upstairs to the BBC bar and they introduced me to Andy Hamilton, a small, hunched, bearded writer and stand-up who I'd previously seen being very funny on the Edinburgh Fringe, and who was friendly, smart, and had a great line in showbiz gossip. They suggested we go for a meal, and we headed off to a little Italian place in Shepherd's Bush. As soon as we were inside the door they insisted they'd pick up the bill. It dawned on me that this wasn't a casual meeting at all; the sexy smiles from Denise, Jim strolling into my dressing room, the apparently arbitrary encounter with Andy; they were softening me up for something. I didn't mind. They were ridiculously confident, intelligent people who gave off an aura of potential success; I was flattered they should think I was worth the bother. I told them I had a suspicion I was being set up, they apologised profusely, and then came clean. In low voices, as though it was a state secret, they told me they wanted to make a sketch show unlike anything previously seen on British television. It would feature the work of six writers, all of whom had written for *Not the Nine O'Clock News*. But whereas *Not* was a series of short, snappy sketches, this new show would be the complete opposite. Each item would run for several minutes and would shift seamlessly from one subject to another, more a comic essay than a series of punchlines. Its tone would be tough, political and vulgar, and it would be fronted by an ensemble of half a dozen performers who'd present as well as perform the sketches. Andy wanted the playing style to be naturalistic rather than blatantly comic, and because he'd liked the understated way I played Baldrick, and the similar kind of work I'd done with Mel and Griff, Jimmy had suggested I'd be perfect for the show. On the basis of the evening's conversation, said Andy, they thought he was right. For some time they'd been in talks with Thames TV, but now Channel 4 had offered them an hour-long show. Was I up for it?

An hour-long sketch show was virtually unheard of, a gargantuan task, but an intensely attractive one. It sounded like a 1980s version of *That Was the Week That Was*, which was my favourite TV programme of all time.

'Oh,' added Andy, 'and it'll be going out live.'

'Fuck, that's scary,' I said. 'Count me in,' I added.

I didn't realise that my three new friends had virtually no experience of running a television show. They were about to embark on the biggest comedy undertaking in Channel 4's history, and all they had to fall back on was their sublime confidence and their unswerving belief in the project and the writers. But even if I'd known what freshmen they were I'd probably have said yes. Despite her reputation I was already besotted by Denise, Jimmy had an edge of danger that I warmed to, and Andy wore an aura of unpretentious brilliance that made you believe that anything he was involved in would turn out well.

Their offices and rehearsal rooms were at Limehouse Studios on Canary Wharf, a location which today is the epitome of multinational deals and megawealth. But this was long before the wharf became swamped by money. London's world-renowned docks had collapsed when containerisation transformed international shipping. Canary Wharf had been abandoned, its inhabitants had left, and it was now destitute and surrounded by stinking, untended water, just like the old King George V Dock where we'd shot *Brannigan* eight years previously. The only new buildings were two neat, double-storeyed TV studios which protruded like tiny white teeth from the decay, Studio A where we worked, and Studio B currently occupied by *Spitting Image*. A small boat which acted as a canteen and bar was moored next to them. We'd meet up there with the *Spitting Image* crowd after work, but it was a gloomy place, and most of the talk, even from new comedy talent like Harry Enfield and Steve Coogan, was about politics, cars and VAT legislation.

The cast and writers worked collectively on *Who Dares Wins a Week in Benidorm*, just as we later would on *Blackadder II*, although here the arguments were much more brutal. This wasn't just down to Jimmy; his writing partner was equally combative. Deep down Rory McGrath was a lovable, lugubrious man, in many ways the most gifted of all the writers on the show. He had a surreal sense of humour, and some of his ideas were breathtakingly innovative. If Benny Hill had written *Waiting for Godot*, it would have been like one of Rory's sketches. But he was his own worst enemy. He'd turn nasty and have blazing rows for no reason, his copy tended to arrive late and badly edited, and he'd go walkabout for hours, sometimes days on end. This was particularly frustrating because he was also one of the team of performers, so rehearsals would grind to a halt while we waited for him to reappear. He always did, and each time we forgave him, and Denise and the other women in the office would mother him and give him a severe talking-to, after which he'd be as good as gold for a few days.

The pre-filming went well. The expensive filmed shots in *The Black Adder* tended to be views of castles, galloping horses, peasants in carts and the like. They gave the show texture, although they didn't add much to the comedy. But the *Week in Benidorm* writers used film to create elaborate comic set-ups, into which lots of different ideas were woven. They were funny, innovative and unique. However strong they might be, though, *Week in Benidorm* would stand or fall on the quality of the live studio show into which they were to be inserted, and this turned out to be one of the most nerve-jangling hours of my life.

The set changes were so complex that we were constantly dodging the stage flats, doors, tables and chairs that were being whisked hither and thither between sketches; cameras and cameramen hurtled around trying to find their shots; make-up artists rushed across the studio floor dropping wigs and half-glued facial hair; and as it was a topical show and we'd hardly had any time to learn our lines, we were grabbing our scripts in darkened corners and frantically mugging them before going back out front to face the cameras again. Although I remember the backstage chaos vividly, I recall absolutely nothing about the show itself, except watching a terrified actor having a fit of hyperventilation so severe that I feared for his life. Somehow we got through it, there was lots of applause, friends and supporters took us out for a swanky Chinese banquet in Limehouse, and they said they were sure we'd got a hit on our hands.

We were pleased, proud and on an enormous adrenaline rush; but the next day the sky fell in. Suddenly there were endless meetings, lots of shouting and interminable phone calls. Lawyers were consulted, and the press persistently approached us with smiling faces but with knives behind their backs, attempting to wheedle us into talking to them. It was as though there'd been a national political crisis, and it was all our fault.

The first problem was our Jesus on the cross sketch. Everyone in Britain knew the Hamlet cigar ads: there was the one where a piano teacher was driven wild by the inept playing of his young pupil, the Wimbledon spectator fruitlessly trying to follow the play while wearing a neck brace, Michelangelo inadvertently knocking an arm off his nearly completed statue; and at the end of each advert a shot of these put-upon men easing their frustrations by smoking a Hamlet cigar to the accompaniment of Bach's *Air on the G String*, with a voiceover of the famous strap line 'Happiness is a cigar called Hamlet'. But until *Who Dares Wins* no one had made a Hamlet ad featuring the crucified Christ, with him pulling his hands from the nails in order to take a drag from his cigar, toppling forward and disappearing from sight. We'd thought it was pretty funny, but apparently people in high places hadn't.

The other source of outrage was a song called 'The Welsh are Appalling'. Phil Pope, who performed it, was the mildest-mannered man you could possibly meet. It never occurred to him that Jimmy and Rory's lyrics might be construed as a vitriolic attack on the Welsh nation. Stereotyping was still staple comedy fare in the early eighties – the Mexicans were untrustworthy, the Americans loud, the French homosexuals. Even the most respectable mainstream comedians would regularly bash other nations, just as we assumed they'd bash us. And taking the piss out of the Welsh seemed harmless enough – they were our friends, our relations, and our next-door neighbours. But times were changing, although comedians like us who prided ourselves on being cutting edge didn't seem to have noticed it yet. Many Welsh people viewed the song very differently. To them it was rank anti-Welsh bigotry, the antithesis of the new attitude towards Wales that Channel 4, with its remit to give a voice to minorities, should be promulgating. The Welsh representative on the Channel 4 board threatened resignation, Channel 4 Wales refused to broadcast any future episodes, and questions were asked in the press about whether the channel was fulfilling its brief properly. We could have tried to defend ourselves by pointing out that the song's last line was, 'The Welsh are appalling, but compared to the Scots they're not bad'. But we decided not to.

The Channel 4 bosses didn't mind controversy – in fact, they positively thrived on it – but the proviso was that they should be made aware of the contents of every show before it was aired. In our case things weren't so clear-cut. Had the *Benidorm* scripts been properly signed off? Had the commissioning editors been made aware of any possible problems? Had the company lawyers seen the controversial sketches? Andy and Denise pleaded not guilty to all charges, but a lot of accusing fingers were pointed at us and there was ceremonial public

hand-washing by a senior Channel 4 executive on a TV interview. The previous Friday we'd been a potential smash hit, a
flagship programme that would help define what Channel 4
was all about. By the following Tuesday we were irresponsible
idiots who'd given its arch-enemy the *Daily Mail* an open goal,
and threatened its very existence.

But in those days the channel was an extraordinary phenomenon. It weathered, absorbed and spat out criticism like no
other organisation I'd ever come across. For a few days we were
a national outrage, then there was silence, and finally a couple
of months later with no fuss or press releases, we were commissioned to make a further eight episodes. The first was called
Who Dares Wins . . . a Sunshine Cruise on the Persian Gulf, and
the second one was *Who Dares Wins . . . a Quiet Meal For Two
With Princess Di's Brother*, but eventually Andy ran out of
topical ideas and it became known simply as *Who Dares Wins*.
The only change the channel had insisted on was that in future
we record the shows the night before they were transmitted so
the lawyers could view them and put the scissors in if necessary. The series did well, was never less than controversial, the
following year we were given an eight-part series, likewise the
next year, and another six just over a year later.

Returning characters are the stock-in-trade of comedy
shows; if you create an amusing vicar or hilariously idiotic
landowner, it's fairly easy to write a similar sketch about them
the following week. But it was a badge of honour for us that
every sketch should involve original characters and ideas.
There was one exception to this rule: the pandas. Jimmy and I
hated playing Terry and Wang Wang. The costumes were huge
and unwieldy, and the heads weighed a ton, pressed hard into
your neck and shoulders, and choked you. You had to shove one
hand up their throat to operate their mouths, there were no
earholes which meant you couldn't gauge the audience's laughter, and your field of vision was so restricted you kept bumping
into the set and falling over. But on screen they were the cutest,

cuddliest animals you've ever seen. Everyone loved them, and whenever they appeared there was an audible 'Aaaahhh!' from the audience. Consequently the scriptwriters used them as vehicles for their darkest, most vile thoughts. In one sketch we even described a baboon masturbating over Princess Margaret, but because they were so sweet, we didn't get one single complaint about it. Jimmy said in retrospect Phil ought to have been dressed as one when he sang 'The Welsh are Appalling'.

The characters the team played were extensions of our real selves. Julia Hills was a bright young English rose with a lovely voice like a dirty-minded Julie Andrews, Phil didn't say much but was perky and cute, Jimmy was perpetually aggressive, Rory was affable, relaxed and a bit of a smart-arse, and I was an insecure, tub-thumping leftie. But the driving force behind the show was the writers, Jimmy and Rory, Colin Bostock-Smith, Tony Sarchet, and Andy and his co-writer Guy Jenkin who, thirty years later, are still producing comedy hits like *Outnumbered*. Week after week they handed in innovative sketches, tailor-made for the five of us.

The most notorious was a modern parody of the Hans Christian Andersen story about the emperor's new clothes, in which a pair of highly manipulative tailors played by Jimmy and Rory tried to sell me a suit.

Jimmy: Why don't you come out and let's have a look at it.
(Tony comes out of the changing room. He is naked.)
Jimmy: Ah yes, fantastic.
Tony: I'm just not sure.
Jimmy: What's wrong with it?
Tony: I can't quite put my finger on it. Oh look, there's a hole in it.
Rory: It's a button.
Tony: It's got a bit of fluff in it. And what's that?
Jimmy: What's what?
Tony: That dangly thing.

Rory: It's a piece of sartorial whimsy.

Tony: It's a bit big, isn't it?

Rory: Believe me, I've got something similar on one of my
    suits. Any smaller it'd look ridiculous.

(Tony takes scissors from Jimmy's breast pocket.)

Tony: I don't think I like it. I'll cut it off . . .

Jimmy: Look at the back of the suit. Look at the way it hangs.

Tony: There's a tear in it.

Jimmy: That's a vent.

Rory: It lets the air in.

Jimmy: Or out.

I wasn't really naked, I wore the front part of a jockstrap
which had been fixed to my pubic hair with velcro, although
the viewers couldn't see this cute little pouch because it was
constantly obscured by Jimmy or Rory, or simply by the angle
of the shot. Nevertheless thousands of people were fooled, and
believed they'd seen something they hadn't. For weeks afterwards people would call out to me in the street, 'Saw your
todger on the box last night, Tone,' or 'Hullo, Tone, get it out
again, will ya!'

I was often exhausted by the long hours and frustrated by
the continual bickering, but it was an enormous privilege to
have been part of *Who Dares Wins*. If *Blackadder* was classical
comedy, *Who Dares* was an hour of non-stop punk. I even got a
spiky haircut during the first run to indicate where my cultural
allegiances currently lay. In addition to the five main cast members, it also provided a seedbed for young talent like Jeremy
Hardy, Mark Steel, Caroline Quentin and Clive Anderson.
There was nothing else like it on television, and that's always
a source of pride.

When Michael Grade became the new controller of BBC1, this
was the pitch John Lloyd made to him: '*The Black Adder* is the

only show in history that looked a million dollars, but actually cost a million pounds. How about if we do a second series, but on the cheap? No expensive pre-filming, only a dozen extras, and no unnecessary dwarves in cages. We'll shoot the whole thing in studio, and be in and out in six weeks.'

By the late spring of 1985 we were back in the rehearsal studios. The most significant change to the show apart from the reduced budget was that Rowan had stepped down as co-writer, and Ben Elton had taken his place. I assumed that Richard, who was renowned for his storytelling, would be in charge of the plots, and Ben would add lots of jokes. But it didn't work out like that. Ben quickly found himself parodying Richard's work, and vice versa. Within a couple of weeks none of us had a clue who'd written which bits. The two men passed each episode back and forth, amending and rewriting. They only had one rule: never reinstate. In other words, if one of them cut something, the other couldn't put it back into the next draft. This gave their scripts a rigour and coherence that had been sadly lacking from series one.

I thought I'd find Ben intimidating. When you saw him on TV, you got the impression that he was hyper-aggressive, but in real life he was the exact opposite; his brashness hid a deep lack of confidence. He idolised Richard, but this hero-worship wasn't one-way. Richard was a big fan of *The Young Ones*, and knew he could never write the kind of knockabout, no-holds-barred humour that Ben was so good at. The two men were totally unalike; Richard was the typical ex-Harrow public schoolboy, self-deprecating, polite and earnest, with an intense concern and genuine affection for people. Ben was an intellectual barrow boy, a chipper south Londoner educated at Manchester Uni, who talked at a hundred miles an hour. They were two of the most talented people I'd ever met. They made up for each other's shortcomings, and worked superbly well together.

We talked a lot about how we could make series two better

than series one. Ben made the observation that in real life Rowan was quite sexy, and we should incorporate that quality into the script. The rest of us pooh-poohed the notion; we were fond of Row, but certainly didn't want to shag him, and couldn't imagine why anyone would; physically he was like a big goblin. Nevertheless we couldn't deny that he'd had a succession of stunning girlfriends, and we'd seen his technique in action. A new make-up assistant appeared on set. She was remarkably beautiful, of Ugandan Asian extraction. Every man in the show tried to impress her with their wit, charm and flashing eyes, except Rowan, who for the first two days ignored her, then on day three arrived in the make-up room bearing a Dire Straits tape and a small posy of flowers. It was hard to predict which she'd throw in the rubbish bin first. The answer was neither. By the end of the week he and Sunetra were an item.

The writers had decided to set the new series in Elizabethan England, which seemed a shrewd idea. Tudor history is far less complicated than the Wars of The Roses; every viewer would at least have heard of Sir Francis Drake and the Spanish Armada. Suppose our Queen Elizabeth found The Black Adder, or Edmund Blackadder as he was now to be known, attractive. Every episode would then revolve around the changing fortunes in Edmunds's relationship with her. She'd see him as saturnine and charismatic, although actually he'd be an idiot, a cross between Iago and Inspector Clouseau. He'd consistently try to exploit her, and she'd fancy him madly one minute, and grow so bored with him the next that she'd threaten him with execution.

There'd only be a handful of regular supporting characters, so even though the show was going to be set in one of the most opulent courts in British history, it would, like all the best sitcoms, have a domestic feel to it. The Queen would need a confidante, someone she could talk to and who wasn't scared of her, and that character became Nursie, played by Patsy Byrne. And of course we'd have a villain, for which John recruited

Stephen Fry, who he and Ben had worked with on the Granada sketch series *Alfresco*. Stephen was to be Lord Melchett, a composite of all the wily chancellors the real Queen Elizabeth had surrounded herself with, and his prime motivation in life would be to bring down Blackadder.

Baldrick and Percy had much more to do in the second series. They'd become like Sergeant Bilko's henchmen, united in their commitment to further Edmund's plans. But they'd be even more stupid than in series one; in fact, the new Baldrick would be the thickest person in human history. I gave him the deadpan look I'd learnt to exploit over the previous few years, but unfortunately some tiny speck of intelligence still occasionally flickered, and it wasn't until the fourth series that I managed to extinguish it completely.

These new ideas seemed a big step forward from the comedy chaos of the original show, but there was one problem, Queen Elizabeth. She was to be played by an interesting new actress called Miranda Richardson, who'd recently been a big hit as the executed murderess Ruth Ellis in the film *Dance With a Stranger*. She needed to be the linchpin of the series and carry a lot of the comedy. Unfortunately the lines Ben and Richard had written for her were as uninspiring as Baldrick's had been in the pilot. For the first couple of days everyone's focus was directed on one question, 'What shall we do with the Queen?' Miranda was a remarkable performer, and had an appealing quirkiness about her that was perfect for our kind of comedy, but we had to give her the space to find the right character. John Lloyd paced the rehearsal room all day, borrowing Stephen's cigarettes, and puffing away like a steam train as he and Miranda tried to create a plausible but funny Virgin Queen. Then out of the blue, Miranda discovered the character she'd been looking for, a teenager on the cusp of ponies and sex, a spoilt little brat who was the most powerful person in the western hemisphere but craved attention and affection. Immediately

Ben and Richard knew how to write for her, and from then on her performance dominated the series.

After the first show had been recorded Ben approached me about the following week's episode.

'Tone,' he said, 'I've got a great comedy idea for you.'

I waited for the revelation.

'Baldrick,' he continued triumphantly, 'likes turnips.'

'And that's funny because . . . ?'

'Oh, come on, Tone,' he persisted. 'The shape.'

'Ben, what shape is a turnip?'

'Well, it's long and thin, and you know, like a willy.'

'That's a parsnip.'

'Is it?'

'Yes, a turnip's round.'

'It's still pretty funny.'

'You're saying that it'll be funny if Baldrick likes a vegetable that looks like a willy, except it doesn't look like a willy, it's vaguely circular.'

'It'll be brilliant.'

'Will it?'

'Here's an idea. Baldrick finds a turnip that's shaped like a willy.'

'And that will make people laugh, will it?'

'Trust me, Tone. They'll fall about.'

I'd been in show business for over twenty-five years. I knew what was funny and what wasn't, and this wasn't. Or so I thought. But from the moment Baldrick first expressed his passion for circular root vegetables the audience fell about, and it became a comedy mainstay of the series – although to this day I don't quite understand why.

I'd never worked with such an extraordinary group of people as the *Blackadder* team and I was enjoying myself enormously. There was an instinctive understanding between us about what was funny and why. We seldom needed to finish a sentence, because everyone got the point almost as soon as one of us started speaking. No one was a dead weight; everyone was contributing something the others couldn't.

Each Monday morning we'd be presented with the new script, and as soon as we started reading it, we'd fall about laughing. At the end of the read-through Richard and Ben would leave, and the rest of us would start poring over the text. We were paranoid perfectionists, determined not to let a single word remain that wasn't dead right. Was the plot crystal clear? Was the set-up for the next joke economical enough? Was its rhythm right? Was the punchline a few syllables too long? We'd rewrite each joke and each line of dialogue time and time again. When we were finally satisfied, we'd read it to each other out loud. If it was still wrong, we'd go back to the drawing board; if it was right, we chorused 'Yeesss!!' and moved on to the next problem.

This kind of manic textual analysis didn't leave much time for rehearsing. Some actors, particularly those who were only in one episode and weren't used to our way of working, felt insecure by the lack of rehearsal and by what they saw as our time wasting. Wilfred Brambell, who'd played Harry H. Corbett's tetchy dad in *Steptoe and Son* and had been cast as a bitchy lord of the realm, walked out on us after a couple of days saying he'd never worked with such a bunch of inexperienced and unprofessional actors in his entire life. But we couldn't stop fiddling with the lines. And given that we had a lead actor who was fastidious about every aspect of the show, and a producer determined to wring perfect comedy out of each scene, there was no one to divert us from our course. From Monday to Wednesday we worked on the text, on Thursdays the technicians came to the rehearsal room and we discussed how the show would work in studio, on Fridays we polished the lines and decided on the important things like where to stand and when to sit down, and on Saturday we recorded the show, by which time we'd scrutinised the script so thoroughly that nothing about it seemed remotely funny anymore.

Series one had been performed to a tiny audience of friends. Once it had been edited, it was then shown to 150 people in a small cinema in the West End, and the reaction to that viewing provided the laugh-track. But *Blackadder II* was played in front of a full-scale audience in a large studio in the bowels of Television Centre. As we waited for them to file into their seats, we would sit in the make-up room listening to their excited chatter over the tannoy. We'd be intensely nervous. The confidence we'd felt earlier in the week would have drained away by now. The current week's show always felt flabby and verbose, and the jokes not funny enough. In half an hour's time we'd finally be exposed as the incompetents we really were.

No one talked much. Miranda and Patsy would whisper their lines together for the umpteenth time, Stephen would disappear to the loo every five minutes, and Row would sit nervily on his own, fretting and occasionally leaping to his feet to discuss some small problem with the lighting director or the studio manager. Eventually we'd hear Ben introducing himself to the audience – 'Good evening, my name's Ben Elton' – then slip effortlessly into a confident five-minute warm-up. Tim and I would smile at each other. Ben was seen as at the epitome of contemporary comedy, but with his sharp suits, speed-of-light patter and *double entendres*, he reminded us of the legendary comics of the 1950s like Max Miller and Charlie Chester.

Eventually we'd be summoned onto the studio floor one by one to be introduced to the audience. When Row's turn came he'd nod shyly and disappear again as swiftly as possible to deal with whatever tiny concern was niggling away at his brain. Stephen would greet the audience in languid and fulsome tones, and would tell an anecdote or two, which invariably ended with a gross vulgarity guaranteed to generate a combination of shock and hysteria. I'd do a couple of minutes' chat too, partly to warm myself up, but also because I was a relative unknown, and wanted to be able to establish a relationship with the audience before we began. Finally the show would get underway. It was a tremendous relief when we got our first laugh; then the pressure was off, and we could start enjoying ourselves.

Not every day was a bundle of laughs. It wasn't easy being part of a team all of whom were ten years younger than me, but in many ways were more sophisticated, with a contempt for authority, a blithe intellectual arrogance, and a singular lack of interest in anything that didn't immediately stimulate them. They were highly competitive, and masters of the casual put-down, a technique I suspect they'd learnt in the hothouse environment of their public schools to defend themselves from being bullied, and which would serve them well in the new sub-genre of comedy panel games at which they soon became adept.

On Stephen's thirtieth birthday we were invited to his party in a private dining room at the Savoy Hotel. Rik Mayall and Ade Edmondson from *The Young Ones* were there, Hugh Laurie and Robbie Coltrane from *Alfresco*, Angus Deayton and Geoffrey Perkins from *Radio Active*, the towering figure of Douglas Adams who'd created *The Hitchhiker's Guide to the Galaxy*; all the comedy tribe chiefs had come to pay homage at the feet of the great warrior, Fry. The food was superb and the conversation dazzling, but I had nothing to contribute, no trenchant observations, not even a good knob joke, and I sneaked out after an hour or so and went home. Thirty years later I had dinner with Ben at his home in Freemantle, Australia, and told him how isolated I'd felt in those days. 'You too?' he said. 'I thought it was just me!' Maybe it was all of us – although probably not Stephen.

None of this mattered much, though. We all had a deep affection for each other, and for most of us any tensions were simply an undercurrent. But for Richard and Ben they were corrosive. Every Monday they'd leave their scripts in our tender care, and by Friday when they returned, we'd tweaked, cut and pummelled them into a different shape altogether. Although they were philosophical about this and admitted we often made their jokes much funnier, there was no doubt it rankled.

We finished recording *Blackadder II* in July 1985. The following weekend Bob Geldof's charity spectacular Live Aid was due to be transmitted, and Richard invited us to his cottage in rural Oxfordshire to watch it. We all went, along with our partners. Laura and Luke were the only children in this little comedy tribe, and had been adopted by virtually everyone. Richard had even given Laura his rare copy of Stevie Nicks and Lindsey Buckingham's album *Buckingham Nicks* because he knew how much she liked Fleetwood Mac.

It was the kind of July day you dream about. Miranda organised the volleyball and frisbee competitions, we drank lots of tangy white wine, ate cake, and watched the extraordinary musical epic unfold on a little black and white telly which Richard had propped up on a chair on the lawn, its lead snaking back in through the kitchen window. We were mesmerised by the way Geldof and his friends had been able to get the support of so many talented musicians, and how the show engaged millions of viewers who probably hadn't previously given the politics of the developing world a single thought. But none of us could have possibly guessed quite what an effect this show would have on Richard.

18

THE DISCREDITED PRESIDENT

'Order! Order!'

'Resign! Resign!'

'Order!'

'Get off the stage, racist!'

No drama had ever shaken the West End to the core like the one that took place on 28 April 1985 at the Royalty Theatre. But it wasn't *Hair*, *Oh! Calcutta!* or an assassination in the royal box that caused the furore; its backdrop was much more prosaic, almost laughable – the agenda of an Equity annual general meeting. These AGMs were a hangover from the time when the union only had a handful of members. In those days everyone in Equity could sit in the stalls of a single theatre and debate the future of their profession. But now, even though the membership numbered in the tens of thousands, the procedure remained the same: the AGM took place each spring in a West End theatre, and anyone could attend and vote on union policy as long as they were a fully paid-up member.

The president that year was Derek Bond, a silver-haired military cross-winning ex-Grenadier Guard whose slightly pudgy good looks had landed him leading roles in films and on television. He was a Tory and a passionate supporter of Act for Equity, the right-wing campaigning group, an elegant but stubborn man, with a look of permanent outrage at the many and various assaults perpetrated on him by life in general and socialism in particular. He'd recently returned from South Africa where he'd been touring in a production of J. B.

Priestley's *An Inspector Calls*, a dated but moderately entertaining play in which he doubtless excelled. But for an Equity
president to act in direct contravention of Equity policy on
South Africa was incendiary. Perhaps he knew he'd unleash an
explosion of anger and was deliberately stoking the flames, or
maybe he was simply naive, badly advised and blind to anyone's
opinion other than his own. Equity currently had a council
made up almost totally of Act for Equity members, so perhaps
he thought majority opinion would be on his side. But if that
was his calculation, he couldn't have been more wrong. Equity
supporters might vote for the conservatively minded Act for
Equity because they feared change within the union would
open the doors to the Trots, but in general actors were liberal
and a little bohemian; theirs was a profession of itinerants and
misfits who knew the pain of being stigmatised, and tended to
sympathise with the outsider. Support for the anti-apartheid
movement in general, and the imprisoned Nelson Mandela in
particular, was widespread.

A lot more members than usual were expected to turn up
that day, partly because of Mr Bond's behaviour, but also
because the new generation of actors were beginning to make
themselves heard – articulate, often university-educated young
people, who didn't kowtow to the status quo, and saw it as their
right and duty to express their concerns loudly and firmly. No
one, though, could have predicted the queues that snaked
round the block and along Kingsway long before the theatre
opened, the eager lurch forward as the doors opened, and the
sprint, like shoppers in a Selfridges sale, to bag a strategically
placed seat. The Afro-Asian sub-committee representing the
various ethnic minority communities took up their station in
the first two rows of the stalls. Those of us who wanted to speak
in favour of the anti-apartheid motion calling on Mr Bond to
resign deliberately spread ourselves round the rest of the
theatre. The Workers' Revolutionary Party sat in a clump, eyes

to the front, staring haughtily at the stage, ignoring anyone who wasn't of their persuasion.

At 10 a.m. the meeting began in a straightforward and businesslike fashion. A few rule changes were debated, an appeal was made on behalf of the Evelyn Norris retirement home for elderly actors, and Paul Eddington gave a report on the International Committee for Artists' Freedom. It wasn't until item twelve, 'External Policy', that the meeting exploded.

Several motions about Mr Bond's activities in South Africa, particularly his performances in front of white-only audiences, had been tabled. But how could they be debated if he was in the chair? How could he be impartial when he had a vested interest in the outcome of the debate? Speaker after speaker called on him to stand down while the subject was discussed, but he adamantly refused to do so. Anyone in the theatre who might have been undecided about the propriety of his actions was no longer in any doubt. The tension ramped up. Members were marching down to the front of the stage waving their order papers; there was slow hand-clapping, hooting and whistling. The Standing Orders Committee, which was responsible for making decisions about how the meeting should be run, was called on to rule that Mr Bond should leave the chair, but its chairman, Geoffrey Edwards, was another leading supporter of Act for Equity, an otiose man renowned for letting his political bias govern his decisions. He came to the lectern and, staring over his half-moon glasses, told the meeting that the rulebook stated that the president had to be in the chair if he was in the room, and as Mr Bond was indeed present he must remain chair. His speech and the haughty tone in which he delivered it were greeted with cat-calls and derisive laughter, but it meant we now only had two alternatives: either charge the stage and forcibly remove Derek Bond, or withdraw our demand that he step down, in order to make sure the bigger issue of his presence in South Africa was properly debated. We chose the latter course.

The meeting was now irrevocably split between Mr Bond's council cohorts on the stage, and the outraged membership crammed into the seats and gangways. Speaker after speaker railed against Mr Bond's visit, and demanded that he give up the presidency, although many of us went further than that, arguing that Equity's current attitude towards South Africa was half-hearted, and the boycott needed to be extended. The first half of my speech decrying the evils of apartheid went down well, but the second half was more contentious. Rather than supporting anti-apartheid, the WRP had tabled its own amendment. It was overwritten and portentous, using phrases like 'the courageous struggles of the African workers and youth to overthrow the racist Botha regime and the apartheid state of South Africa', it split the opposition by failing to call for Mr Bond's resignation as president, and was wholly against the spirit of the meeting which was trying to build a consensus, not calling for 'immediate expulsion' for all members who breached the policy without further debate. At least that's what I thought, and I urged the meeting to kick it out.

After the votes had been taken, and every motion condemning the president's action including the WRP's amendment had been overwhelmingly carried, Derek Bond came to the lectern. Immediately the Afro-Asian Committee got to their feet and turned their backs on him. Then they slowly walked up the gangways and out of the auditorium. It was a superbly orchestrated display of contempt, and totally unexpected. Virtually everyone followed their example, leaving the president addressing an empty theatre.

The stalls bar was buzzing with excitement. The WRP were furious that their proposal had been criticised, and cornered those of us who had spoken against it. They squared up to us, hectored us, and tried to shout us down when we argued back. Little crowds gathered round us and joined in. Malcolm Tierney, one of the most austere of the WRP's members, loomed up behind me.

'Pabloite!' he hissed. 'We're watching you.'

I ignored him, partly because I thought his party's behaviour had been contemptible, but mainly because I had no idea what a 'Pabloite' was.

Then word went round that Mr Bond's speech had come to an end. We immediately stopped arguing and rushed back into the auditorium. Council, assuming the confrontation was now over, was attempting to move on to the next item on the agenda, but we weren't going to let that happen. The president had lost all credibility, we said. The meeting had made clear that he should do the proper thing, step down from the chair immediately, and resign as president. We certainly had no intention of allowing such a discredited man to run our AGM. The atmosphere became even more febrile. For the next three hours chaos reigned. Those on stage refused our demands, while those in the audience wouldn't let business proceed till they did. Eventually at 7.30 p.m., an hour and a half after it was supposed to have come to an end, the meeting ground to a halt. The following day at 11 a.m. Derek Bond finally relinquished the chair. The meeting was told he 'had an engagement outside London'. He later resigned as president, and a complete ban on sales of our TV programmes to South Africa and live performances by our members there was put in place.

The ramifications of that AGM were huge for Equity. At last a majority of our members realised that the way we ran our affairs was antiquated and out of touch with the needs of the day. A thirst for change swept through the union, and though it took many years to resolve, eventually we got the structure we needed, and Act for Equity quietly sank beneath the waves.

But its effect was felt far beyond the UK. After Nelson Mandela was released from prison he met our general secretary and his eyes filled with tears. 'You will never begin to know how crucial your ban on the sale of TV programmes was in changing the opinions within our white-minority population,' he said. 'For those of us involved in the struggle, it served as a constant reminder that we were not alone and had the support of thousands outside our country who were not prepared to compromise with apartheid.'

Actors are often slagged off for expressing social commitment, and some do make idiots of themselves by sounding off without being properly briefed, but even though we spend most of our lives on the periphery of political events, just occasionally we can make a difference.

19

THE BLOKE OFF THE TELLY

It wasn't until I took Laura to Alton Towers that I realised how prescient John Lloyd's prophesy had been. I was now 'famous' – well, sort of. We arrived at the amusement park early, and at first had the place virtually to ourselves. I loathe fairground attractions, but Laura, who was ten at the time, was a big fan, particularly of the biggest, most dangerous-looking ones. Fortunately she was quite little for her age, so whenever she wanted to go on anything remotely terrifying, I told her there was a height restriction.

After we'd spent half an hour or so tacking across the park trying to find rides that were safe enough for me but scary enough for her, I realised we were being followed. Half a dozen primary school kids were tagging along behind us, the boys behaving as though they'd overdosed on E-additives, barking, crowing and saying in bizarre Chinese accents, 'Looky, looky,' while the girls, particularly when I tried to engage them in conversation, laughed so hysterically I feared they'd wet themselves.

Eventually they began to wander off, but just when I thought we were on our own again, they came back, only now accompanied by about thirty of their colleagues, all of whom were in a mild, gibbering frenzy. I was the object of this agitation, even though they apparently had no idea who I was. The boldest of them finally plucked up the courage to ask me, 'Are you famous?', which is a difficult question to answer without appearing either boastful or falsely modest.

I spent a few minutes explaining what my job was, while Laura grew more and more irritated at my lack of interest in the Hundred-Foot Death Drop, or whatever other terror-inducing piece of machinery it was she wanted to expose us to next. We moved on, or at least attempted to, but more children kept arriving, asking for my autograph on scrappy bits of paper torn from their exercise books, bus tickets and sweet wrappers, touching me like lepers round the hem of the messiah, and asking the same question, 'Are you famous?'

There was a ruined stately home in the grounds which had given Alton Towers its name. I was keen to have a look at it, and Laura seemed reasonably happy to come with me in order to get away from the swarms of children. We headed off towards it, but it was no use. A huge crowd of youthful obsessives was following us, and there was no escape. It was as though I was the Pied Piper luring an entire primary school class to their deaths. When we got to the old ruin, we were turned away by security staff who gave me a good talking-to about not putting children's lives at risk by encouraging them to leave the designated pathways. We reluctantly retreated back to the amusement park.

I tried to keep Laura happy by taking her on the least crowded rides, but she said they were rubbish. I attempted to buy her a Slush Puppy, but we were swamped by the queue which morphed into a tight circle round us. Piping voices demanded 'What you on?', a question I assumed referred to my television appearances rather than to any hallucinogens I might have ingested. We did our best to feed the ducks, but they flew off because there was so much noise. It was no use. The kids had heard I was famous, and that made me irresistible. We gave up and made our way to the exit, driven ever onwards by cries of 'I've seen you in summit, 'n I?', 'Are you that bloke?' and most irritatingly, 'Timmy! Timmy! Where's your mallet?'

We drove back to Bristol, watched *The Fly* on TV and ate our tea. We all enjoyed it, although when Jeff Goldblum shed his human skin and turned into a giant fly, Luke vomited his spaghetti bolognese over the carpet.

Several of my friends in TV comedy had written at least one book, including Ben who was rapidly establishing himself as the country's leading satirical novelist and, once *Blackadder* had finished its second season, I was free to try one too, or would have been if I'd felt capable of it. My feeling of inferiority didn't make much sense. I'd written sketches, speeches, programme notes, election statements, several children's series like *Tales from Fat Tulip's Garden*, and countless other bits and pieces for television. But none of this seemed like writing a proper book. Books were what people who'd been to university wrote. I had four O-levels, and as many chips on my shoulder. If I tried to write one, everyone would see how inept I was. But in late 1985 the book publishers Hutchinson approached me, and wouldn't take no for an answer. So I suggested to them that I retell the story of *The Iliad* for a young readership. I wasn't sure that I particularly wanted to write for children, but I thought it would be less pressured than writing adult fiction, particularly as I'd already researched the story for my TV series.

Hutchinson were happy to take up my proposal, but the moment I'd said yes I became absolutely terrified. I'd no idea how to write a book, or even where to start, so I asked Richard Curtis if he'd help me.

'You don't need me,' he said. 'You're more than capable of knocking out thirty thousand words.'

'I'm not.'

'Have a go at a first chapter, and I'll take a look at it.'

'OK,' I said, 'but I don't want you doing this for nothing. We'll split the profits fifty-fifty, OK?'

This was ridiculous. Richard was already one of the most sought-after comedy writers in Britain. He didn't need 50 per cent of the pittance I was going to make, and would happily have done it for nothing. But I insisted, and he graciously accepted.

I had a go at chapter one, and with some trepidation drove to his Oxfordshire cottage with my copy. He was generous with his praise, and incisive with his criticism.

'Your first three pages are just introduction,' he said. 'They're waffle really, a bit like a long description of reversing your car out of the garage before you set off on a grand adventure. Who wants to know? Ask yourself if we need all that stuff. And if we do, does it have to be at the beginning of the book? Start by painting the picture, hooking the readers, giving them something to invest in!' He sent me for a walk round the garden, and began scribbling a new beginning.

> *Deep in the bushes the tiny puppy stood completely still. Occasionally its eyes flicked up to the boy crouched beside it. He was sixteen, short, with dark hair. In one hand he held a rope and in the other a spear.*
>
> *Suddenly the puppy's ears pricked up. The moment he and the boy had been waiting for had arrived. First there was a crashing sound, then a snorting sound, then a thundering sound, and suddenly a huge wild boar crashed, snorted and thundered out of the forest, coming straight at them.*

I went home with a first chapter about three times as good as the one I'd brought him, and started chapter two.

Hutchinson were complimentary about the book, and commissioned two more. By the time we'd finished our third I needed to make another trip to Oxfordshire.

'Richard, would it be all right,' I asked him, 'if I write the next book on my own? I've got your voice in my head now. I know what you're going to say before you say it. I don't need to come all the way over to Oxfordshire. You're here with me all the time I'm writing. Is that all right?'

'Absolutely!' he said. 'It's the moment I've been waiting for. Have another ginger nut!'

I've written over twenty children's books now, and four for adults. I won the *Blue Peter* non-fiction prize for *The Worst Children's Jobs in History* in 2007, and won it again in 2014 for *Tony Robinson's Weird World of Wonders – World War II*. Maybe it's not surprising that I've done OK. I spent two years being taught how to write by the man who became Britain's most successful Hollywood screenwriter ever, and his tutorials cost me 50 per cent of bugger all.

In the spring of 1986 I accepted an offer from the Arts Council to join the board of directors at the Bristol Old Vic in order to try and stop the rot. At one time it had been the country's number one repertory theatre, but it was a deeply conservative institution which had failed to change with the times, its programme was now as dull as ditch water and it was losing money hand over fist.

Walking back through the ugly 1970s foyer as a board member was like being the little guy in a fifties Hollywood film who's spoken out against the big organisation because he wants to save it from itself, has got fired, and a decade later comes back to sort it out.

My old friend Ted Braun, another fierce critic of the Vic, was now a professor and had recently been given a place on the board as the university's representative. In addition a new Bristol City Council had been elected, the Old Labour leadership had been replaced by a younger more radical group of councillors, and two of them, Hedley Bashforth and Bob Walton, were also now board members.

Our first meeting was the AGM. Could we muster sufficient support to oust the old chairman, Sir Alec Merrison, an academic and businessman who'd held office for well over a decade, and who in our eyes epitomised the ancient regime? It depended on who showed up, and whether any waverers could be persuaded to support us.

The meeting began at 10 a.m. The new board members were politely welcomed, but any searching questions were batted away by Merrison with a patrician distain. He looked like Laurence Olivier as the villain Crassus in *Spartacus*. Hopefully he was about to suffer a similar fate.

At 11.15 we broke for coffee. Ted and I nonchalantly wandered out of the room, then sprinted downstairs to the gentlemen's lavatories adjacent to the studio theatre. A few seconds later we were joined by Hedley, then by Bob, who leant against the door so no one else could come in. We went through the numbers in hushed whispers. One of our side hadn't turned up, but one of theirs hadn't either, and a waverer we thought would probably have joined the other camp had left early to go to the dentist.

'So do we go for it?' asked Hedley.

'Go for it!' replied Ted.

The next item was 'Election of Officers'. The local Tory leader, a wily old fox called Sir Bob Wall, proposed Alec Merrison be re-elected as chairman, there was a pause while Merrison went through the motions of looking round the room to see if there were any alternative candidates, and when none were forthcoming he started to say, 'In that case . . .' I put my hand up. 'Chair,' I began – I knew the word 'chair' rankled him – 'I'd like to propose Professor Ted Braun. You've given long and distinguished service, but I think you'll be the first to agree it's time for a change.' Merrison who, among the many posts he held, was vice-chancellor of the university, stared at the upstart professor long and hard.

'Are you happy to accept the nomination, Professor Braun?' he asked icily.

Ted looked as though the whole thing had come as a complete surprise to him. 'Er . . . yes, I think so. Yes, Alec, certainly.'

You could see in Merrison's face he knew his number was

up. He asked for a show of hands and when Ted won by two votes, he left the room, and never returned. Bob Wall hissed to me that this was a shabby way to treat a man who had contributed so much over the years. I smiled and said, 'You've had your time, Bob.' Ted took the chair, and I was elected vice-chair.

But this wasn't the last reel of a movie; there was a lot of hard work to do, and the next year was fraught with difficulty. The artistic director left, we made redundancies, and the theatre received wave after wave of bad press. But we held our nerve. We brought in an outside arts consultant, Pete Boyden, who produced an excoriating report on the way the organisation was run, and we began to put its recommendations in place. Under Ted's leadership, we eventually turned the Old Vic round, although it took a number of years before it was sailing in calmer waters. Without our intervention in those dark days it would undoubtedly have closed, but it slowly regained its former status, and now, three decades on, the dreadful front entrance has been demolished, the beautiful Georgian building has once again been revealed in its former glory, and it's currently producing some of the most successful shows in the provinces. If there was a happy ending for me, it came when the new artistic director, Paul Unwin, asked me to play Andrei in his production of Chekhov's *The Three Sisters*. It was a long time since I'd trodden the boards of the Bristol Old Vic but it felt like coming home.

Blackadder had become the most popular comedy series on television; the critics loved it, and the sales overseas were astronomical. A third series was a foregone conclusion. But before Ben and Richard began writing it, two perennial questions needed to be resolved: what period should it be set in, and which characters should be in it? Georgian England seemed, on the face of it, a ridiculously bad choice. Who knew who the Georgians were or what they did? Did anyone care about the

War of the Spanish Succession, or the Treaty of Vienna? And all the British kings were Germans called George; who was who and which did what? I didn't have a clue and I was a history fanatic; how could we expect the viewing public to be interested?

But Richard and Ben were keen on diving into the uncharted waters of Georgian comedy. 'If you want to write a funny *Blackadder* series,' Ben said, 'all you've got to do is buy the relevant Ladybird book. They've got six chapters, and we need six episodes. We've got Johnson and his dictionary, the French Revolution, highwaymen, duels, the Duke of Wellington, rotten boroughs . . . that's the plots done in five minutes, and it cost me less than a quid!'

Then Tim dropped a bombshell: he didn't want to play Percy any more. He still wanted to be known as a serious actor, and was worried he was in danger of being typecast as an idiot. We told him that a) he was an idiot, and b) this wasn't the 1960s; audiences liked seeing their favourite actors in different roles. But he was adamant.

I was gutted. He could be a prickly sod sometimes, but he was my friend and comedy partner. The three-way relationship between him, Rowan and me had always been a pleasure. The rehearsals had been fun, and the comedy flowed effortlessly. I'd have to say goodbye to that now.

Oddly, though, Tim's absence worked in my favour. I was now Rowan's only sidekick, the Ernie to his Eric. My role became even more important, and this was reflected in the opening credits. An unknown hand picked up a book in a library, and on the spine were revealed the words 'Rowan Atkinson'. The hand returned, and picked out another book which announced 'Tony Robinson'. I'd got second billing! What a promotion! I tried to tell myself this kind of thing didn't matter, what was important was the work, not the frills and furbelows. But the child actor in me thought differently. Actors either made it or they didn't, and now I had. I'd always been an achiever, and now

I'd achieved – I wouldn't have to worry anymore. I could sit back and enjoy the rest of my life. What a relief!

I even had my own punchline, although it wasn't originally mine. At least four characters, including Percy and Blackadder, had mentioned their 'cunning plans' in the first two series. But in the second episode of series three Baldrick accidentally destroyed Dr Johnson's newly written dictionary and wanted to replace it. 'I have a plan,' he said according to the script. I suggested I add the word 'cunning' to my line, to make it seem a more considered plan, one that was devious and unique, something I was deeply proud of no matter how ridiculous it might turn out to be. And when the others agreed this was a good idea, I remember thinking that it might be useful if I used the phrase in future episodes, because it could be deployed to put nonsensical strategies in Blackadder's mind which he wouldn't otherwise have thought of. Thirty years later at least one person a day still comes up to me and says, 'Ere, Tone, you got a cunning plan?', and I smile and nod with amusement as I'm bound to do.

Apart from losing Tim, the other big change was bringing in Hugh Laurie as the Prince Regent and future King George IV. We never doubted that he'd fit into the team, he'd already been in a couple of episodes of *Blackadder II* and was Stephen's writing partner, but none of us had expected that he'd have his performance nailed from day one. His Prince was an extraordinary creation, outrageous but subtle, extrovert but thoughtful, daft but absolutely believable. He had no idea how good he was, and was riddled with doubt, particularly prior to recordings. We thought of him as our brilliant new star, but he saw himself as the alien arrival who the audience would turn against for messing up the balance of the show. Nowadays he's a cool TV megastar with an underplayed wit, sexual magnetism, and complete control of his surroundings, but in those days he was a troubled neurotic who beat us all hands down in the insecurity stakes.

There wasn't a major part for Miranda or Stephen in this series, but they agreed to be in one episode each, as did Tim (he was the Scarlet Pimpernel, Stephen was the Duke of Wellington and Miranda a squirrel-hating highwayman), so it didn't seem as though the ensemble or our friendships were going to be irredeemably fractured.

Having Hugh on board meant we'd added another writer to the cast who was as opinionated as the rest of us about the scripts, and Richard and Ben got more and more frustrated by this. Ben, whose latest novel was currently flying off the shelves, said to me, 'When I'm with literary people I'm one of the country's most successful authors; when I'm at *Blackadder* rehearsals, I'm a fucking idiot. Which would you rather be?' But there was no doubt this collegiate way of working was producing some terrific gags, although they did tend to get more and more elaborate.

In the historic Samuel Johnson scene when I said for the very first time, 'I have a cunning plan, sir,' George replied, 'Hoorah!' and Blackadder said drily, 'Well, that's that. then, I wouldn't get overexcited, sir.' We all agreed this was a dull and rather pointless exchange, and that the key to making it better would be to provide Blackadder with a more interesting line. So throughout the rehearsal week we added new words and phrases to it until eventually Rowan's line was transformed into, 'I wouldn't get overexcited, sir. I have a horrid suspicion that Baldrick's plan will be the stupidest thing we've heard since Lord Nelson's famous signal at the Battle of the Nile: "England knows Lady Hamilton's a virgin. Poke my eye out and cut my arm off if I'm wrong."'

But the finest example of this kind of collective joke-building never made it into the show, because Rowan bottled out of saying it. In the episode entitled 'Dish and Dishonesty', Blackadder was made a lord and entered the palace kitchen proudly displaying his robe of state with ermine trim.

Mrs Miggins: Ooh, very nice! Ooh, it's real cat, isn't it?

Blackadder: This is not a cat, Mrs Miggins. This is finest leather-trimmed ermine with gold medallion accessories.

Mrs Miggins: Oh, go on, Mr Blackadder. It's cat. Ooh, look, they've left the little collars on!

In the script, Rowan then said:

Blackadder (reading a collar): 'Mr Frisky. If found, please return to Emma Hamilton, Marine Parade, Portsmouth.' Oh God! Who cares about a dead cat now that I'm a fat cat.

It was an excellent comic set-up but the punchline about the cat wasn't great. So the actors got to work, and eventually came up with the idea of Rowan reading the collar, and saying, "'If found, please return to Emma Hamilton, Marine Parade, Portsmouth.' Never in my wildest dreams did I think that one day I'd be up to my neck in Lady Hamilton's pussy.'

A great line that tragically went to waste.

20

THE SPRIGHTLY ROOFER

In the great gale of 1987 our house in Amhurst Road split in two, and it was all my fault. For some time Dad had been getting anxious and forgetful, and was losing interest in hobbies, like tending his chrysanthemums, that had previously given him a lot of pleasure. At first I assumed this was merely a symptom of old age, but when it showed no sign of abating, I suggested he might take up transcendental meditation which worked so well for me when I felt under pressure. This was completely out of his comfort zone but, to his credit, he agreed to give it a try, and got some relief from it.

In addition Mum and I decided that I should take as much weight as possible off his shoulders, particularly in the running of 138 Amhurst Road. The roof had started leaking, and with every bout of heavy rain it got worse. I was getting complaints from the tenants, and wanted to help, but I wasn't sure what to do. The income from the house wouldn't cover a major re-roofing, and none of them were inclined to pay more rent.

The problem seemed to solve itself when a sprightly young cockney bounded up our front steps and told me he'd been looking at our roof from the road. It was obviously in need of a major overhaul, he said, and he could do the job in a single day for £500 cash. This was 60 per cent less than any of the previous quotes I'd had, and I leapt at it. The following Monday a team of noisy young men carrying hods of brick tiles trudged up to the top of the house, and lugged piles of cracked and moss-covered slates back down.

'You don't want to use slates again. Dead old-fashioned,' the roofer had counselled.

As evening fell Tim Munro, Gareth and I stood outside the house gazing up at the newly completed roof. It looked sound, well laid and very pink.

Organising this kind of thing was obviously something I was pretty good at, so I decided to take on the job of renovating all the flats. En suite bathrooms would be installed, new kitchens assembled and fitted, defective windows replaced, and the whole place freshly painted from top to bottom. I contacted Hackney Council to find out what grants might be available and Carol, a shy young woman with a curly afro and big round glasses, came knocking at the door. She went round the house painstakingly making notes, asking questions and offering advice. When she'd finished, we went across to the Sandringham Arms, cancelled our evening appointments and drank and chatted till closing time. The following afternoon she came back with extra paperwork. I'd got a bottle of wine in, and she finally went home very much later than was appropriate.

Why had I bought that wine? Because I was lonely and a selfish sod? Because I was a hippy persuaded by Steve Stills' stricture 'If you can't be with the one you love, love the one you're with'? Whatever the answer, retribution was about to rain down on me.

The next day Carol phoned me to say that while she was happy to continue seeing me on a social basis, she'd compromised her ability to give me objective advice about the house and had spoken about this to one of her senior colleagues, who was going to take over the job. I felt a little remorseful, but understood her position, and booked an appointment with him a couple of days later.

I have seldom met a more unpleasant man. He was like Mr Mackay, the Scottish prison officer in *Porridge*, beaming with sadistic pleasure as he slowly made his way through the property seizing on various safety hazards and council restrictions

I hadn't even known existed. He shook the doors violently to test their stability and they came away at the hinges, he jumped up and down on the stairs and the wood crumbled beneath his feet. He deemed every one of the flats structurally unsound, and when he came to mine chuckled with sarcastic glee at the potential inferno I had on my hands. My kitchen was adjacent to the front door; all the other rooms ran off it. If my toaster caught fire and a blaze took hold, there'd be no escape for anyone, and we were four floors up.

Then he delivered his *coup de grâce*.

'Is the roof new?' he demanded.

'Brand spanking,' I said proudly.

He nodded at the ceiling.

'And what's that?'

'A trapdoor.'

'To?'

'The attic. We don't use it.'

'Mind if I . . . ?' he said, and clambered onto the kitchen units.

When he came back down, he couldn't quite conceal his pleasure.

'The roof tiles are totally inappropriate,' he said. 'You were ripped off. Cowboy was he? They weigh four times as much as the slates you should have up there. The pressure they put on the rest of the house is downright dangerous. You'll have to whip them off again.'

The next day he sent me a list of other dangerous items that needed immediate replacement. It was pages long. I didn't fancy being responsible for mass carnage and having to spend the rest of my life in Wormwood Scrubs for negligence and serial manslaughter, but Dad didn't have the money available for such a major structural overhaul, not right now. It would have to be a long-term project.

I phoned Mr Mackay, but he didn't return my calls. I went round to see him, but he was never in. I eventually wrote to him pleading for time, but he dug his heels in. My priapic adventure had cost me dear.

Eventually he relented a little and gave me an appointment. He scribbled a drawing on a piece of paper. 'It's a temporary wooden joist,' he said. 'It'll cost you a few hundred quid, but with a fair wind, it should stop the roof collapsing while you get everything else sorted out.'

The wind of 16 October 1987 was not fair. It tore through south-east England like a wild beast, uprooting trees, whipping off chimneys, and flattening fences and gardens. My roof didn't stand a chance.

I was in Bristol that night and avoided most of the mayhem, but the following morning I got a bewildered phone call from Gareth.

'I'm in bed,' he said, 'and I can see daylight.'

'Try closing the curtains.'

'They are closed. It's the wall. It's split.'

'It's what?'

'I can stick my hand through and wave at the people outside.'

Things worked out well for Gareth, and for the rest of Dad's tenants. They were given freshly renovated council flats close by, far nicer than anything I'd been planning for them. Hackney Council also bought 138 Amhurst Road to add to their social housing stock, and gave Dad a good price for it even though it was completely wrecked. I'd have to get a flat somewhere else, but *Blackadder II* was continually being repeated on the BBC, was selling well overseas, and the third series was proving equally popular, so getting a mortgage shouldn't be difficult.

The big loss was the house itself. It had been in the Robinson family for the best part of a century until my inept attempt to save money had destroyed it. I'd also lost the opportunity to live with people I could talk to, laugh with, and share ideas and dreams with. The spirit of Fred Place had lingered on at Amhurst Road, and now it had gone.

In the summer of 1988 following the last series of *Who Dares Wins*, I agreed to join the rest of the team on a live national tour, a final farewell to the TV show. It was the closest I ever came to living the rock and roll life. We were driven from town to town in a luxury coach with black-tinted windows, played poker all night, drank too much, and most of us put far too many dodgy substances into our bodies, and ordered vast amounts of food from the local Chinese restaurants which we never finished. We hardly knew where we were or who we were. In classic Spinal Tap fashion, I opened the show in Southend with the greeting, 'Hullo, Margate!'

We performed the 'Emperor's New Clothes' sketch, but took it one step further than on TV. Now I appeared naked as nature intended, and a couple of minutes after the sketch ended and I'd left the stage, I'd reappear in the stalls, announce that Jimmy and Rory had hidden my clothes, and make my bare-arsed way through the audience looking for them under the seats. At least I did until Lincoln.

The venue was the old Ritz cinema where there was no pass door between backstage and the foyer. In order to get into the stalls at the end of the sketch I had to exit the stage door, walk through the car park and come back into the theatre again. Tony Harper, the stage manager, was briefed to look after me, but he didn't have much time to spare because he had to nip swiftly back to the prompt corner to cue a sound and lighting change.

That night I left the stage, grabbed my dressing gown and slippers, and Tony and I sprinted through the car park to the side of the theatre where there was a door that led straight into the stalls. I whipped off my dressing gown, wrapped my slippers up in it, threw the bundle at Tony, and opened the door to make my entrance. At least I attempted to open it. It wouldn't budge. I pushed again, but there was still no movement. I turned to get Tony's help, but he was racing back towards the stage door again, and when I called him he didn't hear, and disappeared between the cars. I pummelled the door with my fists, but the realisation swiftly dawned that no one was going to open it, so bollock-naked, and trying to keep in the shadows as much as possible, I edged round the building looking for another entrance. There wasn't one on that side of the theatre, so I worked my way back to the stage door, but it was an unmanned fire door and the bar was down. I rattled and shook it, but no one came. I ran round the back of the theatre hammering on every door and window, but nobody answered. Once I'd checked the doors on three sides of the cinema, I realised I'd have to go out into the street, and walk back in through the front. I hid behind a large bin until there were no cars or people about, then strode purposefully onto the pavement towards the cinema entrance. I entered the foyer without further incident, and interrupted two young programme sellers who were checking the ice cream money. They looked startled, but I nodded in a reassuring fashion, and strode past them into the theatre.

I was late for my entrance – in fact, so late that my scene had finished, and Phil and Julia were halfway through the next one. But I walked through the stalls anyway, and got my laughs. My feet were bleeding and I felt a complete idiot, but at least I hadn't messed up the show.

'Sorry I was off,' I murmured apologetically to Jimmy when the curtain had fallen.

'Were you?' he replied. 'Yes, I suppose you were. It didn't matter, it was brilliant, we just made stuff up.'

Jimmy had become as crazy as Rory, and the two of them were on a roll. They seldom slept, and their lives were chaos, but they churned out top-class comedy ideas twenty-four hours a day. They were consistently funny, great storytellers and overwhelmingly generous, but woe betide anyone who they thought was an idiot or who got in their way.

At school there'd been a boy in the year below me who'd decided he wanted to be my friend. He was a genius at maths, but a loner who ignored the norms of school life, and was constantly in trouble. One day he stole a little green van and took me for a joyride through the lanes of Woodford Green. He drove at lunatic speed, furiously applying opposite lock as the vehicle skidded from one side of the road to the other. I was in the back, rolling round like the last Smartie in the tube, desperately trying to grab on to something to stop my face smashing against the sides. It eventually came to a halt, he opened the back doors, and I stumbled out. I was flushed, giggling and completely terrified, but I felt utterly alive. That was what it was like being in Jimmy and Rory's orbit.

They survived the crazy eighties and beyond surprisingly well, like aging rock stars who have defied the laws of nature by not being dead yet. Rory's now a household name, his short bursts of surreal, scabrous wit tailor-made for quiz shows and panel games. He even stole my thunder in 2012 by presenting a series on Channel 5 about pub archaeology, the perfect vehicle for his polymathic mind. Jimmy became the most successful of us all; these days he's an international producer, jetting across the Atlantic, pitching ideas and negotiating deals with the same energy he had thirty years ago. He's deeply committed to his sobriety now, but whenever I see him, I'm immediately sucked back into his orbit, intoxicated by the scent of excitement he generates. I love him in the same way I loved Steve Marriott, but I could never be like him. I don't have the staying power.

In 1989 we made the fourth and final series of *Blackadder*. John Lloyd was highly influenced by the classic BBC comedies of the 1960s like *Hancock's Half Hour* and *Steptoe and Son*, and wanted to create a *Blackadder* series that would be set in a similar tightly enclosed world, with scripts focussing on the hero and his close circle of acquaintances to the exclusion of virtually any other characters.

Ben and Richard came up with the idea of the First World War, a period Ben was passionate about. Initially this seemed to me a bit gruesome and rather bizarre, but the more I thought about it, the more convinced I became. The war would give us lots of different storylines, it was history with which our viewers would be familiar, there'd be plenty of opportunity for satire, and the trenches would create the required sense of claustrophobia. We were worried that a comedy about such recent carnage might upset people who remembered it, but Ben was adamant that if we made it clear we were satirising the madness that caused the war, rather than taking the piss out of those who died, we'd give no cause for offence.

Two years after we'd completed *Blackadder the Third*, Rowan, Stephen, Tim, Hugh and I met up at Colchester Barracks to shoot the opening titles of *Blackadder Goes Forth*. It was sheer pleasure to be with the old team again. They were confident, dazzlingly inventive, and at the top of their game. It was like suddenly finding yourself playing in the Brazilian national football team. John Lloyd and the director, Richard Boden, were in a playful mood. There was plenty of improvising, Stephen fell off his horse, and we did a lot of silly marching round the parade ground which the editor made look grainy and jerky in post-production, like a piece of archive film. The soldiers stationed there enjoyed the messing about, and couldn't have been more helpful. They took a particular shine to me because they had a regimental goat called Baldrick. I told them how flattered I was, but in fact by this time virtually every platoon in the British army had a small, scruffy animal or inept private soldier who was named after my character.

Rehearsals went better than ever, at least from the actors' point of view. We were ultra-sensitive to each other's way of working by now, and I don't remember a cross word between us.

But the writers weren't happy with what we were doing. We weren't only trying to improve their gags, we were altering scenes, and even the plots of entire episodes. The crunch came when John Lloyd invented a brand-new character, a suspected German spy, cast the actor Bill Wallis (who'd previously played Ploppy the jailor), and inserted him into the show. Ben and Richard were furious. What made it doubly humiliating was that the people apparently sidelining them weren't only colleagues, they were their close friends.

Despite the charged atmosphere, the feedback from the technicians and guest actors was that episodes one to five were our best yet; although when it came to episode six we seemed to have a disaster on our hands. From our earliest discussions we'd agreed that Blackadder and Baldrick should die at the end of the series, given that this was the fate that befell so many British soldiers. There wasn't anything particularly unusual about this ending; characters had died at the end of every series so far, including Blackadder himself on two occasions. But the First World War was indiscriminate slaughter. Shouldn't Hugh's character, George, die too? He was a lieutenant, and the death rate among junior officers was even higher than that of the other ranks. And what about Captain Darling?

Tim McInnerny's return to the series had been a triumph. He'd agreed to come back on condition that he wouldn't have to play a reincarnation of Percy, but his new character had seemed rather dull, an embittered officer called Cartwright who had a deep loathing for Edmund Blackadder. Stephen suggested we change the character's name to Darling so he could say things like, 'Take this down, Darling', and 'How do I look, Darling?', and although we were sceptical, the more times Stephen's General Melchett said the name the funnier it became. Part of the reason Edmund detested Darling was that he was safe behind the Allied line far away from the fighting. Should he stay there for the whole final episode and survive, or should he be sent to the front too? This wasn't resolved till the last week of rehearsals when we all agreed that the only survivor should be Stephen's oafish general. Officers of his rank and class were seldom close enough to the action to be killed by the rain of German bullets that fell on those who acted on their orders.

The final scene was to be set in no-man's land between the British and German trenches where the four of us would charge across a muddy field to our deaths. But this required a lot of space. Our normal studio, the biggest at the BBC, was taken up by our usual sets and the banks of audience seating, so we'd need a second one.

In those days every show recorded at Television Centre had to finish at 10 o'clock on the dot; our electricians were insistent on that. Even a thirty-second overrun would result in a black-out or fiercely punitive overtime. This episode was particularly complex even without taking the final scene into account, and we didn't finish recording in our first studio till quarter to ten. We then hurtled round the basement corridor to our second studio pursued by the cameras and the production crew. When we arrived, we saw the set for the first time. The scene painters had been under similar time constraints to us. No-man's land looked like the set of a student production of *Waiting for Godot*, with a couple of blackened trees, wet paint and random pieces of exposed polystyrene sticking up hither and thither.

But there was no time to be critical; it was now ten minutes to ten, and once everyone was in position and instructions had been given, a further five minutes had gone by. We'd only be able to do one take. We crouched at the edge of the set out of sight, Richard Boden called action, and we clambered out into no-man's land, although my webbing got tangled up in the ladder, and by the time I'd sorted myself out, I was four or five paces behind everyone else. The sound effects were to be dubbed on in the edit, so when we were sufficiently close to camera, Richard shouted, 'Bang! Bang! Bang!' and we all fell to the ground dead. But because the set was made of polystyrene we bounced. And that was that! We'd run out of time! An episode that had been planned to culminate in an emphatic statement about honouring those who fell in the Great War ended with a frozen frame of four British soldiers a couple of inches off the ground.

That night the celebrations were muted. We were offered a glass of wine in a soulless reception room at Television Centre, and Stephen made a speech thanking everyone for their contribution. He thought he included Richard Curtis and Ben, but they were adamant that he hadn't, were deeply hurt, and after a drink or two everyone went home.

We didn't know how Richard Boden, John and our excellent editor, Chris Wadsworth, had tackled the problem of the non-ending until the show was transmitted. Their solution has become legendary. They slowed down the shot of us running towards camera, so we no longer looked like ducks waddling along in uniform but more like half-seen images in a dreamscape; they created a misty wash around us which obscured the unfinished set; they gradually withdrew the colour from the picture until no-man's land became black and white like a silent movie; and they froze the shot at the moment when we began to fall to the ground, then mixed through to an empty field, brought the colour back, and finally mixed again to reveal a landscape of blood-red poppies. And all the while an elegiac rendition of the *Blackadder* theme tune was being played on a piano, accompanied by the beating of a solitary drum. A major cock-up had given birth to great art!

Life in 1989 was looking good. I was co-starring in Britain's number one comedy series, more job offers arrived every day, and my newfound celebrity meant Luke and I got free lanes at the bowling alley, and could jump the queue at McDonald's.

But it took a single telephone call to make all this irrelevant, and for reality to intervene in the cruellest way possible.

21

THE USELESS DOCTOR

Mum never phoned anyone after seven thirty at night because she didn't think it was polite. So when she called my new flat in Acton at quarter to eleven, I knew something was wrong straight away.

'I've rung the doctor,' she said. 'Dad woke me up and made me go downstairs and get the cups out of the cupboards. He said I had to put them on the kitchen table and make all the handles point north-east, but I don't know where north-east is,' and she began to cry.

Dad's behaviour had been getting erratic recently, but Mum never wanted to talk about it. 'You've got enough on your plate,' she'd say. 'He's just a bit of a worrier.' That was certainly true; he always had been. Years previously, when I'd got my first decent wage packet, I bought the pair of them a Goblin Teasmade so they wouldn't need to go downstairs for their early-morning cup of tea. But I never saw them use it and eventually found it in the spare room wardrobe, still in its box, hidden under a tea towel. Apparently Dad was scared of it; he didn't like having anything electric switched on when he was asleep.

But now she admitted his anxiety had got much worse. He was patrolling the house before he went to bed, pulling every plug out of its socket, checking again five minutes later to make sure he hadn't missed one, then doing the whole thing again in the middle of the night. And he was more obsessive, insisting that all his bits and pieces be packed away tidily – his shoes in a long line, his socks in rows. He'd get agitated for no reason, ask Mum to do things she didn't understand, and when she tried to get him to explain, he'd get angry and shake her.

I asked her to put him on the line, but it was a scary conversation – in fact, not really a conversation at all. He kept tapping the phone and making noises into the receiver. Luke used to do the same thing when he was tiny. I'd phone home from London to tell him how much I loved him, but he didn't understand what a telephone was for. He'd blow fart noises into the receiver, do farmyard impressions, or just wander away when I was in mid-conversation.

'Hello, Dad,' I said gently.

'Hellooooo!' he went. 'Hellooooo!'

'It's me, Dad. Tony.'

'Hellooooo!'

Our chats had always been peppered with daft gags and stupid impressions, but this helloooing wasn't funny, it was eerie. I talked to him for a long time. I told him in graphic detail what I'd been doing that day. I said the doctor was going to come and see him any minute now, and that he didn't have to worry because he'd be better soon. I even sang him a bit of Gilbert and Sullivan like I used to as a boy: 'A wandering minstrel I, a thing of shreds and patches . . .' But he'd gone completely silent. I'd no idea if he was still listening or even if he had his ear to the phone, but I couldn't shut up. I was terrified that if I stopped talking I'd hear the 'hellooooo' again, and I couldn't stand the thought of that.

Eventually the doorbell rang and a locum arrived. He took Dad back to bed, and I stayed on the phone while he administered a tranquilliser. It was either a very strong one, or he felt reassured by the doctor's presence, because he drifted off almost straight away. The locum said he probably wouldn't wake up for about eight hours, and that Mum and I should get some sleep. 'You'll need your strength for tomorrow,' he said. 'Nothing more's going to happen tonight, he's exhausted, bless him!'

I drove across London to Raymond Avenue first thing. Dad woke up about half past nine, and at first seemed more like his old self, although maybe a bit more dozy than usual. But I soon realised he wasn't behaving towards me like he usually did, and it was a bit unsettling. Since I was a child we'd disagreed about politics, my career and my dress sense, but he'd always adored me and was particularly prone to embarrassing public displays of affection. Now he was being polite and detached. I tried to fool around with him, hug him, and tell him how rubbish Leyton Orient had been lately, but this only seemed to agitate him. He grew more and more hostile and it eventually dawned on me that he had no idea who I was. Why had this stranger come into his house? Why was I being overly familiar with him and his wife? Mum said I should leave the room for a while to see if he'd calm down. I paced around the hall for what seemed like hours, feeling I'd abandoned Mum, but not knowing what to do for the best. We'd managed to get an appointment at the doctor's surgery, but not till 4.30. It felt like a lifetime away. What were we going to do with him until then?

Mum eventually managed to get him into my car, and we drove round Epping Forest and down to Westcliff-on-Sea and back. He was talking non-stop in a disjointed fashion, sometimes coherently, and sometimes like the Mad Hatter. 'Don't say crabs. I don't want to hear it. They're like . . . you know, that singer . . .' I didn't dare stop driving; I was scared he'd open the door and run away.

When I eventually pulled up outside the surgery he was mumbling away about privet hedges. I told him where we were, he chattered for a few seconds as though he hadn't heard me, then suddenly stopped, and a miraculous transformation took place. By some extraordinary act of willpower he'd pulled himself together, and was sane, sociable Leslie Robinson again. It was as though the previous sixteen hours had been a performance, a weird practical joke to wind us up, and now he'd decided to stop.

'Let's get going,' he said.

The doctor was running behind and we had to sit in the waiting room for half an hour. Dad didn't say much. Occasionally he whistled a snatch of 'Three Little Maids from School', beamed at the receptionist, or nodded at the other patients, but there were no more monologues, nothing about hedges or crabs. A battered wooden table dominated the room and on it were piles of tattered magazines. Mum read *Woman* and *Women's Realm*, and I flicked through the *Reader's Digest*, but we couldn't concentrate. Time dragged by, other patients came and went. There was a girl with her arm in a plaster cast covered in signatures, an old man who sneezed a lot, and a grizzling child being placated by sweets. Eventually the receptionist called Dad's name, we trooped into the surgery, and sat in stiff, high-backed chairs facing the doctor's desk.

'What's the problem, Mr Robinson?' he asked.

'Oh, nothing really. Just the usual aches and pains,' said Dad.

'Tell the doctor what's been happening, Mum,' I insisted.

Her previous doctor had recently retired, and she didn't know this man. She tried to explain what had been going on, but she made it sound as though it was nothing, just a silly bit of nonsense hardly worth bothering about. Why was she behaving like this? Was it out of politeness, or loyalty to Dad? Either way it wasn't helping us.

I interrupted her and started describing the business about the cups, Dad's attitude towards me, the stream of nonsense, the whole nightmare of the last twenty-four hours. But the doctor didn't seem to be listening; he just smiled and nodded. When I finally ground to a halt, he winked at Dad and said, 'Well, that all sounds rather dramatic. I suppose your son is looking for a cunning plan, Mr Robinson,' which I thought was a pretty crass remark in the circumstances.

'Yes,' said Dad. 'That sounds a good idea. A cunning plan, please, doctor.'

'Let's have a look at you then.'

He felt Dad's pulse and listened to his heart. Dad made a joke about the coldness of the stethoscope, and they both chuckled.

'Doesn't seem to be much the matter with you,' he said. 'We all get funny turns as we get older. Have a good rest, pop in again on Monday, and we'll see if you're still OK. That cunning enough?'

'Cunning enough,' replied Dad cheerily.

'Thank you,' said Mum, and she and Dad left the room. I stayed where I was. I'd never felt so angry in my life, or more abandoned. I pleaded with the doctor to understand that the man he'd been examining wasn't the man we'd been dealing with all day.

'It's probably an infection,' he said. 'Old people do tend to go a bit peculiar when they catch a bug. He's right as rain now, isn't he? I'll give him something to put your minds at rest. How old is he again?' He glanced down at his notes. 'Seventy-five? Yes, these things happen.'

I walked back to the car clutching a prescription for some antibiotics. I was still seething, but not only with the doctor. I was angry with Mum too for not speaking up, and with myself for coping with the situation so badly. And what was Dad playing at? He'd not only wilfully avoided getting the help he needed, he'd also made me look a complete fool.

We drove back in silence. My head was throbbing, and my shoulders were knotted tight. Then Dad started whistling again.

'He's very tricky,' he said.

'Who's tricky?' Mum asked. 'The doctor?'

'Him. In the front. He's very tricky.'

I'd been the apple of Dad's eye. He'd lovingly put together leather-bound scrapbooks of my entire career, and showed them to visitors at every opportunity. Now I was his enemy. It was like when he was cross with me as a child: I felt guilty, abandoned and absolutely bereft.

When we got home, Kate Reeve came round. She was a widow, ten years or so younger than Mum. She lived over the road, and had been Mum and Dad's best friend since Sue Pears' parents had died. She plonked herself down next to Dad and held his hand. She said how nice his chrysanthemums were looking, and told him she was going to Stratford to see *As You Like It*, and that he and Mum ought to come too. The fear and suspicion that had plagued him all day melted away, and were replaced by a quiet sadness. He was like someone recently bereaved; half of him was with us, the other half locked away somewhere else nursing his pain.

Eventually his eyes closed, and we tiptoed into the kitchen where Mum was polishing the taps.

'I think it's Alzheimer's,' Kate said.

The thought hadn't crossed my mind. No one spoke about Alzheimer's in those days. If you didn't think about it, it might pass your family by. I'd assumed he had some sort of pressure on his brain, or food poisoning maybe. We sat in the kitchen for a long time, not saying much, but sharing the knowledge that there were going to be some very dark days ahead.

I was rehearsing in London, so I was able to stay at 14 Raymond Avenue for the next few weeks. I'd been given my biggest commission yet by the BBC children's department. My inspiration had come from watching Laura play football in the playground when I went to collect her from school. She was tiny, useless at passing, and raced around chasing the ball like a crazy person trying to catch a butterfly. But by sheer force of personality she'd become one of the twin strikers in the school football team, which was comprised of ten other athletes almost as inept as she was. She'd yell words of exhortation, willing them on to greater acts of sporting prowess, while they bumbled about, hoofing the ball hither and thither, falling over with expressions of terrible agony on their faces, then getting up and racing off again. I thought to myself, *If she'd been born eight hundred years ago and had hung out with Robin Hood, it wouldn't have been him who ran the gang*, and the image stuck in my mind.

At the time I was writing a thirteen-part series for Children's BBC about my childhood hero, the mythic Greek traveller Odysseus. It had been a labour of love. For a year my sitting room floor was covered with typed-out translations of *The Iliad* and *The Odyssey*, books on the Mycenaeans, and various other stories about Odysseus that cropped up in Greek and Roman manuscripts. Eventually I pieced them all together and wrote a saga called *Odysseus: The Greatest Hero of Them All*, which encompassed not just the Trojan War, but his whole life.

Given that this was a three-thousand-year-old myth about someone whose name most kids couldn't even pronounce, the show got surprisingly high viewing figures. We picked up some good reviews and a BAFTA, a Royal Television Society Award, and the International Prix Jeunesse. On the strength of this the children's department asked me to write more shows inspired by ancient legends, and I agreed to try, but now I wanted to be more ambitious than simply telling stories to camera. I knew how much kids liked *The Young Ones*, *Blackadder* and *The Lenny Henry Show* – Laura and Luke's friends couldn't get enough of them when they came round to our house and raided my VHS library – so I came up with the idea of creating a full-scale half-hour comedy series based on the Robin Hood saga, keeping the spirit of the original, but with the buzz of alternative comedy about it. I'd call it *Maid Marian and Her Merry Men*.

I developed the idea with producer Dave Bell, a curly-haired hippy who I'd collaborated with on my Greek mythological programmes, and to our astonishment the children's department accepted the idea straight away. I went ahead and wrote the scripts, and suddenly we'd been given a half-a-million-pound budget, a design team, and a wardrobe and costume department. Dave cast the brilliantly stroppy but idealistic Kate Lonergan to play the brilliantly stroppy but idealistic Maid Marian, and a team of talented and eccentric actors to play the Merry Men, while ex-Poldark regular Forbes Collins, who had a voice like a randy bull seal, became King John. We debated long and hard about whether I should be Robin or the Sheriff of Nottingham, but I'd been playing sweet, innocent Baldrick for years now, it would be a refreshing change to be an incompetent Sheriff who our viewers could enjoy seeing humiliated each week. It would also allow me to write a part in which I could dictate the tempo of the show, like a grumpy, dysfunctional circus master cracking his whip.

As soon as we started rehearsing I knew we had something special on our hands. Dave was a sensitive director; his casting was inspired, his leadership skills held the team together, and he gave me the space to develop the comedy in whatever way I wanted. He and I particularly enjoyed working with the composer/musicians, writing songs for the show inspired by current pop genres.

> *Marian!*
> *Why don't you carry on*
> *With what you're doing*
> *Coz there's always trouble brewing.*
> *You've got to find a way,*
> *To make a better day,*
> *Oh, Marian!*

The performers blossomed, our design team were inspired, and our costumes were quirky but with a strong sense of period. The days were exciting and creative, but each night I had to go back to a demented dad and a mum who was barely coping. I did my best, but I was exhausted.

Mary and the kids came up from Bristol each weekend. Dad was extraordinary with the children. In an act of will similar to the one he'd demonstrated when he first went to the doctor's surgery, he immediately stopped being angry and aggressive when they were around. He'd still be bonkers, but in a charmingly dotty way like a Dickens character. The kids were unfazed by the fact that he didn't behave like other people, and adored his antics. One day we were mucking about on the sitting room floor with Dad looking on when he suddenly turned to Luke and said, 'Look out of the window, would you, Charlie Winklesnitch.'

'What am I looking for Grandpa?'

'Can you read my number plate?'

'Yes,' said Luke, and he read it out.

'No, that's not right,' said Dad, 'It's AAA-AAA-AAAA-AAAA . . .'

'AAA-AAA-AAAA . . .' we all chorused.

Eventually Dad petered out.

'It must make it hard for you to overtake,' I said. 'I expect you're whacking into other cars all the time with a number plate that long.'

He wagged his finger at me, and gave me a long, sad smile. He knew he was being daft, knew he no longer had a grasp on the real world, and knew that I knew it too. I felt closer to him than I had for a long time.

I was deeply grateful for the work Mary was putting in with Mum and Dad. She was always on hand and invariably sympathetic, although when we were on our own she seemed distant. I asked her why, but she was vague and said it was nothing to worry about, which somehow worried me even more. When I pressed her, she told me to forget about it.

It gnawed away at me. In rehearsals, when the cast went to lunch, I'd lie on the floor and try to meditate, but I couldn't stop thinking about my troubles at home. I told her that if there was a problem between us I'd rather know what it was than get more and more anxious, and eventually she admitted she'd found someone else. I couldn't blame her. For years I'd been a lousy partner. I spent most of my time in London with my own circle of friends and the occasional lover, I was obsessed by my work, and when I came home I poured my energies into my children rather than into my relationship with her. I still loved her deeply, but I was useless at sustaining that love.

I asked her if she was leaving me, and she told me not to be silly. The priority was Dad and Mum. She promised me unconditional support. Anything else could be dealt with at some time in the future.

The following evening on the way back from rehearsals, I stopped off at a pub in Leytonstone. I couldn't face seeing Dad without a drink or two, and the words 'at some time in the future' kept ringing round my head. The saloon bar was empty except for a beefy, tanned man in his forties with a gold chain round his neck, and another round his wrist. I thought he was probably a cabbie. He was chatting to the barman in a cheery, confident cockney accent. I went to the other end of the bar, and when the barman came over I ordered a light ale and a small Bell's. After a while the man sidled up to me.

''Ere, you're Tony Robinson, right?'

I agreed that I was.

'You are a cunt!' he laughed.

He didn't mean it maliciously. It was a London thing. I'm as good as you, he was saying, but respect where respect's due, mate, you're well known, and you're funny. At least I think that's what he meant.

But I sat there for a long time thinking how right he was. Dad was horribly ill and Mum was worn to a frazzle, but I didn't even have the decency to go straight back to South Woodford after work to help them out. I'd failed in my relationship with the mother of my children, she'd probably leave me and I'd lose my kids; I had huge responsibilities at work which were weighing me down, and I couldn't think straight. I was also feeling very sorry for myself.

I was indeed a cunt.

Maid Marian was filmed in the woods on the slopes of Porlock Hill in Devon, and was as big and complex an operation as the original *Blackadder* shoot in Alnwick, only we had ten times more filming to do. We nicknamed it the 'Smoke and Chickens Show'. To create a misty, medieval atmosphere the special effects department swathed each and every set with smoke via four deafeningly loud machines, and on 'Action' an animal handler would rush into frame and dot the ground with live chickens.

We seldom managed to achieve the effect we were after. In seconds the smoke was blown away by the coastal breezes, and the chickens invariably sprinted back to their cages the moment their claws hit the ground. But we carried on with our 'Go smoke! Go chickens!' routine as an act of faith.

We were like a huge gypsy camp. There were lots of extras, inordinate numbers of costumes, prop-makers, special effects and countless lorries, but we felt completely cut off from the rest of humanity, surrounded by thick woods, uninhabited countryside and beyond it an enormous expanse of sea. There were no phone boxes nearby, and I had the only mobile phone. It was new on the market, an enormous contraption made by British Telecom, complete with an extending aerial, a massive battery pack and charger, and a big black plastic case to put it all in. But since there was virtually no reception on the north Devon coast, I lugged it about all day for no good reason.

There were quiz evenings at the Foresters Arms in Dunster, sports days and larks in the holiday cottages in which everyone was billeted, but I seldom joined in. I felt the need to go back to Bristol every night. It was a mad commute; I'd spend an hour and a half driving through winding country roads, then twenty minutes speeding up the motorway. Mary told me I didn't need to come back so often, and part of me knew it would have been wiser to give her the space she needed, but I wasn't feeling wise, and those four hours a day gave me an illusory sense of control over my life which was sadly missing elsewhere.

My only solace during *Maid Marian* was the company of David Lloyd and Mark Billingham who played my henchmen, the Norman guards Gary and Graeme (although I can never remember who played which!). They were both talented but inexperienced writers, and as demand for more episodes increased, I asked them to come up with some storylines for me. This was an enjoyable and larky process, and eventually I suggested the three of us write a *Maid Marian* episode together. It was called 'Tunnel Vision', was a spoof of Richard O'Brien's *Crystal Maze*, and was one of the most popular we ever made. Dave went on to become a full-time scriptwriter on shows like *Doctors* and *EastEnders*, while Mark wrote crime novels like *Sleepyhead* and *The Burning Girl* and is now one of the most successful and well-respected authors in the country. I like to think that my early encouragement was something of a payback for the help and support I'd been given by Richard Curtis.

Dad seemed to be getting worse. Looking after him was a monumental task, but Mum had built up a network of female friends over the years, 'my girls' as she called them, and they gave her tremendous support, taking her out shopping and on little trips, giving her a shoulder to cry on, and babysitting him. I'd always been sniffy about life in the semi-detached world of South Woodford – 'petit bourgeois' I used to call it – but now I was grateful for the warmth and neighbourliness it offered her.

Three months after Mum had phoned me with the mad story about the cups, Dad had a heart attack and was rushed to Whipps Cross Hospital. At the time it seemed one more dreadful event heaped on top of everything else, but there was a positive outcome, or at least there appeared to be. Dad's behaviour was so odd that a couple of specialists were sent to take a look at him, and yes, he did have some kind of dementia. In a strange way we were relieved to know this. It was the first tentative diagnosis we'd had from anyone other than Kate. Now a place would be found for him in a psychiatric hospital where he'd be properly assessed and looked after by specialist nurses.

The London County Lunatic Asylum, later renamed Claybury, was the East London equivalent of St Lawrence's where we'd filmed *Joey*. It had been built in the 1890s, but despite the stigma of its origin, it had a good reputation among the medical profession, although it terrified everyone who lived in its shadow. For us it was a black hole into which you were cast without hope of rescue. 'If you keep upsetting your mum, she'll end up in Claybury,' Dad used to say to me.

Now he was threatened by the same terrible fate, and this time it was for real. 'Don't bother coming to see me,' he said. 'I won't be good for anything once I'm in Claybury.'

We didn't share his despondency. We were optimistic that there'd be people at the hospital who'd understand what was wrong with him, and a few weeks on her own would give Mum a rest. But our first visit shattered our confidence. It took us a long time to work out in which part of the vast old building Dad was located, and when we eventually found his ward, our way was blocked by two women having a row. They had long, lank hair, and white hospital nightdresses that had turned light grey after countless washes. One of them had accidently tucked the bottom of hers into the back of her pants, and her legs, blotchy and discoloured by varicose veins, were completely exposed. Mum winced and clutched my arm tight, but I knew it wasn't the appearance of the women that distressed her so much. She'd been brought up in a tiny tenement in the poorest part of Hackney, and for her, the demarcation line between her early life and the respectability she'd succeeded in creating for herself in South Woodford was 'language'. She never swore, and was repulsed by anyone who did. But these two women didn't share her qualms. They were effing and blinding as though there was no tomorrow.

'Afternoon, ladies,' I said in my best cheeky-chappy voice. 'Would you mind if we squeezed past so we can see my old man?'

They backed away immediately.

'Thanks. See you!' I said.

'See you!' they chorused.

We walked down the long ward. On either side elderly men and women were curled up asleep, or were sitting silently in their bedside chairs staring at us. A voice murmured something, someone shouted a few indistinguishable words, then there was silence again. We found Dad sitting up in bed dressed in a pair of blue-striped NHS pyjamas. His wig was on the little table beside him next to a half-full glass of water. He was drugged to the eyeballs, and his chin kept dropping onto his chest. We told him our news, and I gave him a lengthy account of the comings and goings of the previous week, and about the family of ramblers who'd unexpectedly come across our Porlock Hill set and had been outraged that its natural beauty had been spoiled by a pretend fourteenth-century village, twenty-five peasants and a location catering van. But his eyes were blank, his hands were cold, and he didn't show a flicker of interest.

Mum stoically visited him every day with fruit, Lucozade and a copy of the *Daily Express*, but I had to go back to Porlock. Each evening on my long return to Bristol, I'd pull into a layby, get out my gigantic phone, check that I could get a signal, then call Mum and ask her how he was. By midweek she said he was up and about again, but that he was 'walking funny'. When I saw him the following weekend I understood what she meant.

Dad's most vivid memories were of his five years in the RAF, but although he had loved the sense of liberation, the lack of responsibility, and the excitement of being the star of a boogie-woogie band, he'd hated the rules and regulations, and being ordered about by men far less clever than him but with more stripes on their arm. He'd resented the draughty barracks, the bunk beds, the interminable corridors, and the smell of unwashed men.

I don't know if he marched round his ward in Claybury because he genuinely thought he was back in a Nissen hut, or whether he was parodying the sense of humiliation and power-lessness he felt being in that kind of environment again. But he called the ward orderlies 'sir' and saluted the nurses, and did it without a hint of a smile.

He desperately wanted to come home. He said the orderlies tricked him and tried to take money off him, and the nurses bullied him. I didn't know how to deal with this information. Deluded people might feel threatened and conned, but that didn't mean they had no cause to feel that way. We eventually saw a consultant. He said he'd keep an eye on things, and assured us he'd no intention of keeping Dad in hospital longer than necessary. It would take some time to get the medication right, but once they had, he could come home.

After six weeks he was back with us. He wasn't frightened anymore, and didn't fly into rages, but he wasn't my dad. He was a puzzled, stoned old man sitting in his comfy chair watching the TV all day, nodding at anyone who popped their head through the door to make sure he was OK.

The *Who Dares Wins* team were asked to take part in a Secret Policeman's Ball gig for Amnesty. It wouldn't be an onerous job; we'd be performing a couple of sketches we already knew, our spot was near the top of the show, and we'd be out of the theatre each night by 8.45. I hadn't stayed overnight at Raymond Avenue for a while, and this would be a good opportunity to spend a bit of time with Dad.

At the Wednesday afternoon rehearsal, John Cleese asked me if I could stand in for Terry Jones. *Monty Python's Flying Circus* were down to do a spot and Terry was supposed to be joining them, but he was stuck in New York. I'd only have to learn a dozen or so lines, he said. He made it sound as though I'd be doing him a big favour, but as far as I was concerned, to be one of the Pythons, even if only for a couple of minutes, was the greatest honour a human being could have bestowed on them.

The first night went fine, and the following morning when Dad woke up I told him I'd got something special to show him. In a few weeks my face was going to be on the front cover of the *Radio Times*, and I'd been sent the polaroids and mock-ups for approval. You didn't often get a genuinely happy reaction from Dad these days, but when he saw my pictures, he beamed, took my hand and patted it over and over again.

I arrived at the theatre for the last night of the show to be told that Terry had finally returned, so I wouldn't be needed for the second half. I'd been planning to drive to Bristol afterwards, but it was early so, on a whim, I decided to pop back to South Woodford first to say goodnight to Dad.

When I got there, Mum was at his bedside. He was uncomfortable and kept saying, 'Ow! Ow! Ow!' in a staccato voice like a bad actor. We thought he'd probably had another heart attack and called the emergency doctor who said he'd come straight over. The pain gradually subsided, and Dad asked me to tell him my news. I talked to him about the show and the grandkids and told him how Kate Reeve had been keeping the garden nice for him. We held his hand, and after a while his eyelids closed, the muscles in his face relaxed, and his deep frown disappeared. He didn't look as haggard anymore, nor as old. It was as though the man who'd left us over a year ago had returned for a few moments. There was nothing we could do, or wanted to do, except wait. His breathing became shallower and eventually we weren't sure whether he was alive or not. I asked Mum if she had a mirror we could use to check whether he was still breathing, but we could only find her vanity mirror, a big one with a Bakelite handle, which we couldn't get close enough to his face, and we got a fit of the giggles. We stroked his head and his cheek, and carried on waiting. He was definitely quite still now. When the doctor finally came, in the early hours of 3 September 1989, he confirmed that Dad was dead.

He'd been much smarter than me, had a far wider range of interests, taught me how to think and take care of my finances, and played the piano exquisitely. He'd poured all his thwarted ambition into me, and although this was sometimes a heavy load to bear, it had bred determination and resilience in me, which had ultimately led to my success. I knew he'd taken great pleasure in this. I only wished I'd told him more often that I loved him, and how much I appreciated his faith in me.

After a couple of minutes I realised Mum wasn't there any more. I found her in the spare bedroom going through the wardrobe.

'What are you doing, Mum?'

There was a puzzled frown on her face.

'I think something worrying just happened,' she said, 'but I can't remember what it was, so I thought I'd better look for it.'

I've since learnt that this kind of amnesia is common among people under intense stress, but at the time it was heart-breaking.

The funeral took place a week later. Two months after that Mary left Glendale to start a new life.

22

THE GRIEF MONSTER

Living with the grief monster isn't easy. It picks you up and throws you all over the place. One minute you're in the kitchen wiping the worktops, the next you're staring out the bedroom window with no idea how you got there. It makes you dozy and listless all day, and wide awake all night.

Mary and I had managed to put the practicalities of our lives in order without too much acrimony. The agreement was that I'd look after the children whenever I was at home, and when I was working away she'd have them in the new house I'd bought for her in Hotwells, down by Bristol docks, a stone's throw away from Glendale. Laura was thirteen and Luke was ten, and for the first few weeks after the split-up they looked after me like a pair of tiny parents. I spent hours sitting on the sofa doing nothing, so to encourage me to be a bit more active, Luke built a blow football pitch on the dining room table. He used the green baize from the Subbuteo, and piled books round the edges so the ping-pong ball wouldn't roll on the floor, with two gaps for goals. He'd take me by the hand, lead me to the table and give me a drinking straw and a tissue out of the big Kleenex box, because when you're snivelling the snot tends to run down the outside of the straw and slows the ball down. He always won, even though he was a kid and I'm very good at blow football, because after a few minutes my attention would wander. When he realised I wasn't trying hard anymore, he'd lead me back to the sofa, put the box of Kleenex on my lap and we'd watch *The A-Team*.

Every night Laura clambered into my bed to read me her favourite books, *The Cats of Seroster* by Robert Westall, and Terry Pratchett's *The Colour of Magic*. Her voice was so warm and friendly that I'd nod off after a couple of minutes, and even though the reason she was reading to me was to help me fall asleep, she'd wake me up again and ask me what I remembered, which was only ever the first page. She'd sigh, go back to the beginning and start again, but I'd still nod off in the same place.

I was hurt and angry with Mary for a few months, although I realised I'd got no reason to be. She was a great mum, was generous about organising her arrangements round my work schedule, was supportive of my role as the kids' dad, and I couldn't ask for a better friend. I even had to admit that her new boyfriend Steve was a good bloke, and a far better partner for her than I'd been. I had to let go of her, stop moping, and start a new life. Thanks to my kids I crawled out of my lethargy. I wrote more than I ever had – books, sketches, a two-part *Maid Marian* special called 'Much the Minimart Manager's Son', and scripted and recorded countless episodes of a new series about cartoons called *Stay Tooned*.

The BBC had the rights to the extraordinary animations produced by Warner Brothers and MGM in the 1930s and 40s and were looking for a new way to present them. I was approached by producer and fellow animation-obsessive Nick Freand Jones, and we agreed that it would be fun to go through the entire BBC animation catalogue, find our favourite clips, and build whacky programmes round them. *Stay Tooned* was aimed at children, but we hoped it would also appeal to adults in general and cartoon nerds in particular. Nick would take the Intercity 125 down to Bristol on a Monday morning, we'd spend days huddled in comfy armchairs in my sitting room watching *Daffy Duck*, *Foghorn Leghorn* and *Speedy Gonzales*, then write scripts about cartoon comic devices, Tex Avery and the other great animators, the history of the studios, the use of music and sound effects, etc., and illustrate them with the funniest, most pertinent clips we could find. I'd have been happy to carry on making *Stay Tooned* to this day, but eventually Nick had to break the news to me that the BBC had lost the transmission rights to the new world of satellite and cable TV. It was a sad day.

I was at my happiest at home in Glendale. If I went away, I missed my kids, and started to feel nervous, wobbly and homesick. But I eventually plucked up the courage to go to Rome for a long weekend with Jim Broadbent, Tim McInnerny, Richard Curtis, and our clever young researcher Kevin Lygo (who twenty years later was my boss at Channel 4!). Richard paid for the trip. He'd been given an advance by the BBC to research a new comedy pilot, and we blew the lot.

The programme was to be called *The Chip Show*, and would star Jim, Tim and me as Italians who had their own chat show which they ran from their restaurant Il Cappuccino in Swiss Cottage. Why *The Chip Show*? Because, as Jim's character explained in his ridiculously broad Italian accent, it was *'chip to make'*. He was Franco Giambattista, a kindly and lugubrious restaurateur, and Tim and I were his waiters. Tim played Johnny, a self-declared sex god who danced like George Michael and smoked cigarettes like an Italian movie star, and I was Benni, who was shy, with Dennis Taylor glasses and a Tony Curtis haircut. I can't remember why we thought it was important to go to Rome in order to get to grips with our roles, but it seemed a valid thing to do at the time. We did the tourist bit round the Colosseum, the Forum and the Column of Marcus Aurelius, quaffed Chianti and stuffed ourselves with *osso buco*. Maybe it improved our Italian accents, perhaps we saw the occasional Roman in the street who in some way inspired us, but I suspect it was just an excuse for five blokes to have a big blowout away from home.

We were joined for the pilot by an absentee from the Rome

A publicity
shot of Teri.

With Keith Floyd in Seville;
his new girlfriend can just
be seen on the left.

Blood and Honey in
Israel. The *intifada*
was underway, and
sometimes it got a
bit scary.

Christmas with Mum and Teri at our house in Royal Park, Clifton.

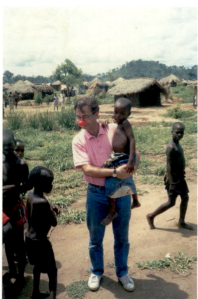

With local kids in Tanzania filming for Comic Relief.

Benni the waiter from *Yes, Minestrone* – the show that never happened.

Blackadder Goes Forth, Chichester Barracks, 1989.
L–R: Tim, Stephen, me, Rowan and Hugh.

Time Team. Working out where to excavate. L–R: Mick Aston,
John Ette from English Heritage, me and John Gater.

Time Team.
Phil Harding.

Time Team.
Mick and me.

Being ducked dressed as a fishwife for *The Worst Jobs in History* at Alnwick Castle.

Fulling wool in a bucket of urine supplied by the film crew over the previous week. St Fagans, Cardiff.

Heli, on a holiday we had in Kenya, November 1997.

Mum on one of her day trips from Harts House.

With Genya the Russian pilot and film director James Cameron as we prepared to dive the *Titanic*.

Luke and me.
Laura and me.

William and me.

June 2011. Louise at our wedding in Ravello with, L–R: Lou's mum Pam, Laura's husband Adrian, Lou's dad Mike, and Laura.

Louise and me on honeymoon in Taormina, Sicily.

trip, Miriam Margolyes, who played Franco's wife, a charming but ruthlessly assertive *signora* with whom he was besotted, but who terrified Johnny and Benni. There was no audience or any other characters in the show, merely a few extras eating pasta at their tables, blithely ignoring the chaos going on around them, and occasionally being served spaghetti and tiramisu by the two waiters. As for its contents, Franco told the viewers it was a magazine-style programme 'by Italians, for Italians, and for everyone else to enjoy', and included items like, '"What Happened to . . . ?", where we get a big star and ask him, "Aay! Whatever happened to you?" and "Watch It!" where you write us a letter about someone who has been getting on your nose, and we say to them, "Aay! Watch it!"'

It was a simple, charming and highly original show, and I was confident the BBC would like it as much as we did. Of course there was a lot wrong with it, but that's the nature of pilot programmes. The *Blackadder* pilot had been pretty dire, but had eventually become one of the biggest money-spinners the BBC had ever produced. Why shouldn't this be something similar? Jim's performance was top drawer, Tim seemed happy to be in a TV comedy again now that he was hidden behind an Italian accent, Richard as always provided strong, funny material, and we had a new title because *The Chip Show* had been deemed too obscure. It was now called *Yes, Minestrone*. What a great package!

But it only took the Corporation a few days to decide they didn't want it. I couldn't understand their decision, and still think they were wrong. Fifteen years later, *The Kumars at No. 42*, based on a similar premise, was a big hit, but the pilot of *Yes, Minestrone* was never even broadcast. It was the one that got away.

At the time I was disappointed, but relieved too. Its rejection meant I could go back home and be with the kids. I had plenty of work in the south-west anyway. For some time I'd been making shows for Radio Bristol. They were cheap, fun and easy to put together, and the station gave me a free hand to do pretty much what I wanted. One of my spoof documentaries got a lot of attention; it was about a small nuclear reactor an elderly couple had built in their garden shed in St Pauls, and the complaints from their neighbours about the fact that it was leaking a bit. I made it sound as much like a news report as possible, in the hope that anyone who casually tuned in would assume they were listening to a genuine piece of reporting, and would only gradually realise they'd been wound up.

Terry Pratchett had been a reporter working at the *Western Daily Press*. He liked my radio shows and made a note of my name. When his publisher decided to make an audio cassette of *The Colour of Magic* Terry suggested I should be the narrator. Baldrick was now a well-known character and a marketable commodity, so the publisher agreed that my profile was sufficiently high to take the job on. It was tailor-made for me. Terry and I had a similar sense of humour, he wrote sparkling prose which was a joy to read out loud, and I loved the challenge of creating a multitude of voices for the army of weird characters who populated his fantasy world. But most importantly *The Colour of Magic* was the book Laura had read to me when I was at my lowest ebb. It meant a lot to me. I'd have been furious if anyone else had been asked to read it.

Terry's publisher drafted in Maurice Leitch, an Irish novelist and BBC radio producer, to oversee the project, and we recorded it at Bedminster's old fire station, which had been converted into a sound studio. The tape sold well, so the publishers decided we should put Terry's entire back catalogue on cassette. Recording sessions were brief but exhausting. I'd read the script at home, and write notes in the margin describing how I wanted each character to sound – 'fat, Leeds and nasal', 'West Country idiot with stammer', 'young James Mason', 'weaselly, stoned, cockney', etc. – then went into the studio and recorded the whole book straight through, only stopping and going back to the beginning of a sentence when I fluffed or got the voices confused. I taped each book in two four-hour sessions, then went back to bed for the rest of the day.

We always felt on edge when Terry showed up. I'd sit in the tiny glass recording booth watching him on the other side of the soundproof window scowling with disappointment. He looked pretty intimidating, but I knew it wasn't personal. Our recordings were adaptations about 30 per cent shorter than the original, and he wanted his audience to hear the books in their entirety.

He dressed in black, a cross between Merlin the Wizard and Johnny Cash, and wore a wide-brimmed black hat which I think was supposed to make him look magical and mysterious. If you'd seen him in the street, you'd probably have assumed he was a bit of a show-off, but he was a shy, solitary man who buried himself away in the gothic writing den he'd built for himself next to his house in Wiltshire. I was invited to a party to celebrate his fiftieth birthday in a private dining room upstairs at The Ivy restaurant. I was very flattered; I didn't think I was sufficiently close to him to be worthy of the invitation, until I realised that virtually all the other guests were work colleagues too; his friends could be counted on the fingers of one hand. The people he seemed closest to were his fans. They were fiercely loyal, dressed themselves as his characters at every opportunity, constantly debated the various elements of his books in fanzines, and held worldwide conferences to celebrate him and his arcane, fictional planet 'Discworld'. In return for their loyalty he spent months on the road wowing them with his spiky wit and quirky observations.

We didn't see each other often, but when we did he treated me like an honorary citizen of this strange universe he'd woven. Maurice and I recorded forty-nine of his books, and each was a pleasure, brimful of social satire, complex set pieces, great gags and lots of common sense.

Towards the end of his life Terry suffered from Alzheimer's disease, and campaigned for more money for dementia research.

He was also keen to publicise his belief that those suffering from debilitating diseases should have the right to decide whether or not they wanted to carry on living, and in 2010 was invited by the BBC to give the Dimbleby Lecture, a yearly live television event which tackled a contentious issue of the day. He was excited by the prospect, but nervous that, given the unpredictability of his condition, he might not be able to get through his speech without help. So a few weeks before the lecture was due to take place, he asked me whether I'd mind coming along, standing by, and reading it on his behalf if he faltered. I was happy to do this, and thought no more about it until the day it was due to be given. I bowled up at the Royal College of Physicians around four o'clock, thinking I'd have nothing to do for the rest of the afternoon other than watch the preparations for the show, but was met at the front doors by an ashen-faced producer. Terry had been feeling poorly and a bit confused. Would I mind giving the entire lecture in his place?

It was due to start in two hours, so I didn't have time to be scared, but I suppose I didn't need to be. My script was on a lectern in front of me, and there was a huge screen at the back of the hall which projected the words via autocue; it would have been virtually impossible for me to forget what to say. Nevertheless it was pretty daunting to be giving the Dimbleby Lecture, one of the most prestigious events in the broadcasting calendar, to an audience of the great and the good, plus five and a half million viewers, at such short notice. Terry sat next to me on the stage in a big armchair. When the time came to speak, I read his words while he smiled and nodded at my side, and just as I'd done in the recording studio over so many years, I was able to revel in his wit, his wisdom and the sound of his exquisite cadences.

'I would like to die peacefully with Thomas Tallis on my iPod before the disease takes me over and I hope that will not be for quite some time to come. If I knew that I could die at any time I wanted, then suddenly every day would be as precious as a million pounds. If I knew that I could die, I would live. My life, my death, my choice.'

Being able to give that lecture was an enormous privilege, and although it was on such a dark and difficult subject, I enjoyed every moment.

By the middle of 1990 I had settled into my new life as a part-time single dad. Luke and Laura seemed happy with the new parenting arrangements, and I felt confident enough to leave Bristol more regularly. IBM were holding an international conference for their executives and senior sales staff in Seville, and I was invited to provide a bit of entertainment in what was otherwise a deadly serious affair. The smell of fear was palpable; if any executive fouled up, they knew their days at IBM were numbered. I was one of four celebs paid to attend, like Gaulish tribe chiefs being led in chains through Imperial Rome. The others were Professor Laurie Taylor, a social scientist who I'd admired for many years, Kate Adie, the renowned television reporter, and Keith Floyd, the restaurateur and *bon viveur*. We were a tight-knit little band, particularly enlivened by Keith's new girlfriend. She was in her late teens, and completely guileless. Keith had been faxed a topless picture of her by her mum explaining that she was his biggest fan, he'd invited them both to lunch at his house in Devon, and he and the young girl had been together ever since. Laurie was also enamoured by her.

'I understand you're a topless model,' he said.

'And bottomless too,' she explained enthusiastically.

I'd brought a friend, Sue Swingler, along for moral support. She was an inveterate people watcher, and during a chat over coffee with some of the senior IBM staff, she mentioned she'd seen the lead singer of The Three Degrees in Seville that morning, and wondered if they were going to be doing a show for us. The room immediately became icy. First the executives told us they had no idea who The Three Degrees were, then they admitted they did know, but they definitely weren't coming to Seville, and finally they blurted out that The Three Degrees were indeed here and were topping the bill, but it was a big surprise; in fact, it was the biggest surprise of the whole conference. Anyone, we were told, who mentioned The Three Degrees would be in breach of their contract, and would be asked to leave the conference immediately. The executives then left the room, and we looked at each other gleefully. Not mention The Three Degrees? Of course we'd mention The Three Degrees. It would be an act of cowardice not to.

The following morning we gave our presentations to three hundred grey-suited men and a few grey-suited women, in a large, soulless, modern lecture theatre with bare white walls and multi-coloured bucket seats.

Laurie introduced us. 'Apart from me,' he said, 'we have three speakers, and all three to varying degrees have important messages to convey.' The three of us immediately applauded vigorously, which must have seemed a bit odd.

I was next, told a few in-jokes about IBM, and gave the audience a comedy résumé of my life. I said I hadn't had much of a formal education, but had recently received a number of honorary awards including three degrees from various British universities, and I was particularly excited by the three degrees. As soon as I said the forbidden words there was more applause from my co-conspirators.

Keith then talked about Spanish cooking, and explained that when making paella you had to raise the temperature of the pan by three degrees (applause), and finally Kate Adie came to the lectern and gave a passionate defence of the BBC World Service which beamed its signal to the world, she said, from three degrees below the horizon (huge applause).

After the session we sat in a windowless basement dressing room congratulating ourselves on our prank and, under Keith's tutelage, drinking far more Spanish sherry than was prudent. I went to my room, had a long sleep, and was eventually woken by Sue, who said that for the last couple of hours a woman called Teri had been trying to contact me from England. Did I know her?

Indeed I did. A couple of weeks previously I'd been invited to a party to celebrate the tenth anniversary of *Preview*, the Bristol listings magazine for which I occasionally wrote. The local museum was the perfect venue. There was a magician doing card tricks among the Egyptian mummies, a fire-eater in front of the stuffed sea birds, and at the end of a corridor lined with cases of dinosaur bones, a small cafe which had been converted into a performance space. Four young women were singing *acapella*, their sound underpinned by a deep, chocolatey baritone. I couldn't work out which of the women had such an extraordinary voice until the prettiest of them stepped forward and gave an unaccompanied solo rendition of Janis Joplin's 'Mercedes Benz'. It was her, and I was transfixed.

When their set finished, she hopped off the little stage like a hippy sparrow, and we started talking. We drank coffee and smoked her roll-ups for a couple of hours, then I went home. Her name was Teri Bramah, and I hadn't seen her since.

Sue gave me the number she'd left, and I called her. She said she'd tracked me down through a mutual friend, wanted to make sure I was OK, and that she'd love to see me when I got back to Bristol. I was very touched, but made it clear I wasn't looking for a relationship. I was still getting over my last one.

That night there was a cabaret, and we all cheered like lunatics when The Three Degrees came on stage. Then we were taken to a posh restaurant, where one of the senior executives had too much to drink and made the mistake of patronising Kate. She tore him to pieces in a polite, measured, analytical way, while his superiors looked on. When she'd finished he wore the look of someone who knew that the following Monday he'd find his desk cleared, and all his things neatly stacked in a little brown box.

We managed to stagger back to the hotel, and Keith decided

to invite The Three Degrees to his room for late-night drinks, but the bar was closed, so we ransacked our minibars. Unfortunately none of us could remember the name of even one Degree, so his attempts to call them via reception came to nothing. Long after we'd demolished the tiny bottles of spirits and I'd gone to bed, I could hear him bellowing down the phone, 'They're called The Three Degrees. You must be able to find them!'

23

THE TASMANIAN DEVIL

In the summer of 1992 two men sat in the Happy Eater on the Honiton bypass, blithely unaware that the conversation they were having would change their lives and the face of British archaeology.

'It's so frustrating that we can't shoot TV digs like Mortimer Wheeler used to in the sixties,' said Tim Taylor. He looked like a confederate officer, with a long coat, full ginger beard and a small-brimmed felt hat.

His friend Mick Aston was opposite him in his ever-present stripy jumper. 'Because . . . ?'

'How long did those excavations take – three months? We couldn't afford the film crews.'

'Wouldn't take that long now,' Mick mused, 'not by a long chalk. They've got all this geophysics, portable computers, ground penetrating radar and the like. They can tell you where to dig in the shake of a whatsit. Saves you all that faffing about.'

'How long?'

'What, for an assessment? What's in the ground, what state's it in, how big it is, that kind of thing?'

'Yeah. A month?'

'Less than that.'

'A week?'

'Less.'

'Three days?'

'Yeah. Three days should do it.'

And that's how *Time Team* was born.

Mick and I had kept in touch since we'd returned from Santo-rini. I'd even developed a couple of TV ideas involving him, me and a lot of old ruins which I'd run past Denise O'Donoghue. She, Jimmy and Rory had started their own TV Company Hat Trick Productions, and it was riding high with programmes like *Drop the Dead Donkey* (written by Andy Hamilton and Guy Jenkin) and *Whose Line is it Anyway?* But no one was inter-ested in an archaeology series starring Baldrick and some Black Country university hippy, so nothing ever came of it.

Tim Taylor was made of sterner stuff, though. He was an ex-teacher who owned a production company in Exeter – a modest outfit, just him, his PA, and a little office. But he was fascinated by archaeology, and was ambitious. He'd taken Mick under his wing, and when he heard that Channel 4 were look-ing for a follow-up to their weekend hit series Anneka Rice's *Treasure Hunt*, he pitched them the idea of 'archaeological dis-coveries in three days'. The channel's light entertainment department thought it was the sort of crazy idea they could make a go of, but even though they fiddled around with it for some time, they couldn't find a way of turning it into a viable show. So it was passed round from department to department, everybody tinkering with the concept thinking it had potential, but no one quite able to find a way to make it work. Eventually it dropped on the desk of the commissioning editor for continu-ing education, Karen Brown. She only had a tiny budget but, even though Tim was untried and untested and the proposal was at such a rudimentary stage, she found enough money for him to make a pilot.

Channel 4 prides itself on its oddball approach, so this new archaeology programme had to be completely different from anything previously seen on television, and Karen started looking for an unconventional presenter to pull it together. In those days comedians did funny stuff, and academics and well-spoken presenters made documentaries, but a VHS had recently dropped on her desk, a low-budget documentary about Bristol Castle which I'd fronted for a friend. She liked what she saw, and when she found out that I knew Mick, who'd already been pencilled in to take part in the show, she called me. We had a long pleasurable whinge about the state of British TV, agreed that most factual television was dogged by antiquated attitudes and elitism, and when she discovered I wasn't only an archaeology fan but actually knew a bit about the subject, she quickly became my champion.

Tim came to my Bristol home and we sized each other up. He was like the Tasmanian Devil, fierce, passionate, and with a whirlwind energy. He talked in a way that brooked no contradiction. It was as if he thought the programme was going to be made by the sheer force of his personality, rather than by addressing prosaic issues like how many cameras we were going to use, or what my role in the show should be. In many ways he seemed the ideal person to drive the project on: he had absolute belief in his vision, and wasn't going to let anyone get in his way. But he'd need a strong guiding hand, and I wasn't in a position to give it to him.

'Is this really something you want to do?' my agent Kate asked me later.

'The producer's difficult,' I said.

'All producers are difficult,' she replied. 'The question is, do you want to be a presenter?'

'God, no,' I said. 'Presenting's crap. How many presenters have a genuine interest in the subject they bang on about? They read their words off autocue or learn them like trained parrots!'

'So, that's a no then?'

'Er . . .'

Despite my reservations there was something about the idea that attracted me, and this was down to Richard Curtis.

He'd been so inspired by 'Live Aid' that when *Blackadder II* came to an end, he'd disappeared to Africa to do charity work. But the local aid workers soon persuaded him that he could be more useful setting up fundraising projects in London. Consequently he came back and started mobilising his friends in the entertainment industry, using them to raise money and public awareness of third-world poverty, and that was how Comic Relief started. I mucked in too, and he sent me to various parts of southern Africa to report on the charity's projects. I even made a forty-minute Comic Relief film for him called *Why Are the Poor So Goddam Poor?*, which raised issues like debt relief and globalisation. It had been my idea, and the words I'd spoken were entirely my own. After twenty-five years repeating other scriptwriters' lines and being told what to do by producers and directors, I'd been the author of a piece of work on a subject I felt passionate about. The idea of doing something similar about archaeology was tempting.

'I'll think about it,' I said.

The *Time Team* pilot was shot in Dorchester in Oxfordshire. Unfortunately all our equipment was sent to Dorchester in Dorset, which was a hundred miles away, because the lorry drivers misread the travel order. This slowed the first day down considerably, and added to the tension that had begun to build up almost from the moment we'd arrived. The problem was that Mick didn't want to have to say his lines more than once.

'I'm an archaeologist, not some poncy actor like Tony,' he said. 'If I repeated anything, it would be fake.'

I tried to point out that on the first take a jumbo jet might fly overhead and drown out his voice, the cameraman might aim his camera at the wrong archaeological find, a disgruntled child might walk by and give him two fingers, a cloud could obscure the sun and plunge him into darkness, or indeed he might balls up his first attempt and want to do it again. But he dug his heels in and, encouraged by his intransigence, the other academics backed him up.

The crew were nonplussed. Had the production team really employed an entire team of experts whose contributions would be unusable? The cameramen did their best to shoot every scene in one take like an experimental film made by a student on a media course, but it was impossible. Fortunately by early afternoon, and after much huffing and puffing, Mick began to understand he was in danger of wrecking the entire project, and reluctantly agreed to do a second take and, if necessary, a third and a fourth. The irony was that he could do it superbly well. He was a teacher, he'd repeated the same points and made the same jokes year after year. He was just as much of a poncy actor as me.

The other problem was the format. It bore the sticky finger-prints of all the various departments that had fiddled with it over the previous eighteen months. It was gimmicky and rid-dled with 'fun' elements. There were clues that had to be solved, hidden keys to be put in hidden locks, and surprise guests who'd appear out of nowhere and reveal the next clue to lead us to the archaeological treasure. This hokum diluted the real purpose of the programme which was to find and understand the archaeology. I tried my best to head off the worst excesses, but I couldn't do much; I was a performer, and on a shoot, if you're in front of the camera, you're at best placated, at worst ignored. We got through the show with much stamping of feet but no further mishap, and went home. It had been a depress-ing experience.

I was amazed when, a few weeks later, Channel 4 told us they'd like to make four more episodes. I said thank you but no thank you, and assumed that was that. But the following day Karen asked me if I'd come and talk to her face to face before I made my final decision. I explained that I already had, but she pressed me to drop by anyway, and as I'd grown fond of her and she'd been so supportive of me, I agreed.

The Channel 4 HQ was in trendy Charlotte Street off Tottenham Court Road. Stylishly dressed media people strode purposefully around ignoring all about them, or headed into glass-sided meeting rooms and entered into passionate discussions observed by everyone else on the entire floor.

Karen and I were in the biggest meeting room. There were just the two of us sitting at a long table like a lord and a lady at dinner.

'What is it you don't like about the show?' she asked.

'Have you got a pen and paper?'

'OK, the big things.'

'It's too trivial. It's supposed to be an archaeology show, but we're not getting excited by the archaeology. It's as though we think everyone will switch off because it's boring, so we're desperately attempting to sex it up.'

'Agreed.'

'The only boring thing is my summary at the end. It goes on forever. The viewers have already seen what we've dug up. Why would they want me to run the whole thing past them again in a church hall in front of the mayor and a couple of hundred locals? It's like the last chapter of a Miss Marple except we haven't got a villain.'

'Absolutely. Cut it out.'

'And the opening isn't working.'

'It certainly isn't.'

We talked for half an hour, and every point I made she blew out of the water by agreeing with it. It's a clever tactic, but very irritating for the person on the receiving end.

'Here's the thing,' she said finally. 'Do you still think the basic idea's sound?'

'Yes.'

'And if we got it right, you'd be happy to be in it?'

'It's a huge "if".'

'Stay on and help me find a way to make it better.'

'Me? How can I help? The producers aren't going to listen to me.'

'They would if you were one.'

'One what?'

'A producer. Associate producer.'

'I can't produce!'

'You wouldn't have to. But you'd be in on all the important meetings, you could argue your case, and you'd have a direct route back to me.'

'Tim would never wear it.'

'Tim would have to wear it.'

How could I turn her down? I agreed to do the series. It was only four episodes; if it was misery, I'd only be miserable for a month. But the odd thing was that once I'd said what I thought, things started to get better. My relationship with Tim certainly improved. He began to listen to me, ran ideas past me, even asked my advice on changes he wanted to make. He had terrible rows with other members of the team, but he and I never did. I think we both came to the conclusion that if we wanted the show to succeed, we'd need to find a way to work together. I even started to like the guy; he had an oddly beguiling nature for someone who could make you so cross.

It was while we were making episode two that I began to real-ise what enormous potential *Time Team* had. Mick took me to the top of a church tower in the market town of Much Wenlock in Shropshire. We could see the whole place laid out below us: the ruins of the Norman Abbey, the way the town had grown out of the little settlement next to it; the original winding main street that ran along the side of the town's original watercourse (known for obvious reasons as 'Shit Brook'), the straight streets of the Norman new town that cut through the old Anglo-Saxon settlement, the Tudor buildings that had replaced them, the Victorian engineering, the 1960s industrial estate. All this history could be seen in one shot from the vantage point of the tower, and Mick's vivid interpretation and some skilful archaeology could slice away layer upon layer of it, and give us a glimpse of the lives of ordinary people who'd lived in that landscape for a thousand years or more. What better way to spend your early Sunday evenings than sitting on the sofa eating your tea and watching that kind of telly? This was a series I wanted to make!

As for the team themselves, they were potential stars – quirky, opinionated, highly intelligent academics with whom the viewers could empathise. Lots of people assumed they'd been put together at random, a bunch of archaeological nutcases who'd met in a pub, turned up for a shoot and picked up a trowel. But they'd been cast with as much thought as the actors in a TV drama. Their chemistry wasn't accidental; we worked hard to get it.

Mick was lead archaeologist, although he was a dreadful leader who hated asserting himself, and would rather grumble in a corner with his mates than tell anyone what to do. But he was loved by the rest of the team, respected nationwide, and his name gave us an entrée onto sites which would otherwise have been off limits. He also had a unique skill. Other top archaeologists were specialists in the Romans or Tudors, but Mick had a firm handle on every period of British history. No matter where we were in the country, what period we were digging, or what techniques we were deploying, Mick could talk with absolute authority.

Although he was an archaeologist, he seldom got his hands dirty. He was more of a thinker, and handed the process of excavation over to his chief digger, Phil Harding, who worked for Wessex Archaeology. Phil was television gold, a self-taught, solitary man whose life revolved round his work. Apart from evenings in the pub, he was at his happiest when he was in a trench reading the subtle changes in the colour and texture of the earth like an archaeological Sherlock Holmes. The words 'personal grooming' meant nothing to him, his fingernails were long and gnarled, and he had long, wiry hairs sticking out of his nose and ears which he adamantly refused to trim. He wore clothes he seldom washed, topped by a sweat-stained cowboy hat, and he spoke with a broad Wiltshire drawl. He was deaf as a post, and could be grouchy and difficult, particularly if he felt the other diggers' work wasn't up to his exacting standards, but he was kind and gentle, and to a TV audience he came across as the sweetest man you could ever meet. He was a one-off, someone for whom the word 'yeoman' might have been invented.

Carenza Lewis was a bright-eyed, blonde field archaeologist, surveyor and academic who'd defend her position to the hilt even when she was in a minority of one. She once reduced a male geophysics expert to tears in front of the rest of us during a disagreement in a hotel lobby about linear features. She gave the impression of being straight-laced, but she'd been wild in her teens, and the devil inside her had never completely been extinguished. On a live *Time Team* dig in Canterbury during a discussion about ninth-century diet she said that if you were a Viking, 'you'd eat beaver if you could get it'. This quote became legendary, but those on the web who thought it had been said innocently didn't know Carenza.

And finally there was me. Who was 'me'? What was my role? I wasn't a presenter, I was far too argumentative and disrespectful for that, and I wasn't a news reporter even though the revelations I referred to unfolded in real time. Nor was I being an actor, although I was in the sense that I was acting a character called Tony Robinson. I could perform some parts of the show with great confidence. I enjoyed interviewing people, teasing information out of them with a series of strategically placed, apparently innocent questions, but that wasn't enough. How could I get across all the information the viewer needed in order to understand the show properly? For the first few programmes, I stayed awake into the small hours reading archaeological tomes to prepare myself for my pieces to camera the following day. Then one of our most perceptive directors, Simon Raikes, took me to one side.

'You're wasting your time,' he said.

'That's a bit harsh, Simon.'

'All that research. It's getting in the way. You're trying to crowbar information into the show we don't need.'

'But it's down to me to tell the viewers what the site's about, and what was going on there in the past.'

'Yes, but you don't have to look that stuff up. You're an inquisitive bastard. You never stop asking questions. Don't try to impress us with what you know; come to the site ignorant, just like the viewers do. Be the viewer. Ask the experts the questions they'd ask, and if you don't understand the answer, ask again in another way until you do.'

So from then on, that's what I did. It was more fun, made my scenes seem fresher, and certainly cut down on the amount of work I had to do.

Many viewers assumed that my main contribution to the show was jabbering away in front of the camera for hours on end, but my writing and directing experience were just as useful. Events moved so fast on a *Time Team* dig that the director had no time to orchestrate a scene, choreograph the moves, or even work out in which order the facts should come out. That was usually down to me. I'd move from one trench to the next identifying what needed explaining, talk to the archaeologists about which of them would tell which part of the story, negotiate with the director about how we should shoot the scene, and when we'd finally got it in the can, move on to the next trench. I had this fantasy that I could create a new way of presenting TV programmes; one that was freewheeling but disciplined, improvised but well constructed, fun but nailing all the important facts. Sadly it would take years before I began to be the kind of presenter I aspired to be. In fact, when Laura first saw *Time Team* she said that with my long hair, baseball cap, scruffy clothes, non-stop tirades and excitable hand-waving I looked and sounded like a low-level drug dealer.

In January 1994 the first series was aired, and Channel 4 were delighted by the response. The ratings were good, the viewers loved it and even better from the point of view of a channel that regarded itself as wayward and counter-cultural, the broadsheets and a lot of academics loathed it. They said we were cheapening archaeology, attempting to turn it into showbiz. Apart from the cardinal sin that a comic actor had been employed to present it (this was long before my contemporaries Stephen Fry and Griff Rhys-Jones had turned to documentary-making), they made allegations about the quality of the archaeology, implying that we were sacrificing scientific rigour in order to attract more viewers. Mick was deeply hurt by this. He believed passionately that ordinary people should have access to continuing education and academic work of the highest quality. *Time Team* archaeologists had to conduct themselves on TV in exactly the same way as they would on any other site. There was no cheating, no shortcuts, and the digs were recorded scrupulously. That any of his colleagues should allege that this wasn't the case was for Mick an act of betrayal.

We now had a wily executive producer, Philip Clarke, on board, a television professional to his fingertips, who held the show together. He'd screw his face up and nod his head from side to side like Ron Moody as Fagin while he poured cold water on our wilder excesses, ensuring every programme was entertaining and fun without sacrificing intellectual integrity. He and Tim were chalk and cheese, one the wild-eyed visionary, the other the quiet but firm pragmatist. No viewer would have had the slightest idea how large Philip's contribution to the programme had been as the credits spun by, but he was central to its quality and its long-term survival.

Demand for the show swiftly grew so strong that we shifted

from four episodes a year to six, then eight, and finally thirteen. Even then we were asked to make more, but Philip told Channel 4 our archaeologists wouldn't be able to cope with such a big workload, and instead offered the channel spin-offs, a pedestrian series about historical archives called *History Hunters* which I fronted rather badly, a daytime show from our historian Robin Bush, and a host of *Time Team* documentaries in which we examined new thinking about aspects of history like the reign of Queen Boudicca or the Viking invasion.

In addition we put out a number of live shows which ran over a whole week and were designed to be as headline-grabbing as possible. We discovered two Roman villas at Turkdean in Gloucestershire, dug Viking York, and a mysterious field in Hampshire that was full of silver Saxon buckets! These shows were particularly tough because the hours were so long, the archaeology so complicated, and we had no time to step back and think.

The most hair-raising by far was at Bawsey Norman church in Norfolk. From the moment we arrived we knew we'd bitten off more than we could chew. There was complex archaeology all over the site from the Neolithic period right through to the Tudors, all of which needed to be untangled. How could we explain it without boring the viewers to pieces? Not only that, but the site was huge, and we'd seriously overstretched our technical capacity; any kind of live show at all was going to be a challenge.

Nevertheless throughout the week we managed to get our hour-long evening programmes on air, plus half-hour lunchtime shows, and sometimes a morning update, although only by the skin of our teeth. Eventually, though, our luck ran out. Our final programme was to be an epic helter-skelter ride through two thousand years of British history, the last third of which would be almost entirely on my shoulders. I had to weave my way across the site, focussing on each aspect of it, telling tales about it, gleaning facts from the various contributors along the way, and finally summarising the whole dig in a few well-chosen words.

The rehearsal was a nightmare. We kept losing the signal, contributors got lost, and pieces of kit vanished or were trodden on. Meanwhile our electricians were getting in the way heaving great wheels of cabling through the mud to try and ensure our lights, sound and cameras were live at the right place and at the right time.

We stopped and started a dozen times, and as the hours went by, got further behind schedule. Finally, forty-five minutes before transmission, a realisation dawned on me. I walked away from the rehearsal and into the scanner, the mobile control room which was the nerve centre of the operation.

'Lawrence,' I said to the director, 'we're not going to finish this sodding rehearsal before we go on air, are we?'

'Seems not,' he replied, while simultaneously listening to half a dozen other questions being yelled at him through his earphones.

'So I'll be standing in front of camera not knowing what comes next.'

'Yep . . . Mike can you give me a tight shot of the femur, please.'

'So what do we do?'

'We wing it . . . No, the femur, it's a bone. Mick'll show you.'

'How do we wing it?'

'We'll talk you through it on your earpiece. You'll have prompt cards, your autocue . . . F-E-M-U-R . . . Won't be a problem. You'll have fun.'

I didn't feel I had his full attention, and was going to try to reason with him, but at that moment the generator packed up and the control room was plunged into darkness. He had other things to worry about.

I went back to the site and tried to work out my route through the show, which locations I was supposed to stop at, and who I was supposed to talk to. I re-marked my cue cards to make them more coherent, and tried to rehearse my pieces to camera with the autocue woman, but she was struggling to get a signal, so we gave up.

It was difficult for me to have any time to myself, because word had got round about the mess we were in, and the contributors were politely panicking. I talked everything through with them, told them it would all be fine, and tried my best to sound convincing. Only Mick was unfazed; he'd never been intimidated by television.

Far too soon the production manager shouted the dreadful words, 'Going live in five, four, three . . .' and we began. There were no hiccups in the first three-quarters of the show. In fact, it went rather well, and we began to give each other tiny confident glances; we were like novice marathon runners who congratulate themselves for sprinting through the first part of the race, only to collapse dehydrated and at death's door with a couple of miles to go.

The voice of doom echoed in my earpiece. 'OK, mate,' said Lawrence, 'We're in uncharted waters now. But no probs. I'll talk you through everything. Enjoy!' He was adopting the calm voice your doctor uses as he pulls a glove on to test your prostate. 'We're on Sandi Toksvig now, we'll come to you in five.'

I just had time to hear Sandi, my co-presenter for the week, say '. . . and you can tell it's live, because I've no idea where we're going, but I expect it's to some sort of trench.'

Lawrence cut to me, I beamed at the cameras, waved my arms, and said, 'Now this is exciting, at least it is for me. Sandi's right, we've got a brand-new trench.'

A specialist handed me a nondescript piece of pottery. I asked what period it was and he told me it was Middle-Saxon, which apparently was doubly exciting. And even better, there was not just one but a whole complex of ditches here; how unbelievably exciting was that! I appeared to be standing at the epicentre of the universe's store of excitement.

Fortunately before I could self-combust, Lawrence cut away

to Hugh Fearnley-Whittingstall who was preparing some kind of ancient wedding feast dressed as a Viking warrior, although the effect was a little muted because he was wearing his glasses. He then dropped to his knees and began proposing to a comely young woman dressed as a Saxon. When he asked her how old she was, she said fifteen, and I heard a gasp of embarrassment from Lawrence's scanner.

He swiftly cut back to me but I was in the wrong place looking for my cue cards, which I'd put down somewhere. So I said a few inconsequential words, and threw back to Carenza, who was squatting in front of her camera, dressed in an eye-wateringly brief pair of shorts, proudly holding up something which looked like a piece of fossilised elephant poo, but was apparently a Saxon loom weight.

When she'd enthused about it for long enough Lawrence ran a VT insert, but it hadn't been cued up properly and we came in halfway through it, which made it completely unintelligible. Then – oh Christ! – it was back to me. As I breathed in to speak, my autocue went black. Bugger! Two of our contributors, Andrew Rogerson and Stephen Heywood, were standing frozen at my side, but none of us had a clue what we were supposed to do next.

'Just chat away while we sort things out,' Lawrence said cheerfully into my earpiece.

I nodded at the camera and said, 'And . . . finally . . . of course . . . the Normans. The Normans that we hoped would be here . . . indeed we were sure they'd be here because of that Norman church . . . but we were sadly unable to . . .'

Andrew and Stephen were brilliant. They waffled away about the absence of Norman evidence being particularly exciting, indeed even more exciting than if we'd found anything, with Stephen ending on the triumphant assertion that we seemed to have evidence of the original apsidal chancel. It was hard to believe our viewers could remain continent after a piece of news like that.

'OK,' said Lawrence, 'start walking up the hill, and I want . . . in the . . . until . . . for . . .' Silence. His voice had cut out. I was entirely on my own.

I began coaxing Andrew and Stephen up the hill towards the church like a pair of skittish bullocks, with my cameraman in tow, his camera wedged between his shoulder and his neck, as he desperately tried to get a decent shot of the three of us. I asked my contributors more pointless questions about the Normans, and received more pointless answers. I had no idea what was going to happen at the top of the hill, but Hugh appeared out of nowhere, his cape billowing, presumably having been sent by Lawrence to guide me to the final set-up.

'Follow me,' he said. 'I was hoping we were going to have a wedding in our finale, but my bride seems to have jilted me. I'm ever so upset, and she was beautiful too. And only fifteen; by ancient standards practically on the shelf . . .'

By now we'd arrived at the church, an impressive maze of ruined walls about ten feet high. A crowd of local onlookers was crammed into what would once have been a side chapel. They backed off like frightened sheep as we approached, revealing four earnest young people in bright cagoules holding sheet music. Someone blew a single note on a recorder, and they began to perform a medieval song, presumably to imbue the end of the show with a suitable plaintive atmosphere. I pulled a spellbound face as I tried to work out where the hell to go and what to do next. Then I had a brainwave! We were supposed to finish the programme talking to a man about a Norman arch he was renovating. I couldn't remember what it looked like or where it was, but I did know what this kind of construction was called.

'Let's take a look at the voussoir,' I said enthusiastically, then turned back to the singers and murmured, 'beautiful! beautiful!' so they wouldn't feel unacknowledged. I ducked through a hole in the wall followed by my cameraman who was now wheezing a little, and headed off down a corridor. Would the voussoir be at the far end of it? No! I was outside the church

again, confronted by a mound of scaffolding and a pile of discarded camera equipment. I desperately clambered over it still
telling the viewers how knee-tremblingly exciting this old arch
would be. But now I found myself in what appeared to be a cul-
de-sac; I'd run out of options. My heart sank and couldn't think
of anything to say. No, wait! Hallelujah! There was a tiny opening at the end, and as I turned into it I practically collided with
my voussoir man and his beautiful voussoir shimmering in the
evening sun. I scrambled over the last of the scaffolding, stumbled up to him, and began to interview him in earnest.

'Wow! What a stunning voussoir! Tell me about its design?'

'What skills are required to make something as intricate as
this?'

'How excited are you feeling?'

Then I realised the voussoir man wasn't miked, so to the
viewers his voice would be sounding like someone calling from
another planet. I couldn't hear the plainchant any more, at some
point my cameraman had disappeared (had he blacked out?),
the voussoir man clearly had nothing else to say, and I felt alone
and deeply depressed, although duty-bound to start my final
piece. Was my voice even being recorded? Was someone shooting
magnificent top shots of Bawsey which would be laid over my
last few well-crafted sentences, or was I just an idiot mumbling
away to himself outside a ruined church, while Hugh, Sandi
and the rest were winding up the show at an entirely different
location?

'It's been a fantastically exciting few days,' I busked. 'If
archaeologists come back here in a thousand years' time . . .
what do you think they'll find? A trowel maybe, a piece of . . .
camera cable, perhaps. And what do you think they'll make of
them? . . . We'll never know.' The familiar *Time Team* music
faded in, the credits rolled, another *Time Team* was over.

However scary that last fifteen minutes had been (and I
lost 4lbs in weight during that show), what held it together
was the trust we had in each other. Whatever went wrong, a

contributor standing next to you, an assistant behind the camera, or a technician in the scanner would bail you out somehow. This was the culture of a show made by people who liked and respected each other, and had worked together a long time. It's a very unusual experience in television, and when *Time Team* eventually came to an end after twenty years, that's what I missed the most about it.

24

THE SNEERY TRAFFIC WARDEN

I woke in pitch-darkness, dangling headfirst out of bed with a pair of hands round my throat.

'I don't fucking need this!' a voice growled. It was Teri. I must have been snoring again.

I'd bought a big house next door to Christchurch primary school in Clifton, courtesy of the sales of *Blackadder* and *Time Team*. Teri and I lived in it on our own, except when the kids and various boy and girlfriends joined us. There were almost always more bedrooms than people, but we needed the space. Teri was like Chita Rivera in *West Side Story*, passionate, mercurial, sexy, with blazing eyes and a personality the size of Puerto Rico. She loved me and would doubtless have killed for me, although she might well have accidentally killed me at the same time. Living with her was like putting your hands into a box of fireworks blindfolded; you never knew if you were going to end up with a golden fountain or a bloody great bang.

I was in awe of her talent. When she sang in a pub or a club she was like Billie Holiday in the black and white film clips, smouldering, exotic and absolutely pitch perfect. I hated the punters chattering away while she was working. I wanted to ask them politely to be quiet, and if they didn't, machine gun them till their viscera dripped down the walls. But I never did. We learnt to scuba dive and went on exotic holidays. We stayed in a luxury, thatched beach hut on a tiny private island near Bali. Our next-door neighbours were Peter Gabriel and his girlfriend. At the end of each day the four of us would go down to the water's edge, watch the sunset, and let the baby sharks nibble our toes.

I was now making TV documentaries non-stop. I worked seven days a week, and never knew what I was going to be doing from one day to the next. My schedule and travel arrangements were so complicated they had to be colour-coded and printed out. Up until now I'd thought of myself as an actor, but I'd been acting for nearly thirty-five years without a break, and my attitude towards my craft was beginning to change. The stage didn't hold much attraction for me anymore; I found performing eight shows a week unbearably repetitive, and the perpetual rhythm of going to the theatre at 5.30, staring at my face in the make-up mirror, winding myself up for the show, and winding myself back down afterwards no longer seemed as romantic as it had. I was happy to do the occasional TV drama, but was seldom available. The rest of the *Blackadder* crew were being offered heavyweight parts on stage and screen, but I wasn't, or if I was, I couldn't do them, and apart from the occasional searing pang of jealousy it didn't bother me.

Instead I travelled worldwide making shows about subjects that fascinated me, and seeing places I'd never visited before. This culminated in a project to retell the major stories of the Old Testament but set in modern-day Israel and Gaza.

When I'd been a kid I'd known all the Bible stories. We learnt them at school, at Sunday school, or at Bible classes with names like the Crusaders and the Covenanters run by enthusiastic ex-army officers. This onslaught of religious propaganda didn't seem to have much effect on us long-term; within a few years we'd become the Sixties generation, more interested in free love than God's love, but it did provide us with a broad understanding of what Christians believed. Almost every aspect of our lives was influenced by Christian morality, and it frustrated me that my children's generation had so little grasp of the stories, particularly as so many of them – Abraham sacrificing his son Isaac, Samson being blinded, David's duel with Goliath – were such ripping yarns.

Moses had promised his people 'a land of milk and honey' and I called my series *Blood and Honey*, but no one noticed the irony. They were tough shows to make. The *intifada* was at its height, and my eyes were often full of tears, not from religious zeal, but from the Israeli army's gas shells. We got trapped in a bomb scare in Jerusalem after a suspicious parcel was found in a rubbish bin on the main road to Bethlehem. The army moved in behind and in front of us, wouldn't let anyone past, and the traffic came to an immediate stop. We'd been halted right next to the suspect bomb, and every time we tried to move away from it we were yelled at and the soldiers waved their rifles at us. We were forced to stay there for an hour, waiting to be blown to smithereens. By the time we were allowed to move, we could hardly speak.

In Jerusalem Old Town we were stoned by young Arabs when we got mixed up in a demonstration, and our sound assistant got badly cut on his head. I went over to a food stall to get falafels for the crew, and was joined in the queue by half a dozen teenage boys smiling at me, nodding and holding rocks in their hands. On the Lebanese border we were shoved, kicked and driven back into Israel even though our documents were in order. The whole enterprise, the work, the ideas, the proximity to danger, were intoxicating, and we returned home triumphant but wired.

In my case a little too wired. I drove back from Heathrow late one night, but there weren't any parking spaces near my house, and I'd got two heavy suitcases. I drove around for a quarter of an hour or so, then saw a driver pulling out of a space directly opposite my front door. The gap was small and adjacent to a yellow line, but when I parked up, all four of my wheels were inside the legitimate parking area, so I thought I had nothing to worry about.

The following morning Teri shouted at me to look out of our bedroom window. A traffic warden was standing next to my car scribbling in his notebook. I was outraged; this was my street, I'd done my best to comply with the law, but some nit-picking bureaucrat was trying to take advantage of me. In Cairo I'd bought a pink-striped *jalabiya*, a long kaftan which made me look almost exactly like Omar Sharif. After a bit of a struggle I managed to get it on, heaved open the sash window, and yelled to the warden that I was coming down so would he please stop what he was doing, in a tone which attracted the attention of several neighbours.

He was a thin, unpleasant young man, probably no more than twenty years old, with a pencil moustache and a sneery look on his face. I explained to him how late it had been when I'd arrived, that there'd been no other available parking places, that the only part of my car which was over the yellow line was the last six inches of the boot, and that any reasonable person would conclude that I hadn't broken the law, or if I had, it was to such a negligible degree that it would be absurd to punish me. But he ignored my protestations, and the more dismissive he became, the more pissed off I got.

It was his little black book in my face that finally made me snap.

'I've already logged the offence!' he said. 'Sorry, chum, there's nothing I can do about it.'

I snatched it back from him and ripped the pages out.

'You've really gone and done it now,' he said.

I tore the pages into tiny pieces and scattered them on the ground. 'No. I've really gone and done it *now*,' I replied, and handed him back the outside covers of his notebook.

'You'll regret that.'

'No, I won't,' I replied defiantly, and strode back to the house seething with anger. 'And I'm not your fucking chum,' I added.

Teri couldn't stop laughing, but the implications of what I'd done slowly began to sink in. It wasn't just the evidence of my alleged parking offence I'd destroyed. I'd torn to pieces the notes on every other case the traffic warden had written up that day.

A few hours later a cheery young policewoman came round to the house. She warned me I'd definitely be charged with the parking offence and probably a great deal more besides, and she tried to keep a straight face but couldn't quite manage it.

'Oh, and is it true you were wearing pink pyjamas?' she asked.

My solicitor put me in touch with Geoff Douglas, a high-powered Bristol lawyer who told me he'd enjoy the challenge of representing me in this particular case, and thought he might be able to get me out of the mess I'd landed myself in. He'd make sure the hearing was at the end of the day because court reporters were a lazy breed and would inevitably have gone home by then, so we should be able to keep my name out of the papers, particularly as I'd be listed as Anthony Robinson rather than Tony. And also, to avoid prying cameras, he said I shouldn't attend unless absolutely necessary.

I was charged with criminal damage and expected a long, humiliating trial, but it was all over in less than fifteen minutes. The prosecution began by saying that because of my celebrity I thought I could get away with anything. Geoff immediately retorted that he hadn't been going to mention what I did for a living, and that this statement confirmed his suspicion that the case was a witch-hunt against someone in the public eye. The magistrate seemed to agree, because I was bound over to keep the peace, and that was that . . . except I had to pay a parking fine. My friends said I was bloody lucky to get away with it, and should have gone down for a five-year stretch, but I was incensed. My wheels weren't over the yellow line, so how could I possibly have been guilty?

To my intense relief by the mid-1990s the Labour Party had returned to sanity and the loonies from the Militant Tendency had been expelled. What had angered me most about them hadn't been their absurd beliefs, or even their obsessive plotting, it was their certainty that they were always right. This is never an attractive character trait, but in politicians it can be downright scary. It makes them incapable of self-criticism, leads them to denounce their opponents as traitors, and gives them a cast-iron justification for their own appalling behaviour and that of their supporters.

I'd seen something similar at close hand in Equity. I'd assumed The Workers' Revolutionary Party would cast a permanent shadow over our union's business, but it had collapsed swiftly, unexpectedly and in a surprisingly tacky way. When I first heard allegations that its leader, a squat, scary Irishman called Gerry Healy, had been involved in a sex scandal I assumed he'd been framed. I knew he'd had some nasty beliefs, he'd announced that the Labour Party was controlled by Jews, an allegation he extended to Margaret Thatcher's government, the BBC, and even more bizarrely the Manpower Services Commission. But the idea that he'd been systematically abusing his female members seemed absurdly far-fetched. It's horrible to admit it now, but when I first heard this story I assumed it was a piece of black propaganda put out by the CIA or MI5 to destabilise the Left. But of course even self-proclaimed moral arbiters are capable of terrible and shameful acts, and are happy to use conspiracy theories to protect themselves from exposure.

The truth began to emerge. Twenty-six women members accused him of cruel and systematic debauchery. 'He wanted only one thing from me,' one said, 'my sexual submission. For a moment I just stared at him; fat, ugly, red-faced . . . Something snapped in me. I guess it was my faith, my belief. The dream that drove me forward now seemed unreal and reality entered, tawdry, petty, dirty, seamy reality.' The evidence these women gave was compelling. Surely all twenty-six of them couldn't be capitalist spies?

Healy was expelled from the WRP, along with Corin and

Vanessa Redgrave and a few others who'd stayed loyal to him. The party imploded and fractured into a dozen factions, each with a tiny membership. Its influence inside Equity evaporated overnight. But the memory of the experience stayed with me. For the moment the hard left was on its knees, but such people are political obsessives, and if the opportunity arose, I knew they'd be back.

By 1994 Mrs Thatcher was out of office, John Major was highly unpopular, and there seemed to be a yearning for change throughout the country. Equity politics tended to reflect national politics, the only significant difference being that the personalities involved had names like Rhubarb the Clown and Roger the Artful, rather than Michael Heseltine or Jim Callaghan. The WRP was no more, and its right-wing counterpart Act for Equity was a fading force, so at last we on the centre-left were riding high. It was our best chance in years to get a progressive leadership. When I'd sat round the council table twenty years previously I'd been a callow youth; now if elected, I'd be one of its most politically experienced members. We won a landslide victory, and I came top of the poll. Shortly afterwards I proposed that Pete Boyden, the arts consultant who'd done such a good job for us at the Bristol Old Vic, should be invited to make a similar appraisal of Equity. He agreed, wrote an effective but ruthless report, and at long last we had a blueprint for change that would stand up to public scrutiny. Two years later I became Equity vice-president, and helped steer the reforms through.

Nowadays it's one of the most successful unions in the country, with a workable rulebook, a burgeoning membership, and sound finances. I occasionally go back to chair contentious meetings, but now I do so as a grey-haired codger, although deep inside I'm still the fiery young actor who used to stand up at Equity AGMs and shout 'Resign!'

*

The show was *Forty Years On*, the venue was the Richmond Theatre, and the date was 1 May 1997, general election day. The curtain fell, then rose again on an empty stage. Fifteen boys dressed in public school uniforms, with soft complexions and respectable haircuts, jogged out from the wings and took their bow. It was a shrewd investment to bring in a fresh batch for each new venue of the tour. Their mums, dads and aunties bought top-end tickets to come and see them, often more than once. They watched the show in a frenzy of excitement, and always gave their darling boys a rousing cheer at the end.

They were followed on stage by the boys with the speaking parts, young professionals who toured with us and spent their days talking about male skincare and the stars they'd worked with. Next were our actresses Antonia Pemberton and Issy Huckle, then Christopher Timothy in his teacher's gown and mortar board, followed by me, dressed likewise. I bowed low and, as I straightened up again, pulled back one side of my gown and exposed the large red rosette I'd pinned to the lapel of my suit jacket. The roar from the audience was deafening. It was a good thirty seconds before Tony Britton, who played the headmaster, could enter, staggering slightly, as older actors tend to do at the end of a play to indicate how hard they've been working. Tony wasn't happy, and stood by my side as we took our company bow grunting and hissing, like the witch in *Hansel and Gretel* when she realises Gretel has locked her in the oven. But my mind was elsewhere. How extraordinary that even here in leafy Surrey, such enthusiasm should be generated by the possibility of a Tony Blair government!

I hadn't planned to return to the theatre, but an offer had come in for me to appear in a revival of the show playing the part Alan Bennett had written for himself thirty years previously. The script was a young man's work, patchy, a bit indulgent and set in a public school, but there was something about it that appealed to me. I'd been a fan of Bennett's since he was a young man playing alongside Jonathan Miller, Dudley Moore and Peter Cook in *Beyond the Fringe*. *Forty Years On* gave me a similar opportunity to be gauche, quirky and very British, the hallmark of that generation of Oxbridge performers. I was also tempted by the freedom of the road. Teri and I had split up eighteen months previously. Our relationship had become so tempestuous it had exhausted us both. When I said I wanted to leave, she'd torn up my Filofax and attempted to flush the pieces down the toilet. I'd spent the next half hour pulling out the soggy, ripped-up addresses and spreading them on the radiators to dry. We were still fond of each other, and I went to see her sing whenever I could, but we were better off apart.

The tour wasn't working out well for me. Tony Britton was a distinguished actor who had once been a minor film star and Shakespearean lead. At first he'd seemed perfectly affable in an old-school actory way, but then apparently decided he didn't like me. I'd no idea why; when I was in the children's TV show *Play Away* his daughter Cherry had been the assistant floor manager, and I'd been quite close to her and her boyfriend Brian Cant. I'd also met her sister Fern a few times, and we'd got on perfectly well. But during rehearsals he became disdainful and deeply sarcastic towards me. Initially I batted it off; he wasn't a young man and had got reams of lines to learn, he was probably feeling insecure. But his behaviour did remind me of my encounter with the petulant Rex Harrison two decades previously, except now it wasn't a vulnerable young assistant stage manager who was the object of the leading man's wrath, it was me, and I'd got decades of experience in the theatre and couldn't stand this kind of nonsense.

Once we were on tour I got lots of local press coverage because I was always off campaigning for Labour, and that seemed to irritate him even more. But I managed to remain reasonably unaffected by his constant sniping, until matters came to a head over a digestive biscuit at the Civic Theatre, Darlington. In act one there was a scene in which, while the rest of us stood round drinking tea, the headmaster made an interminably long speech about how much better things had been in the old days. We had digestive biscuits in our saucers, and I occasionally dunked mine in the cup, but one Saturday matinee I must have dunked a little too enthusiastically, because the whole biscuit collapsed into my tea, which the audience found very amusing. When we came off stage I began to apologise, but Tony erupted into what appeared to be an uncontrollable rage, raving and snarling. It was as though this inadvertent piece of upstaging had confirmed his every prejudice against me. He had a modicum of right on his side as the digestive had made quite a big splash, so at first I tried to mollify him. But suddenly eight weeks' worth of suppressed rage erupted like a shaken can of Coke. I grabbed him by the lapels, heaved him round 180 degrees and slammed him against the theatre wall.

'Shuddup!' I said.

He attempted to extricate himself from me, but we got tangled up in each other's gowns, and it became a wrestling match. We held on to each other, shook each other, tried to push each other down on the ground, and yelled at each other, but very quietly so we wouldn't be heard by the audience.

'You faargin' caaa!' I hissed. 'You stuckarp bassa!'

'Gerroff my face!' he hissed back. 'Don' tushma face!'

The boys in the wings were giggling nervously, which distracted the actors on stage. They glared at the youngsters with 'be quiet' looks on their faces, but then realised why they were behaving so oddly; behind them was the silhouette of the two lead actors going at each other like Mike Tyson and Evander Holyfield. They craned their necks in the direction of the punch-up and gawped, but being true professionals, carried on with the show as they did so.

Eventually the company manager, an old-style theatre man who'd been on the road for decades, wearily stepped between us and told us in no uncertain terms that we were making twats of ourselves. We were both exhausted, and no doubt Tony was as relieved as I was to have the opportunity to stop without appearing to be the loser. We managed to calm down and finish the show without further hostility. Antonia, who'd watched potential trouble brewing for weeks and had a great deal of sympathy for my situation, took me to one side in a motherly fashion, and asked me if I was all right. I said I was, and admitted I'd quite enjoyed the adrenaline rush.

That night I phoned Laura.

'You must promise me you'll not fight him again,' she said.

'I promise.'

'Because he's in his seventies, and you're rubbish at fighting. If he decks you, it'll be really humiliating.'

The following day, after panicked phone calls from the producer, we agreed a ceasefire, and formally shook hands in the green room in front of the rest of the cast.

'I've decided to forgive and forget,' Tony told the assembled actors in a magnanimous voice, which made me want to ram his mortar board down his throat. I restrained myself.

The tour carried on, and although we never became bosom buddies, we'd grunt 'Good evening' when we bumped into each other at the stage door.

Twenty years later we met again when he played the Earl of Kent and I was The Fool in a charity version of *King Lear*, directed by Alan Bennett's old crony, Jonathan Miller. Tony was very elderly and frail by then and had to be helped round the stage. On the first day of rehearsals he greeted me courteously like someone from his past with whom he'd once been friendly, and at the mid-morning break I made him a cup of tea, which he gratefully accepted. We never mentioned our tiff, but I'm pretty sure he remembered it as clearly as I did, although maybe I should have put a digestive in the saucer to jog his memory.

*

Back in Richmond the audience cheered long and hard for the show and Tony Blair's potential victory. When I finally got back to my dressing room, I unpinned the rosette and fixed it on my black Aéropostale bowling shirt, ready for the big night out. I could hear Tony Britton in the next room ostentatiously complaining to someone about my disgraceful behaviour, and how a Labour government would bring the country to its knees. I thought of giving him a rousing rendition of 'Things Can Only Get Better', but decided against it.

My dresser bustled in and I handed her my costume neatly folded on a hanger. Her name was Heledd Mathias and she was small, Welsh and pretty, with dark hair, a serious face, and a tiny silver stud in her nose. We'd been for a walk together across Wimbledon Common between shows the previous day, and she'd told me she didn't have much time for actors and actresses; they were mostly self-absorbed, and if they accidentally peed themselves from exerting too much effort, they never apologised or offered to rinse out their soiled pants. But what irritated her most was that they left their costumes discarded in a bundle on the floor rather than hanging them up, which was unfair on the wardrobe department. I'd committed most of these sins on a regular basis since I was a child actor, but I never would again.

I drove into London, and eventually bumped into Charlotte Cornwell, an auburn-haired fireball who was my fellow Equity vice-president. Sometime after midnight we ended up in Hampstead. The election results were coming in thick and fast, and there were crowds of excited people in the pubs and on the streets chattering non-stop and sharing jokes with strangers. Seventeen years of Thatcherism were about to come to an end, but it felt too good to be true, and we weren't going to believe it till a Labour majority had been formally announced.

'Let's go to David's,' she said, 'and watch it on the telly.'

David was her brother, his pen name was John le Carré, and he lived off Hampstead High Street. I'd never met him before, and when he opened the door I wanted to throw my arms round him and tell him what a huge fan I was, that I thought he'd written some of the most important, intelligent, well-structured novels of the past few decades, and that it was a privilege to share this wonderful night with him. But I didn't. I just said, 'Hi!'

We sat engrossed on his sofa for a long time. The Enfield result was particularly important to me. I'd campaigned for the Labour candidate Stephen Twigg, who looked almost as young as the boys in *Forty Years On*. But despite his apparent youth, he was a shrewd thinker with front-bench potential, and he was up against Michael Portillo, the right-wing cabinet minister. It would be a bitter humiliation for the Tories if Portillo lost the seat, so they'd thrown a lot of resources in his direction. If Stephen took Enfield it would surely be the end of an era. When the result was announced shortly after 2 a.m. Labour had won by a thousand votes, and we began to get a sense of the scale of the landslide.

Early the following morning I appeared bleary-eyed on a chat show at London Weekend Studios with Margaret Hodge, a junior minister who'd successfully defended her Barking seat with an increased majority. We were both knackered, and should have been much more magisterial than we were during the interview. Instead we sat on the studio sofa joking and giggling, and bragging that we'd stayed up all night. I walked the three and a half miles home to Acton. The sky was cloudless, summer had arrived, and given the intensity with which the birds sang, they were probably all Labour supporters too.

Two months later I was invited to a party at Number 10, and asked Laura to come with me. We walked along Downing Street in triumph; it was our street now! I was wearing a natty Italian suit, a rust-coloured T-shirt and a pair of Vans. She was in a sleeveless dress which exposed the dragon she'd had tattooed on her arm when she was fifteen. There were a hundred or so photographers standing on specially erected wooden tiers on the far side of the street. 'Tony! Tony! Over 'ere!' they shouted although, as the whole street was ablaze with flash bulbs, it was impossible to work out where 'over 'ere' was.

The following morning the *Daily Mail*'s headline was 'Tattoos, Bare Midriffs, and Trainers ... How the luvvies met New Labour'. Laura was mortified that they referred to her as my 'tattooed wife, Laura'.

'Why didn't they ask me who I was?' she demanded.

'Because they're lazy, lying wankers?' I suggested.

Tony Blair was brilliant that night. Other Prime Ministers had been creatures of the unions, or the left wing of the party, the right, or the MPs. But Tony didn't have a natural power base; his support came from a handful of progressive intellectuals. So how had he managed to become our unassailable leader? A few minutes in his company and the answer was obvious: it was his charm, his apparent authenticity and his skill at working a crowd. Some people said he was an actor, but if so, he was in the mould of Michael Gambon or Juliet Stevenson, a great performer who never appeared to sacrifice his integrity. He only talked to me for about thirty seconds – he didn't need to invest any more time nurturing me, he already knew I was a supporter. But then he turned to Laura, and flashed a smile as bright as the pressmen's flashbulbs. He asked her if she was a Party member (which she was), what she was studying (which was politics), and what she was hoping for from the new government (which was a lot). He was interested, interesting and made her feel as important as all the government ministers, power brokers, TV stars and business high-flyers chattering away in the rest of the room. He was magnificent. He'd have risen to the top whatever he'd chosen to do with his life.

25

THE FIVE MARGARETS

In the late 1990s I moved with Heledd (or Heli as I called her) into a big, airy flat in Maida Vale. By now the Bristol house was very much my second home, although Laura, who was at Bristol University, was still living in it, and Luke would often stay there when he came down from Birmingham where he was attempting to study engineering. Heli spent most of her time working in the West End while I was off hither and thither filming, but eventually, because we weren't seeing much of each other, she quit her job in theatre wardrobe and became my PA.

As the year 2000 approached, the nation began debating how best to mark the start of the next thousand years, and Richard Curtis was asked to create a special episode of *Blackadder* to be shown for twelve months in the cinema adjacent to the Millennium Dome. We all liked the idea of being part of the national festivities, but the Dome had become hopelessly overburdened by bureaucracy, and by the time contracts had been signed, rehearsals were only a couple of weeks away, and most of the actors had other bookings in place which would limit their availability. So rehearsals were disjointed, and matters were made worse by a black cloud which hung over us – John Lloyd hadn't been invited to be one of the team. Richard had become much steelier after ten years immersed in the world of feature films, and though he was as lovable as he'd always been, he now knew how to get his own way even in the most difficult circumstances. Ben too had become a tougher character. He'd been bruised by systematic personal attacks in the media,

particularly over his decision to work with the conserva-
tive-minded Andrew Lloyd Webber, and didn't want to suffer
more of the pain he'd felt during previous *Blackadder*s. It was
John who'd orchestrated the changes we made to their writing,
but Richard and Ben weren't interested in working like that
anymore. They wanted to write a script, which the actors would
then perform. This was fair enough and we concurred, but it
created a problem. John was a comic genius and an integral
part of *Blackadder*; without him we ran the risk of seriously
diluting the quality of the show.

Maybe the bad feeling between him and the writers was
unavoidable, certainly neither side was completely right or
wrong, but the net result was that we all felt dispirited. We
didn't bond in the way we had previously, and I felt particularly
isolated because my commitment to *Time Team* meant I spent
most days rushing from one show to the other in a breathless
and slightly frenzied fashion. Miranda was back with us, along
with all the other *Blackadder* actors, but I was hardly ever able
to sit down with them for a good natter. Even when I did I felt
alienated from them. They'd once been my friends and inspiration, but now I felt like a virtual stranger.

Only my relationship with Rowan had stood the test of time.
I'd always felt grateful to him; he'd been the star of the show
and, like many famous comics do, could have insisted that the
audience's attention be constantly on him. But on the contrary
he'd allowed me to have innumerable punchlines and the close-
ups to go with them, and never seemed at all bothered when
my role attracted publicity. There was no doubt in my mind that
his generosity had led directly to my success, but just as importantly, our relationship on screen had been the starting point for
a deep friendship. We never spoke about it at the time, indeed
I'm not sure we ever have, but whenever we meet, others comment on the affection we clearly have for each other.

Blackadder Back and Forth was a journey through time
conducted by Blackadder and Baldrick on New Year's Eve 1999.

Our characters visited the Jurassic period, the Battle of Waterloo, the court of Elizabeth I, and for the scenes set in Roman Britain spent a day pretending to be soldiers marching up and down a replica of Hadrian's Wall specially built for us in a field outside Guildford. That day's filming wasn't easy. Hugh and Stephen were dressed as officers, with leather skirts so ridiculously short that we seldom got to the end of a take without someone wrecking the shot with a squawk of supressed laughter. An enormous and over-elaborate machine was fixed to the camera to enable it to pirouette around the wall, and it was so noisy we couldn't hear each other speak. Added to that, our characters were being attacked by the invading Scots, played by a horde of re-enactors specially brought down from Scotland. They were given identical ginger wigs and beards, and on 'Action!' had to charge towards us like angry bees waving their swords and claymores. But the field was so rutted and potholed they kept falling over and hurting themselves, and we had to stop while they were given medical treatment.

Late that evening I was lent one of the production's limousines, the chauffeur made a bed for me in the back, and we drove through the night to the Scottish border. He woke me up at Birdoswald Fort in Northumbria where I spent three days filming a *Time Team* about the brutal, isolated life Roman soldiers experienced on the real Hadrian's Wall, before being driven back to the idiotic nonsense of our fake one in Guildford.

Blackadder Back and Forth wasn't our finest hour. I don't know whether this was due to John's absence, the lack of a studio audience, or the fragmented nature of the rehearsals and the script, but it certainly dampened everyone's enthusiasm for further incarnations of Edmund Blackadder. Nevertheless it had its moments, my favourite being when Baldrick wiped out the earth's dinosaurs by waving his underpants. Nowadays when the show's repeated, I feel much more kindly disposed to it than I did when it was first made, and though I seldom see any of the actors anymore apart from Rowan, I meet up with both Ben and Richard from time to time, and we laugh at each other's bad jokes, and reminisce about the old days.

High political office had never been an ambition of mine. I'd contented myself pottering round Bristol being a local activist. But at long last Labour was in power and I wanted to make a contribution, so in the year 2000 I was persuaded by my friends to try for a place on the National Executive Committee, the body responsible for overseeing the running of the party. After eighteen years of Tory rule it was a liberation to have a radical, reforming government. Throughout its first four months in office Labour announced some new policy initiative every day; a flashy move, but very exciting.

These may have been dizzying times, but the party itself was a mess. Our professional politicians professed undying love for it, 'this great party of ours' as Michael Foot used to call it. But behind the rhetoric there was no sense of a shared enterprise; politicians regarded Party members as at best a nuisance, at worst a force to be neutralised. I had a degree of sympathy with them; members could be unreasonable, factional, obsessive and didn't have the facts at their fingertips like politicians and their phalanx of aides did. Nor did they seem to understand the need for the compromises that were second nature to the professionals. But that didn't mean the politicians had the right to use undemocratic and deceitful measures to get their way. I'd been particularly upset when I'd seen perfectly good motions on House of Lords reform cynically scuppered at Conference, and witnessed the manipulation of constituency shortlists to ensure the selection of favoured allies and political advisors as parliamentary candidates.

This kind of behaviour was happening more and more, and it didn't go down well. The members were the party; they paid for it, campaigned for it, and made personal sacrifices for it. What's more, they did it voluntarily, whereas an MP got £50,000 a year, plus hefty expenses. A tide of resentment was building up, and I feared that unless the party leadership stopped being so manipulative, members would eventually become so disenchanted that they'd turn on them, and start electing demagogues who'd make attractive radical promises while bringing the party to its knees. Over the years I'd gained a lot of experience in politics. I was confident I had something to offer, so why not give it a go and try to help get this kind of nonsense stopped?

In order to stand I needed the endorsement of my own constituency. I'd been filming in London, and caught the train back home for the Bristol West nomination meeting. Laura met me on the platform at Temple Meads looking worried.

'We've been targeted,' she said dramatically. 'The ultra-left have sent Mark Seddon down to challenge you for the nomination.'

Mark was a dishevelled but strangely charming young man whose white lounge suit permanently needed attention from the dry cleaner. He was the de facto leader of the Grassroots Alliance, a left opposition group utterly opposed to Tony Blair and New Labour. He was also the editor of the *Tribune* newspaper, and the party leadership loathed him because, as a member of the NEC, he had access to information the party considered confidential as well as the means to publish material if he thought it was in the members' interests to do so.

The Bristol West constituency hustings were held in a gloomy church hall in Cotham. I won, by twenty-eight votes to eighteen, which wasn't that bad, but Mark had successfully characterised me as the right-wing candidate, a slur I wasn't able to shake off for a long time. If I was having trouble in my own constituency, my campaign wasn't going very well. I needed the support of members all over the country. How was I going to get that?

Laura pulled together a campaign team for me including my old friend Neal Lawson, and Laurie Taylor's son Matthew, a young and original thinker who was beginning to make a name for himself as a policy wonk. When I took their advice I did well, and eventually came top of the poll by a huge margin. Cynics said it was because of my celebrity not because of my politics, and there was probably a bit of truth in that. But I'd covered a few thousand miles listening to the grievances of ordinary members, and I reckoned that had paid off.

The dominant figures on the NEC were all called Margaret. Well, not quite all. Tony Blair wasn't called Margaret, at least not by his cabinet, nor was the implacable Dennis Skinner. There were a few Bills, Bobs and Daves, particularly in the trade union section, but the NEC's backbone, its moral compass and its dynamism, came from a group of women steeped in 1970s feminism, who'd climbed as far up the ladder of the Labour movement as it was permitted for anyone to climb who didn't wear a suit and tie, and a little further still. They were a highly energetic, dedicated and well-oiled machine utterly focussed on protecting and enhancing Tony's position.

Margaret McDonagh was the first woman ever to have become General Secretary of the Labour Party. She was charming when she wanted to be, and scarily fierce the rest of the time. Even hardened trade union leaders were terrified of her. Advancement was in her gift, and she was surrounded by loyal acolytes in a similar mould. Margaret Prosser was the Party Treasurer, a good listener, always reasonable, and spoke in a slow drawl which disguised her iron will. Margaret Wall and Maggie Jones were trade union delegates. Maggie flirted with me, and I with her, but she was the most suspicious of me. Margaret Wall was on the right of the party, and her views and mine seldom chimed, but she was enthusiastic about my attempts to engage more young people in politics, and got me union funding for my various youth projects. The final Margaret was Margaret Wheeler who chaired the NEC's sister committee, the Standing Orders Committee, which ran the party conference. She was like a Jane Austen heroine, with delicate features and the best of manners. Despite heavy lobbying, tactical manoeuvring, and the persistence of obsessive loonies, she held the Labour Party conference together like a headmistress conducting a primary school assembly, while always seeming to ensure Tony Blair got his way.

For better or worse these women dominated my life for the next four years. I'm sure they liked me; they certainly gave me good advice about the rules, rituals, and unspoken power plays within the upper echelons of the party. They made sure I was on influential committees, gave me plenty to do, and covered for me if I made a cock-up. But they didn't trust me and probably rightly so; I was a loose cannon, naive, tactless, and a quixotic champion of causes I couldn't win. I wasn't part of the trade union faction, I wasn't bonded in a common brotherhood of anger and outrage like the Grassroots Alliance, I wasn't a parliamentarian constantly under pressure from the whips' office, nor did I want a seat in parliament or a job in the House of Lords; I was constrained neither by faction nor ambition, so it was hard to predict which way I'd vote on any given issue. The only voices I felt the need to listen to were the members in places like Falmouth and St Helens, Hastings and Aberdeen, and their message was simple, 'Make the Party fairer'.

Over the years, *Time Team* went from strength to strength; there were now many more promising sites available for us than there'd been when we'd started. This isn't as mad as it sounds. Landowners with potentially first-class archaeology in their fields had been reluctant to give us access, but now the series had developed a reputation for archaeological excellence, more and more of them were approaching us with requests to dig their land.

Hopton Castle in Shropshire looked as though it would be particularly productive. So much ancient rubbish is dumped in castle moats that they're often the most exciting part of a site to excavate, and the one at Hopton had been filled with earth, overgrown with grass, and left sealed for centuries. We hired a big mechanical digger and started to go down into it. But the weather was dreadful, and halfway through the afternoon we had to call it a day. On our second morning the rain was still falling in sheets, but our producer rushed up to me in a state of high excitement. Our metal detectorist had been examining the soggy pile of spoil we'd managed to grab on day one, and had found a coin which, at first glance, looked pretty rare; indeed it might be the most valuable find we'd ever discovered on *Time Team*. It had only come up a few minutes previously, would I go over there right away?

Thirty seconds later the camera rolled, I bounded up to the nervous detectorist and said, 'I hear you've got something pretty unusual.'

'Yes, Tony.'

'It's a coin?'

'Yes, Tony.'

'Can you show it to me?'

'Yes, Tony.'

He had a dewdrop on the end of his nose which was getting larger by the second. He placed the coin in my open palm and as he did so the snot dislodged itself and fell into my hand. I wanted to shout and vomit, I wanted to rush to the nearest tap and bathe my defiled fingers in fresh water, but I didn't. Instead I said, 'Gosh, that is interesting. Let's have a look at the other side,' and turned it over with my fingers.

The coin was later identified as a quarter laurel from the reign of King James I in the early seventeenth century. It was probably worth about £3,000, but I'd have paid twice as much never to have held it.

*

Channel 4 were keen to keep me tied into the programme, but I'd have gone bonkers if I'd had to make programmes about digging up old stuff and nothing else, so they offered me a long-term contract which involved me shooting four extra documentaries each year on themes that had nothing to do with archaeology. It was a potentially great arrangement, but who was going to come up with the programme ideas? Who did I know who was quirky but not irritating, a rebel but not indulgent, fun but not a time-waster?

I had a meeting with David Willcock, a glorious eccentric with piercing blue eyes and blond hair, who'd trained for the priesthood, but had had a crisis of faith shortly before he was due to take the cloth, and had moved into television. We immediately bonded. We were both inquisitive about anything and everything, loved the countryside, were fascinated by radical culture and history, and wanted the process of making TV programmes to be fun. In our first year together we went to Italy and made three shows about Roman emperors – the superhuman Julius Caesar, Nero who killed his wife and his mother, and Caligula who went mad and made his horse a senator. We had a rip-roaring time.

On the strength of these shows we were commissioned to make more programmes about the real lives of famous characters from history: *The Real Macbeth*, *The Real William Wallace*, *The Real Robin Hood* and *The Real Richard III*. These culminated in *Britain's Real Monarch*, in which we claimed that King Edward IV had been illegitimate, the Tudor kings and queens had been usurpers, and the true monarchs of Britain were the Plantagenets. The most senior surviving Plantagenet lived on the border between New South Wales and Victoria, and we planned to go there to give him the news that he was the King of England.

In order to fulfil my ridiculously tight filming schedule, I needed to fly to Australia, shoot the sequence, and be back in five days, so there'd be no time to recover from jet lag, a condition which could floor me for a week. David came up with a solution.

'I've borrowed some dieting pills. They're sort of like speed,' he said, with the glee of an unreformed public schoolboy. 'We'll take a handful when the plane gets to Bangkok and hopefully won't fall asleep till Melbourne. Then we'll get a good night's sleep, wake up refreshed and be ready for our drive across Victoria to meet the King.'

The plan seemed to work well. The flight was pleasurable, although we talked more than usual, hardly ate anything, and had to walk up and down the aisles every ten minutes or so to pass the time, but by the time we got into our Melbourne hotel bedrooms the effect appeared to have worn off, and we went out like a light.

The next thing I remember is standing in the middle of the room feeling hazy. My watch said quarter past nine. Where was Dave? Why hadn't he woken me up? I picked up the phone. 'It's not quarter past nine, you idiot, it's quarter to three,' he said tersely, so I climbed back into bed.

When I woke up again the sun was pouring through the window, there was a hammering noise on the door, and my bed-clothes were completely soaked. Oh my God, had I wet myself? I clambered round the bed sniffing the sheets, but they didn't smell uriney. Was there a leak, a flood, some other kind of water crisis? I could hear David calling me. I grabbed my bathrobe, then realised I'd already got my clothes on.

When I finally opened the door David said, 'It's 10 a.m. You've overslept.'

He looked past me into the room.

'Blimey! What's happened?'

My suitcase was lying open on the floor and the contents were strewn about as though I'd been attacked by thieves.

'Did you have problems finding the right stuff?' he asked with a puzzled look on his face. The clothes I was wearing were entirely random: odd socks, shorts and yesterday's shirt with the tail hanging out. We went into the bathroom; the shower was on, the cold tap was running, there was a trail of toothpaste all over the washbasin, and wet towels everywhere.

'You've been sleepwalking, old son.'

Of course he was right. I'd got out of bed in my sleep, showered in my sleep, put my clothes on without drying myself in my sleep, then phoned Dave still virtually asleep.

I put some slightly more co-ordinated things on, repacked, got in the passenger seat of the car, dropped off again, and didn't wake up till we arrived at the tiny town of Jerilderie on the New South Wales border late that afternoon.

Our real monarch Michael Hastings was a staunch republican. He had two daughters, and grandchildren called Caleb, Jet and Zack, which Dave and I thought were very fine names for princes. Michael loved the idea of being King of England, although he insisted he didn't fancy coming back home and ousting Elizabeth Windsor. Instead he knighted me there and then, ten years before I received a knighthood from Prince William. There aren't many people who've been knighted twice!

The following year Dave and I filmed a sequence about the Hundred Years War in the magnificent thirteenth-century nave of Rouen Cathedral. Dave and the cameraman were setting up the next shot while I chatted with Dr Mike Jones, our contributor.

'There's one thing I've always wondered about knights,' I said. 'They're squeezed into all this armour, and they've got no slits, no fly buttons, no sneaky little vents. And yet the battle of Agincourt lasted about ten hours. How did they pee? How did they poo?'

'Ahh,' said Mike. 'There was a special bloke in charge of that.'

I called Dave over.

'If you were a knight in battle,' Mike continued, 'you did what you had to do in your saddle, and at the end of the day when you rode back to camp, a special bloke called the arming squire unbuckled you and took the dirty armour away, and you went to your tent, had a little wash, then feasted with your mates. Meanwhile the arming squire sluiced the armour out, spent the night scrubbing it shiny again with sand and cold water, and buckled you back in the following morning.'

'Blimey!' said Dave. 'That sounds like the worst job in history . . .'

'. . . which is an extremely good name for a TV series,' I added.

'Indeed it is,' said Dave. 'Indeed it is!'

The press loved to portray Dennis Skinner MP as a dour, flinty-hearted Tory-hater, Oliver Cromwell in a duffle coat. But he was a kind, generous-hearted man, and a big fan of my documentaries. I was fond of him too and wrote a *Maid Marian* cartoon book called *The Beast of Bolsover*, a reference to the nickname he'd been given by the press.

He once asked me if I enjoyed making *The Worst Jobs in History*. I replied that it was a bit like asking Paula Radcliffe if she'd enjoyed running a marathon. I'm sure she'd have said she was proud she'd done it, and was pleased with the result, but enjoyment didn't really come into it.

Worst Jobs was undoubtedly my worst ever job. I spent months climbing ridiculously tall buildings, carrying back-breaking weights on my back, and far too much time standing up to my waist in shit. My bones ached, I was constantly pulling muscles, blowing my nose, and hacking up phlegm due to the minor infections brought on by the trillions of bacteria which assailed me.

I could tolerate the smelly jobs. I'd brought up two kids; a dirty nappy held no terrors for me. But I hated heights, so when I was suspended over the edge of a two-hundred-foot cliff on the Gower coast, it wasn't a pleasant experience.

For the first few decades after the Saxons invaded England,

they lived in the coastal regions. They raided further inland, but ran the danger of being cut off, so particularly in winter, they hunkered down by the sea, usually some distance from the high-calorie food they needed for survival. But there was one plentiful source of protein waiting to be devoured: the eggs of the big seabirds that nested on the cliffs. We were on the Gower to demonstrate the job of the Saxon guillemot-egg collector. In order to do this I had to dress in a ludicrously ill-fitting costume, with leather shoes three sizes too big for me. The Saxons would have scaled these heights using sealskin rope with a bucket on the end, but I was safely togged up with modern abseiling equipment. Not that it provided any solace; I'd never abseiled before, nor did I have the slightest desire to do so now.

The instructor, a kindly man with the body of a paratrooper, led me to the top of the chosen cliff. When I saw the sea crashing on the rocks far below, my entire body began to shake. He sent me to the edge, told me to turn round and face him, put my hands on the grass, and push myself off backwards. I didn't want to do this very much at all, but the cameras were rolling and I clung to the modicum of pride I still had, and did what he asked. For a quarter of a second I thought I was plunging to my death, but then the rope pulled me up short. My eyes were now level with his feet.

'Look into my eyes. Look into my eyes,' he said like a comedy hypnotist. Slowly he payed out the line, I began to descend and although I was still terrified, it didn't snap, and I realised I could lean forward and grab the side of the cliff for moral support whenever I wanted.

I was starting to feel almost secure, but then we came to a massive boulder sticking out of the cliff face. I managed to wiggle and push my way over the encumbrance, but once I was below it I'd got nothing to cling on to anymore and was hanging in mid-air. I couldn't see or hear my instructor, he couldn't see or hear me, and I wanted to go home. To my left a cameraman on another abseil line was pointing his camera at me and signalling that he was rolling. I grabbed a chicken's egg which had been placed on a ledge by one of our rock-climbing team half an hour earlier, and attempted an amusing piece to camera about how proud I was that I'd managed to collect it, but that it was a pretty ridiculous thing to do given that no self-respecting hen would lay an egg within fifty feet of a cliff edge. I was dreadful; my voice was high-pitched and jerky like a eunuch being tortured, and my terror was painfully apparent. I got to the end, and waited for something to happen, but nothing did, other than that my instructor must have stopped paying out the rope, because I was now static. Slowly the line spun round until I was facing the sea and the jagged rocks below. Death was imminent. Then my stupid shoes fell off. I watched them descend, swirling this way and that towards the water. It seemed an age before they finally disappeared into the waves. Steve Bowden, our soundman, recorded what I said next for posterity. For some time this outtake was occasionally played at Channel 4 for the amusement of the senior staff.

'Can somebody help me, please,' I called desperately, 'because I'm dangling here . . . like . . . a . . . fucking . . . conker!'

Baldrick's ancestors, and indeed mine, were forced by the poverty rife in Victorian London to scrape a living in a variety of disgusting ways. There were 'cigar-end finders' who looked out for dog-ends to recycle as tobacco, 'tea hawkers' who went from door to door begging for discarded tea leaves, dried them out, mixed them with fresh green tea and sawdust, and resold them to unsuspecting shopkeepers, and 'toshers' who scoured the sewers for coins, cutlery and lumps of old metal that had been dropped down toilets or washed into drains. But in my opinion the very worst job was that of the 'pure collector', and it was that which we were filming one cold Tuesday morning in a recently gentrified garden square in the East End.

The word 'pure' was a nineteenth-century joke; the objects

being collected were the dog faeces used in tanning and similar industries. I worked my way round the square explaining this, occasionally picking up specially prepared sausage-shaped props in my latex-gloved hands, and putting them in a leather satchel. Filming was brought to a halt by an angry resident who alleged we didn't have the required permissions. Once our right to film there had been established I started talking to camera again and collecting more pure, but we were running late now, as I had to be at a meeting by 12.30. The Labour Party's Joint Policy Committee was the only place where the Cabinet, trade union general secretaries and party representatives could meet with Tony Blair on an equal footing in order to come to agreement on party matters. It was the apex of the party's committee structure, and as I was now the lead NEC member on culture and sport, I'd been given a place on it. It was a great honour for a member as inexperienced as me, I didn't want to muck it up, and I certainly didn't want to be late. So in order to ensure that we got everything we needed in the can, and that I arrived at 10 Downing Street on time, David's company had arranged for an ex-police motorcyclist to whisk me across London.

At 12 p.m. I jogged out of the square, slipped the top half of my clothes off, climbed into an enormous bright red quilted PVC motorbike suit, pulled on a bike helmet and boots, and rode pillion in the direction of Westminster, looking like a large child in a Babygro. The city was crowded and bedevilled by roadworks, and it was just after half past twelve before I arrived at Number 10. The security guard asked me to hand over my mobile phone, but it was buried somewhere in the pockets of my voluminous suit, so I told him I didn't have one. I turned left into the large marble loo by the front door for a quick pee, but when I unzipped, I realised I'd left my shirt back in East London with the crew. Rather than attend the meeting bare-chested, I zipped myself up again, clambered up the elegant staircase to the Cabinet Room, discreetly opened the double doors and, so that everyone would understand why I was wearing a Babygro, waved my crash helmet vaguely in the direction of my fellow JPC members who were seated round the cabinet table in their business suits and ties of various shades of red. The meeting was already underway, and there was an empty chair at the far side of the room. I edged my way past dour Gordon Brown, grumpy John Prescott and urbane Jack Straw, mouthing my apologies. Then Tony Blair rose to speak, and as he did so my phone started ringing. I searched my pockets as I shuffled along, but it was difficult while holding a crash helmet. I unzipped the top of my suit with my free hand and began groping around inside the pockets of my jeans, but I still couldn't locate the familiar rectangular lump. Eventually the phone stopped. 'Sorry, Tony,' I murmured, and sat down in my seat.

The reason I'd been so desperate to get to this particular meeting on time was that I had an important speech to make. Tony was keen for us to endorse his plan for new 'super casinos' to be built in some of our poorer towns and cities to help regenerate them. This was deeply unpopular within the party both on moral grounds and from a policing point of view, but my little culture committee didn't have the clout to stop the policy in its tracks. Our best shot was to side with those trying to persuade the government to agree that only one or two casinos should be given the go-ahead, preferably in genuinely impoverished areas like Blackpool, rather than in London and Manchester which had pro-casino lobbies orchestrated by big business.

Only a couple of minutes after I arrived I was called upon to speak.

'Tony, fellow committee members,' I began, 'I'd like us to look a little more closely at—'

Brrring-bring! Brrring-bring!

Back then if someone left a voicemail on my mobile it would ring every few minutes until I picked up the message. I didn't want to unzip my Babygro again because it would make me look ridiculous. But I'd been through my speech countless times in my head, and I knew I could recite it without thinking too hard, so while I jabbered away about negative precedents in other countries, I let most of my mind concentrate on working out a way to shut the phone off. I'd identified the noise as probably coming from somewhere adjacent to my left buttock, and I pressed my thumb firmly in that area hoping it would depress the 'end call' button. It didn't. I repeated the same action on my right buttock, but still the phone kept ringing. I worked my way up my body pressing on both sides with my thumbs. When that failed I tried hitting myself with my fist as though emphasising a point in my speech, in other words trying to deliver a socio-political analysis while beating myself up. Eventually the phone stopped, and a couple of sentences later my speech came to an end.

'Thank you,' said Tony drily. 'That gives us something to think about. Sort that phone out, would you?'

'Yes,' I replied. 'Good idea.'

'Have you tried your top left-hand pocket?' he asked.

I hadn't, but it was there. I took it out, switched it off, placed it ostentatiously in front of me alongside my crash helmet, and smiled wryly. No one smiled back, not even the Margarets. For the next three-quarters of an hour various ministers of state held forth, but I wasn't listening. The meeting ended, and when I got back outside Number 10, I retrieved my message. It was from David Willcock.

'Sorry,' he said, 'can you come straight back. I've just been looking at this morning's tapes. The fake stuff we used didn't look authentic enough. We're going to have to shoot the scene again with real poo.'

26

THE CONFUSED MUM

Tony Blair was reluctant to tell the NEC whether or not he was planning to go to war with Iraq. He absolutely didn't want to, he said, and would do his best to stop such a thing from happening, but we needed to give him some leeway for a while, because:

1. The NEC was leaky – there were secret negotiations going on with other countries and the United Nations, and a leak would scupper them.
2. He didn't want to give anything away in case Saddam Hussein got to hear about it.
3. Britain had secret agents on the ground whose lives would be at risk if the information they'd got hold of was made public.

He said it was easy to support a leader when you had all the facts at your disposal; the big test of loyalty was whether you continued to give him that support when you were left in the dark. At the time this seemed a perfectly reasonable case to make.

That was in September 2002. Eight months later when the initial fighting was over, and Iraq began to fracture and our television screens showed heart-rending pictures of terror, confusion and chaos, the scales fell from my eyes. We hadn't joined the war on the basis of any hard evidence, but simply because George Bush had wanted us to. Even worse, there'd been no plans in place for putting the country back on its feet once it had been defeated. Tens of thousands of innocent people had been killed, the infrastructure was in ruins, old tensions had been laid bare, and all for nothing – well, worse than nothing, now that the entire Middle East was becoming destabilised. The irreplaceable artefacts of the Babylonian Empire had been shattered and smashed, and so had my faith in Tony. It was the most radicalising experience of my adult life.

Apart from my work on the NEC my time was divided between looking after my poorly mum, immersing myself in horrible jobs, and digging holes in people's back gardens. It was extraordinary that *Time Team* was still firing on all cylinders after so long. We had rows, mostly about the conflicting demands of television and archaeology, but everyone involved looked forward to the digs. The excavations had got more complex; now there were at least fifty people on site every day, researchers, production staff, an army of young diggers, re-enactors, several camera crews, all of whom were as much part of *Time Team* as those on screen. The three days we had together were always special; we worked hard, but there was a party atmosphere which usually involved lots of late-night drinking, and even though most of the team were terrified of Tim Taylor, he made a point of joining in, and brought out his battered guitar and played till dawn while the diggers sang along to his renditions of Leonard Cohen and Bob Dylan.

But it wasn't only the parties and booze that held us together. Three days of digging for ten hours a day under constant scrutiny were made bearable by a stream of practical jokes.

In the early days they'd been fairly straightforward. One misty morning I clambered into a freezing river on the Somerset levels to retrieve the fish traps we'd woven out of willow to demonstrate how peasants in the early Middle Ages got their protein. But when I pulled them to the surface and presented them to the camera, someone had filled them with tins of salmon and small jars of pickled mussels.

As time went by, the pranks became more complex. Our soundman, Steve Bowden, was famous for falling into a deep sleep after five or six drinks, and one night he collapsed in the bar and couldn't be woken up. So the younger archaeologists bound him from head to toe in camera tape, painted him blue, covered his face in make-up and lipstick, and wrote tasteless phrases in eyeliner on his cheeks and forehead. He now looked like an Egyptian mummy decorated by Tracey Emin. Then they scrubbed him up again and dumped him in an empty hotel room. The next morning he had no idea where he was or what had happened to him; at least not until he found the incriminating polaroids scattered on his duvet.

These jokes grew into full-scale works of art. I had a white Range Rover, which was particularly handy when we were working off-road. On a shoot in the Lake District, I drove it two-thirds of the way up a small mountain on a slithery dirt track till I got to our forward camp, locked it, left it for the day, and yomped off to film the excavation of a Roman copper mine.

When I got back at six that evening a police car had parked up with its blue light flashing, but there were no policemen about and my Range Rover had disappeared. I wandered anxiously round the surrounding hillside but couldn't find it anywhere. When I returned twenty minutes later, a few archaeologists were sitting around drinking from their thermos flasks before starting the long trudge homewards.

'Have you seen my motor?' I said, but they hadn't.

'You should ask the coppers,' someone suggested. 'See if their car's open. If you beep the horn, that should get them back, shouldn't it?'

'I'm not sure you're allowed to . . .'

I approached it apprehensively. On the passenger seat were a lot of items which seemed familiar: something that looked like my wet-weather gear, my North Face jacket, my books, my dried mango slices . . . Shitty McShit! How could I possibly have been such an idiot? It wasn't a police car at all, it was my Range Rover meticulously disguised with coloured camera tape, specially printed police logos, and false number plates bearing the registration number 'TT1 FU'. As for the blue lamp, it was the original one from Doctor Who's Tardis, which had been borrowed from the props department at BBC Cardiff.

I didn't want to waste the rest of my time on the NEC moaning about everything that Labour had done or said. The government was moving forward on issues like equal pay, child poverty, gay rights, and even improved investment in the arts, all of which I passionately supported. However dreadful our foreign policy might be, I didn't want us replaced by the Tories; I simply wanted the party to be better than it was. So I decided to stand as Chair of the National Policy Forum, a debating chamber in which members could have their say about Labour's future direction, and which would have been the perfect place to express any unease about Iraq. This hadn't happened, though. The Forum had kept its collective trap shut because its debates were tightly controlled, a lot of its members were hand-picked by party officials, and any opposition firmly squashed. I thought it was time for us to have a major rethink, with the NPF being the perfect place to start. In theory this was a reasonable aspiration, but in practice it was incendiary. The current Chair was Margaret Wall, and she had the support of Tony Blair, Number 10, and all the senior party officials. I could try to fool myself that this was a jolly little election between like-minded colleagues, but deep down I knew that to stand against one of the Margarets was an act of rebellion.

Campaigning was ridiculously difficult. I couldn't lobby anyone face to face because I was in the north-east filming a new series of *The Worst Jobs in History*. All day long I'd crawl along dark tunnels with a rope tied round my waist dragging trucks of coal, hack at rock faces with a tiny pick, or carry vast barrels of drinking water on my shoulders down cobbled streets; then in the evenings I'd climb into bed, snuggle under the duvet, and start phoning the hundred and thirty-odd NPF delegates. Even if I'd been feeling at my best this would have been a tall order, but the weeks of non-stop worst jobs were wearing me down. I shivered all day, and sweated all night. The final day of filming was the worst. Coincidentally I was back at Alnwick Castle where we'd shot the original *Blackadder* series, this time re-enacting a trial by ducking stool, the torture that medieval women were put through in order to determine whether or not they were witches.

The water was icy and I was ducked countless times, brought back to the water's edge while the camera angle was altered, then sent crashing back down into the river again. It was the best part of an hour before the ordeal was over. I grabbed a towel and staggered off to the relative warmth of a draughty antechamber in the castle wall. My dry clothes had inadvertently been left on the far side of the field, so I had to wait, with the towel draped round my dripping clothes, while the runner loped off to get them.

Someone gave me a paper cup with cold water in it, the last thing in the world I wanted, and my glasses and mobile phone. I'd had a message from the macho firebrand Tony Woodley, who was general secretary of the Transport and General Workers' Union, and I needed to return his call right away. If I could get his union's support, more votes would follow. But there was some hard bargaining to be done about which union policies I'd be prepared to endorse if I got the post. I phoned him, and was friendly but firm, courteous but adamant. I'd like his delegates to votes for me, I said, but there were certain lines I wasn't prepared to cross. I didn't mention that I was dressed as a medieval witch with a floppy hat over my eyes and my soaking tights round my ankles, as I felt it might dilute my credibility.

He gave me his blessing, and I could now head for South

Wales with some well-needed union votes in my pocket. I dried off, and had a pork pie, two Nurofen, and a cup of tea.

I drove a hundred miles, had a doze in a layby near Nottingham, then drove another hundred to the Celtic Manor in Newport. The bar was crammed with NPF delegates, and the noise was overwhelming. I wanted to curl up on a sofa and die, but instead bought a large whisky and began working the room. I couldn't remember which delegates were against me, who was a doubter, whose vote was in the bag, or indeed who anyone was, but I beamed at everyone, and mumbled platitudes about how I wanted us to break out of the stranglehold of blah-blah-blah. It was as though I was in an Italian arthouse movie; faces loomed up at me but I couldn't work out what they were saying, arms hugged, squeezed and tugged at me, I was dragged from one side of the room to the other, and harangued and whispered at conspiratorially. A hand passed me more Scotch, and I blundered round clutching two large glasses, too bemused to tip the contents of one into the other.

I woke up next morning on my bed still wearing my clothes, hastily showered, then went down to breakfast with a banging headache for some final lobbying. But the other delegates had already gone to the conference hall, so I crept in at the back nibbling a piece of toast, which made an unbearably loud crunching sound. Eventually the candidates were called on to speak, and when my turn came, I pulled myself together, sprang to life, breathed in and gave a ten-minute improvised tub-thumping speech about how important ordinary members were to the health of the party, how they should be treated with integrity, how our finances should be open and above board, how damaging our failure to debate Iraq openly and honestly had been, and how it was our duty to invest in encouraging young people to join us in our fight for freedom, fairness and social democracy.

The slow smatter of applause when I came to the end of my last rousing line told me my audience was less impressed by my rhetoric than I was, but I no longer cared. I was simply pleased that I'd been able to get through my speech without vomiting. I knew that if I'd said the same things to any group of members in the country it would have been well received, but the trouble with the NPF was that it was deaf; it was simply part of the machine that delivered party loyalty. Margaret Wall and I observed the count to make sure there hadn't been any funny business, and she beat me comfortably. She was gracious in victory, as she'd been throughout the campaign. I broke the news of my defeat to my supporters, went back to bed, and slept for the rest of the day.

In 2004, after four years and an enormous amount of hard work, I decided to leave the NEC and the Margarets, and go back to being an ordinary Party member. Although I was proud of a lot of the work I'd been able to do, I was deeply concerned that the reservations I had about the Party's conduct would ultimately bring about its downfall. The relationship between the members and politicians had been split asunder. Members saw Iraq as a betrayal and they no longer trusted the leadership. Maybe they'd soon start choosing unelectable leaders with whose policies they agreed rather than electable leaders about whom they had reservations but who would give them a chance to make at least some of their dreams a reality. This was a tragedy; politics should be about changing people's lives, not voting for figureheads who make you feel good about yourself.

My worst fear was that at some time the groups and individuals who'd done so much damage in the past would return, become influential again and bring back with them the unsavoury policies and behaviour that had sullied my party and my union throughout the 1970s. I hoped I was wrong.

Eventually *The Worst Jobs in History* came an end, and David Willcock decided to leave television and become a history teacher. But *Time Team* still showed no signs of flagging. There were changes: Carenza left to pursue an academic career in Cambridge and bring up her three children; Mick had a severe blood clot but survived. A few new faces were brought in, we all got older, and the practical jokes became ever more complex.

The most legendary was played on John Gater, who owned the geophysics company we'd used since the first series. John was a dour, bearded Yorkshireman with the softest of hearts. He was deeply loyal to the show, and very proud of the key role geophysics played in it. Virtually every TV viewer in the land now knew what the word 'geophys' meant, and this was down to John and his team, the miles they walked every day to map what was below the surface of each site, and the new and innovative geophysics rigs John bought for his team to use.

There was one particular machine of which he was inordinately proud, a Bartington magnetometer, which had cost him over fifteen thousand pounds, and was highly effective at identifying ditches, pits and kilns. One of our top archaeologists, site co-ordinator Kerry Ely, spent weeks secretly making a copy of it in his garage and it was so well made that even at a few feet it would have fooled the most hawk-eyed scientist.

On day three of our Roman dig at Alfoldean in Sussex I called John on his walkie-talkie and asked him to put his wonder-rig down for a moment, and come over to the far side of our field for an interview. As he walked towards me, Kerry surreptitiously swapped his kit for the dummy one, and propped it up against our Land Rover Discovery.

In the middle of a very pertinent question about the science of magnetometry, John saw the Discovery drive off and his precious instrument crash to the ground. The interview was immediately forgotten. 'Whoa!' he shouted, but no one appeared to hear him.

A large mechanical digger started up and headed towards the fallen machine, the driver apparently unaware of what was in his path. 'Whoa! Whoa! Whoa!' went John, although now at a much higher pitch, but the driver ran straight over his rig and headed off again, leaving it a twisted wreck.

John gave a howl of anguish, and strode towards it, followed by virtually everyone else in the field. 'What's up, John? What happened?' people asked solicitously, but John just shook his head.

When he reached his beloved magnetometer, he looked down at what was left of it, and in a broken voice said, 'Well, that's fifteen-thous—' Then he saw the note fixed to it. 'Gotcha!' it said. He looked round; everyone was laughing and applauding, including the cameramen who had secretly filmed the entire event. Then Kerry popped out from behind his van holding up John's pristine rig.

John seldom swore, but on this occasion, after a cursory inspection of the twisted metal, he said, 'You bastards! You bastards!' and just to make sure everyone knew exactly how he felt, he added, 'You fucking bastards!'

By the mid-2000s Mum had been ill for many years. Back in 1998 she'd been fit and independent and living an active life among her friends and neighbours in Raymond Avenue. Her only problem was that she'd got an ulcerated varicose vein on her leg which refused to heal. The doctor said the solution was a simple one which would require a few days in hospital. On the Sunday before her operation she took Luke, Heli and me out for lunch at a carvery in Buckhurst Hill. When we got to the reception desk there was some confusion about our booking, but she put on her regal, slightly bossy voice, and sorted everything out. Then we settled down to a Sunday roast. It was the last time I ever saw her with her mind intact.

The following Thursday afternoon her neighbour Kate drove her in to Whipps Cross Hospital. Then late the next day I got a phone call.

'Your mum's legs are fine,' her anaesthetist said, 'absolutely top notch. But there was a little problem with the application of the anaesthetic, and things got a bit stormy.'

'What does that mean?' I asked. 'Shall we come in right now?'

'No, it's all good,' he said. 'Everything's right as rain. Pop in tomorrow.'

I accepted his recommendation at face value, and the next morning Heli and I went to Whipps Cross.

'Hullo, Mum, how you going?' I asked.

She had a puzzled look on her face.

'Les hasn't been in,' she said.

'Mum, Dad died nine years ago,' I said. 'You know that.'

'So where is he?'

We asked to see someone in charge, but it was the weekend and there was no one around for us to talk to. When visiting time ended, we went home.

That night we got a phone call to tell us she'd been taken into Intensive Care, and we rushed back to the hospital. She was a horrendous sight. The doctors had put a hole in her throat and inserted a tube in it, and there were drips and lines all over her body. The nurse said she had double pneumonia and pleurisy.

But she didn't die. She was put on twenty-four-hour watch for three days, and remained in Intensive Care for a few weeks after that, but eventually she came out, although she was now in a wheelchair, and more confused than ever. No one seemed to know what had happened to her or why, and half her medical notes appeared to be missing. I felt like a powerless child, or a character in a Kafka novel overwhelmed by impersonal forces he can't understand or control.

We managed to get her out of hospital and into Harts House Nursing Home, a stately Georgian mansion overlooking Woodford Green. We'd planned for her to stay there only until she got better, but eventually it became apparent that she'd never walk again and, like Dad, she'd been struck by full-scale dementia.

The years passed and we continued to collude with the fiction that she'd soon be moving back to South Woodford. Heli and I visited her every week, and took her for trips at weekends. We went to Southend and ate chips on the promenade, to posh pubs where she'd have a sweet sherry and roast beef with Yorkshire puds, and to jolly, nicely painted cafes for afternoon tea. We gatecrashed the Metropolitan Police fair in Chigwell, and were given a high old time by the constables. We took her to see *South Pacific*, *Phantom of the Opera*, and an Italian comedy at the Lyric Theatre where the fire curtain was lowered in the interval and got stuck on its way back up again. We spent the next thirty minutes watching the technicians try to free it, and listening to ever more desperate apologies from the stage manager. Then we were all sent home with our money back. Mum thought this was the best show she'd seen for ages.

Even when she began to find the trips more painful than enjoyable, we still took her out occasionally. But she'd shake, get tetchy, and hated being bumped about in the wheelchair. We took her to our flat for Christmas which meant carrying her up several flights of stairs; I'm pretty sure she'd rather have stayed at Harts House, but it seemed important at the time that she should be with her family pulling crackers and wearing a paper hat.

Dementia had now been the dominant feature in my life for the best part of twenty years. I felt I'd become as much of an expert on the trials and tribulations of dementia care as I was on archaeology. I could reel off the figures and facts; I knew the paltry amount the UK spent on research, how poorly trained and badly paid our professional carers were, how little we knew about how to alleviate day-to-day suffering, how many thousands of people gave up their jobs each year in order to look after a demented loved one, how they got virtually no support, and how exhausted, angry, useless and frustrated they felt most of the time.

In 2004 I wrote an article about this for the *Daily Mail*. It was long and passionate, with pictures of Mum and Dad from the old days before they were struck down. Channel 4 suggested I make a polemical show on the subject, but we agreed it would only work if Mum was involved, because then I'd be able to speak from the heart.

We discussed the idea at length with Laura and Luke who'd always been wary about the demands TV people make, and came to the conclusion that it would only be a good idea if Mum wanted to do it, and her dignity was protected. Also before we went ahead I needed her permission, not an easy thing to obtain when you're asking someone whose mind is fractured.

'Mum,' I said, 'Channel 4 would like to make a documentary film about you.'

'Ooh yes,' she replied. 'That would be nice.'

'Hang on, Phyllis,' said Margaret Mitchell, the Harts House Head of Care. 'Tony hasn't told you what it would involve.'

'It would be your story, Mum, about what happened after your operation and the trouble you have getting your thoughts together. And it'd show us taking you out on trips. And I'd be in it too, and Heli would make sure you wore the dresses you like, and she'd do your nails.'

'Ooh yes,' Mum said again.

But was she taking the information in, or simply saying 'ooh yes' because I'd come to the end of a sentence?

A couple of hours later we were in the dining room, and I was attempting to feed her a Waitrose sherry trifle, which she usually gobbled up. But she pushed the spoon aside and said, 'You know that thing?'

'What thing?' asked Margaret.

The familiar look of mild irritation crossed her face.

'That nice thing.'

'Yes?'

'When's it going to happen?'

We took that as permission to go ahead.

Mum had always loved acting, although she'd seldom been

given more than a few lines to say, and now at the end of her life here she was starring in her own TV show. We started filming *Me and My Mum* in late autumn 2005, and she had a wonderful time. She charmed the crew and they charmed her. We took countless shots of her in bed, out of bed, upstairs, downstairs, and in the car, and she never complained about having to do retakes. In one sequence Luke and I took her out for a cream tea in an Essex village and she flirted shamelessly with him. He may have been her grandson, but for a few moments she was Scarlett O'Hara and he was Rhett, feeding her pieces of scone and jam from his fork. She slept well after a day's filming.

On the final day of the shoot we interviewed the health minister. His intentions seemed sound enough, but it was obvious there wasn't much he could do to help those suffering from Alzheimer's unless the Treasury gave him more cash, and that was extremely unlikely. We hired a cab so we could drive around Parliament Square while I summed up my feelings about his interview on camera, but my mobile rang before we started rolling. It was Margaret Mitchell.

'I think you ought to get down here right away. Your mum's taken a nasty turn.'

'How bad is she?'

'I think she's probably dying.'

I picked up my car, met Laura in West London and we went straight to Harts House. It seemed to take an age to get there. The crew was following us, but did we want them to film her? We needed space to say goodbye, we didn't want her death throes played out to the nation, but on the other hand the film had seemed to matter to her more than anything else. It was her story. Shouldn't we tell it to the end? What would she want us to do?

We went in to see her. She was awake but barely conscious. Luke and Heli had arrived, and when we were ready we let the cameraman in for a few minutes, but then her eyes closed, and the TV people went away again.

The four of us prepared for the long wait. The room opposite was unoccupied, and the nurses brought in some bedclothes, so when night came, we could take it in turns to rest. We held Mum's hand, mopped her forehead, completed an entire book of *Sun* word games, and ate a monster pack of chicken legs. In the early hours she slipped away with her family by her side.

Me and My Mum exceeded all expectations, and became a rallying cry for those campaigning for a better deal for dementia sufferers. I received more mail in response to that programme than for all the other shows I've ever done put together. They were mostly angry, frustrated, thwarted letters written in long-hand outlining the terrible treatment the writer and their loved one had received at the hands of the state, the NHS, private healthcare or their GP. They complained about the ignorance surrounding dementia, the lack of resources and the institutional cruelty. I became an ambassador for the Alzheimer's Society, and remain one to this day.

27

THE FEROCIOUS DIRECTOR

I wasn't heartbroken when Mum died. I was sad she wasn't around anymore, and I knew I'd miss the countless, comforting little rituals we'd devised since she'd been at Harts House. But I was relieved too. She'd wanted to die, she'd often told me so, and her death was a release for both of us. I'd been mourning her loss since her operation had gone horribly wrong seven years previously; now I didn't have to mourn any longer.

But her death created a big hole in my life, and it was some time before I achieved any kind of equilibrium. Heli and I had morphed from lovers to partners, then when the passion died to close friends, and now she lived across the road from me while still working as my PA. We were constantly squabbling, took the piss out of each other, and were probably a bit codependant, but it worked for us, and still does. The children had left university; Laura was the political officer at the Transport and General Workers' Union, and Luke was in corporate entertainment specialising in sport, which meant we could get tickets for any football match we wanted. What a great job!

I needed a big project now, something that wasn't primarily history or archaeology, and would galvanise me into a new way of thinking. I didn't have to wait long. I was stopped in a corridor at Channel 4 by a remarkably attractive young woman I'd never met before. Her first words to me remain etched in my mind.

'Hi Tony. How would you fancy diving the *Titanic*?'

'Sure,' I replied. 'I'll pop home and slip on my Speedos.'

'I'm serious.'

She was Louisa Bolch, the channel's new commissioning editor for science, and she'd just pulled off a big coup. James Cameron, who'd directed the *Titanic* movie, was about to dive the stricken ship for one last time in order to make a multi-million dollar live TV show called *Last Mysteries of the Titanic* for the Discovery Channel. This was to be Discovery's walking on the moon moment, unique footage that would bring the experience of diving the most iconic wreck in the world into the sitting rooms of the citizens of Milwaukee and Maine. And as every grand project always needs a little extra money, Discovery had agreed to sell Channel 4 access to the project so we could make our own programme alongside the glitzy American one.

Two weeks later I flew to Canada. I had to wait a few days in St John's, Newfoundland for the arrival of the ship that was going to be my home for the next ten days. I wandered the colonial streets of St John's and its brightly painted clapboard houses, Irish bars, cute little independent eateries, and shops selling wet-weather gear and big guns for shooting predators.

'Have you got a cunning plan?' people asked me as usual, but I hadn't. All I had was a slight feeling of sickness, and as much faith as I could muster in the people in charge of our boat, which is how the passengers on the *Titanic* had probably felt as they hurtled towards the iceberg.

Eventually I boarded the big Russian scientific research vessel the *Keldysh* and sailed the four hundred and fifty miles to our destination, although when I got to it there was nothing to see except dark blue sea and towering waves in every direction. I knew that somewhere far below me was the largest vessel early twentieth-century human beings had made, but precisely where it was I couldn't tell. It was impossible to drop an anchor two and a half miles to the bottom of the ocean and keep the boat stable, so the *Keldysh* kept drifting away from her vantage point and then returning with the aid of transponders submerged on the end of long cables. Their little bleeps were party music to the ears of the local whale population. It was as though we were transmitting Russ Abbot's 'Atmosphere' very loud and non-stop. The whales honed in on the sound from fifty miles away and pirouetted, leapt out of the water, and generally caroused for hours on end until the transponders were switched off, whereupon they immediately disappeared.

I'd been given my own room, cold, bleak and monastic, but luxury compared to the quarters occupied by virtually everyone else who, with the exception of James Cameron, the captain and me, were crammed four to a cabin on mattresses and rugs, and even in the gangways. By some callous administrative oversight my camera crew hadn't been given anywhere to sleep at all, were forced to stay on our supply vessel half a mile away, and every morning had to make the dangerous transfer to our ship. We were told the sea was relatively calm but it didn't look like it to me. There was a sixty-foot swell, and stepping between the two ships as they hurtled up and down at different paces was a terrifying ordeal. Will Fewkes had joined *Time Team* many years previously as a wisecracking young camera assistant, and had now become one of our most valued cameramen. We borrowed him for this trip, and nearly lost him. He stepped off his ship a fraction too early and was caught by the *Keldysh* as she hurtled upwards at speed. He managed to step back just in time, but the edge of her deck brushed the front of one of his legs and like a giant potato peeler sliced off all the skin.

I looked forward to my team's arrival even though there wasn't much we could do apart from the occasional brief interview. Everyone else on the ship was obsessed by the objective of getting the big live show up and running. Our programme was a sideshow, no one had time to talk, and I felt pretty isolated.

It was an odd assembly of people; the chatter of Australians, Kiwis, cockneys, a bloke from Birmingham, the drawl of the Californians, all interspersed with the occasional terse word in

Russian. Jim's American team wore cowboy hats and expensive diving watches, they sped around the *Keldysh* in state-of-the-art inflatable ribs, and said 'right on' and 'you betcha'. The Russians were ex-secret service officers who had sailed round the world during the Cold War conducting 'scientific surveys'. Now they sold their talents and their world-class deep-sea technology to the highest bidder. There was no feeling of camaraderie. Maybe somewhere a friendship flourished between a Californian and a Russian, but I saw no evidence of it. The ship felt as divided as Berlin before the wall fell.

Day after day I stayed in my cabin while the rest of the ship's company fiddled with their massive banks of equipment, made test broadcasts to their bosses back in Atlanta, Georgia, produced videotaped packages to play into the live show if the signal went down, rehearsed and rewrote various interviews with their experts, and laid the miles of cable needed to carry the signal, twenty-five thousand feet of it simply to get down to the ocean floor.

Meanwhile I attempted to write a novel about Judas Iscariot, based on the idea that the word Iscariot is a corruption of 'dagger-man', and that Judas had been an armed revolutionary. It was a good starting point and it passed the time, but I never got further than the first half-dozen chapters.

Last Mysteries of the Titanic was a colossal fuck-up. As the Americans had feared, they kept losing transmission, (partly because the ship's funnel got in the way of the signal), communication between the *Keldysh* and Atlanta was sporadic and the director was continually forced to cut away to the experts, who spoke in plodding, earnest voices which drained the programme of any excitement or glamour. The VT packages included superb shots of the interior of the *Titanic*, but they were so polished that they looked like excerpts from a documentary rather than part of the exciting rough and tumble of a live broadcast. It was a dull show with no pace or tension, and not much of a narrative line. The majority of viewers probably switched off after the first fifteen minutes. We all knew the show was a turkey. When it was over everyone sloped off back to their cabins or started packing up their equipment. There was no wild singing or dancing till dawn.

The following day everyone was flat and depressed except me. I was about to dive the *Titanic* for our little show, *Tony Robinson's Titanic Adventure* – at least I thought I was, until the weather forecast announced an oncoming hurricane. My dive was postponed for at least twenty-four hours, and I and my little unit were left on tenterhooks. The ship had to return to St John's; if I didn't dive tomorrow, I wouldn't get down at all, and we'd have no programme to take back to the UK.

All that night the *Keldysh* pitched and tossed, and the next morning the sea was still churning. I was on standby from 8 a.m. Every hour or so I went up on deck to have a look at the weather, but the sky remained dark and ferocious. Then around 3 p.m. I thought I saw a streak of light on the horizon. Were the waves a little less fierce? I wasn't sure. At four I was finally told to kit up and get into my submersible. I put on my thermals and a boiler suit, and took my medications, seasickness pills, charcoal tablets to stop me farting, a necessity in a submarine the size of a large wardrobe, and Imodium to prevent me having a poo. I took a double dose of these; if I was taken short, a small tent would be erected round me, and I'd have to do my business in a small bucket with a lid, which would stay with us for the rest of the dive. I would rather have died than go through such a palaver under the watchful eyes and noses of Genya, our taciturn Russian pilot, and Jim Cameron, one of the most ferocious directors in Hollywood. Finally around 6 p.m. I clambered up a metal ladder and into the hatch of Mir 2, one of two tiny red and white submarines parked on the deck. A winch lifted us into the air and back down again, I felt us bob on the surface for a few moments, then we began our descent.

We were going down at five thousand feet per hour, so it was dark within a minute, and it would be the best part of two hours before we got to the ocean floor, during which time we'd remain in pitch-black. We had to conserve as much energy as possible. We could use our battery-powered electricity either for lighting or heating or operational purposes but not all at once, and Genya was constantly weighing his options, because if we ran out of power, there was no more to be had. This wasn't a theoretical issue. There were horrendous stories of submarines malfunctioning under water. It was only a few years since the Russian submarine Kursk had exploded at depth, and all 118 crew members had died, some of them very slowly.

Time dragged, the silence broken only by occasional crackly instructions over the intercom. Condensation dripped on us from the ceiling. Jim said this was fine as long as the water didn't taste salty. I felt bored, frightened and exhilarated; until that long descent I had never realised you could feel all three of those emotions at once.

I hardly noticed the moment we arrived on the seabed because the touchdown was so soft. I looked out of my porthole – nothing! I checked the monitor screens – again nothing! Then Jim picked up his intercom and softly said, 'Go! Go!' Immediately BAM! The ocean flooded with bright white light emanating from Mir 1, our sister sub, a floating lighting-rig bristling with huge lamps, which had been descending at the same rate as us on the other side of the wreck. I'd expected to see bulbous fish with glowing noses, and gigantic writhing eels with vicious teeth, but there was nothing but white-out, a snowstorm of ocean bed detritus and swirling sand kicked up by our Mir. Slowly it began to clear, and for the first time I could see where I was. Looming up above me was the prow of the *Titanic*, silent, immobile, exactly where it had been since the early morning of 15 April 1912. But then Hollywood intervened, and however hard I tried, I couldn't shift it from my mind, a hundred feet above me was the tiny metal platform on which Leonardo and Kate had stood with outstretched arms against a backdrop of a ridiculously red sunset while a flute and full orchestra played 'My Heart Will Go On'.

Jim turned on the tiny ceiling-mounted cameras and checked that they were sufficiently well aligned to shoot us talking to each other, then picked up a manual control panel like something you'd use in a computer game and brought to life his robotic cameras, a pair of little bugs or 'bots' called Elwood and Gilligan, which were tethered to the Mir on long cables.

He took ages fiddling around trying to make sure they were working properly. Meanwhile I couldn't take my eyes off the hull. It was adorned with brown mounds and stalactites like the dribbled icing on the sides of a wedding cake. A miracle was taking place down here. These strange 'rusticles' were the planet's most primitive life forms, hosts of them building communal homes, and feeding off the metal that made up the steel. The basic constituent of the *Titanic* was pig iron, and in a hundred years' time all the metal would have been leached out of it and it would revert to nature once more. The *Titanic* wasn't a permanent symbol of man's hubris; it would soon disappear and pass into the world of myth and legend.

Genya lifted the Mir's nose, it drifted up alongside the massive ship, with Elwood and Gilligan flying in front of us like toasters on steroids, then we dropped down again onto the main deck. As we did this the whole sub slumped, I died a little, and even Jim gasped. If the deck gave way and the Mir tumbled into the body of the ship, we'd be trapped and no one would be able to rescue us. Like the stricken Russian submariners, it would take us a long time to die, getting colder, hungrier, and ever lower on oxygen. It seemed like forever before the little submarine was safely in position, but by the time we stabilised, the ocean had completely cleared and we could see the wonderful old ship in all her tragic glory. Ahead of us was the long stretch of deck where the terrified passengers, rich and poor alike, had queued and jostled for their lifeboats. Massive chains lay across it dotted with chunky bits of machinery like a set for a modernist opera. It was an awesome sight, achingly sad and very beautiful. But it was also a memorial to a forgotten story. This was where the ship's band had played while the *Titanic* went down, a noble thing to do, but only half the reality. The White Star Line had recently cut the musicians' wages by 30 per cent, and their grieving families didn't even receive all of this reduced wage. The Line decided that as the men had only got three-quarters of the way to New York, the families would receive three-quarters of their pay. As a final insult they were charged for their lost uniforms, a spiteful piece of chiselling that remains a guilty secret buried in the heart of the *Titanic*'s story.

The bots gracefully dived down a rusty hole in the deck, which opened out into a huge cavern which had once housed the ship's grand central stairway, although because it had been made of wood, it had long ago collapsed. All that was left was the stairwell, which allowed the bots free passage into the bowels of the ship without snagging their long leads.

Below the stairway was a large room decorated in a Moorish style with ceramic tiles fixed to its steel walls, their blue and green motifs still visible. This was the ship's Turkish baths, and scattered on the floor were the broken remnants of the passengers' loungers, the original deckchairs on the *Titanic*. Above us were the remnants of wooden domes and neatly carved Star-of-David finials, all made of teak, the only wood to survive the voracious micro-organisms. What a privilege to be so close to this beautiful room and experience the emotions it generated! Then I remembered I was watching this exploration on the sub's television monitors; I was seeing exactly the same images as everyone else high above me on the *Keldysh*, the only difference being that I was cold, squashed in a tiny box, and two hours away from the nearest bathroom. I might as well have been in my cabin watching all this on my telly with a cup of cocoa in my hand!

The bots moved on to a first-class cabin, with a gold-plated brass clock on the mantelpiece, its glass cloudy and opaque. If it was ever brought back to the surface, it could be cleaned and we'd learn at what precise moment the cabin had flooded. But should we do that? The *Titanic*'s archaeology was falling apart; when Jim had dived it a couple of years previously, the main mast had been proud and upright; now it was broken, and lay like a giant worm cast on the deck.

Perhaps the ship should be left lying there. I'd been taught that archaeology should be preserved and celebrated, so that the vividness of the past could be passed down the generations. *Time Team* was built on that premise; indeed it seemed more than a premise, it was a moral imperative. But was it practical, let alone desirable? Museum storerooms were crammed to overflowing with archaeological finds, and there was little money to pay for more suitable, temperature-regulated storage, or the staff to be its custodians. Did we really want to save everything in the world and put it in a glass case? Was it appropriate to spend tens of millions of dollars poking around in the depths in order to drag up the *Titanic*'s hand mirrors and soup tureens, which would inevitably be put on the open market and sold to the highest bidder? Wouldn't it be a more fitting memorial to those like my namesake James William Robinson, the ship's victualling steward, to let the wreckage lie on the seabed until time and the currents took their course?

Our expedition had ground to a halt. Elwood's cable was tangled up, and it couldn't move forwards or backwards, so Gilligan was trying to shake it to and fro until it was free again. It was hours before Jim managed to get the two bots lashed safely to the side of the Mir. The rest of our filming schedule was a write-off.

I sat in the semi-darkness with the tiny ceiling-mounted cameras still rolling and pointing straight at me. I was somewhere virtually no other human being had ever been before and had seen the most legendary ship in the world. We'd been submerged for nearly seventeen hours. Soon we'd break the record for the longest ever dive on the *Titanic*. I'd have a lot of time on my hands while Jim fiddled about. What should I do next? I could try conducting another interview with him; I could see if I could get a laugh out of Genya; I could film a piece to camera about the piles of plates still miraculously stacked on the shelves of the ship's pantry; or look out of the porthole and watch the occasional ghost-grey sea slug.

How had I got here? There'd been no route map, no strategy, no plan cunning or otherwise. I'd worked hard, raised a family, followed my convictions, and I was sad to say had made countless balls-ups along the way. But I was only fifty-nine; with luck I'd have another quarter of a century to get things right.

EPILOGUE

On 25 June 2011 Louise and I were married in a medieval castle in Ravello overlooking the Adriatic. We'd met five years previously. I'd been given a rare afternoon off, and decided to treat myself to lunch before I headed home. Spitz was crowded; there was only one empty place at a table for two. The maître d' asked the woman already sitting there whether she'd mind sharing. She was very beautiful, with long dark hair, impeccable make-up, and a warm and welcoming smile. My first thought was, *She's out of my league*.

She said her name was Louise Hobbs, she was from the Wirral, and had moved south to work as the employment service co-ordinator at a London university. We talked for two hours non-stop. I invited her to come to Wales the following weekend to watch *Time Team* being shot, and within a week a new and amazing chapter of my life had begun.

On 11 July 2013 Louise and I attended two funerals. The first, at the crematorium in Weston-super-Mare, was for Mick Aston. Even though he'd been one of my closest friends, we hadn't seen each other for over a year. *Time Team* had been losing viewers for some time, and the producers had decided that as a one-year experiment we'd make a number of changes to the programme in order to freshen it up.

But Mick was incandescent. He thought we were trying to drive the show downmarket. I tried to explain that the alterations were being introduced in an attempt to ensure the show's long-term survival, but he wouldn't be persuaded, and eventually left the programme.

A year later at his home in Somerset, he went downstairs for a drink of water in the night, collapsed in the hallway, and died. He'd suffered from bleeding on the brain a decade previously and had nearly died then. The doctors had told him he'd be lucky to survive for more than a few years, and that he would have to be careful, but he seldom did what they told him. When they prescribed medication, he only took it for a few days, or refused to take it at all. Stubborn to the last, he survived much longer than less robust people with his condition. I felt his loss keenly, but I wasn't surprised. I'm thankful he lived as long as he did.

We couldn't stay till the end of the funeral because we had to drive forty miles up the M5 to the Memorial Woodlands at Alveston near Bristol where Mary, the mother of my children, was being buried.

She'd learnt a few years previously that she had ovarian cancer, and we were invited by her husband Steve to share her final days with him, Luke and Laura. Louise organised a spoof Desert Island Discs for her; I pretended to be Kirsty Young, and Lou played her favourite songs on a specially made CD. Mary was wryly amused; she said some of the dates were hopelessly muddled and I'd got a lot of the facts wrong. She was probably right, I do tend to do that.

On one of her last evenings I spent an hour or so alone with her. We held hands, said how much we cared about each other, and agreed we'd done a bloody good job bringing up the children. She died with dignity and grace.

THANK YOU

While writing this book I've received inspiration and help from a number of friends and colleagues, including:

Wendy Allnutt, David Bell, Peter Boyden, Teri Bramah, Ted Braun, Martin Brown, Sue Brymer, Adrienne Burgess, Nick Cohen, Philip Clarke, Raksha Dave, Hannah Davies, Howard Davies, Michael Douglas, Ben Elton, John Gater, Teresa Hall, Andy Hamilton, Graham Hamilton, Gavin Henderson, Greg Hicks, Huw Illingworth, Kate Illingworth, Will Knightley, Guy Jenkin, David Lloyd, Liz Mansfield, Mel Morpeth, Jimmy Mulville, Tim Munro, Joyce Nettles, Steve Page, Martin Parr, Sylvie Pierce, Andy Robertshaw, Barrie Rutter, Sue Sparkes, Robert Spicer, Dudley Sutton, Sue Swingler, Laurie Taylor, Bardy Thomas, Michael Thomas, Rob Wilkins, and David Willcock.

Many thanks to Heledd Mathias who has been living with this project for the past year, researching, typing, scrutinizing the text and giving me honest and sometimes ruthless critiques. Her help and friendship have been invaluable.

Thanks too to my editor Ingrid Connell, who insisted I write this autobiography even though I was determined not to. Her enthusiasm, excitement and wise counsel have imbued me with a confidence I wouldn't otherwise have had.

For the last fifteen years Sarah Dalkin has been my agent, manager, friend and collaborator. She has a passion for this project, and I'm deeply indebted to her.

I've received thoughtful and detailed advice from Laura and Luke Shepherd-Robinson, and they've given me permission to include episodes about their father that no child would want to be made public. I love them very much.

Thanks to my long-time colleagues Gaby Morgan, the editor of my children's books at Pan Macmillan, and Non-Fiction Communications Director, Dusty Miller.

Thanks also to Jeremy Hicks, Julie Dalkin and Charlotte Leaper at JHA.

And finally to Louise, who only appears on the first and last pages of this book, but is my devoted companion, and has given me support and shrewd advice throughout its inception.

Tony Robinson
26.05.2016

INDEX

Picture Acknowledgements

All photographs are from the author's collection with the exception of the following:

Page 5 courtesy of The Royal Central School of Speech and Drama
Page 9 courtesy of Sue Sparkes
Page 10 middle left and middle right courtesy of Tim Munro
Page 12 bottom © Martin Parr
Page 15 bottom and page 19 top © BBC
Page 19 bottom and page 20 © Steve Shearn
Page 21 © Spire Films Ltd
Page 22 bottom © Mel Morpeth
Page 23 top left and right © Adrian Scottow
Page 23 bottom © Jonathan Brady/PA Archive/Press Association Images
Page 24 top © Debra and Paul Simpson